The **R**

written and researched by

Martin Dunford and Phil Lee

with additional contributions by

Suzy Summer and Loïk Dal Molin

ROUGH GUIDES

NEW YORK · LONDON · DELHI

www.roughguides.com

Contents

Belgian beer colour
section following p.112

Belgian food colour
section following p.208

Colour maps following
p.305

3

Introduction to

Brussels

**Brussels gets a bad press among European cities. It's
known as the home of the European Union, and has a
reputation as a dull centre of business, bureaucracy
and men in grey suits. Yet the EU neither defines nor
dominates Brussels – it merely forms one layer of a city
that since the middle of the last century has become
a cosmopolitan, thriving metropolis. It's a surprisingly
dynamic place, with a rich ethnic mix, architecture and
museums that rank among the best in Europe, a superb
restaurant scene and energetic nightlife. Moreover, most
of the key attractions are crowded into a centre that's
small enough to be absorbed over a few days. Arguably,
then, the perfect short-break destination.**

The **centre** of Brussels is roughly the shape of a
diamond with the top cut off, defined by a ring of
inner-city boulevards known as the "petit ring". Its
layout embodies historic class divisions. For centuries
the ruling class lived in the **Upper Town**, an area of
wide boulevards and grand mansions which looks
down imperiously on the tangled streets of the **Lower
Town**, traditionally the home of shopkeepers and workers. This rarified
atmosphere persists to this day: the streets are wider and less congested
in the Upper Town, and the air is sweeter, given its height above the
maelstrom. This divide in landscape and class is further complicated by
the **language divide** between Belgium's French-speaking Walloons and
Dutch-speaking Flemish. Rather cumbersomely, the city is Belgium's only

4

officially bilingual region, in which all road signs, street names and all published information must by law be in both languages. French-speakers make up the majority of Brussels' population, but many of the surrounding suburbs are Flemish-speaking, and the ancient Brussels dialect (known as Brusselse Sproek or Marollien) is a strange mixture of the two languages. As if this wasn't complicated enough, the city is as ethnically diverse as any European capital, with immigrants from North Africa, Turkey, Greece and other parts of the Mediterranean, as well as from Belgium's former African colonies – not to mention a host of expats working for the EU, NATO and other multinational organizations based hereabouts – who comprise a quarter of the population. There is perhaps no more international – or more linguistically complex – city in the world.

Brussels has been messed about by the planners over the past hundred years or so, particularly in the 1960s when misguided development left parts of the city disfigured by some hideous modern architecture and carved up by new arterial roads. The centre is still something of a hotchpotch, with pock-marked facades and peeling paint quite a feature of many of the streets of the Lower Town. But that's part of Brussels' charm – it's not a city that stands on ceremony to any degree. In spite of this, the city has picked itself up over the last few years and is looking better than it has done for some time. There's more of a sense of pride in the place these days: some of the most run-down parts of the city centre have been spruced up, and the shabbier buildings renovated; and beyond the centre, Brussels' fast-gentrifying inner-city districts have been lent vitality by the city's patchwork of ethnic groups.

What to see

Visitors to Brussels are often surprised by the vigour of the **city centre**. It's not neat and tidy, and many of the old tenement houses are shabby, but there's a buzz about the place that's hard to resist, and it's here you'll find the majority of the city's sights and attractions, restaurants and bars. The centre is also surprisingly compact, sitting neatly within the rough pentagon

◄ The Grand-Place

Art Nouveau Brussels

Brussels is the birthplace of the **Art Nouveau** movement in architecture, which originated here in the late nineteenth century. The style embraced modern materials and building methods, making use of stone, wrought iron and glass, but moulded these into organic forms that were almost deliberately anachronistic. Its chief exponent was **Victor Horta**, and the house he built for himself is now open as a museum and is as complete and undisturbed an example of Art Nouveau architecture as you're ever likely to see. This is just as well, as it's also one of the disappointingly few Art Nouveau buildings you can routinely visit in Brussels, with others either in use as offices or private residences and never open to the public, or only open on certain days of the year or to specialist tours (if you'd like to get inside those buildings normally closed to the public, consider taking a **tour** with the heritage group, Arau – see p.26). We've detailed the best and most accessible Art Nouveau sights throughout the Guide, but the following are those we consider must-sees.

Centre Belge de la Bande Dessinée This Horta-designed ex-department store, now Brussels' comic-strip museum, retains some original interior features. See p.59.

Le Cirio Arguably the most unchanged and charming of a number of Brussels' *fin-de-siècle* cafés. See p.203.

Hôtel Hannon The windows are the main attraction here – a fantastic example of the period. See p.93.

Hôtel Tassel Horta's first real Art Nouveau masterpiece. See p.99.

Maison Autrique The building on which Victor Horta cut his teeth. See p.124.

Maison Cauchie The facade here is one of Brussels' finest examples of sgraffiti, Art Nouveau's fanciful paint-and-brickwork. See p.117.

Maison Cyr Among the most unusual and elegant facades in the city. See p.113.

Musée des Instruments des Musique The 1899 Old England department store building houses this great museum. See p.77.

Musée Victor Horta The best Art Nouveau sight in the city – unmissable. See p.97.

of boulevards that enclose it – the **petit ring** – which follows the course of the fourteenth-century city walls, running from place Rogier in the north, close by the Gare du Nord, to Porte de Hal in the south, close to the Gare du Midi. The larger, westerly portion of the city centre comprises the Lower Town, spreading out from the Grand-Place, while up on the hill to the east lies the smaller Upper Town. Broadly speaking, the boundary between the two zones follows the busy boulevard that swings through the centre under several names – Berlaimont, L'Impératrice and L'Empereur.

The magnificent **Grand-Place**, with its exquisite guildhouses and town hall, is the unquestionable centre of Brussels, a focus for tourists and locals alike. It's also the hub of the **Lower Town**, whose cramped and populous quarters are bisected by a major north–south boulevard, variously named Adolphe Max, Anspach and Lemonnier, which roughly follows the route of Brussels' river, the Senne, which was covered over and diverted during the nineteenth century. The Lower Town fans out from the Grand-Place – to the **south** the narrow lanes of the St-Jacques district, to the **west** the gentrified streets of St-Géry and Ste-Catherine, and to the **north** the small quarter of Ilot Sacré and the restaurant ghetto of rue des Bouchers. The area further north has less obvious appeal, with dreary rue Neuve, a street of mainstream shops and department stores, leading up to the clumping skyscrapers that surround **place Rogier** and the **Gare du Nord**. This is an uninviting part of the city, but relief is at hand in the precise if bedraggled Habsburg symmetries of the **place des Martyrs** and at the Belgian Comic Strip Centre, the **Centre Belge de la Bande Dessinée**. To the south of the Grand-Place are the more inviting **Marolles district**,

a former working-class quarter that's now known for its antiques shops and excellent flea market, and the depressed and predominantly immigrant quarter around the **Gare du Midi** – though the presence of the Eurostar means that even this area is up-and-coming these days.

Quite different in feel from the rest of the city centre, the **Upper Town** is a self-consciously planned, more monumental quarter, with statuesque buildings lining wide boulevards and squares. Appropriately, it's the home of the Belgian parliament and government departments, formal parks and the original **Royal Palace**

◀ The European Parliament

– a huge, empty building that's no longer occupied by the Belgian royals. More promisingly, its lower slopes also accommodate Brussels' **Cathedral**, a fine Gothic edifice with wonderful stained-glass windows, some of the city's swishest shops clustered around the picturesque **place du Grand Sablon**, and, further up, the superb **Musées Royaux des Beaux Arts**, arguably Belgium's best collection of fine art. There's also the excellent **Musée des Instruments de Musique**, housed in the Art Nouveau Old England building, and, marking the end of the Upper Town's main spine, **rue Royale**, the preposterous bulk of the **Palais de Justice**, which lords it over the rest of the city, commanding views that on clear days reach way across the suburbs.

Brussels by no means ends with the petit ring. During the nineteenth century Léopold II pushed the city limits out beyond the course of the old walls, grabbing land from the surrounding *communes* to create the irregular boundaries that survive today. To the east, he sequestered a rough rectangle of land where he laid out **Parc Léopold** and across which he ploughed two wide boulevards, Belliard and La Loi, designed to provide an imperial approach to the **Parc du Cinquantenaire**, whose self-glorifying monuments were erected to celebrate Belgium's golden jubilee and now house three of the city's largest **museums**. The boulevards were soon colonized by the city's bourgeoisie, but in the last few years they have been displaced by the brash modern blocks of the **EU Quarter**, whose flashy **European Parliament building** is probably the best example of the area's largely undistinguished building boom.

▲ Le Cinquantenaire

Comic-strip Brussels

One of Belgium's greatest contributions to world culture is the **comic strip**, and it's from Brussels that the greatest comic art has emerged, either in its French incarnation – *bandes dessinées* – or the Flemish *stripverhalen*. The best known, of course, is **Tintin**, the creation of Georges Remi, better known as Hergé, who dreamed up his bequiffed hero back in the 1920s. The industry really blossomed after World War II, when magazines like *Bravo* and *Spirou* published the strips of Belgian folk hero comic artists like **Jijé** (along with Hergé, considered the granddaddy of Belgian comic art), **Maurice Tillieux**, **Frank Pé**, **Morris** (who invented Lucky Luke), **Peyo** (creator, alas, of the Smurfs, but of much else besides) and **Edgar-Pierre Jacobs** (creator of the peerless Blake & Mortimer). Nowadays comics are still as popular here, but Belgium is less dominant, both at home and abroad, and only *Spirou* survives from the old days. Inevitably, Japanese manga and American publications have stolen some of the European ground, but there is still a core Belgian comic industry in Brussels, with big publishers like Depuis, Standaard and Lombard (founded by Raymond Leblanc and for years publisher of *Tintin* magazine) producing regular comic magazines and graphic novels.

Taking in the shops, museums and sights related to the glories of Belgian comic art would make an enjoyable weekend for the enthusiast. The following are the places not to be missed on any **comic-strip tour**.

Centre Belge de la Bande Dessinée The best general display of comic-strip content, with work by most of the great names, regular exhibitions, and one of the city's best comic bookshops. See p.59.

Fondation Raymond LeBlanc This new museum, hosting temporary exhibitions devoted to all aspects of comic-book art, is located in the famous *Tintin* magazine building near the Gare du Midi. See p.67.

Maison de la Bande Dessinée This excellent comic bookstore has its own exhibition space devoted to *Spirou* and in particular the work of Jijé. See p.224.

Murals All over the city, murals fill spare walls on the side of buildings – there are a couple of very central ones on rue du Marché au Charbon. See p.63.

Nine City One of the city's best comic shops – out of the centre but definitely worth a trip for the comic devotee, with four floors of comics and comic-related stuff, and even a bar. See p.224.

Outside the city centre proper, to the south, are perhaps the city's most cosmopolitan districts: **St Gilles** and neighbouring **Ixelles**, whose streets hold a handful of designer stores and an ever-growing number of chic bars and restaurants. Ixelles is bisected by **avenue Louise**, a prosperous corridor that's home to much of the city's most upscale shopping territory, and overall these two *communes* boast much of the best of the city's **Art Nouveau architecture**.

On the other side of the city centre, the suburb of **Anderlecht** is famous for its soccer team and is also worth a visit for its local brewery. Adjacent to this area, **Koekelberg** is the site of the Basilique du Sacré Coeur, another whopping pile built by Léopold II, and the *commune* of **Jette**, just north, was for many years home to the surrealist painter René Magritte, whose house is now a museum. To the north of the city centre, beyond the partly Turkish districts of **St Josse** and **Schaerbeek**, is leafy **Laeken**, city residence of the Belgian royal family, and **Heysel**, with its notorious stadium and the Atomium, a leftover from the 1958 World Fair. Finally there's the suburb of **Tervuren** to the southeast, whose giant Africa museum is one of the city's biggest, as well as being one of the larger relics of Belgium's shameful colonial past; and beyond here the famous battlefield of **Waterloo**, the furthest draw among Brussels' outlying suburbs.

And then of course there's the **rest of Belgium**, much of which is

within a couple of hours of the city. We've included the pick of the many excursions you could make from the capital, including, of course, **Bruges** – one of the most beautiful towns anywhere, and only an hour away by train – and **Ghent**, its underrated larger neighbour, which is less than half the distance. Belgium's second city, **Antwerp**, is just a forty-minute train ride away, and a much cooler place than Brussels could ever be. Finally, less than half an hour by train are the ancient student city of **Leuven** and the lovely cathedral town of **Mechelen**.

When to go

Brussels – like all of Belgium – enjoys a temperate **climate**, which is easy to plan for. Expect a dose of **rain** every two to three days, more showery in summer, more drizzly in winter. Severe summer heat waves and winter cold snaps are uncommon, and the weather is generally mild, with little difference in temperature between late spring and early autumn, though June to August are the warmest months. April and May, when the light has the clarity of springtime and the city isn't swarming with tourists, are especially appealing. Similarly September, when the weather is usually still comfortably warm and the crowds that much more bearable, can be a pleasant time for a visit.

Brussels temperatures

	Jan	Feb	Mar	Apr	May	Jun	Jul	Aug	Sep	Oct	Nov	Dec
Average daily temperature												
Temp °C	3	4	8	10	14	16	19	18	15	12	7	4

15 things not to miss

It's not possible to see everything Brussels has to offer on a short trip – and we don't suggest you try. What follows is a subjective selection of the city's highlights, ranging from our favourite things to eat to the best museums, all arranged in colour-coded categories to help you find the very best things to see, do and experience. All entries have a page reference to take you straight into the Guide, where you can find out more.

01 **The Grand-Place** Page **39** • Quite simply one of the most uniformly beautiful enclosed city squares in the world.

02 **Musée Gueuze** Page **121** • A traditional brewery specializing in a beer that is only brewed in Brussels.

04 **Mussels** Page **190** • You can't leave Brussels without having mussels, best enjoyed in season with a generous side of frites.

03 **Cathedral** Page **69** • Brussels' cathedral is a fine Gothic building, but its stained-glass windows are the real draw.

07 Musées des Beaux-Arts
Page **78** • A great museum, combining a wealth of old masters with a fine modern art collection.

05 Musée René Magritte
Page **123** • The former home of the Surrealist painter is familiar from many of his paintings.

06 Frites
Page **190** • There's no better place to eat them than on the street, smothered in mayonnaise, out of a paper cone.

08 Centre Belge de la Bande Dessinée
Page **59** • This Art Nouveau ex-department store is a homage to one of Belgium's national obsessions – and it's not just Tintin.

10 Place du Grand Sablon Page **89** • The Upper Town's most elegant square, perfect for hanging out on a summer's afternoon.

09 Art Nouveau Page **6** • Brussels is the birthplace of Art Nouveau architecture, best represented by some great private houses, a couple of which – the Horta house and the Cauchie house – are open to the public.

11 Place du Jeu de Balle Page **67** • Not as cheap as it once was, but still what a flea market should be, full of delectable old junk.

12 Waterloo Page **133** • This sleepy Brussels suburb made European history in 1815.

13 Musée des Instruments de Musique Page **77** • Housed in the renovated Art Nouveau Old England building, this great museum has a fine collection, as well as wonderful views over the city centre from its top-floor restaurant.

14 Beer Page **206** • One of the city's greatest pleasures. Belgium has more brewers per head than any other country in the world, and Brussels has a fantastic array of bars to sample them in.

15 Adoration of the Mystic Lamb, Ghent Page **164** • It's worth the half-hour train journey to see this incredible painting by Jan van Eyck in the setting it was painted for.

Basics

Basics

Getting there

There are direct and stopover flights to Brussels from every corner of the globe, and the city is also well connected by rail and bus to a multitude of European cities. The Eurostar rail link is particularly speedy, making the journey from London to Brussels in a little under two hours.

Fares usually depend on the season, with the highest prices being around early June to the end of August; the lowest are normally available from November to March (excluding Christmas and New Year).

Flights from the UK and Ireland

Brussels international airport is easily reached **from the UK**, with regular flights from London and a number of regional airports. There's also Brussels-Charleroi airport, whose name is somewhat deceptive – it's actually on the edge of Charleroi, an industrial town about 50km south of the capital. British Airways, bmi and SN Brussels Airlines all fly regularly to Brussels from London Heathrow; SN Brussels flies from Gatwick; and VLM from London City airport. As for **regional airports**, British Airways has flights to Brussels from Bristol, Southampton, Birmingham, Newcastle, Manchester, Aberdeen, Edinburgh, Glasgow and Belfast, as does the Dutch airline KLM, which also flies from Cardiff and Norwich; Air France flies to Brussels from Southampton; VLM from Southampton and Liverpool; SN Brussels from Birmingham, Newcastle and Glasgow; bmi from East Midlands, Leeds Bradford, Edinburgh, Belfast and Dublin; flybe links Brussels with Manchester and Southampton; and Ryanair flies to Brussels-Charleroi from Glasgow. **Flying times** are insignificant: London to Brussels takes a little over an hour, one hour and twenty minutes from Newcastle.

Flying **from Ireland**, there's much less choice, but Ryanair charges very reasonable rates for flights from either Dublin or Shannon to Brussels-Charleroi.

Travelling at convenient times at the weekend between April and September, **fares** are usually around £100 return (including taxes) with the low-cost airlines, £150 with one of the full-service carriers. Weekday travel will cost £50–60 with a budget carrier, and maybe £100 or so with a full-service airline. Of course if you want more flexibility with your ticket you'll pay more, as you will if you book at the last minute – economy return tickets from London to Brussels can cost anything up to £400. All carriers offer their lowest prices online.

Flights from the US and Canada

From the US, you can fly direct to Brussels from New York City (American, Delta or Continental from Newark) and Chicago (American), but you'll usually find cheaper deals if you're prepared to stop once, either in the US or mainland Europe. Fares to Brussels can be found for as little as $800 if you're prepared to change; otherwise reckon on spending around $1300–1600 return. From Chicago, non-stop fares cost around $2300, but you can cut this to around $1300 with one stopover. There are no direct flights from the West Coast, but plenty of carriers will get you to Brussels with one stop, for as little as $1300 return.

From Canada, the best deals are offered by Air Canada, which flies non-stop to London Heathrow, with onward connections to Brussels. From Toronto to Brussels, expect to pay around Can$1900 in high season and Can$1400 in low season, while typical fares from Vancouver are around Can$2100 in high season and Can$1500 in low season.

Fly less – stay longer! Travel and Climate Change

Climate change is perhaps the single biggest issue facing our planet. It is caused by a build-up in the atmosphere of carbon dioxide and other greenhouse gases, which are emitted by many sources – including planes. Already, **flights** account for three to four percent of human-induced global warming: that figure may sound small, but it is rising year on year and threatens to counteract the progress made by reducing greenhouse emissions in other areas.

Rough Guides regard travel as a **global benefit**, and feel strongly that the advantages to developing economies are important, as are the opportunities for greater contact and awareness among peoples. But we also believe in travelling responsibly, which includes giving thought to how often we fly and what we can do to redress any harm that our trips may create.

We can travel less or simply reduce the amount we travel by air (taking fewer trips and staying longer, or taking the train if there is one); we can avoid night flights (which are more damaging); and we can make the trips we do take "climate neutral" via a carbon offset scheme. **Offset schemes** run by climatecare.org, carbonneutral .com and others allow you to "neutralize" the greenhouse gases that you are responsible for releasing. Their websites have simple calculators that let you work out the impact of any flight – as does our own. Once that's done, you can pay to fund projects that will reduce future emissions by an equivalent amount. Please take the time to visit our website and make your trip climate neutral, or get a copy of the *Rough Guide to Climate Change* for more detail on the subject.

www.roughguides.com/climatechange

Flights from Australia and New Zealand

There are **no direct flights** from Australia or New Zealand to Brussels. Most itineraries will involve two changes, one in the Far East – Singapore, Bangkok or Kuala Lumpur – and then another in the gateway city of the airline you're flying with: usually Paris, Amsterdam or London. You can get tickets to Brussels from Sydney or Melbourne for Aus$1500–2000 if you shop around, and from Auckland for slightly more.

Flights from South Africa

There are **no direct flights** from South Africa to Brussels, but KLM does offer direct flights from Cape Town and Johannesburg to Amsterdam, a short train ride from Brussels. Alternatively, South African Airways flies direct to London and Frankfurt, from either of which it's a short hop to Brussels; Lufthansa also links South Africa with Frankfurt. Flights with KLM from Cape Town to Amsterdam cost around ZAR7400, ZAR8200 from Johannesburg. Flights via London or Frankfurt cost around ZAR8000.

By train from the UK

Eurostar trains running through the Channel Tunnel put Brussels within easy striking distance of London's St Pancras International and Kent's Ebbsfleet train stations. Considering the time it takes to check into any of London's airports, Eurostar is often faster than a flight: the journey time from St Pancras to Bruxelles-Midi is a very competitive one hour and fifty minutes, and there are around ten services a day. **Fares** are also very competitive: the least expensive Standard Class return tickets cost about £60, depending on availability and the flexibility of the ticket – with the cheapest tickets you cannot change your times or dates; a fully flexible Standard Class ticket at a peak period costs around £300. One other Eurostar perk is that their tickets are valid for travel to any Belgian station – not just Brussels.

If you're visiting Brussels as part of a longer European trip, it may be worth considering a **European rail pass**. There are lots to choose from – see the website of **Rail Europe** (Ⓦwww.raileurope.com), the umbrella company for all national and international passes, for a rundown of the options. Note that some passes have to be bought before leaving home, and others can only be bought in specific countries.

Driving from the UK – and Eurotunnel

The easiest way to reach Brussels **by car or motorbike** from the UK is to use **Eurotunnel**'s shuttle train service through the Channel Tunnel from Folkestone to Calais. There are up to four trains per hour (one per hr midnight–6am) and the journey takes 35 minutes (45min for some night-time departures); you need to check in at Folkestone at least thirty minutes before departure. It is possible to turn up and buy your ticket at the toll booths (exit the M20 at junction 11a), though at busy times booking is advisable.

Fares depend on the time of year, time of day and length of stay; it's cheaper to travel between 10pm and 6am, while the highest fares are reserved for weekends in July and August. Prices are charged per vehicle, with the standard single fare starting from as little as £49, though the cheapest fares require advanced booking and fixed departure times. Alternatively, a more flexible, five-day "Flexiplus" fare costs around £150 each way; look out also for special offers. Finally, note that Eurotunnel only carries cars (including occupants) and motorbikes, not cyclists and foot passengers. From the Eurotunnel exit in Calais, it's just 50km or so to De Panne, on the Belgian coast, 120km to Bruges and 200km to Brussels.

By bus from the UK

Cheap flights may be readily available, but long-distance bus is still likely to be the cheapest (if not the most comfortable) way of getting there. **Eurolines**, part of National Express, has four daily departures from London's Victoria coach station to Bruxelles-Nord train station in Brussels, with a journey time of between seven and eight hours. Return tickets cost about £40–50, with small discounts for travellers aged under 25 and over 60. **Anglia Lines** has one departure a day from London to Brussels,

charging as little as £20 return; the journey takes just over seven hours and passengers are dropped at avenue Fonsny 2a, 100m from the Bruxelles-Midi station.

By train from continental Europe

A veritable raft of rail lines runs into Belgium from its three neighbours – France, Germany and the Netherlands – and most services pause or stop in Brussels. In particular, Brussels is the hub of the **Thalys** international rail network, a combined project of the Belgian, Dutch, French and German railways, with regular services to Brussels from – among many destinations – Rotterdam, Amsterdam, Paris and Cologne.

Airlines and agents

Online booking

ⓦ **www.expedia.com**
ⓦ **www.lastminute.com** (UK)
ⓦ **www.opodo.com**
ⓦ **www.orbitz.com** (US)
ⓦ **www.travelocity.com**
ⓦ **www.travelonline.co.za** (South Africa)
ⓦ **www.zuji.com.au** (Australia)

Airlines

Aer Lingus Republic of Ireland ☎0818/365 000, UK ☎0870/876 5000, US and Canada ☎1-800/IRISH-AIR, NZ ☎1649/3083355, SA ☎1-272/2168-32838; ⓦwww.aerlingus.com.
Air Canada US & Canada ☎1-888/247-2262, UK ☎0871/220 1111, Republic of Ireland ☎01/679 3958, Australia ☎1300/655 767, NZ ☎0508/747 767; ⓦwww.aircanada.com.
Air France US ☎1-800/237-2747, Canada ☎1-800/667-2747, UK ☎0870/142 4343, Australia ☎1300/390 190, SA ☎0861/340 340; ⓦwww.airfrance.com.
Air India US ☎1-800/223-7776, Canada ☎1800-625/6424, UK ☎020/8560 9996 or 8745 1000, Australia ☎02/9283 4020, NZ ☎09/631 5651; ⓦwww.airindia.com.
Air New Zealand NZ ☎0800/737000, Australia ☎0800/132 476, UK ☎0800/028 4149, Republic of Ireland ☎1800/551 447, US ☎1800-262/1234, Canada ☎1800-663/5494; ⓦwww.airnz.co.nz.
American Airlines US & Canada ☎1-800/433-7300, UK ☎020/7365 0777, Republic of Ireland

☎01/602 0550, Australia ☎1800/673 486, NZ ☎0800/445 442; ⓦwww.aa.com.
bmi US ☎1-800/788-0555, UK ☎0870/607 0555 or 0870/607 0222, Republic of Ireland ☎01/283 0700, Australia ☎02/8644 1881, NZ ☎09/623 4293, SA ☎11/289 8111; ⓦwww.flybmi.com.
bmibaby UK ☎0871/224 0224, Republic of Ireland ☎1890/340 122; ⓦwww.bmibaby.com.
British Airways UK ☎0844/493 0787, Republic of Ireland ☎1890/626 747, US & Canada ☎1-800/AIRWAYS, Australia ☎1300/767 177, NZ ☎09/966 9777, SA ☎114/418 600; ⓦwww.ba.com.
Continental Airlines US & Canada ☎1-800/523-3273, UK ☎0845/607 6760, Republic of Ireland ☎1890/925 252, Australia ☎1300/737 640, NZ ☎09/308 3350, International ☎1800/231 0856; ⓦwww.continental.com.
Delta US & Canada ☎1-800/221-1212, UK ☎0845/600 0950, Republic of Ireland ☎1850/882 031 or 01/407 3165, Australia ☎1300/302 849, NZ ☎09/9772232; ⓦwww.delta.com.
easyJet UK ☎0905/821 0905, ⓦwww.easyjet.com.
Emirates US & Canada ☎1-800/777-3999, UK ☎0844/800 2777, Australia ☎1300/303 777, NZ ☎05/0836 4728, SA ☎0861/364 728; ⓦwww.emirates.com.
flyBE UK ☎0871/700 2000, Republic of Ireland/International ☎0044/13922 68500; ⓦwww.flybe.com.
JAL (Japan Air Lines) US & Canada ☎1-800/525-3663, UK ☎0845/774 7700, Republic of Ireland ☎01/408 3757, Australia ☎1-300/525 287 or 02/9272 1111, NZ ☎0800/525 747 or 09/379 9906, SA ☎11/214 2560; ⓦwww.jal.com or www.japanair.com.
Lufthansa US ☎1-800/3995-838, Canada ☎1-800/563-5954, UK ☎0871/945 9747, Republic of Ireland ☎01/844 5544, Australia ☎1300/655 727, NZ ☎0800-945 220, SA ☎0861/842 538; ⓦwww.lufthansa.com.
Malaysia Airlines US ☎1-800/5529-264, UK ☎0871/423 9090, Republic of Ireland ☎01/6761 561, Australia ☎13 26 27, NZ ☎0800/777 747, SA ☎11-8809 614; ⓦwww.malaysiaairlines.com.
Qantas Airways US & Canada ☎1-800/227-4500, UK ☎0845/774 7767, Republic of Ireland ☎01/407 3278, Australia ☎13 13 13, NZ ☎0800/808 767 or 09/357 8900, SA ☎11/441 8550; ⓦwww.qantas.com.
Ryanair UK ☎0871/246 0000, Republic of Ireland ☎0818/303 030; ⓦwww.ryanair.com.
Singapore Airlines US ☎1-800/742-3333, Canada ☎1-800/663-3046, UK ☎0844/800 2380, Republic of Ireland ☎01/671 0722, Australia ☎13 10 11, NZ ☎0800/808 909, SA ☎11/880 8560 or 11/880 8566; ⓦwww.singapoeair.com.

SN Brussels Airlines US ☎1-516/740-5200, Canada ☎1-866/308-2230, UK ☎0905/609 5609, Republic of Ireland ☎01/844 6006, Australia ☎02/9767 4305; ⓦwww.flysn.com.
South African Airways SA ☎11/978 1111, US and Canada ☎1-800/722-9675, UK ☎0870/747 1111, Australia ☎1300/435 972, NZ ☎09/977 2237; ⓦwww.flysaa.com.
United Airlines US ☎1-800/864-8331, UK ☎0845/844 4777, Australia ☎13 17 77; ⓦwww.united.com.
Virgin Atlantic US ☎1-800/821-5438, UK ☎0870/574 7747, Australia ☎1300/727 340, SA ☎11/340 3400; ⓦwww.virgin-atlantic.com.
VLM Airlines (Vlaamse Luchttransport-maatschappij; Flemish Airlines) UK ☎0871/666 5050, ⓦwww.flyvlm.com.

Travel agents

ebookers UK ☎0871/223 5000, Republic of Ireland ☎01/431 1311; ⓦwww.ebookers.com. Low fares on an extensive selection of scheduled flights and package deals.
North South Travel UK ☎01245/608 291, ⓦwww.northsouthtravel.co.uk. Friendly travel agency offering discounted fares worldwide. Profits are used to support projects in the developing world, especially the promotion of sustainable tourism.
Trailfinders UK ☎0845/058 5858, Republic of Ireland ☎01/677 7888; ⓦwww.trailfinders.com. One of the best-informed and most efficient agents for independent travellers.
STA Travel US ☎1-800/781-4040, UK ☎0871/2300 040, Australia ☎134 782, NZ ☎0800/474 400, SA ☎0861/781 781; ⓦwww.statravel.com. Worldwide specialists in independent travel; also student IDs, travel insurance, car rental, rail passes and more. Good discounts for students and under-26s.

Train contacts

Belgian Railways ⓦwww.b-rail.be.
Eurostar UK: ☎0870/518 6186; Brussels: ☎02 528 28 28; ⓦwww.eurostar.com.
French Railways (SNCF) ⓦwww.sncf.fr.
German Rail ⓦwww.bahn.de.
International Rail (UK) ☎08700/841 410, ⓦwww.international-rail.com.
Netherlands Rail ⓦwww.ns.nl.
Rail Europe ☎08448/484 064, ⓦwww.raileurope.co.uk.
Thalys ⓦwww.thalys.com.

Bus contacts

Anglia Lines ☎ 0870 608 8806, ⓦ www
.anglia-lines.co.uk.
Eurolines ☎ 08705 808 080, ⓦ www
.nationalexpress.com/eurolines.

Eurotunnel

Eurotunnel ☎ 08705/35 35 35, ⓦ www
.eurotunnel.com.

Arrival

Brussels has an excellent public transport system (see p.24), which puts all the main points of arrival – airport, train and bus stations – within easy reach of the city centre.

By air

Most flights to Brussels land at the city's **international airport** in the satellite suburb of Zaventem, 13km northeast of the city centre. There is a **Tourisme Information Brussels (TIB)** information desk (daily 8am–9pm) in the arrivals hall, dispensing assorted blurb on the city, including free maps. It shares its space with **Espace Wallonie**, representing OPT, the Wallonian tourist board, who have information on – and make accommodation bookings in – Wallonia (French-speaking Belgium). The arrivals hall also has all the other facilities you would expect of a major airport, notably bureaux de change, car rental, a post office and ATMs.

From the airport, trains run every ten to twenty minutes to the city's three main stations – Bruxelles-Nord, Bruxelles-Centrale and Bruxelles-Midi. The journey time to Bruxelles-Centrale, the nearest station to the Grand-Place, is about twenty minutes and costs €3 one-way; buy tickets at the airport train station. Trains run from around 5.30am until just before midnight, after which you'll need to take a **taxi** into the city centre – reckon on paying around €40 for the trip. The airport also has its own **bus station** with a number of services to the capital, including hourly bus #12 running to Métro Schuman in the EU Quarter (6am–10pm; tickets €3, or €4 from the driver).

Some airlines – principally Ryanair – fly to **Brussels-Charleroi airport**, which is also sometimes called Brussels South, though it is in fact some 50km south of central Brussels. This secondary airport, which is currently being expanded at a rate of knots, has a reasonable range of facilities including car rental and ATMs, plus an Espace Wallonie **tourist information desk** (daily 9am–9pm). An hourly bus service to Brussels (8.30am–11.30pm) departs from outside the terminal building and drops passengers just outside

---

Visitors soon adjust to the city's **bilingual signage** (in French Flemish), but on arrival it can be very confusing, especially with regard to the names of the city's three main train stations: **Bruxelles-Nord** (in Flemish it's Brussel-Noord); **Bruxelles-Centrale** (Brussel-Centraal); and, most bewildering of the lot, **Bruxelles-Midi** (Brussel-Zuid). To add to the confusion, each of these three train stations adjoins a Metro station – respectively the Gare du Nord (Noordstation), Gare Centrale (Centraal Station) and Gare du Midi (Zuidstation). Note that for simplicity's sake, we've stuck to using the French versions in this Guide.

Bruxelles-Midi train station at the junction of rue de France and rue de l'Instruction; tickets are sold inside the airport terminal. Note that it is a good idea to double-check pick-up locations. Depending on traffic, the journey takes about an hour and costs €13 one-way, €22 return. Alternatively, you can take a local TEC bus (every 30min–1hr; 15min) from the airport to **Charleroi Sud train station**, from where there are regular services to Brussels' three main stations (every 30min; 50min); the combined train and bus fare is €10.50 one-way, €21 return.

By train

Brussels has **three main train stations** – Bruxelles-Nord, Bruxelles-Centrale and Bruxelles-Midi. Almost all domestic trains stop at all three, but the majority of international services only stop at Bruxelles-Midi, including Eurostar trains from London and Thalys express trains from Amsterdam, Paris, Cologne and Aachen.

Bruxelles-Centrale is, as its name suggests, the most central of the stations, a five-minute walk from the Grand-Place; **Bruxelles-Nord** lies among the bristling tower blocks of the business area just north of the main ring road; and **Bruxelles-Midi** is located in a depressed area to the south of the city centre. Note that on bus timetables and on maps of the city transport system, Bruxelles-Nord appears as "Gare du Nord", Bruxelles-Centrale as "Gare Centrale" and Bruxelles-Midi as "Gare du Midi", taking the names of their respective métro stops. If you arrive late at night, it's best to take a taxi to your hotel or hostel – and you should certainly avoid the streets around Bruxelles-Midi. The taxi fare from Bruxelles-Midi to the Grand-Place can cost anywhere between €6 and €18, depending on traffic.

If you need to **transfer** from one of the three main train stations to another, simply jump on the next available mainline train; there are services between the three stations every ten minutes or so, the journey only takes a few minutes and all you'll have to do (at most) is swap platforms. Bruxelles-Midi and Bruxelles-Nord are also linked by underground tram – the **prémétro** – with several services shuttling underneath the city centre between these two stations, but it's surprisingly difficult to pick out the correct tram and platform. There are two ways to reach the Grand-Place from either Bruxelles-Nord or Bruxelles-Midi: take either a mainline train to Bruxelles-Centrale, or the prémétro to the Bourse station; from either, it's a brief walk to the Grand-Place.

By bus

Most **international bus** services to Brussels, including those from Britain, are operated by Eurolines, whose terminal is in the Bruxelles-Nord station complex. Belgium's comprehensive rail network means that it's unlikely that you'll arrive in the city by long-distance domestic bus, but if you do, Bruxelles-Nord is the main terminal for these services too.

Getting around

The easiest way to get around the centre of Brussels – the rough oval contained within the boulevards of the so-called "petit ring" – is to walk, but to get from one side of the centre to the other, or to reach some of the outlying attractions, you'll need to use public transport.

Operated by **STIB** (☎070 23 2000, ⒲www .stib.be), the city's public transport system runs on an integrated mixture of bus, tram, underground tram (prémétro) and Metro lines that covers the city comprehensively. It's a user-friendly network, with every Metro station carrying Metro-system diagrams; route maps are available free from the tourist office and from most major Metro stations, and timetables are posted at many bus and tram stops.

Tickets

Tickets, which can be used on any part of the STIB system, are available from ticket offices and automatic machines at Metro stations, or from newsagents displaying the STIB sign; tram and bus drivers will only issue single-journey tickets. **Prices** are very reasonable: a single ticket costs €1.50 if prepaid, €2 from the driver; a carnet of five tickets (*carte jump de cinque voyages*) €6.70; and ten (*carte jump de dix voyages*) €11. A **day ticket** (*carte jump d'un jour*), for €4, allows for 24 hours of unlimited, city-wide travel on public transport; at the weekend, it covers two passengers. At the beginning of each journey, you need to **stamp tickets** yourself, using one of the machines on every Metro station concourse or inside every tram and bus. After that, single tickets are valid for an hour, during which you can get on and off as many trams, Metros and buses as you like (note that **doors** on Metros, trams and buses mostly have to be opened manually). The system can seem open to abuse, as ticket controls at Metro stations are almost non-existent and you can get on at the back of any tram without ever showing a ticket. Bear in mind, however, that there are roving inspectors who impose hefty on-the-spot fines for anyone caught without a valid ticket.

By Metro, prémétro and tram

The **Metro** system consists of two underground lines – #1 and #2. **Line #1** runs west–east through the centre, and splits into two branches (#1A and #1B) at either end to serve the city's suburbs. **Line #2** circles the centre, its route roughly following that of the petit ring up above. Currently, the two Metro lines only intersect twice – at Métro Arts-Loi and Métro Simonis – but an extension is currently under construction to link Delacroix Metro station on Line #2 with Gare de l'Ouest on Line #1B. Brussels also has a substantial **tram** system serving the city centre and the suburbs. Trams are at their speediest when they go underground to form what is

sometimes called the **prémétro**, that part of the system which runs underneath the heart of the city from Bruxelles-Nord, through De Brouckère and Bourse, to Bruxelles-Midi, Porte de Hal and on underneath St Gilles.

Times of operation and frequency vary considerably among the multitude of routes, but key parts of the system operate from 6am until midnight, with a supplementary Noctis night bus service running on Friday and Saturday nights (see below). Lone travellers should try to avoid the Metro late at night.

By bus

STIB **buses** supplement the trams and the Metro. A network of Noctis **night buses** operates on twenty routes on Friday and Saturday nights, running every thirty minutes or so until 3am; one single journey on a night bus costs €3. In addition, **De Lijn** (☎070 220 200, ⓦ www.delijn.be) runs buses from Brussels to the Flemish-speaking communities that surround it, while **TEC** (☎010 230 53 53, ⓦ www.infotec.be) operates services to the French-speaking areas. Most of these buses run from – or at least call in at – the Gare du Nord complex. Both companies also run services to other Belgian cities, but they can take up to four times longer than the train.

By local train

Supplementing the STIB network are **local trains**, operated by Belgian Railways (ⓦ www .b-rail.be), which shuttle in and out of the city's four smaller train stations, connecting different parts of the inner city and the outskirts. These four stations are Bruxelles-Chapelle, Bruxelles-Quartier Léopold, Bruxelles-Schuman and Bruxelles-Congrès. Unless you're living and working in the city, however, you're unlikely to need to use them.

By car

There's no real reason to hire a car if you are staying in Brussels, but the major car rental operators have branches at both Brussels airport and at the Gare du Midi train station. Two reliable options are Europcar (Gare du Midi ☎02 522 95 73, airport ☎02 721 05 92; ⓦ www.europcar.be) and Hertz (Gare du

Midi ☎02 524 31 00, airport ☎02 720 60 44, ⊛www.hertz.be).

Taxis

Taxis don't cruise the streets, but can be picked up at ranks across the city – notably on De Brouckère, at Porte de Namur, at train stations and outside smarter hotels. The **tariff** is based on two elements – a fixed charge of €2.40 (€4.40 at night) and the per-kilometre rate (€1.35 inside the city). If you can't find a taxi, phone Taxis Verts (☎02 349 49 49), Taxis Orange (☎02 349 43 43) or Autolux (☎02 411 12 21).

Cycling

The city council has recently developed a **public bicycle scheme** (premium line ☎0900 11 000, ⊛www.cyclocity.be), in which bikes can be taken from any of the stands dotted across the city centre and returned after use to another. There are 23 stands at the time of writing, though more are planned, and 250 bikes. Costs are very reasonable – €0.50 for the first 30 minutes, then €0.50 for each subsequent hour – and the tourist office on the Grand-Place (see p.34) has all the latest information.

Guided tours

Guided tours are big business in Brussels and the TIB (see p.34) has details of – and takes bookings for – about twenty operators. On offer is everything from a quick stroll or bus ride round the city centre to themed visits – following, for example, in the footsteps of René Magritte or visiting the pick of the city's Art Nouveau buildings. As a general rule, the more traditional tours can be booked on the day, while the more exotic need to be booked ahead of time, either direct with the company concerned or via the TIB, who normally require at least two weeks' notice. Among the many more straightforward options, Brussels City Tours, rue de la Colline 8 (☎02 513 77 44, ⊛www.brussels-city-tours.com), operates breathless, three-hour **bus tours** round the city and its major sights for €27 between two and three times daily. They also run the rather more agreeable Visit Brussels Line, a hop-on, hop-off bus service which loops round the city, visiting twelve of its principal sights (daily 10am–5pm; tickets, valid for 24hr, cost €18).

More promising still is **ARAU** (Atelier de Recherche et d'Action Urbaines), boulevard Adolphe Max 55 (☎02 219 33 45, ⊛www.arau.org), a heritage action group which provides **architecture tours**, with particular emphasis on Art Nouveau, from early June to November. Prices vary with the length of the tour and the itinerary, but average about €12 per person. **Cyclists** are catered for by Pro Vélo, rue de Londres 15 (☎02 502 73 55, ⊛www.provelo.org), which operates several half-day bike tours round the city and its environs; the cost is about €8 per tour, with bike hire an extra €11.

The media

British newspapers and magazines are readily available in Brussels, and American publications are easy to get hold of too. Two of Britain's leading TV channels – BBC1 and BBC2 – are picked up by most of the city's hotels.

The press

British newspapers – from tabloid through to broadsheet – as well as the more popular **English-language magazines** are widely available, either on the day of publication or the day after, right across Brussels. Internationally distributed **American newspapers** – principally the *Wall Street Journal, USA Today* and the *International Herald Tribune* – are also easy to find, though distribution is concentrated around the city centre and the EU Quarter. Train-station bookstands are usually a good bet for English-language publications.

The three main newspapers in **French-speaking Belgium** are the influential, independent *Le Soir*; the right-wing, very Catholic *La Libre Belgique*; and *La Dernière Heure*, which is noted for its sports coverage. **Flemish-speakers** rely on the leftish *De Morgen*, traditionally the favourite of socialists and trade unionists; the right-leaning *De Standaard*; and the populist, vaguely liberal *Het Laatste Nieuws*. There's also an **English-language weekly magazine**, *The Bulletin* (⊛www.thebulletin.be), which primarily caters for the sizeable expat community resident in Brussels. Its news articles are interesting and diverse, picking up on key Belgian themes and issues, and its listings section is first-rate. It also carries a fair-sized classified section – useful if you've just arrived for an extended stay and are looking for an apartment or even work.

TV and radio

British radio stations can be picked up in Brussels: you'll find BBC Radio 4 on 198kHz long wave; the World Service on 648kHz (463m) medium wave; and BBC Radio 5 Live on 909am and 693am. Shortwave frequencies and schedules for BBC World Service (⊛www.bbc.co.uk/worldservice), Radio Canada (⊛www.rcinet.ca) and Voice of America (⊛www.voa.gov) are listed on their respective websites.

As far as **British TV** is concerned, BBC1 and BBC2 are on most hotel-room televisions. Access to cable and satellite channels is common in hotels and bars across the city too. **Domestic TV** is largely uninspiring, though the Flemish-language TV1 and Kanaal 2 usually run English-language films with subtitles, whereas the main Wallonian channels – RTBF 1 and ARTE – mostly dub. For local news and current affairs in French, try the city's own Télé-Brussels; the Flemish equivalent is TV Brussels.

Travel essentials

Addresses

In the **French-speaking** parts of Belgium, addresses are usually written to a standard format. The first line begins with the category of the street (rue, boulevard etc); followed by the name and then the number; the second line gives the area – or zip – code, followed by the town or area. Common abbreviations include *bld* or *bd* for boulevard, *av* for avenue, *pl* for place (square) and *ch* for *chaussée*. An exception is the hyphenated Grand-Place (main square), written in full. In the **Flemish-speaking** areas, the first line gives the name of the street, which is followed by (and joined to) its category – hence Krakeelplein is Krakeel square, Krakeelstraat is Krakeel street; the number comes next. The second line gives the area – or zip – code followed by the town or area. Consequently, Flemish abbreviations occur at the end of words: thus Hofstr for Hofstraat. An exception is Grote Markt (main square), which is not abbreviated. Common categories include *plein* for square, *plaats* for place, *laan* or *weg* for avenue, *kaai* for quay, and *straat* for street. In bilingual Brussels, all signs give both the French and Flemish versions. In many cases, this is fairly straightforward as they are either the same or similar, but sometimes it's extremely confusing (also see box, p.23), most notoriously in the name of one of the three principal train stations – in French, Bruxelles-Midi; in Flemish, Brussel-Zuid.

Costs

By western European standards, Brussels is **moderately expensive** when it comes to accommodation and food, though this is partly offset by the low cost of public transport. If you're prepared to buy your own picnic lunch, stay in hostels, and stick to the less expensive bars and restaurants, you could get by on around €45 a day. Staying in two-star hotels, eating out in medium-range restaurants most nights and drinking in bars, you'll get through at least €110 a day, with the main variable being the cost of your room. On €150 a day and upwards, you'll be limited only by your energy reserves – though if you're planning to stay in a five-star hotel and to have a big night out, this still won't be enough. As always, if you're travelling alone you'll spend much more on accommodation than you would in a group of two or more: most hotels do have single rooms, but they're fixed at about 75 percent of the price of a double.

Restaurants don't come cheap, but costs remain manageable if you avoid the extras and concentrate on the main courses, for which around €15–25 will normally suffice – twice that with a drink, starter and dessert. You can, of course, pay a lot more – a top restaurant in Brussels can be twice as expensive again.

Crime and personal safety

There's little reason why you should ever come into contact with the Belgian **police** force. For one thing, it's statistically unlikely you'll be a victim of crime; for another, the police generally keep a low profile, though they do blitz areas – especially the city's three main train stations – when they feel things are getting out of hand. There are two main types: the Gendarmerie Nationale, who wear blue uniforms with red stripes on their trousers, patrol the motorways and deal with major crime, and the municipal Police, in dark blue uniforms, who cover everything else. Many officers speak English, though a modicum of French can be invaluable. All police are armed.

As regards **personal safety**, it's generally possible to walk around Brussels without fear of harassment or assault, though the city does have its shady areas (for example round the Gare du Midi, the Gare du Nord and in Molenbeek), and wherever you are it's better to err on the side of caution late at night, when – for instance – badly lit or empty streets should be avoided. Using public transport isn't usually a problem either, though lone travellers should avoid the Metro late at night; if in doubt take a taxi.

If you are **robbed**, you'll need to go to a police station to report it, not least because your insurance company will require a police report; remember to make a note of the report number – or, better still, ask for a copy of the statement itself. Don't expect a great deal of concern if your loss is relatively small – and the form-filling and formalities can be time-consuming.

Travellers with disabilities

Brussels is not an easy destination for the traveller with **mobility problems**. Lifts and ramps are scarce, steep steps and uneven pavements are common – and, even when an effort has been made, obstacles are frequent. Nevertheless, although it can be difficult to get around, practically all **public buildings**, including museums, theatres, cinemas, concert halls and hotels, are obliged to – and do – provide access, while hotels, hostels and campsites which have been certified wheelchair-accessible now bear an International Accessibility Symbol (IAS). Other signs of progress are the installation of Braille information panels in some Metro stations; rubber mats at many bus and tram stops to assist the partially sighted; reserved seats for the elderly and those with mobility problems; and new trams with low-level access platforms. There is also a low-cost door-to-door **minibus service** operated by the city's public transport provider, STIB, for people with disabilities (℡02 515 23 65; Mon–Fri 6.30am–8.30pm; French and Dutch only), but note that you need to book the service two days in advance. Finally, bear in mind that a lot of the older, narrower **hotels** are not allowed to install lifts for conservation reasons – so be sure to check first.

Electricity

The **electric current** is 220 volts AC, with standard European-style two-pin plugs. British equipment needs only a plug adaptor to connect; North American apparatus requires a transformer and an adaptor.

Entry requirements

Citizens of **EU and EEA** countries only need a valid passport or national identity card to enter Belgium, where – with some limitations – they also have the right to live, work and study. US, Australian, Canadian, South African and New Zealand citizens need only a valid passport for visits of up to **ninety days**, but are not allowed to work. Passports must be valid for at least three months beyond the period of intended stay. Citizens of **non-EU** countries who wish to visit Belgium for longer than ninety days must get a special **visa** from a Belgian consulate or embassy before departure (see below for addresses). Visa requirements do change and it is always advisable to check the current situation before leaving home.

Embassies in Brussels

Australia rue Guimard 6–8 ☏ 02 286 05 00, ⓦ www.eu.mission.gov.au.
Canada av de Tervuren 2 ☏ 02 741 06 11, ⓦ www.dfait-maeci.gc.ca/brussels.
Great Britain rue d'Arlon 85 ☏ 02 287 62 11, ⓦ www.britishembassy.gov.uk/belgium.
Ireland rue Wiertz 50 ☏ 02 235 66 76, ⓦ foreignaffairs.gov.ie.
New Zealand square de Meeûs 1 ☏ 02 512 10 40, ⓦ www.nzembassy.com.
South Africa rue Montoyer 17–19 ☏ 02 285 44 00, ⓦ www.southafrica.be.
US blvd du Régent 27 ☏ 02 508 21 11, ⓦ belgium .usembassy.gov/index.html.

Belgian embassies and consulates abroad

See ⓦ www.diplomatie.be for links to the websites of Belgian embassies and consulates abroad.
Australia Embassy: 19 Arkana St, Yarralumla, ACT 2600, Canberra ☏ 02/6273 2501.
Also consular representation in Adelaide, Brisbane, Darwin, Hobart, Melbourne, Perth and Sydney.
Canada Embassy: 360 Albert St, Suite 820, Ottawa, Ontario K1R 7X7 ☏ 613/236 7267.
Also consular representation in Edmonton, Halifax, Montréal, Toronto, Vancouver and Winnipeg.
Ireland 2 Shrewsbury Rd, Ballsbridge, Dublin 4 ☏ 01/205 71 00.
Also Honorary Consuls in Cork and Limerick.
Netherlands Embassy: Alexanderveld 97, 2585 DB Den Haag ☏ 070/312 3456. Honorary consulates in Amsterdam, Groningen, Maastricht, Nijmegen, Rotterdam and Vlissingen.
New Zealand Honorary consul: 15A Rarangi Rd, St. Heliers, Auckland ☏ 09/575 6202.
Also consular representation in Wellington and Christchurch.
Poland Embassy: Ulica Senatorska 34, 00-095 Warszawa ☏ 22/551 28 00.
Also consular representation in Katowice and Poznan.
South Africa Embassy: Leyds St 625 Muckleneuk, 0002 Pretoria ☏ 12/440 32 01.
Also consular representation in Johannesburg, Durban and Port Elizabeth.
UK Embassy: 17 Grosvenor Crescent, London SW1X 7EE ☏ 020 7470 3700.
Visa Application Centre: 1–8 Bateman's Building, South Soho Square, London W1D 3EN ☏ 0844 8159839, ⓦ www.vfs-be-uk.com.
USA Embassy: 3330 Garfield St NW, Washington DC 20008 ☏ 202/333 6900, ⓦ www.diplobel.us.

Gay and lesbian travellers

Gay and lesbian life in Brussels does not have a high international profile, especially in comparison with neighbouring Amsterdam. That said, there's still a vibrant scene, though more so for men than women, and the Belgians have a pragmatic tolerance – or intolerance soaked in indifference – that has provided opportunities for legislative change. In 1998 Belgium passed a law granting certain rights to cohabiting couples irrespective of their sex, and gay marriage was legalized, after much huffing and puffing by the political right, in 2003. The legal age of consent for gay men is 16. See pp.243–245 for more on the city's gay and lesbian scene.

Health

Under reciprocal health care arrangements, all citizens of the EU (European Union) and EEA (European Economic Area) are entitled to free, or at least subsidized, **medical treatment** within Belgium's public health care system. With the exception of Australians, whose government has recently entered into a reciprocal health agreement with Belgium, non-EU/EEA nationals are not entitled to any free treatment and should, therefore, take out their own medical insurance. However, EU/EEA citizens and Australians may also want to consider private health insurance, both to cover the cost of items not within the EU/EEA scheme, such as dental treatment and repatriation on medical grounds, and to enable them to seek treatment within the private sector. Note also that the more worthwhile insurance policies promise to sort matters out before you pay (rather than after), in the case of major expense; if you do have to pay upfront, get and keep the receipts. For more on insurance, see below.

In an **emergency**, phone ☎112. Belgium's public health care system is of a good standard and widely available, with clinics and hospitals in all the larger towns. If you're seeking treatment under **EU/EEA reciprocal health arrangements**, it may be necessary to double-check that the medic you see is working within (and seeing you as) a patient of the public system. That being the case, you'll receive subsidized treatment just as the locals do. Technically you should have your passport and your **European Health Insurance Card (EHIC)** to hand to prove that you are eligible for EU/EEA health care, but often no one bothers to check. You can anticipate that some hospital staff will speak English in Brussels, though a rudimentary grasp of French is much more useful. Your hotel will usually be able to arrange an appointment with a doctor, but note that this will almost certainly be on a private basis.

For **minor complaints**, go to a **pharmacy** (French *pharmacie*, Flemish *apotheek*): pharmacists are highly trained, willing to give advice (often in English), and able to dispense many drugs which would only be available on prescription in many other countries. Pharmacies are to be found all over the city.

Insurance

It's a good idea to take out an **insurance policy** to cover against theft, loss and illness or injury. Before paying for a new policy, however, it's worth checking whether you already have some degree of cover: for instance, EU/EEA health care privileges apply in Belgium (see p.29), some all-risks home insurance policies may cover your possessions when overseas, and many private medical schemes include cover when abroad.

For those that still need to take out travel insurance, a typical policy usually provides cover for loss of baggage, tickets and – up to a certain limit – cash or cheques, as well as cancellation or curtailment of your journey and medical costs. Most of them exclude so-called **dangerous sports** – climbing, horse riding and so forth – unless an extra premium is paid. Many policies can be chopped and changed to exclude coverage you don't need – for example, sickness and accident benefits can often be excluded or included at will. If you do take medical coverage, ascertain whether benefits will be paid as treatment proceeds or only after your return home, and whether there is a 24-hour medical emergency number. When securing baggage cover, make sure that the per-article limit will cover your most valuable possessions. If you need to make a claim, keep **receipts** for medicines and medical treatment. In the event you have anything stolen, you must obtain a **crime report** statement or number.

Internet

Many of the city's hotels and hostels provide internet access for their guests either free or at minimal charge, which is a good job as internet cafés are noticeably thin on the ground. The useful website ⓦwww.kropla.com gives details on using your laptop abroad, as well as information on phone country codes and electrical systems around the world.

Left luggage

Bruxelles-Midi and Bruxelles-Centrale train stations have both left-luggage offices and coin-operated lockers. The luggage office in Bruxelles-Midi, located near the Thalys and Eurostar departure lounge, is open 24 hours. In Bruxelles-Centrale, it is open daily from 6.20am–9.30pm. Expect to pay €3–4 per day, depending on size of bag. There is no left-luggage facility in Bruxelles-Nord.

Lost property

For items lost on an aircraft flying into Brussels international, ring the airport on ☎02 723 60 11; if lost at the airport itself, call ☎02 753 68 20. The lost property office for STIB's Metro, tram and bus network is at avenue de la Toison d'Or 15 (☎02 515 23 94). For Bruxelles-Midi train station, call ☎02 224 88 62, and for Bruxelles-Centrale, ☎02 224 60 04.

Mail

Belgium has an efficient postal system. In Brussels, **post offices** are fairly plentiful and are mostly open Monday to Friday 9am to 4/5pm, with the larger ones also open on Saturday mornings from 9am to noon. The main central post office is in the Gare Centrale complex (entrance on blvd de l'Imperatrice; Mon–Fri 8.30am–5.30pm & Sat 9am–noon). **Stamps** are sold at a wide range of outlets, including many shops and hotels. Post to the US takes seven days or so, within Europe two to three days.

Maps

The **maps** in this Guide should be more than adequate for most purposes, but if you need one on a larger scale, or with a street index, then pick up the free city map with index issued by all of the TIB tourist offices (see p.34). These maps do not, however, extend to the **outer suburbs**; for these districts, the best map currently on the market is Michelin's the widely available *Bruxelles* (1:17,500). As for Belgium in general, a very good-value national road map is the clear and easy-to-use De Rouck Geomatics' (ⓦwww.derouckgeomatics.com) *Belgium and Luxembourg* (1:250,000) map.

Money

The **currency** of Belgium – like most of the rest of the EU – is the euro (€), with each euro comprising 100 cents. There are seven euro notes – in denominations of €500, €200, €100, €50, €20, €10 and €5, each a different colour and size – and eight different coins, including €2 and €1, then 50, 20, 10, 5, 2, and 1 cents. All euro notes and coins can be used in any of the fifteen euro-zone – sometimes "euroland" – states. At the time of writing the **rate of exchange** for €1 is £0.79; US$1.57; Can$1.56; Aus$1.64; NZ$1.99; ZAR12. For the most up-to-date rates, check the currency converter website ⓦwww.oanda.com.

ATMs are liberally dotted across the centre of Brussels, with a particular concentration on and around the Grand-Place, including one at Grand-Place 7, though note that they are notorious for running out of money late on Saturday night. Most ATMs give instructions in a variety of languages and all accept a host of **debit cards** without charging a transaction fee. **Credit cards** can be used in ATMs too, but in this case transactions are treated as loans, with interest accruing daily from the date of withdrawal. All major credit cards, including American Express, Visa and

MasterCard, are widely accepted in Brussels and, for that matter, all of Belgium.

All well-known brands of **traveller's cheque** in major currencies can be exchanged, as can foreign currency, for euros at most **banks**, which are ubiquitous. Banking hours are usually Monday to Friday from 9am to 3.30pm, with a few banks also open on Saturday mornings; all are closed on public holidays (see below). Outside regular banking hours, most major hotels, many travel agents and some hostels will change money at less generous rates and with variable commissions, as will the **bureaux de change** at the three mainline stations: Bruxelles-Nord (Mon–Fri 8am–8pm & Sat 10am–5pm); Bruxelles-Centrale (Mon–Fri 9.30am–4.30pm); and Bruxelles-Midi (daily 8am–8.30pm).

For **lost or stolen credit cards**, call ☏02 676 26 26 for American Express, ☏02 626 50 04 for Diner's Club, ☏070 34 43 44 for MasterCard and ☏0800 18 397 for Visa. See p.28 for how to report a crime.

Opening hours and public holidays

Typical **business hours** run from Monday to Friday 9.30/10am to 4.30/5pm, whereas regular **shopping hours** are Monday to Saturday 10am to 6pm. That said, many smaller shops open late on Monday morning and/or close a tad earlier on Saturdays, while many supermarkets and department stores are likely to have extended hours, with late-night opening on Fridays (until 8/9pm) especially popular, and the tourist-oriented shops in and around the Grand-Place generally open seven days a week until the early evening. Finally, a smattering of convenience stores (*magasins de nuit*) stay open either all night or until 1am or 2am daily.

The majority of the city's **museums** are state-run and these almost invariably conform to a pattern: closed on Monday, and open Tuesday to Sunday from 10am to 5pm, though the most important ones usually open on Mondays during the summer months too. **Church** hours vary considerably, but the most-visited are normally open Monday to Saturday from around 9am to 5pm, with shorter opening hours on Sunday. Most **restaurants** are open for dinner from about 6pm or 7pm, and though many close as early as 9.30pm, a few stay open past 11pm; many open for a couple of hours at lunch time too – from around noon to 2pm – and some close one day a week. **Clubs** generally function from 11pm to 4am during the week (though few open every night), and stay open until 5am at weekends. Precise opening hours for shops, museums, churches, restaurants and clubs – as well as many other attractions – are given in the Guide.

In Belgium, there are twelve national **public holidays** per year and, for the most part, they are keenly observed, with most businesses and many attractions closed, and public transport reduced to a Sunday service. For the dates of **festivals and special events**, which can be similarly disruptive to the normal ebb and flow of the city, see pp.246–250.

Phones

Brussels has excellent **mobile phone** (cell phone) coverage; the network is at GSM900/1800, the band common to the rest of Europe, Australia and New Zealand. Mobile phones bought in North America need to be of the tri-band variety to access this GSM band. If you intend to use your mobile phone in Brussels, note that call

---

Public holidays

Note that if a public holiday falls on a **Sunday**, the next day becomes a holiday.

New Year's Day	Whit Monday	(Aug 15)
Easter Sunday	Flemish Day (Flemish-	Walloon Day (French-
Easter Monday	speaking Belgium only	speaking Belgium only
Labour Day (May 1)	July 11)	Sept 27)
Ascension Day (forty	Belgium National Day	All Saints' Day (Nov 1)
days after Easter)	(July 21)	Armistice Day (Nov 11)
Whit Sunday	Feast of the Assumption	Christmas Day

International calls and useful telephone numbers

Phoning home from Brussels

To make an international phone call from Brussels, dial the appropriate international access code as below, then the number you require, omitting the initial zero where there is one.

Australia ☎0061

Canada ☎001

Republic of Ireland ☎00353

New Zealand ☎0064

South Africa ☎0027

UK ☎0044

US ☎001

Phoning Brussels from abroad

To call a number in Brussels, dial the local international access code, then ☎32 for Belgium, followed by the number you require, omitting the initial zero where there is one. Most Brussels numbers begin with ☎02.

Operator numbers

Domestic directory enquiries Flemish ☎1207, French ☎1307

International directory enquiries & operator Flemish ☎1204, French ☎1304

Emergency numbers

Police, fire brigade & ambulance ☎112

---

charges can be extortionate – particularly irritating is the supplementary charge that you often have to pay on incoming calls – so check with your provider before you depart. **Text messages**, on the other hand, are usually charged at ordinary rates.

Domestic and international **phone cards** – *télécards* – for use in public phones can be bought at many outlets, including post offices, some supermarkets, railway stations and newsagents. They come in several denominations, beginning at €5.

To make a **reverse-charge** or collect call, phone the **international operator** (Flemish ☎1204; French ☎1304) – they almost all speak English. Remember also that although virtually all hotel rooms have phones, there is almost always an exorbitant surcharge for their use.

There are no **area codes** in Belgium, but Belgian numbers mostly begin with a zero, a relic of former area codes, which have

now been incorporated into the numbers themselves. Telephone numbers beginning ☎0900 or 070 are premium-rate, ☎0800 are toll-free. There's no distinction between local and long-distance calls in Belgium – in other words calling Ostend from Brussels costs the same as calling another number in Brussels.

Time

Belgium (and Brussels) is on **Central European Time** (CET) – one hour ahead of Greenwich Mean Time, six hours ahead of US Eastern Standard Time, nine hours ahead of US Pacific Standard Time, nine hours behind Australian Eastern Standard Time and eleven hours behind New Zealand. There are, however, variations during the changeover periods involved in daylight saving. Belgium operates daylight saving time, moving its clocks forward one

Smoking

In 2007, smoking was **banned** in all restaurants, and those bars and cafés which serve food are now obliged to have a non-smoking area. Smoking is also forbidden in all public places, from theatres through to town halls. All public transport is no-smoking too, as are the confined spaces of train stations, but you can still light up on open-air platforms.

hour in the spring and one hour back in the autumn.

Tipping

There's no need to tip when there's a service charge – as there often is – but when there isn't, restaurant waiters will anticipate a ten to fifteen percent tip. Taxis display a sign saying that tipping is neither necessary nor expected, but often people will simply round up the fare.

Toilets

Public toilets are comparatively rare, but many of the city's cafés and bars operate what amounts to an ablutionary sideline with a €0.20–0.50 fee to use their toilets; you'll spot the plate for the money as you enter, or "Madame Pipi" (as she is endearingly known) will be happy to remind you.

Tourist information

Belgium has two official tourist boards, one covering the French-speaking areas, the other the Flemish-speaking regions; they share responsibility for Brussels. These boards are respectively the **Office de Promotion du Tourisme (OPT) Wallonia-Bruxelles** and **Toerisme Vlaanderen** (Tourism Flanders). Both have all-encompassing websites (see p.35), covering everything from hotels and campsites to forthcoming events. In addition, there are tourist information desks at both of Brussels' main airports (see p.23).

Right in the centre of the city, in the Hôtel de Ville on the Grand-Place, is the extremely useful **Tourisme Information Bruxelles (TIB)** office (Jan–Easter Mon–Sat 9am–6pm; Easter–Sept daily 9am–6pm; Oct–Dec Mon–Sat 9am–6pm & Sun 10am–2pm;

☏02 513 89 40, ⓦwww.brusselsinternational .be). It stocks a wide range of handouts, including free city **maps**, has details of forthcoming events and concerts, makes reservations on **guided tours** (for more on which, see p.26), and sells inexpensive general- and specialist-interest guides, the most useful of which is the detailed Brussels Guide and Map. TIB also issues a free booklet detailing all the city's (recognized) hotels and can make last-minute **hotel reservations** for free – the deposit you pay is subtracted from your final hotel bill. This is especially attractive as TIB can often offer substantial discounts on published rates; for more on accommodation, see p.181. It can help with public transport too, selling the 24-hour pass (see p.25) and handing out free public transport maps. Finally, TIB sells the **Brussels Card** (see box below). There's another TIB tourist information desk (May–Sept daily 8am–8pm; Oct–April Mon–Thurs 8am–5pm, Fri 8am–8pm, Sat 9am–6pm & Sun 9am–2pm) in the main concourse at **Bruxelles-Midi train station**, one of the city's three main train stations and the Eurostar terminus, but it's geared up to cater for new arrivals and does not offer the same range of services as the main office.

Toerisme Vlaanderen (Tourism Flanders) has an information office just metres from the Grand-Place at rue Marché aux Herbes 61 (April–June & Sept Mon–Sat 9am–6pm, Sun 10am–5pm; July & Aug daily 9am–7pm; Oct–March Mon–Sat 9am–5pm, Sun 10am–4pm; ☏02 504 03 00, ⓦwww.visitflanders .com). They also operate a hotel room reservation service, but it's for Flemish Belgium, not Brussels.

As for local news and reviews, the weekly **Bulletin** (€3; ⓦwww.thebulletin.be) is the city's main English-language magazine, with a thorough **entertainment listings** section,

---

The Brussels Card

The **Brussels Card** (ⓦwww.brusselscard.be) provides free access to most of the city's key museums, unlimited travel on the STIB public transport network, and discounts of up to 25 percent at specified restaurants and bars. There are three versions – 24hr (€20), 48hr (€28), and 72hr (€33), and each is valid from the first time it is used, rather than the day of issue. The card is on sale online on the website and at the tourist office on the Grand-Place (see above); there are no concessionary rates for seniors or children. It's issued with a booklet detailing all the concessions and discounts.

detailing what's on where and when; it's on sale at most central newsagents.

Tourist-office and related websites

Belgian Tourist Office for the Americas
ⓦwww.visitbelgium.com. Reliable website providing standard tourist information with an American slant.
Expatica ⓦwww.expatica.com. Advice on how to go about being an expat in several EU countries, including Belgium. Covers housing, employment and so forth.
Museum Talks ⓦwww.museumtalks.be. Official site with free, downloadable Mp3 audio guides covering a number of the city's museums, recorded by artists, musicians and assorted experts.

Tourisme Information Bruxelles (TIB) ⓦwww .brusselsinternational.be. Official city tourist board website.
Toerisme Vlaanderen ⓦwww.visitflanders.com. Detailed and competent multilingual guide to the capital and the northern, Flemish-speaking half of Belgium.
Wallonia–Bruxelles ⓦwww.belgiumtheplaceto .be. Portal site with lots of useful links, plus details of everything from golfing holidays to festivals. Operated by the official Wallonia-Bruxelles tourist board, covering the capital and the southern, French-speaking half of the country.

B

BASICS | Travel essentials

The City

The City

The Grand-Place

O ne of Europe's most beautiful city squares, the **Grand-Place** is an almost entirely enclosed, pedestrianized rectangle tucked away amid the tangle of ancient cobbled lanes that lies at the heart of Brussels. It's the Gothic magnificence of the **Hôtel de Ville** – the town hall – which first draws the eye, but in its shadow is an exquisite sequence of late seventeenth-century **guildhouses** whose gilded facades, with their columns, scrolled gables and dainty sculptures, encapsulate the Baroque ideals of exuberance and complexity. There's no better place to get a flavour of Brussels' past, and, as you nurse a coffee watching the crowds from one of the pavement cafés, its Eurocapital present.

The Hôtel de Ville

From the south side of the Grand-Place, the newly scrubbed and polished **Hôtel de Ville**, or town hall, dominates proceedings, its 96-metre spire soaring high above two long series of robust windows, whose straight lines are mitigated by fancy tracery, striking gargoyles, solid statuettes and an arcaded gallery. The town hall dates from the beginning of the fifteenth century, when the town council decided to build itself a mansion that adequately reflected its wealth and power. The first part to be completed (in the 1410s) was the **east wing**, and the original entrance is still marked by the twin lions of the Lion Staircase, though the animals were only added in 1770. Work started on the **west wing** in 1444 and continued until 1480. Despite the gap, the wings are of very similar style, and you have to look hard to notice that the later wing is slightly shorter than its neighbour, allegedly at the insistence of Charles the Bold who – for some unknown reason – refused to have the adjacent rue de la Tête d'Or narrowed. The niches were left empty and the statues you see now – which represent leading figures from the city's past – are modern, part of a heavy-handed nineteenth-century refurbishment.

Tours

There are regular **guided tours** of the Hôtel de Ville in English (April–Sept Tues & Wed at 3.15pm & Sun at 10.45am & 12.15pm; Oct–March Tues & Wed at 3.15pm; €3), which last about forty minutes and are confined to a string of lavish official rooms used for receptions and town council meetings. The most

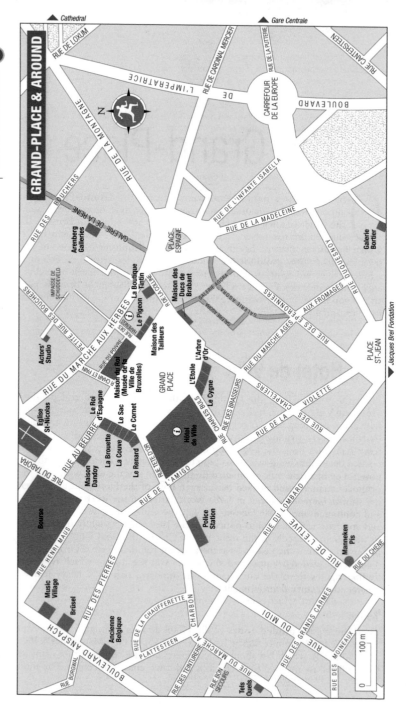

GRAND-PLACE & AROUND

▲ Cathedral

▲ Gare Centrale

N

RUE DE LOXUM

RUE DE L'IMPÉRATRICE

RUE DE CARDINAL MERCIER

RUE DE LA PUTTERIE

RUE CANTERSTEEN

CARREFOUR
DE L'EUROPE

BOULEVARD

DE

RUE DE LA MONTAGNE

RUE DES BOUCHERS

GALERIE DE LA REINE

RUE DE L'INFANTE ISABELLA

RUE DE LA MADELEINE

Arenberg
Galleries

PLACE
ESPAGNE

GALERIE AGORA

GALERIE AGORA

Galerie
Bortier

IMPASSE DE
SCHUDDEVELD

PETITE RUE DES BOUCHERS

La Boutique
Tintin

Le Pigeon

RUE DE LA COLLINE

Maison des
Ducs de Brabant

GALERIE AGORA

RUE DUQUESNOY

RUE DES ÉPERONNIERS

AUX FROMAGES

RUE DU MARCHÉ AUX HERBES

Actors'
Studio

RUE DES HARENGS

Maison des
Tailleurs

RUE DU MARCHÉ AUX

RUE DU POIVRE

L'Étoile

L'Arbre
d'Or

RUE DE LA

PLACE
ST-JEAN

▼ Jacques Brel Fondation

RUE DU CHAR ET PAIN

Maison du Roi
(Musée de la
Ville de
Bruxelles)

GRAND
PLACE

Le Cygne

RUE DES CHAPELIERS

VIOLETTE

Église
St-Nicolas

Le Roi
d'Espagne

Le Sac

Le Cornet

i

Hôtel
de Ville

RUE CHARLES BULS

RUE DES BRASSEURS

RUE DE LA

RUE DES

RUE AU BEURRE

La Brouette

La Couve

Le Renard

RUE DU TABORA

Maison
Dandoy

RUE DE LA TÊTE D'OR

RUE DE L'AMIGO

Police
Station

RUE DU LOMBARD

RUE DE L'ÉTUVE

Manneken
Pis

RUE DU CHÊNE

Bourse

RUE HENRI MAUS

Music
Village

Brüsel

RUE DES PIERRES

Ancienne
Belgique

RUE DE LA CHAUFFERETTE

CHARBON

DU MIDI

RUE DES GRANDS CARMES

BOULEVARD ANSPACH

RUE BORGWAL

PLATTESTEEN

RUE DU MARCHÉ AU

RUE DES TEINTURERS

RUE BON
SECOURS

Tels
Quels

RUE DES

MOINEAUX

0   100 m

The Grand-Place in history

Originally marshland, the **Grand-Place** was drained in the twelfth century, and by 1350 a **covered market** for bread, meat and textiles had appeared, born of an economic boom underpinned by a flourishing cloth industry. The market was so successful that it soon expanded beyond the boundaries of the square – hence the names of the warren of narrow streets around it: rues au Beurre and des Bouchers, marchés aux Herbes, aux Poulets and aux Fromages. On the square itself, the city's merchants built themselves their headquarters, the guildhouses that cemented the Grand-Place's role as the commercial hub of the emergent city.

In the fifteenth century, with the building of the **Hôtel de Ville**, the square took on a civic and political function too, with the ruling dukes descending from their Upper Town residence to hold audiences and organize tournaments. Official decrees and pronouncements were also read here, and rough justice was meted out with public executions. In the 1480s, Brussels, along with the rest of the Low Countries, became a fiefdom of the **Habsburgs** and the role of the Grand-Place was transformed by that most Catholic of kings, **Philip II of Spain** (1555–98), who turned the square's public executions into religious events as he strove to crush the city's Protestants. These were the opening shots of a bitter religious war that was to rack the Low Countries for the next hundred years, although Brussels, after changing hands a couple of times, was finally secured by the Catholics in 1585. In victory, the Habsburgs were surprisingly generous, granting a general amnesty and promising to honour ancient municipal privileges. The city's economy revived and the Grand-Place resumed its role as a commercial centre. Of the square's medieval buildings, however, only parts of the Hôtel de Ville and the lower floors of two guildhouses survive today, the consequence of a 36-hour **French artillery bombardment**, which pretty much razed Brussels to the ground in 1695.

Unperturbed, the city's **guilds** swiftly had their headquarters rebuilt, using their control of the municipal council both to impose regulations on the sort of construction that was permitted and to ward off the Habsburg governor's notions of a royal – as distinct from bourgeois – main square. The council was not to be trifled with. In an early example of **urban planning**, it decreed: "(We) hereby forbid the owners to build houses on the lower market [ie the Grand-Place] without the model of the facade … first being presented to the Council … Any construction erected contrary to this provision shall be demolished at the expense of the offender." By these means, the guilds were able to create a homogeneous Grand-Place, choosing to rebuild in a distinctive and flamboyant Baroque which made the square more ornate and more imposing than before. This magisterial self-confidence was, in fact, misplaced, as the factories that were soon to render the guilds obsolete were already colonizing parts of the city. The industrialization of the city effectively becalmed the Grand-Place and accidentally preserved it in its entirety.

dazzling of these is the sixteenth-century **Council Chamber**, decorated with gilt moulding, faded tapestries and an oak floor inlaid with ebony. The **entrance chamber** at the top of the first flight of stairs is also of interest for its assortment of royal portraits. Empress Maria Theresa of Austria is pictured side-saddle with her little feet (of which she was inordinately proud) poking out from her extravagantly lacy dress, while a gallant-looking **Charles II** (see p.43) sits astride his handsome steed, courtesy of Jan van Orley. This must have stretched Orley's imagination to the limit: Charles, the last of the Spanish Habsburgs, was – according to the historian J. H. Elliott – "a rachitic and feeble-minded weakling, the last stunted sprig of a degenerate line". Tours begin at the reception desk off the interior quadrangle; be prepared for the guides' overly reverential script.

▲ The Hôtel de Ville during the Tapis de Fleurs flower festival

The tower

By any standards, the **tower** of the Hôtel de Ville is quite extraordinary, its remarkable slender appearance the work of Jan van Ruysbroeck, the leading spire specialist of the day, who also played a pivotal role in the building of the cathedral (see p.69) and SS. Pierre et Guidon in Anderlecht (see p.120). Ruysbroeck had the lower section built square to support the weight above, choosing a design that blended seamlessly with the elaborately carved facade on either side – or almost: look carefully and you'll see that the main entrance is slightly out of kilter. Ruysbroeck used the old belfry porch as the base for the new tower, hence the misalignment, a deliberate decision and not a miscalculation prompting the architect's suicide, as legend would have it. Above the cornice protrudes an octagonal extension where the basic design of narrow windows flanked by pencil-thin columns and pinnacles is repeated up as far as the pyramid-shaped **spire**, a delicate affair surmounted by a gilded figure of **St Michael**, protector of Christians in general and of soldiers in particular.

The Guildhouses

Flanking and facing the Hôtel de Ville are the **guildhouses** that give the Grand-Place its character, their slender, gilded facades swirling with exuberant, self-publicizing carvings and sculptures. Decorated with semicircular arches and classical motifs, scrollwork, supple bas-reliefs and statuettes, they represent the apotheosis of **Italian-Flemish architecture**, a melding of two stylistic traditions first introduced into the Low Countries by artists and architects returning from Italy in the early seventeenth century. Each guildhouse has a name, usually derived from one of the statues, symbols or architectural quirks decorating its facade – and the more interesting are described below. Most of the old guildhouses have ground-floor **cafés**, which spill out across the cobbled square. As you might expect, they all charge premium rates, but *La Brouette*, at nos. 2–3, with its tasteful repro furniture and fittings and open fire, is nonetheless particularly appealing and its first floor offers an attractive view of the square; a good second bet is *La Chaloupe d'Or* at no. 24, which is kitted out in similar style.

The west side: Nos. 1–7

On the west side of the square, at the end of the row, stands the **Roi d'Espagne** at no. 1, a particularly fine building, which takes its name from the bust of Charles II (see box below) on the upper storey, but was the headquarters of the guild of bakers. A Moorish and a Native American prisoner, symbolic trophies

---

The health of Charles II

Philip IV of Spain (1605–65) had no fewer than fourteen children, but only one of his sons – **Charles II** (1661–1700) – reached his twenties. With women banned from the succession, the hapless, sickly Charles became king at the tender age of four and, much to everyone's surprise, survived to adulthood. After his first marriage in 1679, there were great hopes that he would be able to sire an **heir**, but none arrived, probably because Charles suffered from premature ejaculation. A second marriage, twenty years later, was equally fruitless and, as it became increasingly clear that Charles was unable to procreate, Europe focused on what was to happen when Charles died and the Spanish royal line died out. Every ambassador to the Spanish court wrote long missives home about the health of Charles, none more so than the English representative, **Stanhope**, who painted an especially gloomy picture: "He (Charles) has a ravenous stomach and swallows all he eats whole, for his nether jaw stands out so much that his two rows of teeth cannot meet... His weak stomach not being able to digest the food, he voids it in the same (whole) manner."

In the autumn of 1700, it was clear that Charles was dying and his doctors went to work in earnest, replacing his pillows with freshly killed pigeons and covering his chest with animal entrails. Surprise, surprise, this didn't work and Charles died on November 1, his death leading directly to the War of the Spanish Succession (1701–14).

of war, flank the bust of Charles, while balanced on the balustrade up above are allegorical statues of Energy, Fire, Water, Wind, Wheat and Prudence, presumably meant to represent the elements necessary for baking the ideal loaf. The guildhouse now holds the most famous of the square's bars, *Le Roy d'Espagne*, a surreal if somewhat dingy affair with animal bladders and marionettes hanging from the ceiling – and repro pikes and halberds in the toilets.

At nos. 2–3, the **Maison de la Brouette** was the tallow-makers' guildhouse, but it takes its name from the wheelbarrows etched into the cartouches. The figure at the top is St Gilles, the guild's patron saint. Next door, the three lower storeys of the **Maison du Sac**, at no. 4, escaped the French bombardment of 1695, but they are really rather unremarkable, unlike the upper storeys whose pilasters and caryatids resemble the ornate legs of Baroque furniture, an appropriate design given that this was the guildhouse of the carpenters and coopers.

The **Maison de la Louve**, at no. 5, also survived the French artillery, and was originally home to the influential archers' guild. The pilastered facade is studded with sanctimonious representations of concepts such as Peace and Discord, and the medallions just beneath the pediment carry the likenesses of four Roman emperors set above allegorical motifs indicating their particular attributes. Thus, Trajan is above the Sun, a symbol of Truth; Tiberius has a net and cage for Falsehood; Augustus is depicted with the globe of Peace; and Julius Caesar with a bleeding heart for Disunity. Above the door, there's a charming bas-relief of the Roman she-wolf suckling Romulus and Remus, while the pediment holds a relief of Apollo firing at a python; right on top, the Phoenix rises from the ashes.

The **Maison du Cornet**, at no. 6, headquarters of the boatmen's guild, is a fanciful creation of 1697 sporting a top storey resembling the stern of a ship. Charles II makes another appearance here – it's his head in the medallion, flanked by representations of the four winds and a pair of sailors.

The house of the haberdashers' guild, the **Maison du Renard**, at no. 7, displays animated cherubs in bas-relief playing with haberdashery on the ground floor, while a scrawny, gilded fox – after which the house is named – squats above the

▲ The Grand-Place's ornate guildhouses

door. Up on the second storey a statue of Justice proclaims the guild's honest intentions and is flanked by statues symbolizing the four continents, suggesting the guild's designs on world markets – an aim to which St Nicolas, patron saint of merchants, glinting above, clearly gives his blessing.

Just past the Maison du Renard, a few metres off the square at 9–11 rue de la Tête, the small **Musée du Cacao et du Chocolat** (Tues–Sun 10am–4.30pm; €5; Ⓦ www.mucc.be) is an unashamed attempt to cash in on the thing that's on most people's mind in the environs of the Grand-Place: chocolate. Indeed, the smell is pretty overpowering as you enter; and by the time you leave, having viewed an exhibition of cocoa cultivation, along with chocolate moulds, cocoa beans and old tins, and received your free biscuit dipped in chocolate from a dripping wheel, you may be heartily sick of the stuff.

The south side: Nos. 8–10

On the south side of the square, beside the Hôtel de Ville, the arcaded **Maison de l'Etoile** (no. 8) is a nineteenth-century rebuilding of the medieval home of the city magistrate. In the arcaded gallery, the exploits of one **Everard 't Serclaes** are commemorated: in 1356 the Francophile Count of Flanders attempted to seize power from the Duke of Brabant, occupying the magistrate's house and flying his standard from the roof. 'T Serclaes scaled the building, replaced Flanders' standard with that of the Duke of Brabant, and went on to recapture the city for the Brabantines, events represented in bas-relief above a reclining statue of 't Serclaes. His effigy, the work of one Julien Dillens (1869–1904), is polished smooth from the long-standing superstition that good luck will come to those who stroke it – surprising really as 't Serclaes was ultimately hacked to death by the count's mates in 1388. The figure was in fact black originally and is currently being restored to its natural colour.

Next door, the mansion that takes its name from the ostentatious swan on the facade, the **Maison du Cygne**, at no. 9, once housed a bar where Karl Marx regularly met up with Engels during his exile in Belgium. It was in Brussels in February 1848 that they wrote the *Communist Manifesto*, only to be deported as political undesirables the following month. Appropriately enough, the Belgian Workers' Party was founded here in 1885, though nowadays the building shelters one of the city's more exclusive restaurants.

The **Maison de l'Arbre d'Or**, at no. 10, is the only house on the Grand-Place still to be owned by a guild (the Union of Belgian Brewers) – not that the equestrian figure stuck on top gives any clues: the original effigy – of one of the city's Habsburg governors – dropped off, and the present statue, of the eighteenth-century aristocrat Charles of Lorraine, was moved here simply to fill the gap. Inside, the small basement **Musée de la Brasserie** (daily 10am–5pm; €5; Ⓦ www.beerparadise.be) has various bits of brewing paraphernalia, old and new, and shows a short film extolling the virtues of Belgian ale; the price of admission includes a beer, which you can enjoy in the pleasant rustic bar.

The east and north sides: Nos. 13–27

The seven guildhouses **(nos. 13–19)** that fill out the east side of the Grand-Place have been subsumed within one grand edifice, the **Maison des Ducs de Brabant**, named after the nineteen busts of dukes of Brabant that grace the facade's pilasters. This building, more than any other on the Grand-Place, has the flavour of the aristocracy, as distinct from the bourgeoisie, and needless to say, it was much admired by the city's Habsburg governors.

The guildhouses and private mansions **(nos. 20–39)** running along the north side of the Grand-Place, just to the right of the Maison du Roi (see below), are not quite as distinguished as their neighbours, though the **Maison du Pigeon** (nos. 26–27), the painters' guildhouse, is of interest as the house where Victor Hugo spent some time during his exile from France – he was expelled after the crushing of the French insurrection of 1848. The house also bears four unusual masks in the manner of the green man of Romano-Celtic folklore. The adjacent **Maison des Tailleurs** (nos. 24–25) is appealing too; the old headquarters of the tailors' guild, it is adorned by a pious bust of St Barbara, their patron saint and now home to one of the square's better bars.

The Maison du Roi

Much of the northern side of the Grand-Place is taken up by the late nineteenth-century **Maison du Roi** (King's House), a fairly faithful recon-struction of the palatial Gothic structure commissioned by Charles V in 1515. The emperor had a point to make: the Hôtel de Ville was an assertion of municipal independence and Charles wanted to emphasize imperial power by erecting his own building directly opposite. With its angular lines, spiky pinnacles and lacy stonework, the original Maison du Roi was an impressive building, but although its replacement, which was completed in the 1890s, is still fairly grand, the arcaded galleries – which were an addition – interrupt the flow of the design. Charles spared no expense in the earlier construction. When it turned out that the ground was too marshy to support the edifice, the archi-tects began again, sinking piles deep into the ground and stretching cattle hides between them to keep the stagnant water at bay.

Despite its name, no sovereign has ever taken up residence in the Maison du Roi, though this was where the Habsburgs sometimes stayed when they visited the city. They also installed their taxmen and law courts here, and used it to hold their more important prisoners – the counts of Egmont and Hoorn (see p.255) spent their last night in the Maison du Roi before being beheaded outside in the Grand-Place. The building was also used as a sort of royal changing room: the future Philip II donned his armour here before joining a joust held in the Grand-Place, and the archdukes Albert and Isabella dressed up inside before appearing on the balcony to shoot down a symbolic target that made them honorary members of the guild of crossbowmen.

Musée de la Ville de Bruxelles

The Maison du Roi holds the **Musée de la Ville de Bruxelles** (Tues–Sun 10am–5pm; €3), a wide-ranging if patchy collection whose best sections feature medieval fine and applied art.

The ground floor

To the **left of the entrance**, there's a room full of **Gothic sculpture** retrieved from various city buildings. Pride of place goes to the eight prophets from 1400, complete with heavy beards and eccentric headgear, who once decorated the porch of the Hôtel de Ville. Two rooms further on you'll find a small but charming sample of eighteenth-century **glazed earthenware**, for which the city was once internationally famous. The finest work is by Philippe Mombaers

▲ The Maison du Roi

(1724–54), whose workshop, on rue de Laeken, is credited with developing table decorations in the form of vegetables or animals – hence the splendid turkey, codfish, duck and cabbage soup tureens and casserole dishes.

The first of the rooms to the **right of the entrance** boasts superb **altarpieces** – or retables – the intricacy of which was a Brussels speciality, with the city producing hundreds of them from the end of the fourteenth century until the economic slump of the 1640s. Their manufacture was similar to a production line, with panel- and cabinet-makers, wood-carvers, painters and goldsmiths working on several altarpieces at any one time. The standard format was to create a series of mini-tableaux illustrating Biblical scenes, with the characters wearing medieval gear in a medieval landscape. It's the extraordinary detail that impresses most – look closely at the niche carvings on the whopping **Saluzzo altarpiece** (*The Life of the Virgin and the Infant Christ*) of 1505 and you'll spy the candlesticks, embroidered pillowcase and carefully draped coverlet of Mary's bedroom in the *Annunciation* scene, while the adjacent *Nativity* comes complete with a set of cute little angels. Up above, in a swirling, phantasmagorical landscape (of what look like climbing toadstools) is the *Shepherds Hear the Good News*. Also in this room is the *Wedding Procession*, attributed to either Pieter Bruegel the Younger or Jan Bruegel, a good-natured scene with country folk walking to church to the accompaniment of bagpipes.

The second room to the right is devoted to four large-scale **tapestries** from the sixteenth and seventeenth centuries. The earliest of the four – from 1516 – relates the legend of Notre Dame du Sablon, the tedious tale of the transfer of a much revered statue of the Virgin from Antwerp to Brussels (see p.88), though fortunately the tapestry is much better than the story. A second tapestry, dating from 1580, tells the Arthurian legend of Tristan and Isolde, but easily the most striking is the *Solemn Funeral of the Roman Consul Decius Mus*, based on drawings by Rubens. Decius was a heroic figure who had won a decisive victory against the Samnites, thus securing Roman control of Italy in the third century BC. In this extraordinary tapestry, he is shown laid out on a chaise-longue and surrounded by classical figures of muscular men and fleshy women. Even

Tapestry manufacture and design

Brussels was once renowned for its tapestries, the manufacture of which began in the middle of the fifteenth century and soon came under the control of a small clique of manufacturers who imposed a rigorous system of quality control. This was codified even more precisely in 1528, when every new tapestry made in Brussels was obliged to bear the town's trademark – two "Bs" enclosed in a red shield. Brussels' tapestries were famous for their lavish raw materials – especially gold thread – and this also served to keep control of the industry in the hands of the few. Only rarely were weavers able to accumulate enough money to buy their materials, never mind their own looms. The first great period of Brussels tapestry-making lasted until the middle of the sixteenth century, when religious conflict overwhelmed the city and many of its Protestant-inclined weavers migrated north to rival workshops. There was a partial revival at the beginning of the seventeenth century, but later the French occupation and the shrinking of the Spanish market led to diminishing production, with the industry finally fizzling out by the end of the eighteenth century.

Tapestry production was a cross between embroidery and ordinary weaving. It consisted of interlacing a wool weft above and below the strings of a vertical linen "chain", a process similar to weaving. However, the weaver had to stop to change colour, requiring as many shuttles for the weft as he had colours, as in embroidery. The design of a tapestry was taken from a painting to which the weaver made constant reference. Standard-size tapestries took six months to make and were produced exclusively for the very wealthy, the most important of whom would often insist on the use of gold and silver thread and the employment of the most famous artists of the day for the preparatory painting. Amongst many, Pieter Paul Rubens, Jacob Jordaens and David Teniers all had tapestry commissions.

inanimate objects join in the general mourning – with the lion head of the chaise-longue, for instance, glancing sorrowfully at the onlooker.

The first and second floors

Up the grand staircase, the **first floor** has a number of interesting scale models depicting Brussels from the thirteenth century to around 1650, along with lots of nineteenth-century paintings of the city – one showing the seventeenth-century bombardment of the Grand-Place, another an abortive plan to build a funicular from the Lower to the Upper Town. There are also some good photographs of the city as it is today. Several of the paintings, sketches and photographs displayed on the **second floor** are also worth a look, notably a curiously detailed N. van der Horst (1598–1646) canvas showing the state arrival of the Spanish Infanta, Isabella, in Brussels in 1622, and a crudely painted, anonymous sixteenth-century diptych depicting – and named after – the anti-Jewish myth behind the Saint Sacrement de Miracle (the Miracle of the Sacrament, see p.73). On the same floor you also get to put faces to some of the names that crop up on street signs all over the city: the moustachioed burgomaster Adolphe Max for one, pictured with his faithful Jack Russell, as well as Rouppe, Rogier, De Brouckère and others that will ring a bell if you've explored the city centre at all – though Brussels' most famous character gets a section to himself, where there's an extensive sample of the vast wardrobe of the **Manneken Pis** (see p.62). There are around a hundred costumes in all, ranging from Las Vegas-era Elvis to a Russian cosmonaut, all of them gifts from various visiting dignitaries for the cheeky little statue that has become the city's mascot.

2

The Lower Town

The **Lower Town** is the commercial centre of Brussels, a sprawling, bustling quarter that's home to most of the city's best restaurants, shops and hotels. At its heart is the Grand-Place (see Chapter 1) and fanning out from here is a labyrinth of narrow, cobbled lanes and alleys whose layout remains essentially medieval, their names often revealing their original purpose as markets – rue du Marché aux Fromages, for example. This medieval street pattern is interrupted by the boulevards that were constructed during the nineteenth century, giving the Lower Town the shape it maintains today: bordered to the north, south and west by the boulevards of the petit ring, and running east to the foot of the steep slope which marks the start of the Upper Town (see Chapter 3), along the line of boulevards Berlaimont, L'Impératrice and L'Empereur. Along with boulevards Anspach and Adolphe-Max, these nineteenth-century boulevards were part of a drive to modernize a city which had become – even by the standards of the day – notably squalid, a refit that included the demolition of acres of slum and the covering and eventual re-direction of the fetid River Senne. Nevertheless, they did little to disturb the jostle and jangle that gave – and still give – the Lower Town its character, with almost every street crimped by tall and angular town houses. There's nothing neat and tidy about all of this, and much of the city centre is scarred by thoughtless Sixties redevelopment. But it's perhaps this more than anything that makes Brussels so intriguing – dilapidated terraces stand next to prestigious mansions, which are in turn side-by-side with ugly concrete office blocks.

The Lower Town is dotted with superb buildings and, although you definitely have to know where to look, worthwhile sights are to be found whichever way you decide to walk from the Grand-Place. **West** takes you to the Bourse and the Ste-Catherine district beyond; **north** to Brussels' shopping quarter and the engaging **Centre Belge de la Bande Dessinée** (Belgian Comic Strip Centre), housed in a fantastic Art Nouveau department store; **south** to the Manneken Pis and some of the city centre's most enjoyable streets for nightlife, St Géry and St Jacques – and to the Marolles district beyond; **east**, you begin to climb the hill to the cathedral, the Gare Centrale and the Upper Town (for which see Chapter 3).

West of the Grand-Place

One of the most diverting parts of the Lower Town, the jumble of narrow streets and pocket-sized squares that spreads **west of the Grand-Place** to

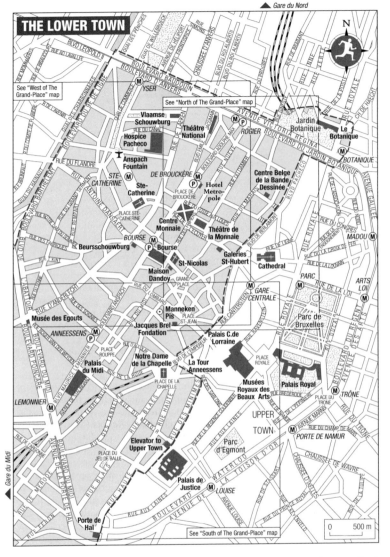

place Ste-Catherine is crowded by the elegant, though often down-at-heel town houses of the late nineteenth-century bourgeoisie. These days, this is the most fashionable part of the city, in an urban-chic sort of way, and there are lots of great bars, plus a couple of especially fine buildings, the Victorian **Bourse** and the Baroque church of **St-Jean Baptiste au Béguinage**.

The Church of St-Nicolas

Walking northwest out of the Grand-Place along **rue au Beurre**, you soon reach one of the city's best-known confectioners, **Maison Dandoy**, at no. 31,

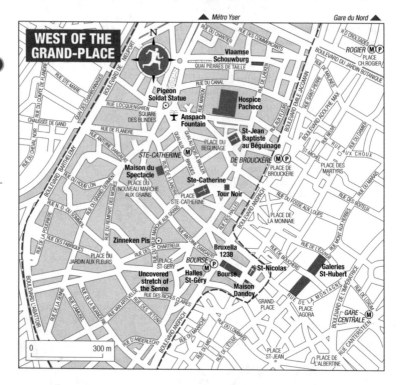

whose tasty specialities are macaroons and *speculoos*, a sugary brown, gingery biscuit that's prepared in a variety of traditional and intricate moulds – and served up in a determinedly old-school atmosphere. Close by, squeezed into its surroundings just across the street, is the church of **St-Nicolas** (Mon–Fri 8am–6.30pm, Sat 9am–6pm & Sun 9am–7.30pm), dedicated to St Nicholas of Bari, the patron saint of sailors, or, as he's better known, Santa Claus. The church dates from the twelfth century, but has been heavily restored on several occasions, most recently in the 1950s, when parts of the outer shell were reconstructed in a plain Gothic style. The church is unusual in so far as the three wide aisles of the nave were built at an angle to the chancel, in order to avoid a stream. It also carries a memento of the French bombardment of 1695 in the cannon ball embedded high up in the third pillar on the left of the nave. Otherwise, the interior hardly sets the pulse racing, although – among a scattering of *objets d'art* – there's a handsome, gilded copper reliquary shrine in the right-hand aisle. The shrine was made in Germany in the nineteenth century to honour a group of Catholics martyred by Protestants in Gorinchem in the Netherlands in 1572.

The Bourse and Bruxella 1238

Opposite St-Nicolas rises the grandiose **Bourse**, the home of the city's stock exchange since the mid-nineteenth century, and a Neoclassical edifice of 1873 caked with garlands of fruit, fronds, languishing nudes and frolicking putti. This breezily self-confident structure sports a host of allegorical figures (Industry, Navigation, Asia, Africa, etc), which both reflect the preoccupations of the nineteenth-century Belgian bourgeoisie and, in their easy self-satisfaction, imply that wealth and pleasure are synonymous. The twin lions flanking the main staircase add a cautionary note – one (with head up) signifying how stocks can rise, and the other (with head down) how they can fall. Partially destroyed by fire in 1990, the building has been well restored inside and out and nowadays houses the Brussels branch of the Euronext network, which has incorporated the Brussels, Paris and Amsterdam exchanges since September 2000.

The Bourse is flanked by sterling town houses, the setting for two of the city's more famous cafés, the Art Nouveau *Falstaff* (see p.202), on the south side at rue Henri Maus 17–23, and the fin-de-siècle *Le Cirio* (see p.203) on the other side at rue de la Bourse 18. In front of *Le Cirio* are the glassed-in foundations of a medieval church and convent, unearthed by archeologists in the 1980s and now known rather grandly as **Bruxella 1238**. There are regular guided tours of the site (first Wed of each month at 10.15am in English, 11.15am in French & 2pm in Dutch; €3; ☏02 279 43 55 for reservations), but they are only of specialist interest – the Maison du Roi on the Grand-Place has further information and sells tickets.

Place St-Géry and around

The square in front of the Bourse – **place de la Bourse** – is little more than a heavily trafficked pause along boulevard Anspach, but the streets on the other side of the boulevard have more appeal. Take rue Jules van Praet for **place St-Géry**, an attractive little square crowded by high-sided tenements whose stone balconies and wrought-iron grilles hark back to the days of bustles and parasols. The square is thought to occupy the site of the sixth-century chapel from which the medieval city grew, but this is a matter of conjecture – no archeological evidence has ever been unearthed, and the only clue to the city's early history is in its name, literally "settlement in the marshes". Place St-Géry has one main attraction in the refurbished, late nineteenth-century covered market, the **Halles St-Géry**, an airy glass, brick and iron edifice now used for art and photography exhibitions. The elegance of the interior is marred, however, by a huge stone fountain plonked right in the middle – moved here from the town of Grimbergen to the north of Brussels. Just off the square, through a brickwork archway on its southwestern corner, there's a courtyard where you can see the only uncovered stretch of the **Senne** in the city centre, running through a tunnel under an office building, with the old quaysides clearly visible. It's clean enough, apart from the coins that are regularly chucked in, due to the fact that the river proper was diverted around the city centre decades ago. For more on the Senne and its nineteenth-century obliteration, see p.68.

Rue Antoine Dansaert and Rue du Flandre

From place St-Géry, it's a couple of minutes' stroll to place Ste-Catherine, past Tom Frantzen's canine answer to the Manneken Pis on the corner of rue des Chartreux and rue du Vieux Marché aux Grains – **Zinneken Pis**, basically a bronze of a dog cocking its leg up in homage to the famous weeing little boy. Just before the square, **rue Antoine Dansaert** is where the most innovative and stylish of the city's **fashion designers** have set up shop amongst the careworn old houses that stretch up towards place du Nouveau Marché aux Grains; see Chapter 12 for the best of these. **Place du Nouveau Marché aux Grains**, a short walk up to the left, is a pleasant, open square lined with trees and decorated with a suitably pensive statue of **Jean-Baptiste van**

Helmont (1578–1644), a Brussels-born physician and chemist who coined the word "gas" to explain the results of some of his experiments. Beyond lies the **canal** – a run-down stretch that marks the edge of the city centre but which is rapidly becoming the centre of some of its most cutting-edge nightlife and bars.

Running roughly parallel with Rue Antoine Dansaert, and meeting it at the canal, **Rue du Flandre** is home to a few decent restaurant and bars, as well as the **Maison du Spectacle** at rue du Flandre 46, an arts centre whose enclosed courtyard you can access during office hours for a view of one of the city's most impressive (and most secret) facades, built at the end of the seventeenth century and likely to last a good few hundred years more in this sheltered environment. Certainly you're able to study its fanciful stonework in detail – the bust of Bellona, Roman goddess of war, over the entrance, and the medallions of Roman emperors and intricate craving on the pilasters.

Place Ste-Catherine and around

At the bottom of Rue de Flandre, **place Ste-Catherine** is, despite its dishevelled appearance, at the heart of one of the city's more fashionable districts, a pleasantly leafy square flanked by fish stalls and home to a small ghetto of seafood restaurants. Presiding over the square is the **church of Ste-Catherine** (Mon–Sat 8.30am–5.30pm, Sun 8.30am–noon), a battered nineteenth-century replacement for the Baroque original, of which the creamy, curvy belfry beside the west end of the church is the solitary survivor. Venture inside Ste-Catherine and you'll see – behind the glass screen that closes off most of the nave – a fourteenth-century Black Madonna and Child, a sensually carved stone statuette that was chucked into the Senne by Protestants, but landed rather fortuitously on a clod of peat and was fished out.

Butting up against the church on the left side you'll notice Brussels' oldest **pissoir** – dating from 1845 and still in use today – while right behind the church the **Tour Noir**, a twelfth-century leftover from the city's original

▲ The church of Ste-Catherine

defences, is oddly encased within the wings of the *Novotel* – a jarring juxtaposition which is in many ways the essence of Brussels.

The quais aux Briques and aux Bois à Brûler ❷

The quai aux Briques and the parallel **quai aux Bois à Brûler** extend northwest from place Ste-Catherine on either side of a wide and open area that was – until it was filled in – the most central part of the city's main **dock**. Strolling along this open area, you'll pass a motley assortment of nineteenth-century warehouses, shops, restaurants and bars which maintain an appealing canalside feel – an impression heightened in the early morning when the streets are choked with lorries bearing trays of seafood for the restaurants here, whose speciality is almost exclusively fish. At the end of the old quays, the fanciful **water fountain**, with its lizards and dolphins, honours burgomaster Anspach, a driving force in the move to modernize the city during the 1880s, while beyond, on **square des Blindes**, a smaller fountain of a woman releasing a pigeon into flight recalls the "*pigeon soldats*" of the first world war – testimony not only to the use of carrier pigeons in the conflict but also to the fact that Belgium is the home of pigeon-racing, with perhaps 60,000 people following the sport even today.

St-Jean Baptiste au Béguinage and around

Lying just to the east of quai aux Bois à Brûler, **place du Béguinage** is a semi-circular piazza dominated by **St-Jean Baptiste au Béguinage** (Mon–Fri 10am–5pm, Sat & Sun 11am–5pm), a supple, billowing structure dating from the second half of the seventeenth century. This beautiful church is the only building left from the Béguine convent founded here in the thirteenth century. The convent once crowded in on the church, and only since its demolition – and the creation of the star-shaped place du Béguinage in 1855 – has it been possible to view the exterior with any degree of ease. There's a sense of movement in each and every feature, a dynamism of design culminating in three matching gables where the upper portion of the central tower is decorated with pinnacles that echo those of the Hôtel de Ville. The church's light and spacious interior is lavishly decorated, the white stone columns and arches punctuated by solemn-faced cherubs intent on reminding the congregation of their mortality. The nave and aisles are wide and open, offering unobstructed views of the high altar, but you can't fail to notice the enormous wooden **pulpit** featuring St Dominic preaching against heresy – and trampling a heretic under foot for good measure.

Around the back of the church, a short street (rue de l'Infirmerie) takes you through to a slender, tree-lined square reminiscent of provincial France, and framed by the austere Neoclassicism of the **Hospice Pacheco** (no access), built to house the destitute in the 1820s. It's a peaceful spot today, but the stern wall that surrounds the complex is a reminder of times when the hospice was more like a prison than a shelter, and draconian rules were imposed with brutal severity. From the Hospice Pacheco, you can cut through to down-at-heel **rue du Laeken**, which leads up to the petit ring and the unappetizing area around the Gare du Nord, past the impressive bulk on the left of the **Vlaamse Schouwburg**, an impressively balconied, refurbished warehouse that is a further reminder that this was formerly Brussels' dockside area. The street behind is known as the quai aux Foins (Hay), and like the nearby Ste-Catherine quays it still sports a small stretch of water in the middle, though these days it's finished off with a decorative waterfall.

North of the Grand-Place

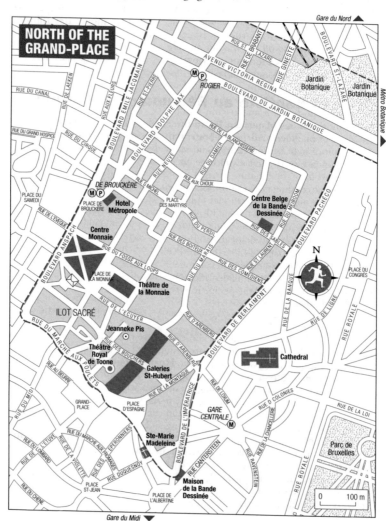

The busy streets between the Grand-Place and the Gare du Nord are not especially enticing, though the area on and around **rue des Bouchers** heaves with restaurants and **rue Neuve** possesses many of the city's biggest shops and department stores. The prime architectural sight hereabouts is the **place des Martyrs**, a handsome square built by the Austrian Habsburgs in their pomp, whilst the most interesting attraction is the **Centre Belge de la Bande Dessinée** (Belgian Comic Strip Centre). Belgian artists and writers produce the best comics in the world – or so they would argue – and the centre contains a vast range of their work, including the most famous comic character of the lot, **Tintin**, who first appeared as long ago as 1929.

Ilot Sacré

The area immediately north of the Grand-Place, on the far side of rue Marché-aux-Herbes, is known these days as the **Ilot Sacré**, since a 1950s plan to redevelop the narrow streets here (mainly by knocking the houses down and widening the streets) was defeated, and a series of planning restrictions was imposed. Nowadays it's Brussels at its most touristy, with **petite rue des Bouchers** and **rue des Bouchers** at its heart – the city centre's restaurant ghetto, whose narrow cobblestoned lanes are transformed at night into fairy-lit tunnels where several dozen restaurants, with elaborate displays of dull-eyed fish and glistening molluscs, vie for custom. It's an atmospheric neighbourhood, but the bad news is that most of the restaurants are fronted by touts to lure you in and have a reputation for charging over the odds; you won't necessarily have a bad meal, but there are one or two places that are reliably a cut above the rest (see pp.191–202 for our recommendations).

A narrow alley off petite rue des Bouchers (there's another entrance down impasse Schuddeveld off rue Marché aux Herbes) leads to the **Théâtre Royal de Toone**, which puts on puppet shows in the Bruxellois dialect known as Brusselse Sproek or Marollien. It's very much a city institution and there are regular performances from Tuesday to Saturday (see p.242) – as well as an excellent bar (see p.207). Another alley, impasse de la Fidélité, off rue des Bouchers, leads to the fountain-cum-statue of **Jeanneke Pis**, a spirited answer to the more famous Manneken Pis, in the shape of a small girl taking a leak, the work of one Denis Adrien Debouvrie in 1985. It's a very Brussels type of sight – out of sight behind railings, and rarely working – but a nice echo of its better-known brother, and a welcome escape from the food mayhem on rue des Bouchers.

In the opposite direction, rue des Bouchers crosses the **Galeries St-Hubert**, whose trio of glass-vaulted galleries – du Roi, de la Reine and the smaller des Princes – were opened by Léopold I in 1847. The *galeries* were one of Europe's first shopping arcades, and the pastel-painted walls, classical columns and cameo sculptures still retain an air of genteel sophistication – with deluxe shops to match. It's a good place to escape the weather, have a coffee or lunch – and shop for chocolates, of course. There are a number of good alternatives, but the most historic is the city's original chocolatier, **Neuhaus**, at no. 23, where the Swiss Jean Neuhaus first created the praline in what was once a pharmacy specializing in medicinal sweets.

Place d'Espagne and around

Just by the entrance to the Galeries, the triangle of **place d'Espagne** is always busy, surrounded by chain hotels and cafés. The fountain in the middle remembers Charles Buls, burgomaster of Brussels from 1881 to 1899, who helped to preserve parts of historic Brussels, including the Grand-Place itself. He certainly seems like a pleasant old chap, sitting as he is with his faithful dog at his side, and invites lots of snapping tourists. Up the hill from here, the brick **church of Ste-Marie Madeleine** is an originally Gothic church whose interior arches form an attractive contrast with the modern lines of its contemporary stained glass. Across the way, the **Maison de la Bande Dessinée**, at boulevard de l'Imperatrice 1 (Tues–Sun 10am–6pm; €2), is a comic shop with a small museum attached – mainly devoted to showcasing the art of the illustrators of *Le Journal de Spirou* magazine, a Belgian institution that has been going for over seventy years. There's a bust of one of the most famous of the *Spirou* artists, **Jijé**, the pen-name of the prolific and influential Joseph Gillain (1914–80), who specialized in tales of derring-do, of cowboys and fighter pilots, Vikings and other heroes, and there are lots of original pieces of artwork and vintage copies of the magazine – sheer delight for fans of the period.

Place de la Monnaie and place de Brouckère

At the far end of the Galeries St-Hubert, a brief walk down rue de l'Ecuyer takes you to **place de la Monnaie**, a dreary modern square that's overshadowed by the huge **centre Monnaie**, housing offices, shops and the main post office. The only building of interest here is the **Théâtre de la Monnaie** (for tickets and performance information, see p.220), Brussels' opera house, a Neoclassical structure built in 1819 and with an interior added in 1856 to a design by Poelaert, the architect of the Palais de Justice (see p.90) and much else in Brussels, and spruced up in the 1980s when the American Expressionist Sam Francis contributed the foyer's ceiling paintings and Sol Lewitt the black-and-white floor.

The company here has a reputation for quality and innovation, but the building's real claim to fame is as the starting-point of the revolution against the Dutch in 1830: the nationalistic libretto in Auber's *The Mute Girl of Portici* sent the audience wild, and they poured out into the streets to raise the flag of Brabant, signalling the start of the rebellion. The opera told the tale of an Italian uprising against the Spanish, and with such lines as "To my country I owe my life, To me it will owe its liberty", one of the Dutch censors – of whom there were many – should really have seen what was coming, as a furious King William I pointed out. The opera house's prices are predictably high, but so is the quality of what you'll see here, and you can peek in to appreciate the lobby whether you're an opera-lover or not.

On the far side of the Centre Monnaie is traffic-clogged boulevard Anspach, which forks and widens at **place de Brouckère**, a major junction laid out in nineteenth-century French style that still evokes parts of Paris. Its major building

▲ The historic Théâtre de la Monnaie

is the **Hôtel Métropole** (see p.185), whose splendidly ornate lobby and bar date from 1895, and were once the haunt of the likes of Sarah Bernhardt and Isadora Duncan.

Rue Neuve and place des Martyrs

From place de la Monnaie, **rue Neuve** forges north, a workaday pedestrianized shopping street that's home to a string of big chain shops – Zara, H&M, Dutch department store Hema and so forth. About halfway up, turn right along rue St-Michel for the **place des Martyrs**, a cool, rational square, quite at odds with the plastic commercialism of rue Neuve, that was superimposed on the city by the Habsburgs in the 1770s. It was in a shocking state until recently, but its restoration is now almost complete, and there's no mistaking the architectural elegance of the ensemble, completed in the last years of Austrian control. The square's imposing centrepiece was added later: it comprises a stone plinth rising from an arcaded gallery inscribed with the names of those 445 insurrectionists who died in the Belgian revolution of 1830, and is surmounted by a female representation of Belgium, the Motherland.

Centre Belge de la Bande Dessinée

Cutting through on rue du Persil from the place des Martyrs, it takes about five minutes to walk to the city's only surviving Horta-designed department store, the **Grand Magasin Waucquez**, situated amongst run-down offices and warehouses at rue des Sables 20. Recently restored after lying empty for thirty years, it's a wonderfully airy, summery construction, with light flooding through the glass and stained glass that encloses the expansive entrance hall. Completed in 1906, it was built for a textile tycoon, and exhibits all the classic features of Horta's work (see p.96) – from the soft lines of the ornamentation to the metal grilles, exposed girders and balustrades.

In the entrance hall is a good comic bookshop, a small display on the building's history, a reference library (Tues–Thurs noon–5pm, Fri noon–6pm, Sat 10am–6pm; free) and a café-restaurant, the *Brasserie Horta* (see p.195). From the hall, a flight of stairs leads up to the museum itself, the **Centre Belge de la Bande Dessinée** (Belgian Comic Strip Centre Tues–Sun 10am–6pm; €7.50; Ⓦ www.cbbd.be), whose displays are extensive and diverting. Most of the labelling is in French and Dutch, but free and very thorough English notes are available at the reception.

The exhibits begin with a modest first-floor section outlining the processes involved in drawing comic strips, and another on cartoon animation. There's also a small auditorium showing cartoons and documentaries about the comic strip. But you really get down to business on the next floor up with the grandly titled **Museum of the Imagination**, which traces the development of the Belgian comic strip from its beginnings in the 1920s up until 1960, with sections on – and examples of the work of – all the leading practitioners. First up – appropriately enough, given his perennial popularity – is **Tintin**, the creation of Brussels-born **Georges Remi**, aka Hergé (1907–83). Remi's first efforts (pre-Tintin) had been sponsored by a right-wing Catholic journal, *Le XXème Siècle*, and in 1929, when this same paper produced a kids' supplement – *Le Petit Vingtième* – Remi was given his first major break. Asked to produce a two-page comic strip, he came up with *Tintin in the Land of the Soviets*, a didactic tale about the evils of Bolshevism. Tintin's Soviet adventure lasted until May 1930, and to round it all off the director of *Le XXème Siècle* decided to stage a

PR-stunt reception to celebrate Tintin's return. Remi – along with a Tintin lookalike – hopped on a train just east of Brussels, and when they pulled into the capital they were mobbed by scores of excited children. Remi and Tintin never looked back. Remi decided on the famous quiff straight away, but other features – the mouth and expressive eyebrows – came later. His popularity was – and remains – quite phenomenal: *Tintin* has been translated into sixty languages, and over twenty million copies of the comic *Le Journal de Tintin*, Remi's own independent creation first published in 1946, have been sold.

Beyond the Tintin section appears the work of Remi's leading contemporaries and successors, with each artist given his own section, however small. To fully appreciate what you see, it does help if you already know something about comic strips and have a working knowledge of French; cartoonists to look out for include **Maurice Tillieux** and **Bob de Moor**, the latter a collaborator of Hergé, and the versatile **Jijé** (whose best work was done in the *Le Journal de Spirou* magazine – see below). **Edgar-Pierre Jacobs'** theatrical compositions and fluent combination of genres – science fiction, fantasy and crime – are displayed in his *Blake and Mortimer*, and there's a mock-up of his desk, complete with pens and brushes, and a half-finished strip. As with several others, Jacobs became popular after his work appeared in *Le Journal de Tintin*, while Belgium's oldest comic-strip paper, the *Le Journal de Spirou*, performed a similar service for the likes of **André Franquin**, the creator of the feckless anti-hero *Gaston Lagaffe*. Sadly, *Spirou* was also where *The Smurfs* first saw light of day, the creation, in 1958, of **Peyo**, who also has a section to himself, with a set of cabinets detailing the evolution of the little blue creatures.

On the top floor, the **Museum of Modern Comic Strips** looks at new trends and themes. The comic strip has long ceased to be primarily aimed at children, and now focuses on the adult (sometimes very adult) market. A series of regularly rotated displays ably illustrates some of the best of this new work and there's also a programme of temporary exhibitions. If all this leaves you with a taste for more, you can check out the museum's bookstore, which has a great stock of comics, as well as other excellent **comic shops** in the city, detailed in Chapter 12.

Le Botanique

Heading north from the Centre Belge de la Bande Dessinée along **rue du Marais**, you'll soon hit the petit ring near the burgeoning skyscrapers of **place Rogier**, from where huge office blocks continue up rue du Progrès to the **Gare du Nord**. This is all predictable stuff – and predictably overpowering – but don't despair: on the north side of the boulevard du Jardin, between rue Gineste and rue Royale, you can escape the concrete and glass, if not the rumble of the traffic, by walking into the **Jardin Botanique** (May–Sept daily 8am–8pm, Oct–April daily 8am–5pm; free). This attractive park divides into two parts: one a hillier, more rustic area, closer to the Gare du Nord, whose woods, lawns and borders are decorated by statues and a tiny lake, and another, more formal half, connected by a bridge on the rue Royale side, with topiary and carefully manicured gardens below **Le Botanique**, whose elegant glasshouses date from 1826. The building once housed the city's tropical gardens, but these were moved out long ago (to Meise – see p.129) and the place is now the city's Francophone cultural centre. It's a peaceful and appealing spot, its long glass corridor punctuated by exotic plants and pools teeming with fish, and there's a café serving drinks and sandwiches, as well as a good Italian restaurant, *Café Bota* (see p.195). It also has regular films and live music – see ⓦ www.botanique.be for programme details.

South of the Grand-Place

The main attraction **south of the Grand-Place** is the city's most visited – the Manneken Pis – but few tourists venture much beyond here, even though the streets of this neighbourhood – loosely called St Jacques – are some of the city's brightest for bars and nightlife, especially of the gay variety. They certainly don't make the ten- to fifteen-minute walk to the increasingly gentrified **Marolles district**, around rue Blaes and rue Haute, or further south to the relatively impoverished area around the **Gare du Midi**. There are, however, a couple of interesting attractions on the northern periphery of the Quartier Marolles – the beautiful church of **Notre-Dame de la Chapelle** and the **Fondation Jacques Brel**, celebrating the country's leading balladeer, and the **Marolles** district itself holds several atmospheric bars and restaurants and has an excellent flea **market**.

Musée de Costume et de la Dentelle

In the 1890s, burgomaster **Charles Buls** spearheaded a campaign to preserve the city's ancient buildings. One of his rewards was to have a street named after him, and this runs south from the Grand-Place in between the Maison de l'Etoile and the Hôtel de Ville to the corner of **rue des Brasseurs** (the first on the left), scene of a bizarre incident in 1873 when the French Symbolist poet

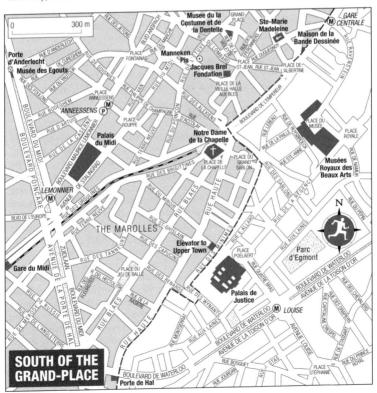

Paul Verlaine shot and wounded his fellow poet and lover Arthur Rimbaud. This rash act earned him a two-year prison sentence – and all because Rimbaud had dashed from Paris to dissuade him from joining the Spanish army.

The next on the left is **rue de la Violette**, where at nos. 4–6 you'll find the revamped **Musée de Costume et de la Dentelle**, or Costume and Lace Museum (Mon–Fri except Wed 10am–12.30pm & 1.30–5pm, Sat & Sun 2–5pm; €3). Brussels was a lace-making centre for three hundred years, but the last of its lace-makers closed down in the 1930s and what you see on sale in the city today comes mostly from the Far East. At its peak in the late nineteenth century the city had no fewer than ten thousand lace-makers, all of them women, and the lace they made was renowned across Europe for the intricacy of its designs.

However, this museum is as much about costume as lace, mounting slickly presented regular exhibitions from its permanent collection that concentrate on historical costumes and the evolution of fashion right up to the present day. The emphasis is very much on the temporary exhibitions, but you will almost certainly be able to view a number of seventeenth-century portraits of the rich and powerful decked out in all their silk trimmings – the portrait of the Spanish queen Marguerite of Austria is especially striking, though her iron-threaded ruff must have given her thunderous neck-ache, while another portrait shows an unknown Dutch woman modelling the boat-shaped neckline that came into fashion during the 1660s. Upstairs, large plan chests hold numerous items of antique lace, including examples that demonstrate the influence Italian lace had on the city's lace-makers, the extraordinarily elaborate lacy fashions inspired by Louis XIV's desire to keep his nobles occupied (and impoverished), and the lighter, simpler Regency style that came to dominate the scene in the eighteenth century. There is also lace from the 1840s onwards, when large and complicated pieces – primarily for shawls, crinoline gowns, overskirts and bridal gear – became increasingly popular in a variety of styles, including Duchesse, Chantilly and *point de gaze* (or *point de rose*). For more on lace, see pp.229–230.

The Manneken Pis and around

From the foot of rue de la Violette, **rue de l'Etuve** crosses busy rue du Lombard down to the **Manneken Pis**, a diminutive statue of a pissing urchin stuck high up in a shrine-like affair protected from the hordes of tourists by an iron fence. The Manneken is supposed to embody the "irreverent spirit" of the city, or at least that is reputed to have been the intention of Jérôme Duquesnoy when he cast the original bronze statue in the 1600s to replace the medieval stone fountain that stood here before. It's likely that Duquesnoy invented the Manneken Pis, whose popularity blossomed during the sombre, priest-dominated years following the Thirty Years' War, but it's possible that his bronze replaced an earlier stone version of ancient provenance. There are all sorts of folkloric tales about its origins, from lost aristocratic children recovered when they were taking a pee, to peasant lads putting out dangerous fires and – least likely of the lot – boys peeing on the city's enemies from the trees and putting them to flight. As a talisman, it has certainly attracted the attention of thieves, notably in 1817 when a French ex-convict swiped it before breaking it into pieces. The thief and the smashed Manneken were apprehended, the former publicly branded on the Grand-Place and sentenced to a life of forced labour, while the fragments of the latter were used to create the mould in which the present-day Manneken was cast. It's long been the custom for visiting VIPs to donate a costume, and the little chap is regularly kitted out in different tackle – often military or folkloric gear, from Country & Western stetsons and chaps to golfers' plus fours and Donald Duck and Mickey Mouse outfits. A good sample of his wardrobe is on display at the Musée de la Ville de Bruxelles (see p.46).

A couple of blocks from the Manneken Pis, in the heart of the St Jacques district, on the corner of rue Plattesteen and rue du Marché au Charbon, there's a nod at Brussels' **comic-strip culture**, in the form of a famous **mural** by the Ixelles-born cartoonist Frank Pé showing his most famous character, Brousaille, crossing the very same road with his girlfriend; the same mural can be seen in the background – a nice touch. Opposite, on rue du Marché au Charbon, another **mural** by Francis Carin does the same thing, showing his creation, secret agent Victor Sackville, in the same location – the church tower of Notre-Dame du Bon Secours is clearly visible in the background. There are murals like this all over Brussels but these are among the best known and most central. Rue du Marché au Charbon is also the heart of gay Brussels, and sports some of the city centre's best bars (gay and straight) – see p.244 and pp.207–209 for more.

▲ Brussels' most famous landmark: the Manneken Pis

A block from here, rue du Midi leads down to **place Rouppe**, a scruffy square that was once home to the Gare du Midi and is now best-known as the location of the city's fanciest Michelin-starred restaurant, *Comme Chez Soi*, which nestles unassumingly in one corner and is still riding high despite having recently lost one of its coveted stars. It's a very unlikely spot for a gourmet restaurant, as the cheerful but unashamedly downscale arcades of the **avenue de Stalingrad**, leading south from place Rouppe, and its parallel neighbour, **boulevard Lemonnier**, testify. It's almost entirely Moroccan these days, with food stores, teashops, bakeries and kitchenware emporiums taking over the wide and often deserted thoroughfare – and even the the giant bulk of the **Palais du Midi**, which sits between the two boulevards.

Place St-Jean, the Fondation Jacques Brel and beyond

A short walk from the Manneken Pis, up rue du Lombard, the memorial in the middle of **place St-Jean** commemorates the remarkable **Gabrielle Petit**. Equipped with a formidable – some say photographic – memory, Petit played a leading role in the Belgian Resistance movement during the German occupation of World War I. When captured, she refused to appeal, even though as a woman her sentence would almost certainly have been reduced. Instead, she declared that she would show the Germans how a Belgian woman could die. And that is precisely what she did: the Germans shot her by firing squad in 1916.

Just to the south of the square, the pretty triangular place de la Vieille-Halle aux Blés is home to the **Fondation Jacques Brel** (Tues–Sun 10am–6pm; €5; Ⓦ www.jacquesbrel.be), which celebrates the life and times of the Belgian singer Jacques Brel, who was born in Brussels – in Schaerbeek – in 1933, and died in Paris in 1978. Brel became famous in the 1960s as a singer of mournful

A Jacques Brel playlist

Amsterdam Brel's deliberately repetitive, climactic tale of sailors in seedy ports is a fantastically evocative song, and one his most intense live numbers.

Les Bonbons This is Brel at his funniest and most unforgiving, poking fun at Sixties hippies.

Le chanson de Jackie Brel in autobiographical mode, looking back in fantastically rumbustious fashion on his career and forward into his future.

Mathilde One of Brel's greatest love songs, brilliantly covered by Scott Walker.

Le Moribond The tormented and yet curiously upbeat lament of a dying man that gave rise to the Terry Jacks hit of 1974.

Ne me quitte pas Brel's most anguished love song, and perhaps one of the most affecting ever written, memorably covered by Nina Simone.

Quand on n'a que l'amour "When we have only love" was one of Brel's earliest songs, and his first hit single.

La Quete "The Impossible Dream" has been covered by just about everyone and is quite rightly one of Brel's best-known songs, but his version naturally stands out.

Je suis un soir d'été This late and very atmospheric study of summer ennui in provincial Belgian towns is one of Brel's most beautiful songs.

Au Suivant Brel is typically satirical in this biting rant against war, militarism and middle-class bourgeois values.

chansons about death and love, and his music still reaches into the depths of many a French-speaking soul. English-speakers may know him from the cover versions of Scott Walker, or maybe from the 1970s hit single, *Seasons in the Sun*, which borrowed the melody of one of his songs – though this hardly does justice to his music, which is heartfelt and original. His live performances were famous for their intensity, and the museum is principally a cinema showing footage of his later concerts – and, in the foyer, a rare, thirty-minute televised interview with Brel (in French, with Dutch subtitles). You can also buy CDs and books on the singer, and view photos and his original scribbled lyrics. Or you can just ask to see a mock-up of his dressing-room through a door off the foyer, complete with a half-eaten baguette and an ashtray full of Gauloises.

From the Fondation, it's a short walk north back to **boulevard de l'Empereur**, a busy carriageway that chews up this part of the centre. Across the boulevard, you'll spy the crumbling brickwork of **La Tour Anneessens**, a chunky remnant of the medieval city wall, while to the south looms the Baroque pepperpot spire of **Notre-Dame de la Chapelle** (see below).

Notre-Dame de la Chapelle

The city's oldest church, founded in 1134, **Notre-Dame de la Chapelle** (daily 9am–7pm) is a sprawling, broadly Gothic structure that boasts an attractive if somewhat incongruous Baroque bell tower, added after the French artillery bombardment of 1695 had damaged the original. Inside, heavyweight columns with curly-kale capitals support the well-proportioned **nave**, whose central aisle is bathed in light from the soaring clerestory windows. Amongst the church's assorted bric-à-brac, the **pulpit** is the most arresting, an extraordinarily flashy affair consisting of an intricately carved hunk of timber showing Eli in the desert beneath the palm trees. The prophet looks mightily fed up, but then he hasn't quite realized that there's an angel beside him with bread. Also of interest is the statue of **Our Lady of Solitude**, in the second chapel of the nave's north aisle, to the left of the entrance. The Flemings were accustomed to religious statues whose clothing formed part of the original carving. It was the Spaniards who first dressed their statues in finery – and this is a much-revered example, given to the church by the Spanish Infanta in the 1570s. Look also at the delicate statue of St Margaret of Antioch in the next chapel but one, which dates from 1520. The church's main claim to fame, however, is the memorial plaque to Pieter Bruegel the Elder. It was made by his son Jan and is located high up on the wall on the right-hand side of the south side-aisle's fourth chapel; the other plaque and bronze effigy in the chapel were added in the 1930s. Pieter is supposed to have lived and died just down the street from the church on **rue Haute** (see p.67).

After visiting Notre-Dame de la Chapelle, the obvious route is to press on into the Quartier Marolles – alternatively, you could backtrack north to **rue de Rollebeek**, a pleasant pedestrianized lane dotted with cafés and restaurants that clambers up to the place du Grand Sablon (see p.88) in the Upper Town.

The Quartier Marolles

South of Notre-Dame de la Chapelle, **rue Blaes**, together with the less appealing **rue Haute**, form the double spine of the **Quartier Marolles**, stacked on the slopes below the Palais de Justice (see p.90). This old working-class district is the linguistic heartland of **Brusselse Sproek** or Marollien,

▲ Notre-Dame de la Chapelle, Brussels' oldest church

a traditional dialect based on Flemish, which has, over the centuries, been influenced by the languages of the city's overlords. Relatively few people speak it today, and there's a real danger that it will die out altogether, which is a pity as it's a colourful, ribald dialect. If you wanted to have a go yourself, you could make a start with *dikenek*, "big mouth"; *schieve lavabo*, "idiot" (literally "a twisted toilet"), or *fieu*, "son of a bitch"; or pay a visit to the Toone puppet theatre (see p.242), which makes it own efforts to preserve the dialect.

A free **public elevator** (daily 7am–midnight), just off Rue Haute on rue Notre-Dame de Graces, whisks you up to Place Poelart and the Palais de Justice, cutting out the long trek between the Marolles and the Upper Town.

The Quartier Marolles grew up in the seventeenth century as a centre for artisans working on the mansions of the nearby neighbourhood of Sablon. Industrialized in the eighteenth century, the Marolles remained a thriving working-class district until the 1870s, when the paving-over of the Senne led to the riverside factories closing down and moving out to the suburbs. The workers and their families followed, initiating a long process of decline, which turned the district into an impoverished slum. Things finally started to change in the late 1980s, when outsiders began to snaffle up property here, and although the quartier still has its rougher moments, it is now a hugely gentrified district: rue Haute and Blaes – or at least those parts from Notre-Dame de la Chapelle to place du Jeu de Balle – are now lined with antique and interior-design shops, and there's an ever-increasing number of trendy bars and restaurants to supplement the earthy ones that have existed here for decades.

Place du Jeu de Balle, the square at the heart of the Marolles and has long been home to the city's best **flea market** (daily 7am–2pm). It's at its most hectic on Sunday mornings, when the square and its immediate surroundings are swamped by pile after pile of rusty junk, alongside muddles of eccentric bric-à-brac – everything from a chipped buddha, rococo angel or African idol, to horn-rimmed glasses, top hats and stuffed bears.

Beyond the market there's not much to see in the Marolles – it's more a place for aimless wandering and window-shopping than specific sights – but you might be interested to know that Pieter Bruegel the Elder used to live at **rue Haute 132** (it's not open to the public but a plaque marks the spot). Otherwise just walk the length of the district to the **Porte de Hal** on the petit ring, a fourteenth-century city gate that was saved from being torn down with the rest of the city walls due to its use as a prison in the late eighteenth century. It was heavily restored in the nineteenth century and has recently opened as part of the **Museés Royaux des Beaux-Arts** (Mon–Fri 9.30am–5pm, Sat & Sun 10am–5pm; €5), with displays devoted to the history and culture of Brussels.

Gare du Midi

Just outside the petit ring, the **Gare du Midi** is now the city's busiest train station and the terminus of most international services, including those operated by Eurostar from the UK. The station has already been expanded and modernized on several occasions, but work continues with the construction of more platforms and facilities. The area around the station, however, is still a rather depressed and seedy quarter with an uneasy undertow by day, and sometimes overtly threatening feel at night. The only good time to visit the district is on a **Sunday morning**, when a vibrant, souk-like **market** (6am–1pm; see p.230) is held under the station's rail arches and along boulevard du Midi, selling food, clothing, music and much more.

In front of the Gare du Midi at avenue Henri-Paul Spaak 7, the **Fondation Raymond Leblanc** (Wed–Fri & first weekend of every month noon–6pm; €3, Ⓦ www.fondationrleblanc.be) opened in late 2006 on the sixtieth anniversary of the Lombard publishing house. Housed on the second floor of the Tintin magazine building, it houses exhibitions that both remember and promote the best of Brussels' comic heritage.

Musée des Egouts

Five minutes' walk north of the Gare du Midi, bang in the middle of the petit ring in the Porte d'Anderlecht, is the city's **Musée des Egouts**, or Sewer Museum (admission by tour in French or Dutch only; Thurs & Fri 10am, 11.30am & 1.30pm; reservations obligatory; €3; ☎02 500 70 32). The museum provides some interesting background on the history of the city's river, the Senne, which once flowed through the heart of Brussels but by the nineteenth century had become intolerably polluted. To quote the Brussels writer, Camille Lemonnier, it was "the dumping ground, not only of industry, but also of the houses lining the river: it was not unusual to see the ballooned stomach of a dog mixed pell-mell with its own litter". An outbreak of cholera in 1866, which killed over 3500 citizens, was the last straw, and after this the city's mayor at the time, Jules Anspach, came up with a plan to cover the river on its journey through the city centre. This was carried out in 1867, and permitted the construction of boulevards Anspach and Adolphe-Max, which now bisect central Brussels.

Tours take in displays on the topography of Brussels and its rivers, including some marvellously evocative nineteenth-century photos, and give a good sense of the scale of the engineering achievement – not only in 1867, but also in 1931, when the main river Senne was diverted around the city centre (it now disappears underground just south of the Gare du Midi and emerges again a little way north of Laeken). You can learn about the city's two million or so rats too, as well as the other creatures that live down below, and about how the 350km of sewers were constructed, before moving on to take in a stretch of the fast-flowing Senne, and a few of the adjoining tunnels, including one that originates in a nearby abattoir.

3

The Upper Town

From the heights of the **Upper Town**, the Francophile ruling class long kept a beady eye on the proletarians down below, and it was here they built their palaces and mansions, churches and parks. Political power is now concentrated elsewhere, but the wide avenues and grand architecture of this aristocratic quarter – the bulk of which dates from the late eighteenth and nineteenth centuries – have survived pretty much intact, lending it a stately, dignified feel that's markedly different from the cramped bustle of the Lower Town.

The Lower Town ends and the Upper Town begins at the foot of the sharp **slope** which runs north to south from one end of the city centre to the other, its course marked – in general terms at least – by a traffic-choked **boulevard** that's variously named Berlaimont, l'Impératrice and l'Empereur. This slope is home to the city's **cathedral**, a splendid Gothic edifice that's recently been restored, but otherwise is little more than an obstacle to be climbed by a series of stairways. Among these the most frequently used are the covered walkway running through the **Galerie Ravenstein** shopping arcade behind the Gare Centrale, and the open-air stairway that climbs up through the stolid, modern buildings of the **Mont des Arts.** Léopold II named this steep slope in anticipation of a fine art museum he intended to build there; the project was never completed, and the land was only properly built upon in the 1950s.

Above the rigorous layout of the Mont des Arts lie the **rue Royale** and **rue de la Régence**, which together form the Upper Town's spine, a suitably smart location for the outstanding **Musées Royaux des Beaux Arts**, the most comprehensive of Belgium's many fine art collections, as well as the surprisingly low-key **Palais Royal**. Here, also, are the entertaining **Musée des Instruments de Musique (MIM)** and the enjoyable salons of the **Palais de Charles de Lorraine**. Further south, rue de la Régence clips through the well-heeled **Sablon district**, whose antique shops and chic bars and cafés fan out from the medieval church of **Notre-Dame du Sablon**. Beyond this is the monstrous **Palais de Justice**, traditionally one of the city's most disliked buildings.

The cathedral

It only takes a couple of minutes to walk from the Grand-Place to the east end of rue de la Montagne, where a short slope climbs up to the **cathedral** (Mon–Fri

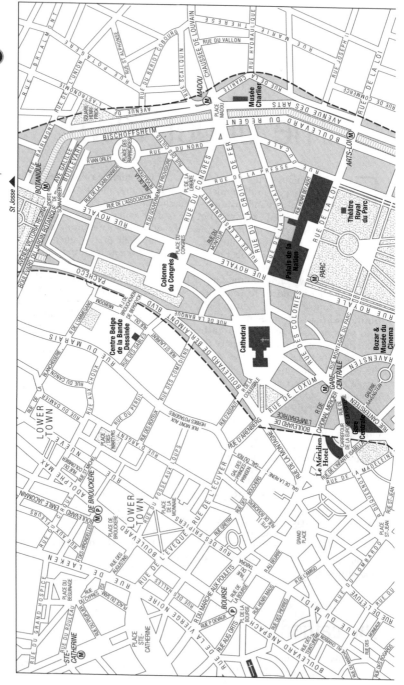

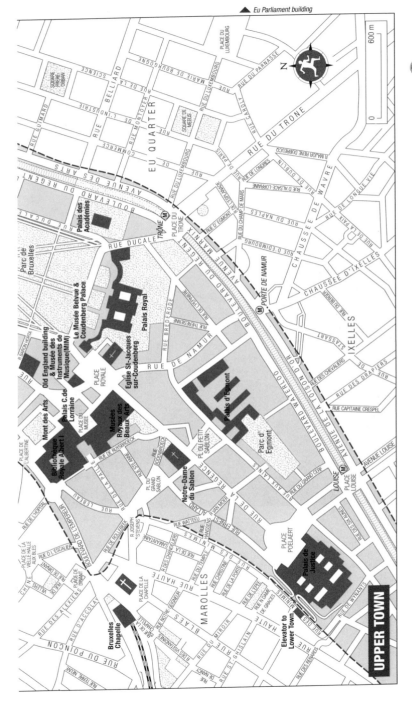

▲ The cathedral

7am–6pm, Sat & Sun 8.30am–6pm; free), a fine Gothic building whose commanding position has been sorely compromised by a rash of modern office blocks. Begun in 1215, and three hundred years in the making, the cathedral is dedicated jointly to the patron and patroness of Brussels: St Michael the Archangel, and St Gudule, a vague, seventh-century figure whose reputation was based on her gentle determination – despite all sorts of shenanigans, the devil could never put her off her prayers.

The cathedral sports a striking twin-towered, white stone **facade**, whose central double doorway and twin side-doors are trimmed by fanciful tracery and adorned with statues of the Apostles, angels and saints and – on the central column – the Three Wise Men. The facade was erected in the fifteenth century in High Gothic style, but the intensity of the decoration fades away inside with the airy triple-aisled **nave**, completed a century before. Other parts of the interior illustrate several phases of Gothic design, beginning with the chancel, the oldest part of the church, built in stages between 1215 and 1280 in the Early Gothic style. The interior is also short on furnishings and fittings, reflecting the combined efforts of the Protestants, who ransacked the church (and stole the shrine of St Gudule) in the middle of the seventeenth century, and the French Republican Army, who wrecked the place a century later. Unfortunately, neither of them dismantled the ponderous sculptures that are attached to the columns of the nave – clumsy seventeenth-century representations of the Apostles, which only serve to dent the nave's soaring lines. Another, much more appealing survivor is the massive oak **pulpit**, an extravagant chunk of frippery by the Antwerp sculptor Hendrik Verbruggen. Among several vignettes, the pulpit features Adam and Eve, dressed in rustic gear, being chased from the Garden of Eden, while up above the Virgin Mary stamps on the head of the serpent-dragon.

The stained-glass windows

The cathedral boasts some superb sixteenth-century **stained-glass windows**, starting above the main double doors with the hurly-burly of the Last Judgement. Look closely and you'll spy the donor in the lower foreground with an angel on one side and a woman with long blonde hair (symbolizing Faith) on the other. Each of the main colours has a symbolic meaning with green representing hope, yellow eternal glory and blue heaven.

There's more remarkable work in the **transepts**, where the stained glass is distinguished by the extraordinary clarity of the blue backgrounds. These windows are eulogies to the Habsburgs – in the south transept, Charles V kneels alongside his wife beneath a vast triumphal arch as their patron saints present them to God the Father, and in the north transept Charles V's sister, Marie, and her husband, King Louis of Hungary, play out a similar scenario. Both windows were designed by Bernard van Orley (1490–1541), long-time favourite of the royal family and the leading Brussels artist of his day.

Chapelle du Saint Sacrement de Miracle

Just beyond the north transept, flanking the choir, the cathedral treasury (see p.74) is displayed in the Flamboyant Gothic **Chapelle du Saint Sacrement de Miracle**, named after a shameful anti-Semitic legend whose key components were repeated again and again across medieval Christendom. Dating back to the 1360s, this particular version begins with a Jew from a small Flemish town stealing a communion wafer from his local church. Watched by his wife, he then presents the Host at the local synagogue on Good Friday and he and his fellow Jews proceed to stab it with daggers. The wafer then starts to bleed and, terrified, the Jews disperse. Shortly afterwards, the original culprit is murdered in a brawl and the wife moves to Brussels, taking the Host with her. Repenting, the woman tries to save her soul by giving the wafer to the city's cathedral – hence this chapel, which was built to display the retrieved wafer in the 1530s. The four **stained-glass windows** of the chapel retell the tale, a strip cartoon that unfolds above representations of the aristocrats who paid for the windows. The workmanship is delightful – based on designs by van Orley and his one-time apprentice Michiel van Coxie (1499–1592) – but the effects of this unsavoury, anti-Semitic legend on the congregation are not hard to imagine.

Trésor

Inside the Chapelle du Saint Sacrement de Miracle, the **trésor**, the cathedral treasury (Mon–Fri 10am–12.30pm & 2–5pm, Sat 10am–12.30pm & 2–3.30pm, Sun 2–5pm; €1) is smartly turned out, but the exhibits themselves are, for the most part at least, a fairly plodding assortment of monstrances and reliquaries. The main exception is a splendid Anglo-Saxon reliquary of the **True Cross** (item 5), recently winkled out of the ornate, seventeenth-century gilded silver reliquary Cross (item 4) that was made to hold it. There's also a flowing altar painting, *The Legend of St Gudule*, by Michiel van Coxcie (item 3), who spent much of his long life churning out religious paintings in the High Renaissance style he picked up when he visited Italy early in his career. Behind the chapel's high altar, look out also for the more-than-usually ghoulish **skull** of St Elizabeth of Hungary (1207–31). In her short life, this Hungarian princess managed to squeeze in just about everything you need to get canonized. She was a faithful wife (whose husband died on a Crusade), a devoted mother, and a loyal servant of the church, renouncing the world to become a nun and devote herself to the care of the poor and sick.

Chapelle de Notre-Dame de la Délivrance and the crypt

Opposite the treasury, next to the south transept, the **Chapelle de Notre-Dame de la Délivrance** dates from the middle of the seventeenth century, its stained-glass windows depicting scenes from the life of the Virgin on the upper level with the donors posing down below. The windows were designed by Théodore van Thulden, one of Rubens' pupils, and commissioned by the Infanta Isabella in 1649 – perhaps as spiritual compensation for the drubbing the Habsburgs had recently received from the Dutch, who had secured their independence from Spain the year before.

Back in the north side-aisle, near the entrance, a stairway leads down to the Romanesque **crypt** (same times as cathedral; E1), which gives an inkling – but little more – as to the layout of the first church built on this site in the eleventh century.

Galerie Ravenstein and the Musée du Cinéma

Just to the southwest of the cathedral, along boulevard de l'Impératrice, the **carrefour de l'Europe** roundabout is dominated by the curving stonework of *Le Meridien* hotel (see p.183), one of the city's more successful modern buildings. Opposite is the **Gare Centrale**, a bleak and somewhat surly Art Deco creation seemingly dug deep into the slope where the Lower and Upper Town meet. The station was one of the last buildings to be designed by Victor Horta and, opened in 1952, five years after his death, it is in striking contrast to his flamboyant earlier works (see p.96).

Behind the station, on the far side of rue Cantersteen, is the **Galerie Ravenstein** shopping arcade, which is traversed by a pleasant covered walkway that clambers up to rue Ravenstein. A classic piece of 1950s design, the arcade sports cheerfully bright decorative panels and has an airy atrium with a water fountain.

At the far end of the walkway, on rue Ravenstein, is arts venue Bozar, formerly the Palais des Beaux Arts, which occupies a severe, low-lying edifice designed by Victor Horta during the 1920s. The palais was built on the site of the Pensionnat Heger, a finishing school for young ladies where Charlotte and Emily Brontë lodged in 1842. Charlotte didn't like the Belgians much – "singularly cold, selfish, animal and inferior" – but she did take a shine to her tutor and the owner of the pension, Constantin Heger, writing him passionate letters, which he, as a married man, ignored. A plaque on the corner of the building, beside rue Baron Horta, recalls the Brontë's stay here. Bozar itself holds a theatre and concert hall and hosts numerous temporary exhibitions, mostly of modern and contemporary art. Part of the complex accommodates the **Musée du Cinéma** (daily except Thurs from 5.30pm to the end of the film, Thurs from 2.30pm; €2; Ⓦ www.cinematheque.be), which has displays on the pioneering days of cinema and shows early "talkies" and silent movies (with piano accompaniment) most evenings.

From Bozar, you can either climb the steps up to rue Royale and the Musées Royaux des Beaux Arts (see p.78), or stroll south along rue Ravenstein to the top of Mont des Arts and the Musée des Instruments de Musique.

Place de l'Albertine and the Mont des Arts

The wide stone **stairway** that cuts up through the sombre 1940s and 1950s government buildings of the **Mont des Arts** also climbs the slope marking the start of the Upper Town, serving as an alternative route to the Galerie Ravenstein (see p.74). The stairs begin on **place de l'Albertine**, which is overlooked by a large and imposing statue of **King Albert I**, depicted in military uniform on his favourite horse. Easily the most popular king Belgium has ever had, Albert became a national hero for his determined resistance to the Germans in

▲ The Mont des Arts

World War I and there was a genuine outpouring of grief when he died in a climbing accident near Namur, in southern Belgium, in 1934. Opposite him, across the square, is a statue of his wife, Queen Elizabeth.

The stairway clambers up the hill to a wide **piazza**, with water fountains, footpaths and carefully manicured shrubbery, and then it's on up again, offering splendid **views** over the Lower Town with the fanciful tower of the Hôtel de Ville soaring high above its surroundings. Beyond, at the top of the stairs, is rue Ravenstein and MIM (see p.77) and on the right, up a short flight of steps, is the place du Musée.

Place du Musée and the Palais de Charles de Lorraine

Just off the Mont des Arts, the **place du Musée** is a handsome cobbled square edged by a crisp architectural ensemble of sober Habsburg symmetry, whose sweeping stonework dates back to the eighteenth century. The elongated facade that bends round the square was originally covered with a jungle of Neoclassical decoration – cherubs, statues, military insignia in the Roman style and trailing garlands – and although much has disappeared, enough remains to suggest its original appearance. Two sides of the square are now part of the Musées Royaux des Beaux Arts (see p.78), as is the hole in the middle, which allows light to reach the museum's subterranean floors, but on the north side are the five salons of the **Palais de Charles de Lorraine** (Wed & Sat 1–5pm; €3), the surviving portion of the lavish suite of apartments designed for Charles de Lorraine, the Austrian who served as Brussels' governor-general from 1749 to 1780. The salons reflect Charles's avowed enthusiasm for the Enlightenment: he viewed himself as the epitome of the civilized man and fully supported the reforms of his emperor, Joseph II (1741–90), though these same reforms – especially the move towards a secular society – created pandemonium amongst his fiercely Catholic Flemish and Walloon subjects.

The palais begins in style with a statue of **Hercules**, the symbol of strength and courage, guarding a sweeping staircase. There's no false modesty here: if any of his guests bothered to look, they'd see that Charles was at pains to associate himself with Hercules, whose club is inscribed with the Cross of Lorraine, the Teutonic Cross (Charles was a Grandmaster of the Teutonic Order) and the letter "C" (his initial). Neither does it end there: at the feet of Hercules is a salamander, a creature that had long been linked with alchemy, one of Charles's keenest interests. At the top of the staircase behind Hercules, the **doorway** has its own guardian, a cherub sitting on a sphinx with a finger on his mouth – suggesting secrets and silence – and just beyond is a lavish **rotunda** decorated with stuccoed Roman military insignia to emphasize Charles's military prowess. The rotunda boasts an intricate marble floor with chequerboard tiles surrounding a star-shaped central feature consisting of lots of different types of marble, but here again it's all about good old Charles who prided himself on his knowledge of geology. The rotunda leads to five inter-connecting **salons**, each of which holds a miscellany of eighteenth-century bygones illustrative of one or other of Charles's many interests. The first room is mechanical, the second horological and geographical, the third is devoted to hunting and leisure, the fourth is musical and the fifth has a cabinet of porcelain. Few of these bygones were actually owned by Charles, but it is an enjoyable collection, the most interesting pieces being his Masonic trinkets and baubles.

Charles had his own private chapel next door – he was a well-known rake, so presumably it was handy for confession – and this could once be reached from the rotunda, but today you have to go back outside the palais to gain access to what is now the **Eglise Protestante de Bruxelles** (June–Aug Mon–Fri 1–5pm; free). Charles decorated the chapel in suitably ornate style, dripping with delicate stuccowork and glitzy chandeliers, and these have survived it being passed on to the city's Protestants in 1804.

Musée des Instruments de Musique (MIM)

Footsteps from the place du Musée, at rue Montagne de la Cour 2, the **Old England building** is a whimsical Art Nouveau confection, all glass and wrought iron, that started life as a store, taking its name from the British company which had the place built as its Brussels headquarters in 1899. It has been refurbished to house the entertaining **Musée des Instruments de Musique** (Tues–Fri 9.30am–5pm, Sat & Sun 10am–5pm; €5, plus extra charge for some exhibitions; ⓦ www.mim.fgov.be). Spread over three main floors, the museum's permanent collection features several hundred musical instruments, with an international assortment of traditional folk music instruments on the ground floor and European instruments – from antique trumpets and trombones to eighteenth-century Italian violins and clavichords – up above. The special feature is the **infrared headphones**, which are cued to play music to match the type of instrument you're looking at. This is really good fun, especially in the folk music section where, for example, you can hear the sound made by a whopping Tibetan temple trumpet and, amongst all sorts of bagpipes, the whine of the medieval Cornemuse, as featured in the paintings of Pieter Bruegel the Younger. Also here is the dreaded ocarina, a slug-shaped instrument that was once popular with children and drove many an adult to despair; the good news is that there's no sight of that other instrument of audio torture, the kazoo.

Aside from the permanent collection, one floor of the museum holds a concert hall, another has a shop selling a wide range of CDs and books, and the top floor is given over to a **restaurant**, where you'll be rewarded with wonderful views over the Lower Town.

Place Royale

Composed and self-assured, **place Royale** forms a fitting climax to rue Royale, the dead straight backbone of the Upper Town which runs 2km north to the Turkish inner-city suburb of St Josse. Precisely symmetrical, the square is framed by late eighteenth-century mansions, each an exercise in architectural restraint, though there's no mistaking their size, nor the likely cost of their construction. Pushing into this understated opulence is the facade of the **church of St-Jacques sur Coudenberg** (Tues–Sat 1–6pm, Sun 9am–6pm; free), a fanciful, 1780s version of a Roman temple with a colourful frescoed

Routes on from place Royale

Once you've reached the place Royale, the obvious option is to visit the Musées Royaux des Beaux Arts (see below), but if that doesn't appeal, there is a choice of walking routes. It's a short stroll south along rue de la Régence to the Sablon neighbourhood (see p.88), one of the city's swankier quarters; or you can walk round to the Palais Royal (see p.85) and then visit the fine art collection of the Musée Charlier (see p.87).

pediment representing the Virgin Mary as Comforter of the Depressed. Indeed, the building was so secular in appearance that the French Revolutionary Army had no hesitation in renaming it as a Temple of Reason. The church's soaring interior is a well-lit affair with a splendid coffered ceiling, and in the transept, amidst a fairly predictable assortment of furnishings and fittings, you'll find two large and dramatic paintings of the Crucifixion by Jean-François Portaels (1818–95), one-time director of the city's fine art academy.

The French Revolutionary Army destroyed the statue of a Habsburg governor that once stood in front of the church in the middle of place Royale, and its replacement – a dashing equestrian representation of **Godfrey de Bouillon**, one of the leaders of the first Crusade – dates from the 1840s. The statue has Godfrey, all rippling muscles and tree-trunk legs, rushing into battle in a supposedly heroic manner, but the sculptor wasn't quite up to his brief: Godfrey is supposed to be staring determinedly into the distance, but instead it looks as if he needs specs. Nonetheless, it's an appropriate spot for the statue as apparently this was where Godfrey exhorted his subjects to enlist for the Crusade, rounding off his appeal with a thunderous "*Dieu li volt*" (God wills it).

Musées Royaux des Beaux Arts

A few metres from place Royale, at the start of rue de la Régence, the **Musées Royaux des Beaux Arts** (Tues–Sun 10am–5pm; €5; ⓦ www.fine-arts-museum.be) comprises two interconnected museums, one displaying modern art from the nineteenth century onwards, the other older works. Together they make up Belgium's most satisfying all-round collection of fine art, with marvellous examples of work by – amongst many – Pieter Bruegel the Elder, Rubens and the Surrealists Paul Delvaux and René Magritte. A small collection is also on display in the Porte de Hal (see p.67).

Both museums are large, and to do them justice you should see them in separate visits. Finding your way around is made relatively easy by the English-language, colour-coded **museum plan** issued at the information desk behind the entrance. The older paintings – up to the beginning of the nineteenth century – are exhibited in the **Musée d'Art Ancien**, where the **blue** section displays paintings of the fifteenth and sixteenth centuries, including the Bruegels, and the **brown** section concentrates on paintings of the seventeenth and eighteenth centuries, with the collection of Rubens (for which the museum is internationally famous) as the highlight. The **Musée d'Art Moderne** has a **yellow** section devoted to Magritte and his contemporaries, though at the time of writing this is not yet open, as well as a **green** section whose six subterranean levels cover the nineteenth and twentieth centuries.

Both museums also have **red** sections, which are used to host a prestigious programme of **temporary exhibitions** for which a supplementary admission fee is usually charged. For the most popular you'll need to buy a ticket in advance; the ticket may specify the time of admission. The larger exhibitions often call for moves of the permanent collection, so treat any room numbers we've given with a degree of caution. Inevitably, the account below just scratches the surface; the museum's bookshop sells a wide range of detailed texts including a well-illustrated guide to the collections for €15, and an English **audio guide** is available at the information desk for an extra €3.

Musée d'Art Ancien

Well presented, if not exactly well organized, the **Musée d'Art Ancien** is saved from confusion by its colour-coded zones – blue, brown and red. It's a large collection and it's best to start a visit with the **Flemish primitives** in the **blue** section.

Rogier van der Weyden and Dieric Bouts

The museum holds several paintings by **Rogier van der Weyden** (1399–1464), who moved to Brussels from his home town of Tournai (in today's southern Belgium) in the 1430s, becoming the city's official painter shortly afterwards. When it came to portraiture, Weyden's favourite technique was to highlight the features of his subject – and tokens of rank – against a black background. His *Portrait of Antoine de Bourgogne* is a case in point, with Antoine, the illegitimate son of Philip the Good, casting a tight-lipped glare to his right while wearing the chain of the Order of the Golden Fleece and clasping an arrow, the emblem of the guild of archers. Weyden also painted religious canvases, and his *Pietà* is one of the most striking, the solemnity of the scene tempered by the brightening dawn sky.

Usually displayed nearby, the two panels of the *Justice of the Emperor Otto* are the work of Weyden's contemporary, Leuven-based **Dieric Bouts** (1410–75). The story shown here was well known: in revenge for refusing her advances, the empress rushes off to her husband to accuse the nobleman of attempting to seduce her. The nobleman is executed, but the man's wife remains convinced of his innocence and subsequently proves her point by means of an ordeal by fire – hence the red-hot iron bar she holds in her hand. The empress then receives her just desserts, being burnt on the hill in the background.

Hans Memling and the Master of the Legend of St Lucy

The gallery owns several fine portraits by **Hans Memling** (1430–94) as well as his softly hued *Martyrdom of St Sebastian*. Legend has it that Sebastian was an officer in Diocletian's bodyguard until his Christian faith was discovered, at which point he was sentenced to be shot to death by the imperial archers. Left for dead by the bowmen, Sebastian recovered and Diocletian had to send a bunch of assassins to finish him off with cudgels. The tale made Sebastian popular with archers across western Europe, and Memling's picture, which shows the trussed-up saint serenely indifferent to the arrows of the firing squad, was commissioned by the guild of archers in Bruges around 1470. Nearby, the anonymous artist commonly referred to as the **Master of the Legend of St Lucy** weighs in with a finely detailed, richly allegorical *Madonna with Saints* in which, with the city of Bruges in the background, the Madonna presents the infant Jesus for the adoration of eleven holy women. Decked out in elaborate medieval attire, the women have blank, almost expressionless faces, but each bears a token of her sainthood, which would have been easily recognized by a medieval congregation. St Lucy, whose assistance was sought by those with sight problems, holds two eyeballs in a dish.

The Master of the Legend of St Barbara

Also in this section, there's more early Flemish art in the shape of the *Scenes from the Life of St Barbara*, a single panel from an original pair by the **Master of the Legend of St Barbara**. One of the most popular of medieval saints, Barbara, so the story goes, was a woman of great beauty, whose father, Dioscurus, locked her in a tower to keep her away from her admirers. The imprisoned Barbara became a Christian, whereupon Dioscurus tried to kill her, only to be thwarted by a miracle that placed her out of his reach – a part of the tale that's ingeniously depicted in this painting. Naturally, no self-respecting saint could escape so easily, so later parts of the story have Barbara handed over to the local prince, who tortures her for her faith. Barbara resists and the prince orders Dioscurus to kill her himself, which he does, only to be immediately incinerated by a bolt of lightning.

School of Hieronymus Bosch

A further highlight of the blue section is the *Temptations of St Anthony*, a precise copy of the **Hieronymus Bosch** (1450–1516) painting that's in the Museu Nacional in Lisbon. No one is quite sure who painted this triptych – it may or may not have been one of Bosch's apprentices – but it was certainly produced in Holland in the late fifteenth or early sixteenth century. The painting depicts St Anthony, a third-century nobleman who withdrew into the desert, where he endured fifteen years of temptation before settling down into his long stint as a hermit. It was the temptations, rather than the ascetic steeliness of Anthony, that interested Bosch and the central panel has an inconspicuous saint at his prayers, desperately resisting distraction by all manner of fiendish phantoms. The side panels develop the theme – to the right Anthony is tempted by lust and greed, and to the left his companions help him back to his shelter after he's been transported through the skies by weird-looking demons.

Lucas Cranach, Gerard David and Quentin Matsys

Martin Luther's friend, the Bavarian artist **Lucas Cranach** (1472–1553), is well represented by his *Adam and Eve*, which presents a stylized, Renaissance view of the Garden of Eden, with an earnest-looking Adam on the other side of the Tree of Knowledge from a coquettish Eve, painted with legs entwined and her teeth marks visible on the apple. Look out also for a couple of panels by **Gerard David** (1460–1523), a Bruges-based artist whose draughtsmanship may not be of the highest order, but whose paintings do display a tender serenity, as exhibited here in his *Adoration of the Magi* and *Virgin and Child*.

The most important paintings of **Quentin Matsys** (1465–1530) illustrate a turning point in the development of Flemish art. A prime example is his exquisite *Triptych of the Holy Kindred* of 1509, in which Matsys abandons the realistic interiors and landscapes of his Flemish predecessors in favour of the grand columns and porticos of the Renaissance. Notice that each scene is rigorously structured, its characters – all relations of Jesus – assuming lofty, idealized poses.

Bernard van Orley

The gallery also owns several works by **Bernard van Orley** (1488–1541), a long-time favourite of the Habsburg officials in Brussels until his Protestant sympathies put him in the commercial doghouse. A versatile artist, Orley produced action-packed paintings of Biblical scenes, often back-dropped by classical buildings in the Renaissance style, as well as cartoon designs for tapestries and stained-glass windows, several of which were used for the cathedral's windows (see p.73). The pick of his paintings displayed here are the *Haneton Triptych*, whose crowded central panel is an intense vision of the Lamentation, and the *Triptych of the Virtue of Patience*, which tells the tale of Job. At the top of the left-hand panel, Satan challenges God to test Job, his faithful follower. God accepts the challenge and visits calamities on Job – at the bottom of the left-hand panel his sheep, horses, cattle and (peculiar-looking) camels are stolen. Even worse, the fearful central panel shows the roof falling in on Job's family while they are eating, and only on the right-hand panel is order restored, with God telling Job he has passed the test.

The Bruegels

The museum has a superb collection of works by the **Bruegel family**, most notably **Pieter the Elder** (1527–69). Although he is often regarded as the finest Netherlandish painter of the sixteenth century, little is known of Pieter the Elder's life, but it's likely he was apprenticed in Antwerp, and he certainly moved to Brussels in the early 1560s. He also made at least one long trip to Italy, but judging by his oeuvre, he was – unlike most of his "Belgian" contemporaries – decidedly unimpressed by Italian art. He preferred instead to paint in the Netherlandish tradition, and his works often depict crowded Flemish scenes in which are embedded religious or mythical stories. This sympathetic portrayal of everyday life revelled in the seasons and was worked in muted browns, greys and blue-greens with red or yellow highlights. Typifying this approach, and on display here, are two particularly absorbing works, the *Adoration of the Magi* and the *Census at Bethlehem* – a scene that Pieter (1564–1638), his son, repeated on several occasions – in which the traditionally momentous events happen, almost incidentally, among the bustle of everyday life. The versatile Pieter the Elder also dabbled with the lurid imagery of Bosch, whose influence is seen most clearly in the *Fall of the Rebel Angels*, a frantic panel painting which had actually been attributed to Bosch until Bruegel's signature was discovered hidden under the frame. The *Fall of Icarus* is, however, his most haunting work, its mood perfectly captured by Auden in his poem *Musée des Beaux Arts*:

In Bruegel's Icarus, for instance: how everything turns away

Quite leisurely from the disaster; the ploughman may

Have heard the splash, the forsaken cry,

But for him it was not an important failure; the sun shone

As it had to on the white legs disappearing into the green

Water; and the expensive delicate ship that must have seen

Something amazing, a boy falling out of the sky,

Had somewhere to get to and sailed calmly on.

Rubens and his contemporaries

Apprenticed in Antwerp, **Rubens** (1577–1640) spent eight years in Italy studying the Renaissance masters before returning home, where he quickly completed a stunning series of paintings for Antwerp Cathedral (see p.152). His fame spread far and wide and for the rest of his days Rubens was inundated with work, receiving commissions from all over Europe. The museum holds a wide sample of Rubens' work, including a sequence of exquisite portraits, each drawn with great care and attention, which soon dispel the popular misconception that he painted nothing but chubby nude women and muscular men. Look out for the exquisite ruffs worn by the Archduke Albert and his wife Isabella and the wonderfully observed *Studies of a Negro's Head*, a preparation for the black magus in the *Adoration of the Magi*, a luminous work that's one of several huge canvases usually displayed in Room 53. Here you'll also find the *Ascent to Calvary*, an intensely physical painting, capturing the confusion, agony and strain as Christ struggles on hands and knees under the weight of the cross. There's also the bloodcurdling *Martyrdom of St Lieven*, whose cruel torture – his tongue has just been ripped out and fed to a dog – is watched from on high by cherubs and angels.

Two of Rubens' pupils, **Anthony van Dyck** (1599–1641) and **Jacob Jordaens** (1593–1678), also feature in this part of the museum, with the studied portraits of van Dyck contrasting with the big and brassy canvases of Jordaens. Like Rubens, Jordaens had a bulging order-book, and for years he and his apprentices churned out paintings by the cartload. His best work is generally agreed to have been completed early on – between about 1620 and 1640 – and there's evidence of this here in the two versions of the *Satyr and the Peasant*, the earlier work clever and inventive, the second a hastily cobbled together piece that verges on buffoonery.

Close by is a modest sample of Dutch painting, including a couple of sombre and carefully composed works by **Rembrandt** (1606–69). One of them, the self-assured *Portrait of Nicolaas van Bambeeck*, was completed in 1641, when the artist was finishing off his famous *Night Watch*, now exhibited in Amsterdam's Rijksmuseum. Paintings by Rembrandt's pupils are usually displayed in the same room – **Nicolaes Maes** (1634–93), in particular, is well represented by the delicate *Dreaming Old Woman*. There are also several canvases by Rembrandt's talented contemporary, **Frans Hals** (1580–1666), notably his delightful *Three Children and a Cart drawn by a Goat*.

Musée d'Art Moderne

To reach the **Musée d'Art Moderne**, you'll need to use the underground passageway which leads from behind the museum entrance to **Level -2** of the **yellow** section, whose five small floors – two underground and three above – are devoted to Magritte and his contemporaries, or at least will be: at the time of going to print, this area is not yet open. Another stairway, on Level -2 of the yellow section, then proceeds down to the six subterranean half-floors that constitute the **green** section of nineteenth- and twentieth-century works. This section is comparatively small and has an international flavour, with the work of Belgian artists supplemented by the likes of Dalí, Picasso, Chagall, Henry Moore, Miró, Matisse and Francis Bacon. When the yellow section opens, most of the paintings in the green section will be moved around, so the account below is limited to pointing out general highlights.

Magritte and the Surrealists

The gallery holds several of the key paintings of **René Magritte** (1898–1967; see box, p.83), perplexing works whose weird, almost photographically realized images and bizarre juxtapositions aim to unsettle. Magritte was the prime mover in Belgian Surrealism, developing – by the time he was 30 – an individualistic

René Magritte

René Magritte (1898–1967) is easily the most famous of Belgium's modern artists, his disconcerting, strangely haunting images hugely influential amongst artists and the general public alike. Born in a small town just outside Charleroi, he entered the Royal Academy of Fine Arts in Brussels in 1915, and was a student there until 1920. His appearances were, however, few and far between as he preferred the company of a group of artists and friends fascinated with the Surrealist movement of the 1920s. Their antics were supposed to incorporate a serious intent – the undermining of bourgeois convention – but the surviving home movies of Magritte and his chums fooling around don't appear very revolutionary today.

Initially, Magritte worked in a broadly Cubist manner, but in 1925, influenced by the Italian painter Giorgio de Chirico, he switched over to Surrealism and almost immediately developed the themes and images that would preoccupy him for decades to come. His work incorporated startling comparisons between the ordinary and the extraordinary, with the occasional erotic element thrown in. Favourite images included men in bowler hats, metamorphic figures, enormous rocks floating in the sky, tubas, fish with human legs, bilboquets (the cup and ball game), and contrasts of night and day – one part of the canvas lit by artificial light, the other basking in full sunlight. He also dabbled in word paintings, mislabelling familiar forms to illustrate (or expose) the arbitrariness of linguistic signs. His canvases were devoid of emotion, deadpan images that were easy to recognize but perplexing because of their juxtapositions – perhaps most famously, the man in the suit with and bowler hat with an apple hiding his face.

He broke with this characteristic style on two occasions, once during World War II – in despair over the Nazi occupation – and again in 1948, to revenge long years of neglect by the French artistic establishment. Hundreds had turned up to see Magritte's first **Paris exhibition**, but were confronted with crass and crude paintings of childlike simplicity. These so-called **Vache** paintings created a furore, and Magritte beat a hasty artistic retreat behind a smoke screen of self-justification. The experiment alienated him from most of the other Surrealists, but in the event this was of little consequence as Magritte was picked up and popularized by an American art dealer, Alexander Iolas, who made the artist very rich and very famous. Magritte and his wife lived in Jette, a suburb of Brussels, until the late Fifties; their old house is now the **Musée René Magritte** (see p.123). René died in 1967, shortly after a major retrospective of his work at the Museum of Modern Art in New York confirmed his reputation as one of the great artists of the twentieth century.

style that remained fairly constant throughout his entire career. It was not, however, a style that brought him much initial success and, surprising as it may seem today, he remained relatively unknown until the 1950s. Three of the more intriguing canvases are the baffling *Secret Player*, the subtly discordant *Empire of Lights*, and the threatening *L'Homme du Large*, which may well have been inspired by the novels of Joseph Conrad. The other leading light amongst the Belgian Surrealists was **Paul Delvaux** (1897–1994), whose trademark themes of trains and stations and/or ice-cool nudes set against a disintegrating backdrop are clear in his *Evening Train* and *Public Voice*. The museum also owns a fine **Dalí**, *The Temptation of St Anthony*, a hallucinatory work in which spindly-legged elephants tempt the saint with fleshy women, and a couple of nerve-rattling **Giorgio de Chirico** paintings of dressmakers' dummies.

Jacques-Louis David

One obvious highlight of the collection is **Jacques-Louis David**'s much celebrated *Death of Marat*, a propagandist piece of 1793 showing Jean-Paul

Marat, the French revolutionary hero, dying in his bath after being stabbed by Charlotte Corday. David (1748–1825) gives Marat a perfectly proportioned, classical torso and a face which, with its large hooded eyes, looks almost Christ-like, the effect heightened by the flatness of the composition and the emptiness of the background. The dead man clasps a quill in one hand and the letter from Corday in the other, inscribed "my deepest grief is all it takes to be entitled to your benevolence". As a counterpoint, to emphasize the depth of Corday's betrayal, David has added another note, on the wooden chest, written by Marat and beginning, "You will give this warrant to that mother with the five children, whose husband died for his country". The painting was David's paean to a fellow revolutionary – like Marat, he was a Jacobin, the deadly rivals of the Girondins, who Corday supported, and both had voted for the execution of Louis XVI. David was also a leading light of the Neoclassical movement and became the new regime's Superintendent of the Fine Arts. He did well under Napoleon, too, but after Waterloo, along with all the other regicides, he was exiled, ending his days in Brussels.

Social Realists

The museum is strong on Belgium's Social Realists, whose paintings and sculptures championed the working class. One of the early figures in this movement was **Charles de Groux** (1825–70), whose paternalistic *Poor People's Pew* and *Benediction* are typical of his work. Much more talented was **Constantin Meunier** (1831–1905), who is well represented here by one particularly forceful bronze, the *Iron Worker*. Look out also for the stirring canvases of their mutual friend **Eugène Laermans** (1864–1940), who shifted from the Realist style into more Expressionistic works, as in the overtly political *Red Flag* and *The Corpse*, a sorrowful vision which is perhaps Laermans' most successful painting. If the Meunier bronzes whet your interest, you might consider visiting the Musée Meunier (see p.100).

Impressionism and Post-Impressionism

French Impressionists and Post-Impressionists – Monet, Seurat, Gauguin – make an appearance here too, along with their Belgian imitators, one of the most talented of whom was **Emile Claus** (1849–1924), whose charmingly rustic *Cows Crossing the River Leie* is on display here. From the same period comes **Théo van Rysselberghe** (1862–1926), a versatile Brussels artist and founder member of Les XX (see p.105), whose most interesting canvases exhibit a studied pointillism – as in his *Portrait of Mrs Charles Maus*. **Henry van de Velde** (1863–1957), another member of Les XX, changed his painting style as often as Rysselberghe, but in the late 1880s he was under the influence of Seurat, hence *The Mender*.

Symbolists and Expressionists

Amongst the **Symbolists**, look out for the disconcerting canvases of **Fernand Khnopff** (1858–1921), who painted his sister Marguerite again and again, using her refined, almost preternatural beauty to stir a frustrated passion – for she's desirable and unobtainable in equal measure. His haunting *Memories of Lawn Tennis* is typical: a work without narrative, it's a dream-like scene with each of the seven women depicted bearing the likeness of Marguerite. In *Caresses* Marguerite pops up once more, this time with the body of a cheetah pawing sensually at an androgynous youth. **Antoine Wiertz**, who has a museum all to himself near the EU Parliament building (see p.107), features here too, his

La Belle Rosme a characteristically disagreeable painting in which the woman concerned faces a skeleton.

There is also a superb sample of the work of **James Ensor** (1860–1949). The son of a Flemish mother and an English father, Ensor spent nearly all of his long life working in the port of Ostend, his home town. His first paintings were demure portraits and landscapes, but in the early 1880s he switched to a more impressionistic style, delicately picking out his colours, as in *La Dame Sombre*. It is, however, Ensor's use of masks – ambiguous carnival affairs with the sniff of death or perversity – which sets his work apart. His *Scandalized Masks* of 1883 was his first mask painting, an unnerving canvas that works on several levels, while his *Skeletons Quarrelling for a Kipper* (1891) is one of the most savage and macabre paintings you're ever likely to see. **Léon Spilliaert** (1881–1946) also hailed from Ostend, which was the setting for much of his work – typically evocations of intense loneliness, from monochromatic beaches to empty rooms and trains; a good example is his piercing *Woman on the Dyke*. Another noteworthy Belgian is **Constant Permeke** (1886–1952), whose grim, gritty Expressionism is best illustrated here by *The Potato Eater* of 1935.

Contemporary art

The museum holds a diverse collection of contemporary art and sculpture featuring an international range of artists in displays and installations that are regularly rotated. All the same, you're likely to spot an eerie Francis Bacon, *The Pope with Owls*, and the swirling abstracts of Brussels-born and Paris-based **Pierre Alechinsky** (b.1927). A painter and graphic artist, Alechinsky was briefly a member of the CoBrA group, but left in 1951. Thereafter, his work picked up on all sorts of international themes and movements, from Japanese calligraphy through to Nordic Expressionism, with a good dose of Surrealism (and Ensor) thrown in. Look out also for the tongue-in-cheek work of **Marcel Broodthaers** (1924–76), particularly his *Red Mussels Casserole*. Poor for most of his life, Broodthaers was greatly irritated by the connection between money and art, setting up a spoof museum of seventeenth-century art in Brussels in 1972, which he packed with postcards.

Palais Royal and Musée Belvue

Around the corner from place Royale, the long and really rather cumbersome **Palais Royal** (late July to mid-Sept Tues–Sun 10.30am–4.30pm; free; ⓦ www .monarchie.be) is something of a disappointment, comprising a sombre nineteenth-century conversion of some late eighteenth-century town houses, begun by King William I, the Dutch royal who ruled both Belgium and the Netherlands from 1815 to 1830. The Belgian rebellion of 1830 polished off the joint kingdom, and since then the kings of independent Belgium haven't spent much time in the palace. Indeed, although it remains their official residence, the royals have lived elsewhere (in Laeken, see p.125) for decades and it's hardly surprising, therefore, that the **palace interior** is formal and unwelcoming. It consists of little more than a predictable sequence of opulent rooms – all gilt trimmings, parquet floors and endless royal portraits, though three features make a visit (just about) worthwhile: the tapestries designed by Goya; the magnificent chandeliers of the Throne Room; and the *Heaven of Delight* ceiling of the Mirror Room, comprising more than a million jewel beetle carapaces. The Mirror Room was originally designed by Léopold II to evoke the Congo, and his successor Albert added the mirrors; in 2002, Belgium's own Jan Fabre finally capped it all off by decorating the ceiling.

Much better, one of the mansions that makes up the Palais Royal, the Hôtel Bellevue, at the corner of place des Palais and rue Royale, has been turned into the **Musée Belvue** (June–Sept Tues–Sun 10am–6pm; Oct–May Tues–Sun 10am–5pm; museum €3, Coudenberg Palace €4; combined ticket €5; Ⓦ www.belvue.be), which tracks the brief history of independent Belgium. It's all very professionally done, with the corridor displays concentrating on the country's kings, the rooms on Belgium as a whole. Juicing up the displays is a wide range of original artefacts – photographs, documents, letters and so forth – but pride of place goes to the climbing jacket that King Albert II was wearing in 1934 when he fell to his death. One particularly interesting display focuses on those Flemish nationalists who collaborated with the Germans during the occupation of World War II; another is devoted to the protracted conflict between the Catholics and the anti-clericalists that convulsed the country for much of the nineteenth century. It's an appropriate location for the museum too, as it was from this very building that the rebellious Belgians fired at the Dutch army, which was trying to reach the city centre across the Parc de Bruxelles in 1830 (see below).

Dating from the 1770s, the Hôtel Bellevue was built on top of the subterranean remains of the **Coudenberg Palace** (same times as museum), which once stretched right across what is now place Royale, though today you will need a vivid imagination to get much out of an underground visit. A castle was first built here in the eleventh century and was enlarged on several subsequent occasions, but it was badly damaged by fire after a vat of sugar boiled over in 1731. The site was levelled off forty years later, leaving only the foundations. These have recently been cleared of debris, revealing a labyrinth of tunnels and cellars that can only be reached from the Hôtel Bellevue. Further restorative work is planned, but for the moment visitors can wander round these foundations, the most notable feature of which is the massive **Magna Aula**, or great hall, built by the spendthrift Philip the Good in the 1450s, though on this particular occasion the duke made the city council pay the bills.

Parc de Bruxelles and place du Trône

Opposite the Palais Royal, the **Parc de Bruxelles** is the most central of the city's larger parks, along whose tree-shaded footpaths civil servants and office workers stroll at lunchtime, or race to catch the Metro in the evenings. They might well wish the greenery was a bit more interesting: laid out in the formal French style in 1780, the park undoubtedly suited the courtly – and courting – rituals of the times, but today the straight footpaths and long lines of trees seem a little formulaic, though the classical statues dotted here and there do cheer things up a tad.

Beside the park's southeast corner stands the **Palais des Académies**, a grand edifice that once served as a royal residence, but now accommodates a battery of royal academies. The palais is at the foot of **rue Ducale**, where **Byron** took up lodgings at no. 51 during his whirlwind, four-day visit to Brussels in 1816. Byron visited the Waterloo battlefield, ran up a steep debt by ordering a new coach, and "saw the bed where the [Empress] Josephine, Marie Louise, and the Queen of Holland, have been treading fast on one another's heels... Some of [Napoleon's] eagles were yet remaining... [and] the servant seemed a little astonished at our bowing before them".

Rue Ducale leads to **place du Trône**, where the whopping equestrian statue of Léopold II is the work of Thomas Vinçotte, whose skills were much used by the king – look out for Vinçotte's chariot on top of the Parc du Cinquantenaire's triumphal arch (see p.114). From place du Trône, it's a ten-minute walk north along avenue des Arts to the Musée Charlier (see below), or you can double back to the Musées Royaux des Beaux Arts and stroll south along rue de la Régence to reach the affluent Sablon district (see p.88). Alternatively, it's a few minutes' stroll east to the EU Parliament building and the EU Quarter, covered in Chapter 5.

Musée Charlier

The enjoyable if seldom visited **Musée Charlier** (Tues–Fri noon–5pm; €6; Ⓦwww.charliermuseum.be), just off the petit ring near place Madou at avenue des Arts 16, illustrates the artistic tastes of Belgium's upper middle class at the end of the nineteenth century. It holds the fine and applied art collection of a certain Henri van Cutsem, a wealthy businessman who bought two adjacent properties here in 1890. Van Cutsem merged and modified the two buildings so that he could display his collection to best effect, even going to the trouble of having Victor Horta install glass roofs, and he subsequently bequeathed the house and its contents to a sculptor he knew and admired, **Guillaume Charlier** (1854–1925). Charlier kept the collection pretty much intact and so it remains today, comprising everything from Belgian tapestries and antique French furniture through to Chinese porcelain and paintings by a number of Belgian artists, mostly lesser-known figures, but with one or two major artists represented too.

Each of the dozen or so rooms is crammed with Cutsem's bits and pieces, and it's this jumbled diversity that is the museum's principal charm. Nevertheless, there are one or two artistic highlights, most memorably James Ensor's *Flowers and Butterflies*; it's on display in the Concert Room.

Place de la Liberté and place des Barricades

From the Musée Charlier, it's a five-minute walk west across the boulevard to **place de la Liberté**, a leafy little square decorated with a statue of Charles Rogier (1800–85), a member of the insurrectionist Provisional Government of 1830 who went on to become a railway tycoon. The square is at the heart of one of the more attractive parts of the city centre, a pocket-sized district where the mansions of the nineteenth-century bourgeoisie, built with dignified balconies and wrought-iron grilles, overlook wide, straight streets and fetching little piazzas. One of these squares, the **place des Barricades**, is named after the impromptu barricades that were erected here against the Dutch in 1830, and in the middle is a statue of the city's own Andreas Vesalius, a distinguished anatomist who was drowned in a shipwreck off Greece in 1564. Another, much more famous figure, **Victor Hugo** (1802–85), lived on the square, at no.4, from 1866 to 1871 – the house carries a plaque. Hugo had been exiled from France for supporting the revolution of 1848 and was only allowed to return after the fall of the Second Empire in 1870 – a fate he shared with other literary lights, notably Dumas and Baudelaire.

Colonne du Congrès

Off place de la Liberté, at the west end of rue du Congrès, the 47-metre-high **Colonne du Congrès**, on place du Congrès, was erected in 1850 to commemorate the country's first national parliament. The column sports a statue of Léopold I on top and four allegorical female figures down below, representing the freedoms enshrined in the Constitution – of worship, association, education and the press. The lions were added later, guarding the tomb of the unknown soldier, in front of which burns the eternal flame honouring Belgium's dead of the two World Wars. The column dominates a large and bleak **belvedere** that offers a singularly unflattering view over the Lower Town.

From the Colonne du Congrès, it's a five- to ten-minute walk north along rue Royale to Le Botanique (see p.60), or a similar distance west down to the entertaining Centre Belge de la Bande Dessinée – the Belgian Comic Strip Centre.

The Sablon district

The **Sablon district** anchors the southern end of the Upper Town and in its midst is **place du Petit Sablon**, a small rectangular area which was laid out as a public garden in 1890 after previous use as a horse market. The wrought-iron fence surrounding the garden is decorated with 48 statuettes representing the medieval guilds, while inside, near the top of the slope, are ten slightly larger statues honouring some of the country's leading sixteenth-century figures. The ten are hardly household names in Belgium, never mind anywhere else, but one or two may ring a few bells – Mercator, the geographer and cartographer responsible for Mercator's projection of the earth's surface; William the Silent, to all intents and purposes the founder of the Netherlands; and the painter Bernard van Orley. Here also, on top of the fountain, are the figures of the counts **Egmont** and **Hoorn**, beheaded on the Grand-Place for their opposition to the Habsburgs in 1568 (see p.59).

Count Egmont is further remembered by the **Palais d'Egmont** (no entry) at the back of the square. This elegant structure was originally built in 1534 for Françoise of Luxembourg, mother of the executed count; remodelled on several occasions, this was where the United Kingdom signed up for the EEC (now the EU) in 1972.

Notre-Dame du Sablon

Opposite the foot of the park, the fifteenth-century church of **Notre-Dame du Sablon** (Mon–Fri 9am–6pm, Sat & Sun 10am–6pm; free) began life as a

▲ The church of Notre-Dame du Sablon

chapel built for the guild of archers in 1304. Its fortunes were, however, transformed when a statue of Mary, purportedly with healing powers, was brought here from Antwerp in 1348. The chapel soon became a centre of pilgrimage and a proper church – in High Gothic style – was constructed to accommodate its many visitors. The church endured some inappropriate tinkering at the end of the nineteenth century, but it remains a handsome structure, the sandy hues of its exterior stonework enhanced by slender buttresses and delicate pinnacles. Inside, the triple-aisled **nave**, which is closed for refurbishment at the time of writing, is dark and gloomy, making it hard to pick out the Gothic detail, but there's no missing the lofty vaulted ceiling or the fancily carved stone tracery of the windows. The statue of Mary is long gone – the Protestants chopped it up in 1565 – but two carvings of a legendary boat and its passengers recall the story, one in the nave, the other above the inside of the present, rue de la Régence entrance. The woman in the boat is one Béatrice Sodkens, the pious creature whose visions prompted her to procure the statue and bring it to Brussels. The occasion of its arrival in the city is still celebrated annually in July by the **Ommegang** procession (see p.248). Look out, also, for the grotesque **tombstone** of Claude and Jacqueline Bouton, members of Charles V's entourage, which, resting against the wall near the old main entrance, displays two graphically realistic skeletons. More conspicuous is the black-and-white marble facade of the **funerary chapel** in the transept beside the current entrance – a Baroque mausoleum for the earthly remains of the Tour and Taxis family, local worthies who founded the Belgian postal system.

Place du Grand Sablon

Behind the church, the **place du Grand Sablon** is one of Brussels' most charming squares, a sloping wedge of cobblestones flanked by tall and slender town houses of every architectural persuasion, from modest crow-step gables through to grand Neoclassical facades and the occasional Art Nouveau extravagance. The conspicuous **fountain** in the square was funded by the English

▲ Hunting for fine art on the place du Grand Sablon

émigré and Jacobite sympathizer Thomas Bruce, the Earl of Aylesbury, in 1740. Minerva, the fountain's central figure, holds medallions depicting the Empress Maria Theresa and her consort, while three allegorical figures frolic nearby – War, Fame, who blows his trumpet, and the River Scheldt with the overflowing urn. Place du Grand Sablon also is the centre of one of the city's wealthiest districts, and is busiest at weekends, when an **antiques market** (Sat 9am–6pm, Sun 9am–2pm) clusters below the church. Many of the shops on the place du Grand Sablon and the surrounding streets are devoted to antiques and art, and you could easily spend an hour or so window-shopping – or soak up the atmosphere eating or drinking in one of Sablon's many cafés.

Palais de Justice and place Louise

From halfway down place du Grand Sablon, rue Ernest Allard slopes up to **place Poelaert**, named after the architect who designed the immense **Palais de Justice** that dwarfs the square and everything around it. Opened in 1883, it's a real monster of a building, decorated with an eccentric mix of Greek, Roman, Egyptian and Assyrian motifs and capped with a gigantic crown which has recently been restored at colossal expense. It's possible to wander into the main hall of the building, a sepulchral affair with tiny audience tables where lawyers huddle with their clients, but really it's the size alone that impresses. During the construction of the palais, several thousand townsfolk were forcibly evicted to make the necessary space, and Poelaert became one of the most hated men in the capital. Indeed, when he went insane and died in 1879, it was widely believed that a *steekes* (witch) from the Marolles had been sticking pins into an effigy of him. The Marolliens also took more direct revenge: the day after its inauguration, the palais was thrown open to the general public, who urinated in every corner and crevice and slashed the seats.

Place Poelaert is also the site of two **war memorials**: the one on the corner of rue de la Régence, dating to 1923, pays tribute to the Anglo-Belgian alliance; the other in the middle of the square commemorates the Belgian dead with Art Deco soldiers following an Art Deco angel. On the right hand side of the Palais de Justice, a conspicuous modern lift leads down to the Marolles district (see p.65); the palais is also no more than a stone's throw from **place Louise**, part square, part traffic junction, which heralds the start of the city's most exclusive shopping district. It's here and in the immediate vicinity that you'll find designer boutiques, jewellers and glossy shopping malls. The glitz spreads east along boulevard de Waterloo and south down the northernmost section of **avenue Louise**, which is described on p.99.

Both avenue and place are named after the eldest daughter of Léopold II, **Louise-Marie Amélie** (1858–1924), whose life story reads like some sort of soap opera. Louise was shoved and shuffled into an unhappy marriage with a German prince in her teens, but fell in love with a Croatian officer (in the Austro-Hungarian army), a certain Géza Mattachich, and the two hightailed it off to Cannes. The ensuing scandal estranged her from her children, caused her husband and lover to fight a duel, and infuriated Léopold no end. It was, however, Louise's capacity to overspend that brought further disasters: Mattachich was dismissed from the army in disgrace and imprisoned for forging documents to keep the couple solvent, and when Louise's husband agreed to pay off her debts, his conditions were precise: she could either go back to him or opt for an asylum – and she chose the latter. There were further twists: after four years in prison, Mattachich was released and proceeded to help Louise escape. Reunited, the lovers dodged their new creditors in the hope that they would inherit a fortune when Léopold died, but the king did his level best to deny her any inheritance; Louise spent years challenging Léopold's will in the courts, but never hit the jackpot, having to settle for comfortable lodgings with one of her royal relations instead.

St Gilles, Avenue Louise and Ixelles

C obwebbed by tiny squares and narrow streets, home to a plethora of local bars and some of the capital's finest Art Nouveau houses, the neighbouring districts of St Gilles and Ixelles, just south of the petit ring, make a great escape from the hustle and bustle of the city centre. This is Brussels without the razzmatazz, and tourists are few and far between, especially in **St Gilles**, the smaller of the two *communes*, which is often regarded as little more than an example of inner-city decay. Frankly, this is true enough of its most westerly section, comprising the seedy quarter near the Gare du Midi, but St Gilles gets much more appealing the further east it spreads, its run-down streets soon left behind for refined avenues interspersed with dignified squares.

Ixelles, for its part, is one of the city's most interesting and exciting outer areas, with a couple of enjoyable museums, and a diverse street-life and café scene. Typified by its cheek-by-jowl diversity, Ixelles has long attracted artists, writers and intellectuals of many persuasions – Karl Marx, Auguste Rodin and Alexandre Dumas all lived here – and even today it retains an arty, sometimes bohemian feel. Ixelles is divided in two by **avenue Louise**, whose character is entirely different, as befits an administrative anomaly: the boulevard is counted as part of the city centre, and has been home to the haute bourgeoisie ever since Léopold II had the avenue laid out in the 1840s. It's here you'll find some of the city's most expensive shops and hotels, pricey jewellers, slick office blocks and the interesting **Musée Constantin Meunier**, sited in the sculptor's old house and studio.

More than anything else, however, it's the dazzling range of **Art Nouveau buildings** clustering the streets of both St Gilles and Ixelles that really grab the attention. For over two decades (1893–1914) Brussels led Europe, if not the world, in modern architecture and during this period the city sprouted about five hundred Art Nouveau structures, around half of which have survived. Many of the finest examples are concentrated on and around the boundary between the two *communes* – in between chaussée de Charleroi and avenue Louise. Here you'll find Victor Horta's own house, now the glorious **Musée Victor Horta**, as well as examples of the work of Paul Hankar and Armand van Waesberghe. Access to most of the city's Art Nouveau buildings is restricted, so you can either settle for the view from outside, or take one of ARAU's **Art Nouveau tours** (see p.26).

St Gilles

One of the smallest of the city's *communes*, **St Gilles** is also one of the most varied, stretching from the impoverished, sometimes threatening streets around the **Gare du Midi** to the affluent precincts of avenue Louise. Generations of political and economic refugees from the Mediterranean and North Africa have established themselves here, but as the tide of gentrification rolls remorselessly on from east to west, so the district's demographic make-up is being transformed. The prettiest part of St Gilles is just to the south of the **Porte de Hal**, and there is one star attraction, the **Musée Victor Horta**.

The Porte de Hal and the Hôtel Winssinger

The imposing **Porte de Hal**, standing on the edge of St Gilles at the southern tip of the petit ring, is the only one of the city's seven medieval gates to have survived – the rest were knocked down by Napoleon, but this one was left untouched primarily because it was a prison. The gate is a ponderous, heavily fortified affair, with towers and turrets, battlements and machicolations, and – although it was clumsily remodelled in the 1870s – it gives a good idea of the strength of the city's former defences.

Heading south from the gateway, down the **chaussée de Waterloo**, you're soon in the heart of St Gilles, with the elaborate Art Nouveau houses of **rue Vanderschrick** running off to the right and culminating in a popular Art Nouveau café, *La Porteuse d'Eau* (see p.210). Turn left here, up avenue Jean Volders, and it's a few metres to the **parvis de St Gilles**, a particularly attractive square that is the site of a lively fruit and vegetable **market** (Tues–Sun 6am–noon). One side of the square is overlooked by the soaring stone facade of a nineteenth-century parish church, the other by the sweeping curve of a matching pair of tenement buildings, where each apartment sports its own mini-balcony and wrought-iron grille.

From here, it's a short stroll east via rues Jourdan and de la Victoire to Victor Horta's **Hôtel Winssinger**, at rue de l'Hôtel des Monnaies 66. Dating from the 1890s, Horta's most creative period, the building has a wide facade, with multiple ground-floor windows set against striped bands of stone. Up above are a series of delicate balconies and the stylistic centrepiece, an ornate bow window.

The Barrière de St Gilles to the Maison and Atelier Dubois

From the Hôtel Winssinger, push on south down rue de l'Hôtel des Monnaies until you reach the **Barrière de St Gilles** – a seven-road junction that was, until the middle of the nineteenth century, the site of a toll gate. Close by, south again up avenue Paul Dejaer, is the *commune*'s **Hôtel de Ville**, a heavy-duty, pseudo-Renaissance edifice, and behind that, at the top end of avenue Jef Lambeaux, rises the ersatz medieval castle (actually nineteenth century), which holds the **prison**.

Heading east from the prison, take the first right off avenue Ducpétiaux and then the second on the left – avenue de la Jonction – to reach the **Hôtel Hannon**, a fine Art Nouveau edifice designed by the architect Jules Brunfaut in 1903 and located on the corner of avenue Brugmann. The windows, some of which are decked out with Tiffany glass, are a special highlight here – flowing, beautifully carved extravagances set against a facade whose brickwork is

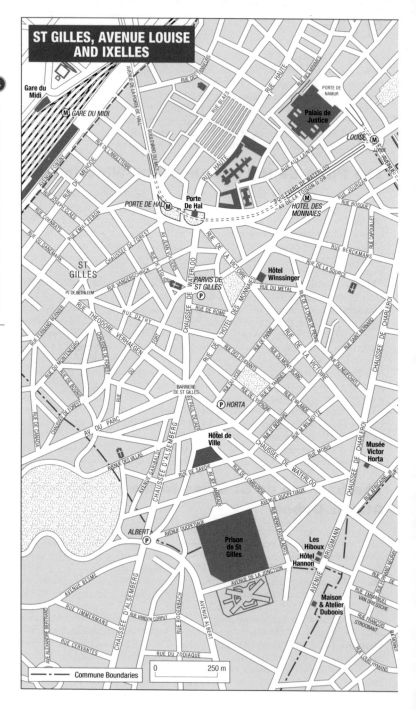

ST GILLES, AVENUE LOUISE AND IXELLES

Gare du Midi

(M) GARE DU MIDI

Palais de Justice

PORTE DE NAMUR

LOUISE (M)

AVENUE DE LA PORTE DE HALL

RUE DES TANNEURS

RUE BLAES

RUE HAUTE

RUE DES MINIMES

RUE AUX LAINES

BOULEVARD DE WATERLOO

AV DE LA TOISON D'OR

(M) HÔTEL DES MONNAIES

RUE JOURDAN

RUE BOSQUET

RUE DE CAPOUILLET

PORTE DE HAL (M) Porte De Hal

PORTE DE HAL

RUE DE LA VICTOIRE

Hôtel Winssinger

RUE BERCKMANS

RUE DE LA SOURCE

ST GILLES

CHAUSSÉE DE FOREST

PL DE BETHLEEM

RUE VANDERSCHRICK

PARVIS DE ST GILLES (P)

CHAUSSÉE DE WATERLOO

RUE DE ROME

RUE DU MÉTAL

RUE THÉODORE VERHAEGEN

RUE DETHY

RUE FERNAND BERNIER

CHAUSSÉE DE FOREST

RUE DU MONTENEGRO

RUE DE LA BOSSE

RUE DES ÉTUDIANTS

RUE FÉLIX

RUE DU MONT BLANC

RUE DE LA VICTOIRE

RUE SAINT BERNARD

CHAUSSÉE DE CHARLEROI

BARRIÈRE DE ST GILLES

(P) HORTA

RUE DE DANEMARK

RUE DU CANADA

AV DU PARC

AVENUE DES VILLAS

AVENUE GARIBALDI

CHAUSSÉE D'ALSEMBERG

RUE DE SAVOIE

Hôtel de Ville

RUE DE NAMUR

RUE D'ESPAGNE

RUE DE L'IRLANDE

RUE ST BERNARD

RUE M. WILLMOTTE

RUE MOBIS

CHAUSSÉE DE WATERLOO

Musée Victor Horta

CHAUSSÉE DE CHARLEROI

RUE AFRICAINE

RUE DE LOMBARDIE

AVENUE DUCPETIAUX

RUE FÉLIX DELHASSE

ALBERT (P)

AVENUE DUCPETIAUX

Prison de St Gilles

Les Hiboux Hôtel Hannon

AVENUE BRUGMANN

AVENUE DE LA JONCTION

AVENUE BESME

AVENUE ALBERT

RUE TIMMERMANS

RUE ALEXANDRE BERTRAND

RUE CERVANTES

CHAUSSÉE D'ALSEMBERG

RUE VANDEN CORPUT

RUE ROODENBACH

RUE DU ZODIAQUE

Maison & Atelier Dubois

RUE EMMANUEL VAN DRIESSCHE

RUE FRANÇOIS STROOBANT

RUE FERNAND NEURAY

RUE LOUIS HYMANS

— · — · — Commune Boundaries

0   250 m

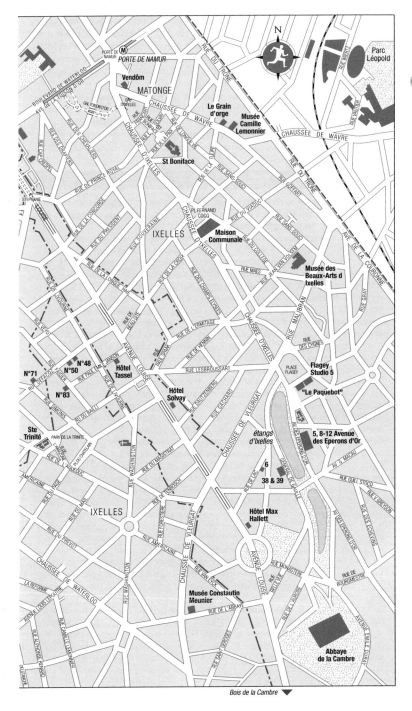

Bois de la Cambre ▼

decorated with strips of stone and a large allegorical stone plaque. Next door, **Les Hiboux** – The Owls' House – is a more modest red-brick affair, but it does carry some attractive wrought-iron grilles and a charming stained-glass window, plus a **sgraffiti** panel depicting two perky little owls – sgraffiti being the decorative technique in which one colour is laid over another and the top coat then partly etched away to create the design.

A couple of minutes' walk to the south, at avenue Brugmann 80, is Victor Horta's **Maison and Atelier Dubois**. Completed in 1906, towards the end of Horta's Art Nouveau period, the building is much simpler than some of his earlier works, though it still bears several of his familiar trademarks: a well-lit interior, exquisite carpentry in mahogany and oak, a mosaic floor and a marble

Victor Horta

The son of a shoemaker, **Victor Horta** (1861–1947) was born in Ghent, where he failed in his first career, being unceremoniously expelled from the city's music conservatory for indiscipline. He promptly moved to Paris to study architecture, returning to Belgium in 1880 to complete his apprenticeship in Brussels with Alphonse Balat, architect to King Léopold II. Balat was a traditionalist, responsible for the classical facades of the Palais Royal – amongst many other prestigious projects – and Horta looked elsewhere for inspiration. He found it in the work of William Morris, the leading figure of the English Arts and Crafts movement, whose designs were key to the development of **Art Nouveau**. Taking its name from the Maison de l'Art Nouveau, a Parisian shop which sold items of modern design, Art Nouveau rejected the imitative architectures which were popular at the time – Neoclassical and neo-Gothic – in favour of an innovative style that was characterized by sinuous, flowing lines. In England, Morris and his colleagues had focused on book illustrations and furnishings, but in Belgium Horta extrapolated the new style into architecture, experimenting with new building materials – steel and concrete – as well as traditional stone, glass and wood.

In 1893, Horta completed the curvaceous **Hôtel Tassel** (see p.99), Brussels' first Art Nouveau building – "hôtel" meaning town house. Inevitably, there were howls of protest from the traditionalists, but no matter what his opponents said, Horta never lacked for work again. The following years – roughly 1893 to 1905 – were Horta's most inventive and prolific. He designed over forty buildings, including the **Hôtel Solvay** (see p.99) and the **Hôtel Winssinger** (see p.93) as well as his own exquisitely decorated house and studio, now the **Musée Victor Horta** (see p.97). The delight Horta took in his work is obvious, especially when employed on private houses, and his enthusiasm was all-encompassing – he almost always designed everything from the blueprints to the wallpaper and carpets. He never kept a straight line or sharp angle where he could deploy a curve, and his use of light was revolutionary, often filtering through from above, atrium-like, with skylights and as many windows as possible. Curiously, Horta also believed that originality was born of frustration, and so he deliberately created architectural difficulties, pushing himself to find harmonious solutions. Horta felt that the architect was as much an artist as the painter or sculptor, and so he insisted on complete stylistic freedom. It was part of a well-thought out value system that allied him with both Les XX (see p.105) and the Left; as he wrote, "My friends and I were reds, without however having thought about Marx or his theories."

Completed in 1906, the **Maison and Atelier Dubois** (see p.96) and the **Grand Magasin Waucquez** department store (p.59) were transitional buildings, signalling the end of Horta's Art Nouveau period. His later works were more Modernist constructions, whose understated lines were a far cry from the ornateness of his earlier work. In Brussels, the best example of his later work is the Palais des Beaux-Arts of 1928 (see p.75).

staircase. The building is not open to the public, but the exterior – a modest but subtle facade with curvaceous windows set off by the careful use of wrought iron – is mightily impressive.

Doubling back along avenue Brugmann, it's a short stroll to the **chaussée de Charleroi**, within easy striking distance of the Musée Victor Horta.

Musée Victor Horta

Musée Victor Horta (Tues–Sun 2–5.30pm; €7; ⓦ www.hortamuseum.be), just off the chaussée de Charleroi at rue Américaine 25, occupies the two houses Horta designed as his home and studio at the end of the nineteenth century, and was where he lived until 1919. The only Horta house fully open to the public, the museum was developed in the late 1960s as part of a sustained

▲ The elaborate staircase of the Musée Victor Horta

campaign to stop the destruction of Brussels' architectural heritage and to publicize the charms of Art Nouveau. The outside of the building is tantalizing, a brace of narrow terraced houses with a fluid facade and almost casually knotted and twisted ironwork, but the interior is even better. Inside is a sunny, sensuous dwelling exhibiting all the architect's favourite flourishes in wrought iron and stained glass, alongside ornate furniture and panelling made from several different types of timber.

The main unifying feature is the **staircase**, a dainty spiralling affair that runs through the centre of the house, illuminated by a large skylight. Decorated with painted motifs and surrounded by mirrors, it is one of Horta's most magnificent and ingenious creations and it gives access to a sequence of wide, bright rooms, most memorably the **dining room**, an inventive blend of white enamelled brickwork and exposed structural metal arches above a parquet floor. Lining the walls of this room are six bas-reliefs carved by Pierre Braecke, five of which portray the arts represented by the muses above the dresser: painting, music, sculpture, literature and architecture – with the sixth holding out a model of the Aubecq mansion, built by Horta in 1899 and demolished in 1950. Also of interest is the modest but enjoyable selection of **paintings**, many of which were given to Horta by friends and colleagues, including works by Félicien Rops and Joseph Heymans.

To **get to** the museum from the city centre by public transport, take **tram** #92 from either place Louise, rue de la Régence or rue Royale.

Western Ixelles

Wedged in between the chaussée de Charleroi and avenue Louise, **western Ixelles** is one of the most fashionable parts of the city, its more prosperous inhabitants occupying graceful late nineteenth- and early twentieth-century town houses, usually of stone and often with attractive grilled balconies. The district holds a fine sample of Art Nouveau houses, with the pick of them on or in the vicinity of **rue Defacqz** and **rue Faider**.

The church of Ste-Trinité and place du Châtelain

Heading east from the Musée Victor Horta, take the first turning on the left – rue Africaine – for the parvis de la Trinité, the site of the sulky **church of Ste-Trinité**, a run-down but still domineering Baroque structure whose heavy-duty stonework fills out the square. The church's most interesting feature is the extravagant main facade, which was originally part of the church of St Augustin (1620), demolished to make way for place de Brouckère in 1896. The facade was moved here block by block and although pollution and years of neglect have left their mark, it remains – with its swirling lines, pointed pediments and pilasters – an impressive structure. There are vague plans to restore the church, but for now the interior is plain and dreary.

Just to the east of the church – along rue de l'Amazone – is **place du Châtelain**, a pleasant, tapering square lined with bars and cafés. Best known for its Wednesday afternoon food market (2–7pm) – where you can buy home-made wines, fine cheeses and a delicious cakes and pastries – it's also a relaxing place for a quiet drink or a spot of lunch.

Rue Defacqz: the Art Nouveau of Paul Hankar

From place du Châtelain, it's a short stroll northwest up rue Simonis to **rue Defacqz**, the site of several charming Art Nouveau houses. Three were designed by **Paul Hankar** (1859–1901), a classically trained architect and contemporary of Horta, who developed a real penchant for **sgraffiti** (see p.96) and multicoloured brickwork. Hankar was widely regarded as one of the most distinguished exponents of Art Nouveau and his old home, at no. 71, is marked by its skeletal metalwork, handsome bay window and four sgraffiti beneath the cornice – one each for morning, afternoon, evening and night. Hankar designed his home in the early 1890s, making it one of the city's earliest Art Nouveau buildings. No. 50 is a Hankar creation too, built for another painter, René Janssens, in 1898, and noteworthy for its fanciful brickwork. Next door, at no. 48, the house Hankar constructed for the Italian painter Albert Ciamberlani in 1897 sports a fine, flowing facade, decorated with sgraffiti representing the Ages of Man.

Rue Faider and the Hôtel Tassel

There are more Art Nouveau treats in store on neighbouring **rue Faider**, where **no. 83** boasts a splendidly flamboyant facade with ironwork crawling over the windows and frescoes of contented pre-Raphaelite women, all to a design by Armand Van Waesberghe. Directly opposite is rue Paul Emile Janson at the bottom of which, at no. 6, is the celebrated **Hôtel Tassel**, the building that made **Horta**'s reputation. The sinuous facade is appealing enough, with its clawed columns, stained glass and spiralling ironwork, but it was with the interior that Horta really made a splash, an uncompromising fantasy featuring a fanciful wrought-iron staircase and walls covered with linear decoration. It's also a striking example of the way in which Horta tailor-made his houses to suit the particular needs of clients. In this case it was built for an amateur photographer, and includes a studio and projection room.

At the end of rue Paul Emile Janson you hit avenue Louise, where a right turn will take you to another couple of vintage Horta buildings: the Hôtel Solvay and, a little further down the avenue, the Hôtel Max Hallet (see below).

Avenue Louise

Named after the eldest daughter of its creator, King Léopold II, **avenue Louise** slices southeast from the petit ring, its beginnings lined with some of the city's most expensive shops and boutiques. Further along, the shops give way to plush apartment blocks, the most visible part of the wealthy residential area that occupies the side-streets to either side of the avenue. It's here you'll find Horta's **Hôtel Solvay** and **Hôtel Max Hallet**, as well as the diverting **Musée Constantin Meunier**, which displays a large sample of the work of the late nineteenth-century sculptor, and the **Abbaye de la Cambre**, whose pleasant gardens and old brick buildings are situated in the midst of what is now a diplomatic zone hogging the end of the avenue.

Horta's Hôtel Solvay and Hôtel Max Hallet

The **Hôtel Solvay**, at Avenue Louise 224 – a couple of hundred metres south of the corner with rue Paul Emile Janson (see above) – is another Horta

▲ High fashion on avenue Louise

extravagance which, like the Musée Horta (see p.97), contains most of its original furnishings and fittings. The 33-year-old Horta was given complete freedom and unlimited funds by the Solvay family (who had made a fortune in soft drinks) to design this opulent town house, whose facade is graced by bow windows, delicate metalwork and contrasting types of stone. Inside, Horta commissioned an artist to paint a scene from the Solvay's summer cottage on the first staircase landing, but typically chose the dominant colours himself.

Also on avenue Louise, five minutes further along at no. 346, is Horta's **Hôtel Max Hallet**, a comparatively restrained structure of 1904, where what was originally a very ordinary, domestic facade is decorated with elegant doors and windows and an elongated stone balcony with a wrought-iron balustrade. Just beyond, the modern **sculpture** stranded in the middle of the traffic island looks like a set of elephant tusks, but is in fact a representation of the "V" for Victory sign of World War II. Named *Phénix 44*, it's the work of the city's own Olivier Strebelle (b.1927), whose speciality has long been large symbolic sculptures crafted in bronze and steel.

From the Max Hallet residence, it's a quick tram ride north (#94) to the smart commercialism of place Louise or a five- to ten-minute stroll south to the Musée Constantin Meunier (see below).

Musée Constantin Meunier

Musée Constantin Meunier (Tues–Fri 10am–noon & 1–5pm; free) is at rue de l'Abbaye 59, just off avenue Louise – and about 500m beyond Victor Horta's Hôtel Max Hallet (see above). It's housed on the ground floor of the former home and studio of Brussels-born Constantin Meunier, who lived here from 1899 until his death at the age of 74 just six years later. Meunier began his career as a painter, but it's as a sculptor that he's best remembered, and the museum has a substantial collection of his dark and brooding bronzes.

The museum's front room holds a dozen of Meunier's paintings and statues, but the collection doesn't really warm up until you reach the corridor behind it, where there are a handful of watercolours, a bronze or two and several interesting sketches of London made during one of the artist's many visits to England. The largest and most important sculptures and paintings are, however, in the old studio at the back, including a series of life-size bronzes of muscular men with purposeful faces, all standing around looking heroic – *Le Faucheur* (The Reaper), *Un Semeur* (A Sower) and *Le Marteleur* (The Metalworker) are typical. Among the paintings in the studio, there are several gritty industrial scenes like the coalfield of *Black Country Borinage* and the gloomy dockside of *The Port*, one of Meunier's most forceful works. Much stranger is Meunier's attempt to equate the harsh life of the Belgian miner with the sufferings of Christ in his *Triptych of the Mine: Descent, Calvary and Resurrection*, a moody but ultimately unapproachable work. Meunier was angered by the dreadful living conditions of Belgium's working class, particularly (like van Gogh before him) the harsh life of the coal miners of the Borinage. This anger fuelled his art, which asserted the dignity of the worker in a style that was to be copied by the Social Realists of his and later generations. According to historian Eric Hobsbawm's *Age of Empire*, "Meunier invented the international stereotype of the sculptured proletarian".

To **get to** the museum by public transport from the city centre, take **tram** #94 from place Louise, rue de la Régence or rue Royale.

The Abbaye de la Cambre

In a lovely little wooded dell just to the east of avenue Louise, a five-to-ten-minute walk from the Meunier Museum – and easily approached via rue de l'Aurore – lies the postcard-pretty **Abbaye de la Cambre** (open access; free). Of medieval foundation, the abbey was suppressed by the French Revolutionary army at the beginning of the nineteenth century, but the soldiers left its eighteenth-century brick buildings standing and, after many to-ings and fro-ings, they are now used as offices by several government departments. An extensive complex, the main courtyard is especially attractive and it serves as the entrance to the charming **abbey church** (Mon–Fri 9am–noon & 2–5pm; free), whose nave, with its barrel vaulting and rough stone walls, is an exercise in simplicity. The church is an amalgamation of styles, but Gothic predominates except in the furnishings of the nave, where beautifully carved Art Deco wooden panelling covers some of the stonework and frames a set of religious paintings of the Stations of the Cross. The church also holds one marvellous painting, Albert Bouts' *The Mocking of Christ*, an early sixteenth-century work showing a mournful, blood-spattered Jesus. Around the abbey's buildings are walled and terraced gardens plus the old abbatical pond, altogether an oasis of peace away from the hubbub of avenue Louise. To **get to** the abbey, take **tram** #94 along avenue Louise.

From the abbey, it's a brief walk south to the Bois de la Cambre (see below) and a minute or two to the mini-lakes and Art Nouveau houses of the étangs d'Ixelles (see p.105).

Bois de la Cambre

Beyond the abbey, at the end of avenue Louise, the **Bois de la Cambre** is unpleasantly crisscrossed by the main commuter access roads in its upper reaches, but much more agreeable around the lake that lies further to the south. It's Brussels' most popular park, bustling with joggers, dog-walkers, families and lovers at weekends, and is the northerly finger of the large **Forêt de Soignes**,

▲ Guarding the entrance to the church of the Abbaye de la Cambre

whose once mighty woodland bears a clutch of dual carriageways, and, more promisingly, scores of quiet footpaths.

Eastern Ixelles

Eastern Ixelles radiates out from the petit ring, its busy streets spined by the workaday **chaussée d'Ixelles**, whose long string of shops meanders down to **place Fernand Cocq** and ultimately place Eugène Flagey. It's the general flavour that appeals hereabouts rather than any specific sight, though there are a few exceptions, notably the first-rate **Musée des Beaux-Arts d'Ixelles**, whose forte is modern Belgian art, and the good-looking church of St-Boniface.

South along the chaussée d'Ixelles to St-Boniface

From the big and hectic square that is the **Porte de Namur**, it's a brief walk south past the shops of the chaussée d'Ixelles to the **Galerie d'Ixelles**, a small shopping concourse that lies at the heart of the Matongé district, which is home to a good part of the city's sizeable Congolese population. Just beyond the *galerie*, turn left off chaussée d'Ixelles along **rue Francart** and then take the first right to reach rue St Boniface, a particularly engaging street that's home to a number of laid-back café-bars including the immensely popular *L'Ultime Atome* (see p.205). The far end of rue St-Boniface is blocked by the imposing gabled facade of the **Church of St Boniface**, a largely Gothic structure, which, with its soaring buttresses, dates back to the fifteenth century. The outside of the church is in a sorry state of disrepair, but the interior is in good nick, its triple-aisled nave supported by mighty columns and illuminated by an impressive series of stained-glass windows.

Musée Camille Lemonnier

The **Musée Camille Lemonnier** (Mon–Fri 10am–noon & 2–4pm, but opening hours can be erratic; free), a brief walk east of St-Boniface at chaussée de Wavre 150, is dedicated to the eponymous Belgian intellectual, writer, dramatist and essayist, who was an influential member of the city's cultural elite for almost fifty years. A sharp-witted Francophone, Lemonnier (1844–1913) started out writing for a literary review, the *Journal des Artistiques*, and subsequently turned his hand to novels, books of art criticism – including the *Histoire de Beaux-Arts en Belgique* (1887) – and political texts. There were also monographs on the artists of the day – for instance Henri de Braekeleer, Alfred Stevens and Constantin Meunier – as well as oodles of stuff on the avant-garde Les XX (see p.105). Inevitably, Lemonnier's acid tongue created hostility, and bitter arguments punctuated his career, most disagreeably with the artist James Ensor.

Set up by Camille's daughter Louise in 1946, the **museum** is housed in a faded late nineteenth-century mansion and holds an eclectic collection of *objets d'art*: everything from sculptures and paintings to gilded books. In the main room upstairs are paintings by Louise, hanging alongside portraits of her father by Emile Claus, Constantin Meunier and Isidore Verheyden. The finest of the sculptures are *The Foolish Song* by Jef Lambeaux and *Eternal Spring* by Auguste Rodin, but the labelling is non-existent and you will have a hard time making sense of it all if you don't read French.

Place Fernand Cocq

From near the Musée Camille Lemonnier, rue de la Tulipe leads south back to the chaussée d'Ixelles and **place Fernand Cocq**, a small, refreshingly leafy square named after a one-time Ixelles burgomaster, and lined with a good selection of bars, including *Volle Gas* (see p.200) and *L'Amour Fou* (see p.209). The square's centrepiece is the **Maison communale**, a sturdy Neoclassical building designed by the Flemish architect Vanderstraeten for the opera singer

Maria Malibran, née Garcia (1808–36), and her lover, the Belgian violinist Charles de Bériot. Malibran was one of the great stars of her day and her contralto voice created a sensation when she first appeared on the stage in London in 1825. Her father, one Manuel Garcia, trained her and organized her tours, but pushed his daughter into a most unfortunate marriage in New York. Mr Malibran turned out to be a bankrupt and Maria pluckily left husband and father behind, returning to Europe to pick up her career. She was fantastically successful and had this Ixelles mansion built for herself and Bériot in 1833. After her death, the house lay uninhabited until it was bought by the Ixelles *commune* in 1849; the gardens in which Maria once practised have been reduced to a small park that now fronts the house.

Musée des Beaux-Arts d'Ixelles

The excellent **Musée des Beaux-Arts d'Ixelles** (Tues–Fri 1–6.30pm, Sat & Sun 10am–5pm; €7; Ⓦ www.musee-ixelles.be), rue Jean van Volsem 71, is located about ten minutes' walk southeast of place Fernand Cocq, via rue du Collège. Established in an old slaughterhouse in 1892, the museum was enlarged and refurbished a few years back and since then it has built up an excellent reputation for the quality of its temporary exhibitions, ranging from Belgian surrealism through to Russian modernism. The permanent collection is mainly late nineteenth- and early twentieth-century Belgian material, but it tends to play second fiddle to the exhibitions and is regularly chopped and changed, so although we mention some of the paintings you're likely to see, there are no guarantees. The museum's temporary exhibitions are almost always held in the **main auditorium**, a substantial warehouse-like affair ringed by two elevated galleries and located to the right of the entrance. The permanent collection is displayed in the long, single-storey **wing** that leads off from this auditorium.

Highlights of the **permanent collection** include several exquisite pointillist canvases, the pick of which is Theo van Rysselberghe's (1862–1926) charming painting of three women having tea in the garden. There's also the playful primitivism of Gustave de Smet (1877–1943), who has around a dozen paintings displayed here, and a wonderful collection of haunting works by Charles Herman, one of a large group of talented Belgian realists. Like his fellow realists, Herman struggled to get his work exhibited in the capital's salons, which until the late 1870s would contemplate only Romantic and Neoclassical works. Look out, also, for the large collection of posters featuring the work of Toulouse-Lautrec (1864–1901) – thirty of his total output of thirty-two are owned by the museum.

Among the more modern artists featured are well-known figures like the surrealist Paul Delvaux (1897–1994) and Marcel Broodthaers (1924–76), who pops up with an eerily abstracted *Casserole de Moules*, through to less familiar names such as Edgar Tytgat and Constant Permeke. There is also a healthy sample of the work of René Magritte (1898–1967), perhaps most appealingly *La Corde Sensible*, in which an over-sized cup and cloud are set against a mountainous backdrop. For more on Magritte, see p.83.

Finally, the museum possesses a smattering of **sculptures**, with the main event being Rodin's *La Lorraine* and *J.B. Willems*. Rodin (1840–1917) used to have a studio in Ixelles, at rue Sans Souci 111, and this was where he designed his first major work, *The Age of Bronze*. When it was first exhibited in 1878, there was outrage: Rodin's naturalistic treatment of the naked body broke with convention and created something of a scandal – he was even accused of casting his sculptures round live models.

Les XX

Founded in 1883, **Les XX** was an influential group of twenty Belgian painters, designers and sculptors who were keen to bring together all the different strands of their respective crafts. For ten years, they staged an annual exhibition showcasing both domestic and international talent and it was here that Cézanne, Manet and Gauguin were all exhibited at the very beginning of their careers. With members as diverse as the painter James Ensor and the architect-designer Henri van de Velde, Les XX never professed to be united by the same artistic principles, but several of its members, including Theo van Rysselberghe, were inordinately impressed by the Post-Impressionism of Seurat, whose pointillist *The Big Bowl* created a sensation when it was exhibited by Les XX in 1887.

Les XX – and the other literary-artistic groupings which succeeded it – were part of a general **avant-garde** movement which flourished in Brussels at the end of the nineteenth century. This avant-garde was deeply disenchanted with Brussels' traditional salon culture, not only for artistic reasons but also because of its indifference to the plight of the Belgian working class. Such political views nourished close links with the fledgling **Socialist movement**, and Les XX even ran the slogan "art and the people have the same enemy – the reactionary bourgeoisie". Indeed, the Belgian avant-garde came to see art (in all its forms) as a vehicle for liberating the Belgian worker, a project regularly proclaimed in *L'Art Moderne*, their most authoritative mouthpiece.

To **get to** the museum by public transport, take **bus** #71 linking Porte de Namur, chaussée d'Ixelles and place Eugène Flagey, and walk from there.

South to the étangs d'Ixelles

From the Musée des Beaux-Arts d'Ixelles it's an uneventful stroll south to **place Eugène Flagey**, whose fortunes are on the up after a long period of neglect: by the 1990s, the square had become a bare, dispiriting expanse, but it is now in the middle of a major revamp. The chain of 1930s modernist buildings that fringes its southern side gives it a sense of style, and a touch of history is provided by the **Delhaize** supermarket on the opposite side, which has the distinction of being the first self-service supermarket in Europe (opened in 1957). The largest building – the former **National Broadcasting Institute** (completed in 1937), a sweeping structure of yellow brick and glass – is regarded with some affection by the locals, who call it **le paquebot** for its resemblance to a luxury liner.

Just to the southwest of place Eugène Flagey lie the **étangs d'Ixelles**, two little lakes – really large ponds – that are flanked by several handsome Art Nouveau villas. **Avenue des Eperons d'Or**, running alongside the first lake, has the pick with **nos. 5 and 8–12** all designed by the Delune brothers in the florid, busy style – with balconies, layered stonework, turrets and high gables – which was their architectural hallmark. Across the lake, **avenue Général de Gaulle 38 & 39** illustrate the work of another Art Nouveau architect, Ernest Blérot, who specialized in ornate, almost abstract, wrought ironwork and demonstrated his virtuosity by building houses in pairs to heighten the effect. Close by, at **rue du Lac 6**, stands another Delune creation, but here the diminutive size of the house prompted the Delunes to extend the top floor above the original building line and protect it with overhanging eaves. A second special feature here is the exquisite stained-glass windows sporting aqua-floral designs inspired by Japanese woodcuts.

5

The EU Quarter and around

A
s Belgium thrived during the nineteenth century, so Léopold II extended the boundaries of Brussels east of the petit ring to incorporate the grandiloquent monuments and grassy parks he had constructed. Smart residential areas followed, plus a series of museums whose large collections reflected, so the king believed, Belgium's proper position amongst the leading industrial nations. Much of Léopold's grand design has survived, most notably in the Parc du Cinquantenaire, which provides the district's key attractions, but today it's overlaid with the uncompromising office blocks of the **EU Quarter**. Known properly as the Quartier des Institutions Européennes, it's home to the **European Commission**, whose civil servants support and advise the EU's ultimate decision-making bodies, and parts of the **European Parliament** (which also sits in Strasbourg). This area of town is hard to like: the streets groan with traffic and a vast building programme has turned whole blocks into dusty construction sites, interspersed with run-down and boarded-up terraces overlooking scraps of waste ground. Walking around the district, you can't help but get the feeling of "Europe" as a huge, unfinished project: there's so much construction going on, so much money being spent, and the buildings are so overblown with their own sense of self-importance. But the odd isolated pocket of charm survives, and there has been a recent wave of repentance in the EU, with the result that its newest buildings are not quite the inhumane monsters of before (the refurbishment of the Berlaymont is a case in point). Nonetheless, despite recent efforts to create a more friendly, human-scale environment, this is certainly not the city's most appealing quarter and to enjoy a visit you'll need to know what you want to see and to follow a clear itinerary – one which allows you to avoid, as much as possible, rues de la Loi and Belliard, the two wide boulevards that serve as the area's main thoroughfares. The best place to start is in the vicinity of **Parc Léopold**, just a few minutes' stroll from the petit ring, where you'll find the intriguing **Musée Wiertz**, exhibiting the huge and eccentric paintings of the eponymous artist, footsteps from the gleaming **European Parliament building**. From here, it's a ten-minute walk east to the Parc du Cinquantenaire, with its three large and wide-ranging museums and a triumphal arch built to celebrate the golden jubilee of Belgian independence.

Square de Meeûs and place du Luxembourg

On the edge of the EU Quarter, **place du Trône** is distinguished by its double lion gates and sooty, life-size statue of Léopold II, perched high up on his horse. From here rue du Luxembourg heads east, bisecting **square de Meeûs**, a small city park whose northern half contains a modest, careworn memorial to Julien Dillens, a popular nineteenth-century sculptor responsible for the effigy of Everard 't Serclaes on the Grand-Place (see p.45). A leafy, well-proportioned open space, it must have been a good deal prettier before the undistinguished boxy office blocks of Euroland arrived. Just along the street, the **place du Luxembourg** is a more characterful square, edged for the most part by nineteenth-century, three-storey, stone-trimmed houses, but shadowed to the east by soaring EU offices. In the middle of the square, a statue remembers John Cockerill (1790–1840), a British entrepreneur who built a steel-making empire in southern Belgium, particularly Liège. His pioneering efforts certainly transformed the local economy – and his company still exists today – but the loyal workers at his feet stretch the point, as does the statue's inscription: Le père des ouvriers ("The father of the workers").

The European Parliament

On the far side of place du Luxembourg, behind the tidily refurbished Gare du Quartier Léopold railway station, rises the veritable cliff-face of the **European Parliament**, a glass, stone and steel whopper that consists of two main blocks. The nearer of the two, the **Spinelli building**, accommodates MEPs' offices and the EU library; it also has an information office which dishes out EU propaganda and can answer questions on the building and advise on guided tours (see below). The information office is beside the capacious passageway that cuts through the middle of the Spinelli – directly behind the railway station – to reach the **Spaak building**, home to the horseshoe-shaped debating chamber and equipped with a curved glass roof that rises to a height of 70m. Completed in 1997, the structure has its admirers, but it's known locally as Le caprice des dieux ("Folly of the gods"), a wry comment on the EU's sense of its own importance.

Thirty-minute **tours** of the Spaak building (usually Mon–Thurs 10am & 3pm, Fri 10am; ☎02 284 34 57, ⓦwww.europarl.europa.eu; free) are fairly cursory affairs, more or less a look at the debating chamber and the stairwell outside, with the aid of headphones that guide you through and explain how the EU works. It's not exactly essential viewing, but you do learn something of the purpose of the building – which, amazingly enough, is here mainly to house the Parliament's various committees (most of the debates take place in Strasbourg). To take the tour, report to the visitors' entrance of the Spaak building fifteen minutes in advance and be sure to take photo ID.

▲ The European Parliament

Musée Wiertz

A couple of minutes' walk from the European Parliament building, up the slope at rue Vautier 62, the **Musée Wiertz** (Tues–Fri 10am–noon & 1–5pm; free) is a small museum devoted to the works of one of the city's most distinctive, if disagreeable, nineteenth-century artists. Once immensely popular – so much so that Thomas Hardy in *Tess of the d'Urbervilles* could write of "the staring and ghastly attitudes of a Wiertz museum" – **Antoine-Joseph Wiertz** (1806–65) painted religious and mythological canvases, featuring gory hells and strapping nudes, as well as fearsome scenes of human madness and

The European Union

The precise organization of the **European Union** is convoluted, but broadly speaking, it is operated by three main institutions, each of which does most of its work in Brussels:

The **European Parliament** sits mainly in Brussels, but transfers to Strasbourg once a month. It's the only EU institution to meet and debate in public, and has been directly elected since 1979; elections to the EP are held every five years. There are currently 785 MEPs, who sit in political blocks rather than national delegations; members are very restricted on speaking time, and debates tend to be well-mannered consensual affairs, controlled by the President, who – along with 14 Vice-Presidents – is elected for two and a half years, by Parliament itself. The President (or a Vice-President) meets with the leaders of the political groups to plan future parliamentary business. The European Commission (see below) submits legislation to Parliament, and it's debated first by committees, who meet in Brussels every month. Their work is then presented to the EP's plenary sessions, which consider the legislation at the same time as the Council of the European Union (see below), though on some issues the Council decides without reference to Parliament.

The Council of the European Union (or the Council of Ministers) is composed of 27 national ministers – one for each state, though the ministers change depending on the subject. There are complex rules regarding decision-making: some subjects require only a simple majority, others need unanimous support. This political structure is underpinned by scores of committees and working parties, based in Brussels and made up of both civil servants and political appointees. The Council of the European Union should not, however, be confused with the **European Council**, where all the heads of state of the EU plus the President of the European Commission meet regularly in "European Summits"; technically, the European Council is not part of the EU.

The **European Commission** acts as the EU's executive arm and board of control, managing funds and monitoring all manner of agreements. The 27 Commissioners are political appointees, nominated by their home country, but once they're in office they are accountable to the European Parliament. The president of the Commission is elected by the European Parliament for a five-year period of office. Over 25,000 civil servants work for the Commission, whose headquarters are in Brussels, in the Berlaymont and adjacent Charlemagne building on rue de la Loi.

In an attempt to simplify the whole EU system, members drew up a proposed EU treaty, but this was rejected in a referendum in Ireland in June 2008, and at time of writing radical changes to the EU look unlikely to proceed.

suffering. The core of the museum is housed in his studio, a large, airy space that was built for him by the Belgian state on the understanding that he bequeath his work to the nation. Smaller pictures on display here include *The Burnt Child*, *The Thoughts and Visions of a Severed Head* and an especially gruesome *Suicide* – not for the squeamish. There are also a number of quite elegantly painted quasi-erotic pieces featuring coy nudes, and a colossal *Triumph of Christ*, a melodramatic painting of which Wiertz was inordinately proud. Three adjoining rooms contain further macabre works, such as *Premature Burial* and *Hunger, Madness, Crime*, in which a madwoman is pictured shortly after hacking off her child's leg and throwing it into the cooking pot. Mercifully, there's some more restrained stuff here too, including several portraits and more saucy girls in various states of undress. There's no doubt that Wiertz was technically accomplished, but eventually he came to believe that he was a better painter than his artistic forebears, Rubens and Michelangelo. Judge for yourself.

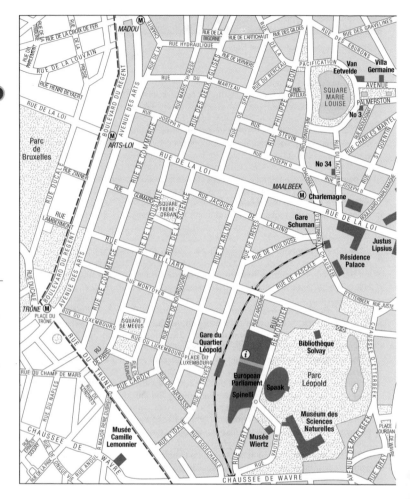

Muséum des Sciences Naturelles

Follow rue Vautier up the hill from the Musée Wiertz and you soon reach the
Muséum des Sciences Naturelles, at rue Vautier 29 (Tues–Fri 9.30am–
4.45pm, Sat & Sun 10am–6pm; €4; ⓦ www.naturalsciences.be), which holds
the city's natural history collection. It's a large, sprawling and somewhat
disorientating museum, whose wide-ranging displays are lodged in a mixture
of late nineteenth-century and 1960s galleries. There are sections devoted to
crystals and rocks, rodents and mammals, and insects and crustaceans, plus a
whale gallery featuring the enormous remains of a blue whale, with excellent
multilingual labels to explain it all. Most impressive of the lot, though, is the
capacious dinosaur gallery with a superb selection of dinosaur fossils. The
most striking ones are of a whole herd of iguanodons, whose fossilized
skeletons are raised on two legs, though in fact these herbivores may well have

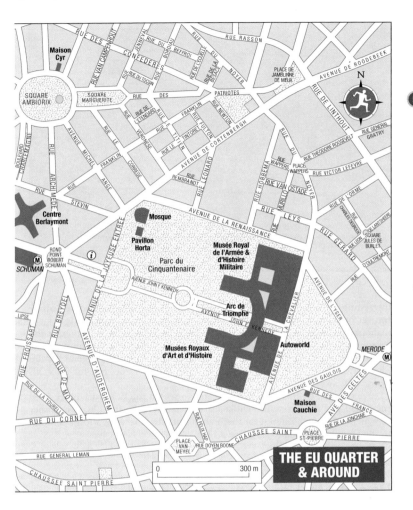

been four-legged. The fossils were discovered in the coal mines of Hainaut in the late nineteenth century.

Parc Léopold

On rue Vautier, almost opposite the Musée Wiertz, a scruffy back entrance leads into the rear of **Parc Léopold**, a hilly enclave landscaped around a lake. The park is pleasant enough, but its open spaces were encroached upon years ago when the industrialist Ernest Solvay began constructing the educational and research facilities of a prototype science centre here. The result is a string of big old buildings that spreads along the park's western periphery. The most

▲ Musée Wiertz

interesting is the second you'll come to, the handsome **Bibliothèque Solvay** (no set opening times), a splendid barrel-vaulted structure with magnificent mahogany panelling. Down below the library and the other buildings, at the bottom of the slope (on the left hand side of the lake), is the main entrance to Parc Léopold, where a set of stumpy stone gates bear the legend "Jardin royal de zoologie". Léopold wanted the park to be a zoo, but for once his plans went awry.

Leave the park by this front entrance and you're on rue Belliard, a block from rue de la Loi – the two traffic-choked main arteries of the EU Quarter, neither of which hold much interest for themselves, but which serve as a route through to the Parc du Cinquantenaire (see p.114).

Rue de la Loi and rue Belliard

The office blocks of the EU are concentrated along and between the two wide boulevards – **rue de la Loi** and **rue Belliard** – which Léopold II built to connect his Parc du Cinquantenaire with the city centre. It's not an enticing area to visit: the EU remains committed to modernistic, state-of-the-art high-rises and street-level is dominated by off-putting facades and lines of traffic with rarely a shop or café in sight. The hub of the area, **rondpoint Schuman**, is perhaps the most interesting spot hereabouts as it accommodates the EU's most notorious construction, the **Centre Berlaymont**, a huge office building that was widely praised for its ground-breaking design – shaped like a giant cross of St Andrew – when it opened in 1967. Twenty or so years later, however, it was abandoned for health and safety reasons when it was discovered the building was riddled with asbestos and (ironically) contravened EU regulations. It has recently reopened after a refurbishment that took twelve years, and certainly looks a lot better – just as well, given its

Belgian beer

No other country on earth produces more beers than Belgium – around seven hundred and counting. There are strong, dark brews from a handful of Trappist monasteries, light wheat beers perfect for a hot summer's day, fruit beers bottled and corked like champagne, and unusual concoctions that date back to medieval times. The centre of Brussels harbours lots of really good bars, some with literally hundreds of beers to choose from. We've listed a selection of our favourites, but don't be afraid to experiment – the bars, the beers, even the glasses – which are specific to each brew – provide some of the city's real pleasures.

Kwak ale, served in distinctive hourglasses ▲

Orval, a refreshing malt beer ▼

Best of the beers

Brugse Zot (Blond 6%, Dubbel 7.5%) De Halve Mann, a small Bruges brewery, produces zippy, refreshing ales with a dry, crisp aftertaste.

Bush Beer (7.5% and 12%) The 12% is the strongest beer in Belgium. It has a lovely golden colour and an earthy aroma; the weaker 7.5% version is a tasty pale ale with a hint of coriander.

Chimay (red 7%, blue 9%) Made by Trappist monks in southern Belgium, Chimay beers are widely regarded as among the best in the world. These two are fruity and strong, deep in body, and somewhat spicy.

La Chouffe (8%) Produced in the Ardennes, this refreshing pale ale with a peachy aftertaste is recognizable by the red-hooded gnome (*chouffe*) on its label.

De Koninck (5%) Antwerp's leading brew is something of a Flemish institution, a smooth pale ale that's very drinkable.

Kriek (Cantillon 5%, Belle Vue 5.2%, Mort Subite 4.3%) A type of beer rather than a particular brew, made from a base lambic beer to which are added cherries or, in the case of the more commercial brands, cherry juice.

Kwak (8%) This Flemish beer is not all that special – it's an amber ale sweetened by a little sugar – but it's served up in style, in a distinctive hourglass that's placed in a wooden stand.

Gouden Carolus (8%) A full-bodied, dark-brown ale with a sour and slightly fruity aftertaste that was the favourite tipple of Charles V. Brewed in Mechelen.

Gueuze (Cantillon 5%) Made by blending old and new lambic beers, gueuze is a lively, slightly sour, cidery concoction that is the essence of Brussels. There are lots of varieties, and the most common

– Belle Vue (5.2%), Timmermans (5.5%) and the exemplary Lindemans (5.2%) – are sold all over the city; Cantillon is the most traditional.

Hoegaarden (5%) A light and extremely refreshing wheat beer, the ideal drink for a hot summer's day.

Lambic beers (Cantillon 5%, Lindemans 4%) A Brussels speciality, lambic beers are tart because they are brewed with at least thirty percent raw wheat as well as the more usual malted barley. The key feature, however, is the process of spontaneous fermentation in open wooden casks over two to three years.

Orval (6.2%) One of the world's most distinctive malt beers, Orval is made in the Ardennes at the Abbaye d'Orval, founded in the twelfth century by Benedictine monks. The beer is a lovely amber colour, refreshingly bitter, and makes a great aperitif.

Rochefort (Rochefort 6 7.5%, Rochefort 8 9.2%, Rochefort 10 11.3%) Rochefort beers are typically dark and sweet and come in these three main versions; Rochefort 10 is a deep-brown ale with a fruity aftertaste.

Rodenbach (Rodenbach 5%, Rodenbach Grand Cru 6.5%) Flemish beer Rodenbach (5%) is a tangy brown ale with a hint of sourness, while the much fuller – and sourer – Rodenbach Grand Cru is harder to find, but delicious.

Westmalle (Dubbel 7%, Tripel 9%) The Trappist monks of Westmalle, north of Antwerp, claim their beers not only cure loss of appetite and insomnia, but reduce stress too. Whatever the truth, the prescription certainly tastes good. Their most famous beer, the Westmalle Tripel, is creamy and aromatic, while the popular Westmalle Dubbel is dark and malty.

▲ Tangy Rodenbach ale

▼ The Trappist-brewed Rochefort

A la Mort Subite ▲

Belgian beer barrels ▼

La Bécasse ▼

A Belgian hopfield ▼

Top ten Brussels beer spots

▶▶ **La Bécasse** The ultimate city-centre beer bar, and one of the only places to serve genuine Brussels lambic by the jug. See p.206.

▶▶ **Beer Mania** Brussels' best beer shop, with a great selection and friendly, expert advice. See p.228.

▶▶ **Cantillon Brewery** The city's best gueuze is produced at this brewery, and you can tour the premises. See p.121.

▶▶ **Chez Moeder Lambic** This smoky haunt has Brussels' best beer list, bar none. See p.210.

▶▶ **Délices et Caprices** This city-centre shop does tastings and has a fantastic selection of Belgian beers, including some you'd be hard pushed to find anywhere else. See p.229.

▶▶ **Maison des Brasseurs** Grand-Place 10. The brewery museum isn't an unmissable sight by any means, but there's something comfortingly appropriate about poking around its dusty artefacts and finishing up with your complimentary beer in the cosy bar.

▶▶ **A la Mort Subite** Originally the site of a brewery, now perhaps Brussels' nicest bar, with an excellent range of beers, delicious snacks and an enjoyable atmosphere to boot. See p.208.

▶▶ **Poechenellekelder** Odd that one of the city's best selections of gueuze should be available right opposite its tackiest tourist attraction, but that's Brussels all over. See p.209.

▶▶ **Restobières** Marolles restaurant that specializes in food cooked with beer, and with a great beer list to wash it down with. See p.196.

▶▶ **In 't Spinnekopke** A longstanding Brussels favourite, in which beer is the main event – in the food and the glass. See p.194.

role as home to the European Commission. To its credit, the building is also kitted out with a string of environmentally friendly features: the glass panels of the exterior can be moved by computer to take account of the weather and the toilets are fed by rainwater. It remains probably the best-known symbol of the EU, and has recently been acquired from the Belgian state by the EU for around €550 million. Next door, the huge **Charlemagne building** houses the rest of the Commission's bloated bureaucracy, while opposite, housing the Council of the European Union, is the boxy, cream-coloured **Justus Lipsius building**, constructed in the mid-Nineties and almost as bland and nondescript as the Berlaymont is flamboyant.

Rue Archimède and squares Ambiorix and Marie-Louise

Although EU behemoths dominate this slice of the city, there's aesthetic relief near at hand on **rue Archimède**, beside the Berlaymont, where a pleasant stretch of shops and cafés serves a mixed bag of eurocrats and expats. Rue Archimède also leads through to two pleasant and leafy plazas – squares Ambiorix and Marie-Louise – which were laid out in the 1870s on what had previously been marshland. By the end of the century, they formed, along with the short avenue Palmerston that linked them, one of the city's most fashionable suburbs, where · the residences of the bourgeoisie included several splendid examples of Art Nouveau – though none, unfortunately, are currently open to visitors. First up is **square Ambiorix**, which is largely overshadowed by modern apartments, but you shouldn't miss the superb facade of the **Maison Cyr**, on the far side of the square at no. 11, one of the city's most ornate Art Nouveau buildings and the one-time home of the painter Georges de Saint-Cyr. The house itself is almost impossibly narrow, but its spidery balconies and swirling window frames make a flamboyant artistic statement nonetheless. "I daresay I have commissioned one of the most beautiful houses on the square", the painter observed modestly – but with some justification.

Just below here, on avenue Palmerston, the **Villa Germaine**, at no. 24, exhibits striking floral patterned tiles and multicoloured bricks, while down at the foot of the street are three wonderfully subtle buildings by Victor Horta: no. 2 is a charming corner house with a delicately carved, fluted stone facade, completed a few years after the adjoining no. 4, which has a functional design of riveted cast-iron softened by arched lintels and mosaics; together they're known as the **Hôtel van Eetvelde**. And finally there's the austere facade of no. 3, across the street, whose white and grey stone trimmings lead round to an exuberant side-entrance.

The south side of **square Marie-Louise** is occupied by a series of big old houses whose stone trimmings, balconies, dormer windows and high gables jostle for attention. Just off the square, back towards rue de la Loi, rue du Taciturne 34 is a lavish structure with an elegant facade of intricate window grilles and slender black columns. It was designed by Paul Saintenoy, who was also responsible for the Old England building at the top of rue Ravenstein (see p.77). If you want to see more of this sort of architecture, see p.117 for the Maison Cauchie; for more on Victor Horta, see p.96.

Rue du Taciturne leads back to rue de la Loi, from where it's a couple of minutes' walk west to Métro Maalbeek.

Le Cinquantenaire and around

The wide and leafy lawns of the **Parc du Cinquantenaire** slope up towards a gargantuan triumphal **arch** surmounted by a huge and bombastic bronze entitled Brabant Raising the National Flag. The arch, along with the two heavyweight stone buildings it connects, comprise **Le Cinquantenaire**, which was placed here by Léopold II for an exhibition to mark the golden jubilee of the Belgian state in 1880. By all accounts the exhibition of all things made in Belgium and its colonies was a great success, and the park continues to host shows and trade fairs of various kinds, while the buildings themselves – a brief walk from either Métro Merode or Métro Schuman – contain extensive collections of art and applied art, weapons and cars, displayed in three separate museums.

The only specific attraction in the park itself is the **Pavillon Horta** (Tues–Sun 2.30–3.30pm; €2.50), tucked away in its northwest corner. A grey, graffitied Neoclassical box, it is subtitled the "pavilion of human passions" on account of the sculpture inside, by Jef Lambeaux, from 1886, which shows writhing naked figures overlooked by a shrouded Death. Designed specifically to hold the sculpture, the pavilion was Horta's first public commission and shows no hint of the later organic decorative work for which he became known. In fact, the building was closed three days after opening due to the controversy the no-holds-barred work caused. The big cream-coloured building next door is Brussels' main **mosque**, built in 1978 in a modern Arabic style by a Tunisian architect, but not in fact a symbol of the city's new multiculturalism – it was, rather, a replacement for an earlier building that dated from 1897.

Musées Royaux d'Art et d'Histoire

The **Musées Royaux d'Art et d'Histoire**, on the south side of the south wing of the Cinquantenaire complex (Tues–Fri 9.30am–5pm, Sat & Sun 10am–5pm; €5; Ⓦ www.mrah.be), is made up of a maddening and badly labelled maze of pottery, carvings, furniture, tapestries, glassware and lacework from all over the world. The galleries contain almost too much to absorb in even a couple of visits, and there's no plan, which makes it even harder to select the bits that interest you most. There are enormous galleries of mostly run-of-the-mill Greek, Egyptian and Roman artefacts, an assortment of Far Eastern art and textiles, medieval and Renaissance carving and religious artefacts, and a decent collection of glasswork from all eras. But perhaps the best thing to do with a large, disorganized museum of this nature is to wander freely and stop when something catches your eye.

To the right of the entrance hall, the **European decorative** arts galleries have perhaps the most immediacy, featuring everything from Delft ceramics, altarpieces, porcelain and silverware through to tapestries and Art Deco and Art Nouveau furnishings. There's little to link one set of objects to another, but highlights to look out for include some striking fifteenth- and sixteenth-century **altarpieces** from Brussels and Antwerp churches, notably The Passion altarpiece, animated with a mass of finely detailed wooden reliefs. Carved in Brussels in the 1470s, it's quite different from The Passion altarpiece three rooms down, made in Antwerp some sixty years later and much more extravagant, sporting a veritable doll's house of figures. Seek out, too, the museum's prime collection of Brussels **tapestries**, dotted here and there and dating from the middle of the sixteenth century, the heyday of the city's tapestry industry. There are also less languid earlier works manufactured during the fifteenth

▲ The Musées Royaux d'Art et d'Histoire

century in Tournai, southern Belgium, depicting scenes of tense and often violent drama as in the Battle of Roncesvalles, in which Christians and Moors slug it out in a fearsome, seething battle scene. Other sixteenth-century Brussels tapestries include the legend of Notre Dame du Sablon (see p.88), while there are also some fine alabasters from Mechelen, just north of Brussels, and a delightful double bed – a fancy, canopied affair produced for a Swiss burgher in the 1680s. Finally, don't leave without poking round the **Art Nouveau** sections, where the display cases were designed by Victor Horta for a firm of jewellers, and now accommodate the celebrated *Mysterious Sphinx*, a ceramic bust of archetypal Art Nouveau design. It was the work of Charles van der Stappen in 1897.

On the other side of the entrance hall are galleries devoted to ancient civilizations. The **Roman collection** focuses on a giant hunting mosaic from

415 AD, which you can view from above and from ground level – it's very vivid and well preserved, showing hunters spearing tigers and chasing lions with dogs. There are also busts of emperors and dignitaries, including a full-length bronze of Septimius Severus, and a number of floor mosaics from villas in Syria. Nearby, the **Greek collection** consists mainly of pottery, while the **Egyptian section** has an array of funerary stelae, sculptures, mummies and cult figurines. In this wing also, the **Asian section** is particularly strong on Chinese and Indonesian artefacts: stone buddhas and bodhisattvas, puppets and theatrical masks, and a huge lacquered Chinese bed – which after this lot you might be tempted to sink into.

Autoworld

Housed in a vast hangar-like building in the south wing of Le Cinquantenaire, **Autoworld** (April–Sept daily 10am–6pm; Oct–March daily 10am–5pm; €6; Ⓦ www.autoworld.be) is a chronological stroll through the short history of the automobile, with a huge display of vintage vehicles, beginning with early turn-of-the-century motorized cycles and Model Ts. Perhaps inevitably, European varieties predominate: there are lots of vehicles from Peugeot, Renault and Benz, and homegrown examples, too, including a 1925 Minerva which once belonged to the Belgian monarch. American vehicles include early Cadillacs, a Lincoln from 1965 that was also owned by the Belgian royals, and some great gangster-style Oldsmobiles. Among the British brands, there's a mint-condition Rolls-Royce Silver Ghost from 1921, one of the first Austins, and, from the modern era, the short-lived DeLorean sports car. Upstairs is a collection of assorted vehicles that don't fit into the main exhibition; it's a bit of a mishmash, but worth a brief look for some early Porsches and Volvos, classic 1960s Jaguars and even a tuk-tuk from Thailand. The museum's major drawback is its lack of recent vehicles – few cars date from after the mid-1970s. That said, there's good English labelling, at least on the downstairs exhibits, and a decent museum shop, with lots of automobile-related gear, including a great selection of model cars. The café is also a bonus if you're flagging.

Musée Royal de l'Armée et d'Histoire Militaire

In the north wing of Le Cinquantenaire, on the other side of the triumphal arch from the other two museums, the **Musée Royal de l'Armée et d'Histoire Militaire** (Tues–Sun 9am–noon & 1–4.45pm; free; Ⓦ www.klm-mra.be) traces the history of the Belgian armed forces from independence to the present day by means of weapons, uniforms and paintings. It's a great museum in its way, with large and clearly – if rather stuffily – displayed collections. There are also discrete sections dealing with "Belgian" regiments in the Austrian and Napoleonic armies, and, more interestingly, the volunteers who formed the nucleus of the 1830 revolution. The hall devoted to World War I is excellent, with uniforms and kit from just about every nationality involved in the conflict, together with a fearsome array of field guns, an early British tank of 1917 and a German Fokker replica (in red, naturally). The courtyard outside has a squadron of tanks and armoured cars from the 1940s – British, American and German – while the largest hall is devoted to aviation, and not just military either, with a Sabena Caravelle among its extensive collection, although the highlights are inevitably the jet fighters – a Belgian air force F16, a Mirage and a MIG23, and the obligatory Hurricane and Spitfire. The large hall overlooking the park covers World War II, depicting the build-up to the war, including the Belgian experience of fascism and Flemish collaboration, plus it has some great blown-up photographs of the end of the conflict and liberation. A welcome bonus to the museum is that you can access the **triumphal arch** and enjoy extensive views over the city from its terrace; you can get there by lift or stairs. All in all, much more interesting than you might expect.

Maison Cauchie

Visible through the trees from the southeast edge of the Parc du Cinquantenaire, the facade of the **Maison Cauchie**, rue des Francs 5 (open first weekend of each month 11am–1pm & 2–6pm; €4), is the epitome of the decorative Art Nouveau tradition, and considered to be one of the finest examples of the style in Brussels. Paul Cauchie, who had the house built in 1905, was a designer and painter who specialized in the "sgraffito" style that decorated the facades of Art Nouveau houses, and the twenty-metre-high frontage is a literal advertisement for his work, elegantly decorated with nine muses evoking the arts. You have to take a tour to see the interior, with the basement and former studio displaying paintings by Cauchie and his contemporaries, and detailing the evolution of the house. Upstairs, the first floor shows the living quarters pretty much as they were when Cauchie died in 1952.

▲ The facade of the Maison Cauchie

The Outlying Districts

Brussels pushes out in all directions from the city centre and the inner suburbs, its present-day perimeter – marked by the ring road, the RO – enclosing no fewer than nineteen *communes*. Within this circle, the city's **Outlying Districts** are little known by tourists but they do hold a handful of first-rate attractions, as well as some lesser sights. All of the places mentioned are within easy reach of the centre by public transport.

On the western edge of the city centre, the gritty *commune* of **Anderlecht** comes high up in the order of places to visit, a tight-knit working-class suburb that has a small-town, provincial feel and is home to one of Europe's most famous football teams (see p.234). It's also the location of the Maison d'Erasme, where Erasmus holed up for a few months in 1521, and the Musée Bruxellois de la Gueuze, devoted to the production of the eponymous brew. **Koekelberg**, just to the north, is the site of the colossal Basilique du Sacré Coeur, visible from just about everywhere in Brussels, while **Jette**, next door, boasts the delightful Musée René Magritte, sited in the artist's old home and studio.

To the north of the centre, **Schaerbeek** holds a charming Art Nouveau mansion, **Maison Autrique**, and beyond, there's leafy **Laeken**, whose sprawling parkland is dotted with the accoutrements of the Belgian royals – their greenhouses, statues and monuments, as well as the palace and regal follies of the Musées d'Extrême-Orient, principally a Japanese tower and a Chinese pavilion. Further north, **Heysel** is best known as the location of the infamous Heysel stadium, scene of the 1985 Liverpool-Juventus football crowd disaster, but it's also home to the Atomium, built for the 1958 World Fair in Brussels, whose giant metal balls are virtually the symbol of the city, as well as a set of attractions that might suit kids. Further out, in **Meise**, the National Plantentuin van Belgie comprises wonderfully lush botanical gardens.

South of the city centre, well-heeled **Uccle** is home to the marvellous Musée David et Alice van Buuren, and next door is the **Forêt de Soignes**, a great chunk of forest criss crossed by footpaths and scattered with picnic spots. On the northern edge of the forest is the small town of **Tervuren**, the site of the Musée Royal de l'Afrique Centrale, whose assorted African artefacts were first brought together by Léopold II. Finally, it's a short train ride south from any of the capital's three mainline stations to **Waterloo**, site of Napoleon's final defeat at the hands of the Duke of Wellington in 1815. In the town, the house where Wellington spent the night before the battle has been turned into an engaging museum and although the battlefield itself has been poorly treated, there are several mildly diverting historical attractions here too.

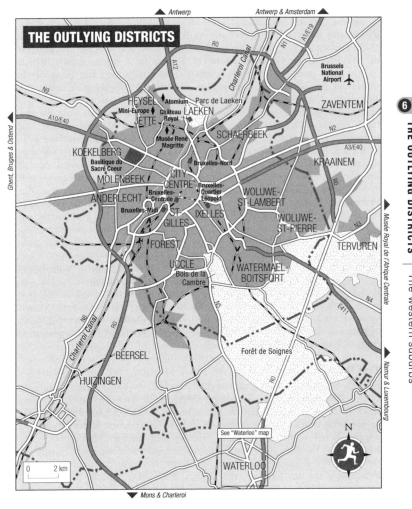

The western suburbs

Brussels' **western suburbs** are a rather dreary collection of grey, industrial districts that, on first impression at least, seem to have little to recommend them. Nevertheless, there are one or two highlights to make a trip out to this part of town worthwhile – and the good thing is that the **public transport** connections make it easy to be selective. The centre of Anderlecht is readily reached by Metro (to St Guidon on line #1B), and is well connected to its neighbours further north by a mixture of tram (line #49) and Metro (lines #1A and #1B).

Anderlecht

No one could claim **ANDERLECHT** is beautiful, but it does have its attractive nooks and crannies, particularly in the vicinity of the Metro station, where the area on and around place de la Vaillance – turn left out of the station and it's a couple of minutes' walk – has the feel of a small Belgian town. The square is a pleasant plaza flanked by cafés and bars and the **church of Sts Pierre et Guidon** (Mon–Fri 2–5pm; free), whose facade, which mostly dates from the fifteenth century, is unusually long and irregular, its stonework graced by delicate flourishes and a fine set of gargoyles. Inside, the church has a surprisingly low and poorly lit nave, in a corner of which is a vaulted chapel dedicated to St Guidon (St Guy), a local figure from the late tenth century. Of peasant origins, Guidon entered the priesthood and proceeded to invest all of his church's money in an enterprise that went bust. Mortified, he spent the next seven years as a pilgrim, a sackcloth-and-ashes figure who walked to Rome and Jerusalem, and in between devoted most of his time to prayer and charitable works. The chapel contains a breezy *Miracle of St Guidon* by Gaspard de Crayer, a local seventeenth-century artist who made a tidy income from religious paintings in the style of Rubens. Elsewhere in the church, several of the walls are decorated with late medieval murals, and although these are incomplete and difficult to make out in the prevailing gloom, one or two make interesting viewing. On the north wall of the nave look out for the *Martyrdom of St Erasmus* – having his guts ripped out – and opposite, in the Chapelle de Notre Dame de Grâce, the *Scenes from the Life of St Guidon*. The chancel is of interest too – it was designed by Jan van Ruysbroeck, who was also responsible for the tower of the Hôtel de Ville (see p.39). It contains two contrasting tombs: the earlier effigy, a recumbent knight wearing his armour, is conservative and formal, whereas the kneeling figure opposite is dressed in lavish, early Renaissance attire, his helmet placed in front of him as decoration.

The Béguinage

Directly behind the church, off rue du Chapelain, the two surviving buildings of the **Béguinage** (Tues–Sun 10am–5pm; €1.25) face each other across a small courtyard, a world apart from the rest of Anderlecht, let alone Brussels. In medieval times almost every town and city in Belgium had a *béguinage*, a semi-secluded community where widows and unmarried women – the **béguines** – lived together, the better to do pious acts, especially caring for the sick. *Béguine* communities were different from convents in so far as the inhabitants did not have to take vows and had the right to return to the secular world if they wished – a crucial difference at a time when hundreds of women were forcibly shut away in convents for all sorts of reasons. Anderlecht's *béguinage* was founded in the 1250s, but the two remaining buildings are fifteenth-century and they have been turned into a small museum, their rooms remodelled much as they would have looked when they were built. It's a low-key attraction certainly, but it's sensitively done, with a small selection of local artisanal and domestic artefacts on one side, and a set of period rooms on the other – a kitchen, rooms that would have been used for lacemaking, a sweetshop and cases showing prayers to St Guidon, the patron saint of peasants and farm animals.

Maison d'Erasme

Turn left out of the *béguinage* and it's just a couple of minutes' walk round to the front of Sts Pierre et Guidon and the **Maison d'Erasme**, at rue du Chapitre 31 (Tues–Sun 10am–5pm; €1.25; ⓦwww.erasmushouse.museum). With its pretty dormer windows and sturdy symmetrical lines, this is Anderlecht's most medieval

Erasmus

By any measure, Desiderius **Erasmus** (1466–1536) was a remarkable man. Born in Rotterdam, the illegitimate son of a priest, he was orphaned at the age of 13 and defrauded of his inheritance by his guardians, who forced him to become a monk. He hated monastic life and seized the first opportunity to leave, becoming a student at the University of Paris in 1491. Throughout the rest of his life Erasmus kept on the move, travelling between the Low Countries, England, Italy and Switzerland, and everywhere he went, his rigorous scholarship, sharp humour and strong moral sense made a tremendous impact. He attacked the abuses and corruptions of the Church, publishing scores of polemical and satirical essays which were read all over western Europe. He argued that most monks had "no other calling than stupidity, ignorance... and the hope of being fed". These attacks reflected Erasmus' determination to reform the Church from within, both by rationalizing its doctrine and rooting out hypocrisy, ignorance and superstition. He employed other methods too, producing translations of the New Testament to make the Scriptures more widely accessible, and coordinating the efforts of like-minded Christian humanists. The Church authorities periodically harassed Erasmus but generally he was tolerated, not least for his insistence on the importance of Christian unity. Luther was less indulgent, bitterly denouncing Erasmus for "making fun of the faults and miseries of the Church of Christ instead of bewailing them before God". The quarrel between the two reflected the growing schism amongst the reformers that eventually led to the Reformation.

spot, a largely sixteenth-century gabled Flemish house set in its own walled garden. The oldest parts actually date from 1468, when it was built to accommodate important visitors to the church, easily the most celebrated of which was Desiderius Erasmus (see box above), who lodged here for five months in 1521. The house is immaculately preserved and hosts a variety of period exhibits squeezed into half a dozen rooms, but contains none of Erasmus' actual belongings. To get the most out of a visit, ask to borrow the (English-language) catalogue from reception. There are lots of portraits of Erasmus, including one by Hans Holbein in the old study (*Cabinet de Travail*), and a varied selection of ancient books, notably early editions of Erasmus' work in the upstairs *Salle Blanche*, which include several altered and amended texts: some show scrawled comments made by irate readers; other changes are the work of the Inquisition and assorted clerical censors. The best paintings are in the *Salle Renaissance*, which boasts a charming triptych, *The Adoration of the Magi*, by Hieronymus Bosch, a gentle *Nativity* by Gerard David, and a hallucinatory *Temptation of St Anthony* by Pieter Huys, a follower of Bosch – though it's hard not to feel that the freakish beasts populating his painting are there as much to titillate as to terrify. Afterwards, be sure to visit the well-maintained walled garden, which is a real delight.

Musée Bruxellois de la Gueuze

The **Musée Bruxellois de la Gueuze**, at rue Gheude 56 (Mon–Fri 9am–5pm, Sat 10am–5pm; €4; ⓦ www.cantillon.be), is ten minutes' walk north of the Gare du Midi Metro station, via avenue Paul Henri Spaak and rue Limnander; to get there direct from Anderlecht's Maison d'Erasme, take tram #81 from Métro St Guidon to the Gare du Midi.

Founded in 1879, the museum is home to the **Cantillon Brewery**, the last surviving Gueuze brewery in Brussels. Gueuze is a Brussels beer speciality, and it's still brewed here according to traditional methods: the beer, made only of wheat, malted barley, hops and water, is allowed to ferment naturally, reacting with natural yeasts peculiar to the Brussels air, and is bottled two years before it's ready to drink. The museum gives a fairly dry explanation of the brewing process, but the brewery itself is mustily evocative, with huge vats in which the ingredients are boiled before being placed in large oak barrels where the fermentation process begins. The results can be sampled at the tasting session at the end of your visit – and of course bought to take home and enjoy.

Koekelberg and Jette

North of Anderlecht, **KOEKELBERG** and **JETTE** merge into each other, workaday neighbourhoods for the most part that would hardly merit a second glance if it weren't for the city's largest church and the former home of René Magritte. You can reach the basilica by taking Metro line #2 to Simonis and walking for ten minutes through the Elisabeth Park, or by taking tram #49 from Anderlecht Metro station. The most straightforward way to get to the Magritte museum from the basilica is to take the Metro one stop up from Simonis to Belgica and then make the ten-minute walk up avenue Charles Woeste.

Basilique du Sacré Coeur

Commissioned by Léopold II, the man responsible for so much of the capital's grandiose architecture, the **Basilique du Sacré Coeur** (church daily: Easter–Oct 8am–6pm; Nov–Easter 8am–5pm; free; dome daily: Easter–Oct 9am–5pm; Nov–Easter 10am–4pm; €3) is a huge structure, 140m long with a 90-metre-high dome, which dominates its surroundings, and indeed the

▲ The Basilique du Sacré Coeur

whole of Brussels. Begun in 1905 and still in part unfinished, the basilica was conceived as a neo-Gothic extravagance in imitation of the basilica of the Sacré Coeur in Montmartre, Paris – an edifice which had turned the Belgian king green with envy, making him even more determined to build Brussels into a capital worthy of taking its place alongside the best of Europe. The construction costs, however, proved colossal and the plans had to be modified; the result is this amalgamation of the original neo-Gothic design with Art Deco features added in the 1920s. Inside it's undeniably impressive, with a modern sensibility that works well with the soft brown bricks and the gently filtered light – the atmosphere is more soothing, and the church cosier, than you might expect from outside. And once you've seen the church, climb up to the top of the dome for some marvellous views of the city.

Musée René Magritte

To the north, Koekelberg fades into the suburb of Jette, home to the enthralling **Musée René Magritte**, rue Esseghem 135 (Wed–Sun 10am–6pm; €7, including guided tour at weekends; @ www.magrittemuseum.be), which contains a plethora of the Surrealist's paraphernalia, as well as a modest collection of his early paintings and sketches. Magritte lived with his wife Georgette on the ground floor of this unprepossessing house from 1930 to the mid-1950s, an odd location for what was effectively the headquarters of the Surrealist movement in Belgium, most of whose leading lights met here every Saturday to concoct a battery of subversive books, magazines and images.

The **ground floor** of the museum has been faithfully re-created as the artist's studio and living quarters, using mostly original ornaments and furniture, with the remainder carefully replicated from photographs. Hanging near the indoor studio is the famous bowler hat which crops up in several of Magritte's paintings. Many features of the house itself also appear in his works: the sash window, for instance, framed the painting entitled *The Human Condition*, while the glass doors to the sitting room and bedroom appeared in *The Invisible World*. Other parts of the interior, including the fireplace and staircase, as well as the lamppost in front of the house, are also prominent in the painter's works. Magritte built himself a studio – which he named "Dongo" – in the garden, and it was here he produced his bread-and-butter work, such as graphics and posters, though he was usually unhappy when working on such mundane projects. His real passions were painted in the **dining-room studio**, where he displayed just one work by another artist – a photo by Man Ray – which is there again today.

You have to don shoe-covers to visit the **first and second floors** of the house, which were separate apartments when the Magrittes lived here, but are now taken up with letters, photos, telegrams, lithographs, posters and sketches pertaining to the artist and his time here, all displayed in chronological order – as well as the blue rug he had made for the bedroom, and work by his fellow Surrealists. There are two fine posters announcing the world film and fine arts festivals which took place in Brussels in 1947 and 1949, as well as Magritte's first painting, a naive landscape which he produced at the tender age of 12. Finally there are a number of personal objects displayed in the **attic**, which he rented, including the easel he used at the end of his life. Overall, it's a fascinating glimpse into the life of one of the most important artists of the twentieth century, and there are plans to extend the museum to the property next door.

For more on the artist and his work, see the box on p.83.

The northern suburbs

The closest of the northern suburbs to Brussels' city centre are **St Josse** and **Schaerbeek**, just to the northeast of the Gare du Nord, both relatively run-down neighbourhoods with significant immigrant populations. More interesting to the visitor are the districts of **Heysel** and **Laeken** further out to the north, where there are a number of leisure attractions, and further north still, Belgium's national botanical gardens at **Meise**.

St Josse and Schaerbeek

Immediately to the northeast of Le Botanique, beyond the petit ring and accessible on tram #92 from rue de la Régence, or a short walk from Métro Botanique, lies **ST JOSSE**, a mainly residential district that has a large Turkish and North African population and is noted for its inexpensive Turkish restaurants, many of which are dotted along chaussée de Haecht, which runs parallel to rue Royale. A few minutes' walk up rue Royale from the petit ring is the area's most obvious architectural attraction, and a reminder that this wasn't always a Turkish neighbourhood: the vast, domed **Eglise de Ste-Marie**, a real nineteenth-century whopper whose cupola rises high above its heavy-duty buttresses and dominates the area around.

North of St Josse, and further up the #92 tram route, **SCHAERBEEK** (Schaarbeek in Flemish) is slightly more prosperous, a post-industrial suburb that grew around the rail yards of the nearby Gare du Nord and was the home of the young Jacques Brel. It's scarcely more interesting for the casual visitor than its neighbour, but it does have one worthwhile sight in the Art Nouveau mansion, **Maison Autrique**, at chaussée de Haecht 266 (Wed–Sun noon–6pm; €6; Ⓦ www.autrique.be), which was one of the first commissions of the young Victor Horta in 1893. Horta designed the exterior in bold style, using contrasting types of stone which he etched with a swirling filigree of decoration before rounding it all off with a top-floor beamed gallery with curved stone lintels. Inside there are a few Horta trademarks: the hallway has a lovely mosaic floor and there are some ornate stained-glass skylights on the stairway landings, while the two main ground-floor rooms have been amalgamated with an exposed girder, one of Horta's favourite design features. It's a fun place to explore, and almost spookily authentic, brilliantly evoked by the life-size figures dotted around the place – the upstairs bedroom and en-suite bathroom have hats and coats and dresses flung carelessly about as if the occupants had just stepped out in a hurry. There are also some unexpected bits and pieces discovered when the house was restored in the 1990s, relating to two of the more eccentric occupants. One was an obscure French painter by the name of Augustin Desombre (1869–1912), a tormented soul who holed up here and left behind a small collection of paintings and a crude and very large early camera. The other was an inventor named Axel Wappendorf, who retreated to the attic to invent away, surrounded by all sorts of clutter – the museum has restored the attic in appropriately disorderly style.

Laeken

A kilometre or so northwest of Schaerbeek, leafy **LAEKEN** is accessible by way of tram #19 from Jette, Metro line #1B to Heysel or Bockstael, or tram #51 from the Gare du Nord. It's home to the royal family, who occupy a large,

out-of-bounds estate and have colonized the surrounding parkland with their monuments and memorials.

Cimitière de Laeken and Notre Dame de Laeken

At the top of avenue de la Reine, the **Cimitière de Laeken** is the last resting place of many influential Belgians, including the artist Jef Dillen, whose tomb is marked by an imitation of Rodin's *The Thinker*, and Maria Felicia Garcia, the famous Spanish soprano better known as Maria Malibran (see p.104). The architect Joseph Poelaert (who designed the Palais de Justice) lies here – fittingly perhaps, because he also designed the neo-Gothic church of Notre Dame de Laeken which stands at the cemetery's entrance, built over several decades in memory of Louise-Marie, Belgium's first Queen. Most of the country's royals are buried here, in the Royal Crypt (Sun 2–5pm).

The Château Royal and the Serres Royales

Further up Laeken's main artery, behind railings off to the right of avenue du Parc Royal, the sedate **Château Royal** (no entry) is the principal home of the Belgian royal family. Built in 1790, its most famous occupant was Napoleon, who stayed here on a number of occasions and signed the declaration of war on Russia here in 1812. Just past the château are the **Serres Royales**, several enormous greenhouses built for Léopold II, covering almost four acres and sheltering a mind-boggling variety of tropical and Mediterranean flora. They're pretty fantastic, but are only open to the public for ten days a year, from the end of April to early May, when the queues to see them can be daunting. During this period, buses #231 and #232 from the Gare du Nord drop you right outside, or take the Metro to Métro Bockstael, then bus #53.

Parc de Laeken and Parc d'Osseghem

Right opposite the royal palace, a wide footpath leads up to the fanciful, neo-Gothic monument erected in honour of **Léopold I**, the focal point of the pretty **Parc de Laeken**, which is also home to the **Stuyvenbergh Castle**, once the residence of Emperor Charles V's architect, Louis Van Bodeghem, and now used to accommodate high-ranking foreign dignitaries. The park stretches out in all directions from the Léopold monument, grassy meadows that slope down from a forested core that is populated by colonies of rabbits, who emerge in warm weather to bask on the grass in their hundreds. A short walk to the north, the park merges into the **Parc d'Osseghem**, whose pretty wooded paths wind around a small lake, beyond which lies the Atomium (see p.127).

The Museés d'Extrême-Orient

Just past the royal greenhouses, off avenue Jules van Praet, are the **Musées d'Extrême-Orient** (Tues–Fri 9.30am–5pm, Sat & Sun 10am–5pm; €4, free first Wed of each month from 1pm), basically the Far Eastern collection of the Musées Royaux d'Art et d'Histoire (see p.114), accessible direct on tram #4 from Bourse. This one of the city's most original and, taken as a whole, most successful collections: a very fine array of Far Eastern artefacts displayed in some wonderful nineteenth-century ersatz oriental buildings and gardens. The first building you see, the **Pavillon Chinois**, is an attractive, elegant replica of a Chinese pavilion built by Léopold II after he had seen one at the World's Fair in Paris in 1900, and a great memorial to that era's fascination

▲ The Pavillon Chinois, part of the Musées d'Extrême-Orient

with all things eastern. It's a gaudy mix of rococo European and oriental styles, housing a first-rate collection of Chinese and Japanese porcelain and furniture (not to mention an Art Nouveau bathroom). And it's not just the Far East that features: India gets a look-in too, with two rooms decorated with carved wooden friezes of Hindu gods. A glorious turn-of-the-century fantasy, it's all deftly done and beautifully restored – much like the matching **Tour Japonaise** across the road, reached by a tunnel from the ticket office. Another of Léopold's follies, this time an imitation Buddhist pagoda with parts made in Paris, Brussels and Yokohama, it's reached through beautifully kept Japanese gardens. You can't actually visit the pagoda itself, but the lower floors of the building next door contain beautiful displays of vibrant seventeenth- and eighteenth-century Japanese porcelain from the Edo period, and, up the stairs, later monumental vases and other items from the late nineteenth and early twentieth centuries, including a marvellous mobile temple. But again it's the building that is the main event: it's brilliantly realized, and after ascending the stairs it's easy to imagine that you're here for an audience with the emperor himself. Finally, back on the other side of the road, behind the Pavillon Chinois in a converted music room, the **Musée d'Art Japonais** includes an excellent display of samurai armour, swords, textiles, gorgeous lacquerwork, and more.

Heysel and beyond

On the other side of the Parc du Laeken, **HEYSEL**, most easily reached by Metro to Heysel station, is a 500-acre estate bequeathed to the authorities by Léopold II in 1909. These days, it's a theme park without a theme – a large area with a diverse array of attractions, the most famous of which are the Atomium and the former Heysel stadium, but there are also a number of other sights aimed specifically at kids. The botanical gardens at **MEISE**, just to the north, are a short bus ride away if you want to make a day of it.

The Atomium

Within easy reach of Métro Heysel, or tram #23 or #51, is Heysel's most recognizable attraction: the **Atomium** (daily 10am–6pm; €9; Ⓦwww .atomium.be), a curious model of a molecule expanded 165 billion times, built for the 1958 World Fair in Brussels. The structure is something of a symbol of the city – and is as popular as ever, judging by the length of the weekend and holiday queues for the lift to its observation deck and panoramic restaurant. **Visits** are in two parts: the lift whizzes you up to the top sphere for the views, after which you take in the other three spheres, accessible by a combination of escalators and stairs. It's all pleasingly retro – the Atomium was quite a feat of technology in its time (its elevator was the world's fastest, the escalator connecting the spheres the world's longest). Its construction is remembered with photos here and there, and there are cool Sixties objects on sale in the classy gift shop. However, the thoroughness of the restoration can't disguise the fact that there's not really that much to see – the spheres are mainly given over to temporary exhibition space and a rather feeble café, and trudging up and down the stairs and escalators can turn into a bit of a slog after a while. It's undeniably impressive from the bottom, and the views from the top are as spectacular as you would expect (enhanced by computer screens identifying what you're looking at). But really the civilized way to see it is to book a prime spot in the top-floor restaurant – not expensive, and undeniably unique (see p.201).

The Bruparck and around

Next door to the Atomium, the **Bruparck leisure complex** is a handy place to take the kids, with **Océade**, a water park with slides, a swimming pool, wave pools and whirlpools (July & Aug daily 10am–9pm, Sept–March Wed–Fri 10am–6pm, Sat & Sun 10am–9pm; April–June Tues–Fri 10am–6pm, Sat & Sun 10am–9pm; €15.50, children €12.50; ⓦwww.oceade.be); a gigantic cinema complex called **Kinepolis**; and – perhaps of most interest to tourists – **Mini-Europe** (mid-March to June & Sept daily 9.30am–6pm; July & Aug 9am–8pm; mid-July to mid-Aug Sat till midnight; Oct–early Jan 10am–6pm; €12.40, children €9.40, €23.50/€17.50 for a combination ticket with Océade; ⓦwww.minieurope.com), where you can see 1:25 scale models of over 100 European buildings: very realistic, right down to the materials used. There are several examples for each country – some obvious, others less so: you can see St Mark's Square in Venice and the leaning tower of Pisa, but there are also dinky models of Dutch canalsides and Finnish castles, not to mention a constantly erupting Vesuvius. It's all very precisely and imaginatively realized, enhanced by models of various European trains and boats fizzing around harbours and running through tunnels and across bridges like a giant train set – great fun, with kids or without. Even the spurious "Spirit of Europe" exhibition you're funnelled through as you leave is not without its charms.

With all this to see, you could spend a good day at the Bruparck if you have kids. There's a "village" with places to eat a huge variety of ethnic cuisines, you can drink in various bars, and of course there are plenty of souvenir shops.

There's also the **National Planetarium**, the other side of the Bruparck, at avenue de Bouchout 10, which puts on regular star shows, some of which are in English (Mon–Fri 9am–4.30pm, Sun 1.30–4pm; €4, children €3; ⓦwww.planetarium.be), though you will probably need to book. There's also a small exhibition on the ground floor, with astronomical instruments and displays on rockets and satellites.

The Parc des Expositions and Stade du Roi Baudouin

Just beyond the Bruparck is the city's large trade fair area – the **Parc des Expositions**, where the World Fairs of 1935 and 1958 were held – and the **Stade du Roi Baudouin** (Tues 1–6.30pm, Wed–Sat 10.30am–6.30pm; €6), formerly the infamous Heysel football stadium in which thirty-nine, mainly Italian supporters were crushed to death when a sector wall collapsed on May 29, 1985. Rebuilt in 1995, and renamed after the Belgian king who had died shortly before its completion, it's now the national stadium, with a capacity of 50,000. International fixtures are held here, and it was the main Belgian venue for Euro 2000 – hosted jointly with Holland – and held one of the semi-finals of the tournament. Buses #250 and #251 from the Gare du Nord drop you right outside.

Inside, you can wander around, following a prescribed route and taking in the home team dressing room, complete with the "Red Devils" strip laid out as for a game, the anti-doping room, complete with an audio session with a nervous player, before walking down the tunnel and out on to the pitch – or at least the running track. The stadium is very much a homage to the Belgian national team, with lots of exhibits relating to the players and their stats, and the shirts of famous players lining the walls. But it's also careful not to forget the pre-Baudouin days, and in particular the Heysel disaster (while not accepting any of the blame). The security room has an array of screens showing not only parts of the stadium, but downtown Brussels too (the stadium can now be evacuated in just 7 minutes, they are keen to point out); and next door the first-aid room used on the day is preserved as shrine to those who died, whose names are listed on the wall. Just outside here, a sculpture in the shape of a sundial – *Stop all the Clocks* – serves as perhaps the most poignant memorial.

Meise: the Nationale Plantentuin van Belgie

Just outside the city limits, ten minutes by bus from Heysel, or half an hour from the Gare du Nord (bus #250 or #251 from either place drops you right outside), the gardens of the **National Plantentuin van Belgie** (Jan–March & Nov–Dec daily 9.30am–4.30pm, April–Sept Mon–Fri 9.30am–6.30pm, Sat & Sun 9.30am–7pm, Oct daily 9.30am–6pm; €4; ⓦwww.br.fgov.be) are so wonderfully tended, expansive and peaceful that they feel as if they've been here forever. In fact the national botanical collection has only resided here in the grounds of Castle Bouchout since the 1960s, when they were relocated from the more familiar glasshouses and park in the city centre. The castle itself, surrounded by a lake in the middle of the gardens, is a picturesque sight, but is home to temporary exhibitions only, and the real point of visiting is to strike out from here along the numerous paths that wind their way through deep woods. On the other side of the water the old orangery houses a small lakeside café-restaurant, and from here you can do a circuit of the gardens (on summer weekends by pony and trap), taking in a long herbaceous border, a glasshouse of succulents and cacti surrounded by a garden of flowering plants, and sculptural clusters of conifers. But the real glory of the place is its **glasshouses**, just to the left of the main entrance, consisting of a steamy series of rainforest houses, a dry house of fantastic cacti and desert species, a house of comestible crops – rice, coffee, cocoa and suchlike – an exhibition on evolution, and a cloudforest house with carnivorous plants. As in the rest of the garden, there's English labelling throughout, and the whole thing is a really good half-day out if you're weary of urban Brussels.

The southern suburbs

Brussels is an unusually green city, and nowhere more so than in its **southern suburbs**, which ease gradually through the wild expanse of the **Forêt de Soignes** and leafy suburbs like Uccle, Forest, Woluwe St Pierre and into the countryside beyond. Tram #44 connects Métro Montgomery with **Tervuren**, a lovely trip which takes you down the chestnut tree-lined avenue de Tervuren and into the Forêt de Soignes before reaching the terminus at Tervuren town. The Forêt de Soignes is also accessible from the park just to the north, the Bois de la Cambre, although you have to cross the unpleasant chaussée de la Hulpe before you reach the forest's peaceful, winding footpaths, or by taking Metro line #1A to the end of the line at Herrmann-Debroux – connected with **Uccle** by bus #41. South, **Waterloo**, site of Napoleon's defeat at the hands of the Duke of Wellington, has long been a popular tourist attraction – both the town itself, where you can visit the house where the duke stayed the night before the battle, and the battlefield itself, a few kilometres south, where a handful of attractions help to make sense of what happened.

Forest and Uccle

South of St Gilles, the leafy neighbourhood of **FOREST** spreads around the parks of Forest and Duden, merging almost imperceptibly into the more upscale suburb of **UCCLE** (tram #92 from rue de la Régence), originally a string of out-of-town hamlets which only became part of the city in the mid-nineteenth century when the aristocracy, attracted by the lush greenery, took up residence here. There's not too much to bring you here, although it's a pleasant way to wind up a day after spending time in Ixelles or St Gilles, and the excellent **Musée David et Alice van Buuren** (see below) is a worthy attraction in itself. There are a few other low-key sites too. The **Chapelle Notre Dame des Afflingés** at rue de Stalle 50, just off avenue Brugmann, is a lovely little church which dates back to the fifteenth century and has a beautiful stucco ceiling added in the seventeenth century. A ten-minute walk along avenue Vanderaey from here is the tranquil **Cimetière Dieweg**, unused for burials since 1958 – apart from Hergé, the creator of Tintin, who was interred here by special permission in 1983. East up Diewag, across avenue de Wolvendael, the **Parc de Wolvendael** is a historic 45-acre estate that makes a lovely place for a picnic and is home to a small white stone **chateau** built in 1753 and a beautiful Louis XV summerhouse – sadly converted into a rather unimpressive restaurant.

Musée David et Alice van Buuren

A few minutes' stroll north of avenue de Fré, at avenue Léo Errera 41, the **Musée David et Alice van Buuren** (Wed–Mon 2–5.30pm; €10, garden only €5) is a

▲ The stylish interior of the Musée David et Alice van Buuren

Some 5km southeast of the city, the leafy suburbs are left behind for the dense beech woodland of the **Forêt de Soignes**, one of Belgium's most beautiful national parks. Originally a royal domain used for hunting, it once covered over 27,000 acres; sadly, more than a century and a half of development has taken its toll. In the 1820s the king of the Netherlands gave the forest to the "General Society for promoting National Industry" and large parts of the land were subsequently sold off, before it was turned over to the government in 1843. Further depletion followed when sections were cleared to make way for country estates, agricultural complexes and country houses, and in 1861 a huge slice was carved off to create a large urban park, now known as the **Bois de la Cambre** (see p.101). Today just over a third of the original forest remains.

What's left stretches from the Bois de la Cambre in its most northerly reaches, 10km southeast to La Hulpe, and from Uccle in the west, some 9km east to the Arboretum Géographique which lies less than a kilometre south of Parc de Tervuren. Despite the piecemeal development, it still remains one of the region's most attractive spaces, criss crossed with paths and bridleways, and is a popular escape for walkers and cyclists, as well as horse riders, golfers and anglers.

wonderful little gallery in a glorious Art Deco house. Once the home of well-connected Dutch banker David van Buuren and his wife Alice, who bought the property in 1928, the house served as a live-in museum for their collection of furniture, carpets and art; a global salon of sorts, with great names like Satie, Magritte, Chanel, Ben Gurion and Lalique all passing through. During World War II, David (who was Jewish) and Alice were forced to leave their home for five long years, but on their return – much to their surprise – the house and the works of art within it remained intact. The house became a museum in 1973, on the death of Alice.

The **interior** is utterly stylish yet extremely comfortable, the creation of a team of Dutch, Belgian and French master craftsmen, and a perfect example of the Art Deco style of the late 1920s. There are Cubist carpets and tapestries by Gidding, woodwork and furniture by the fashionable Dominique studio of Paris, including van Buuren's enormous desk, and a piano in the music room that once belonged to Erik Satie. As for the **art**, it's a small but incredibly diverse collection, spanning five centuries and including Flemish and Italian masters, as well as many twentieth-century artists. The earlier works include still lifes by Fantin-Latour, several landscapes by the sixteenth-century painter Joachim Patenier, a Guardi view of Venice, a Saenredam church interior, and sketches by van Gogh – not to mention a version of the Fall of Icarus by Bruegel the Elder on wood, a work David acquired shortly before his death in 1955 (it's the same as the one in the Brussels' Royal Museum), though its provenance is now considered dubious. Later canvases include a couple of lovely paintings by Gustave van de Woestyne and James Ensor (a still life of shrimps and shells), Max Ernst, Rik Wouters and Constant Permeke. The picturesque **garden**, designed by Belgian landscape architect René Pechère, contains many rare species of rose, as well as 300 yew trees and a genuinely complex maze, in which it's fairly easy to get lost.

Tervuren

Six kilometres southeast of the city, the small town of **TERVUREN** is one of the prettiest and greenest in the Brussels region. Bordered in the south by the beautiful Forêt de Soignes (see box, p.131), dotted with grand old houses, and surrounded by lush woodland, it's no surprise that the area is a popular place to live, particularly with British and Irish Eurocrats, although it remains firmly off the tourist track.

Tervuren is connected to the city by the ten-kilometre-long avenue de Tervuren, a route most easily covered by tram #44 from Métro Montgomery, or on weekends by antique tram from Parc du Cinquentenaire or the **Musée du Tram** at avenue de Tervuren 314 in Woluwe St-Pierre (April to early Oct Sun 2–6pm; Ⓦ www.trammuseumbrussels.be), though the museum itself is being restored (due to open in 2009). The area's main draw is the impressive **Musée Royal de l'Afrique Centrale** situated in the **Parc de Tervuren**, an attractive park of ancient trees, manicured lawns, lakes and flowerbeds.

Musée Royal de l'Afrique Centrale

Without a doubt, Tervuren's main attraction is the **Musée Royal de l'Afrique Centrale**, Leuvensesteeweg 13 (Tues–Fri 10am–5pm, Sat & Sun 10am–6pm; €4; Ⓦ www.africamuseum.be). Only a short walk along Leuvensesteeweg from the Tervuren tram terminal, it's housed in a pompous, custom-built pile constructed on the orders of King Léopold II around 1900. Personally presented with the vast Congo River basin by a conference of the European powers in 1885, Léopold became one of Europe's richest men as a result. His initial attempts to secure control of the area were abetted by the explorer and ex-Confederate soldier Henry Stanley, who went to the Congo on a five-year fact-finding mission in 1879, just a few years after he had famously found the missionary David Livingstone. Even by the standards of the colonial powers, Léopold's regime was too chaotic and too extraordinarily cruel to stomach, and in 1908, one year before the museum opened, the Belgian government took over the territory, installing a marginally more liberal state bureaucracy. Its

▲ The Musée Royal de l'Afrique Centrale

history has been one of the most bloodstained in Africa – no less so since it gained independence as Zaire in 1960.

The museum was Léopold's own idea, a blatantly colonialist and racist enterprise which treated the Africans as a naive and primitive people and the Belgians as their paternalistic benefactors. The collection, however, is undeniably rich, and its antiquated attitudes and presentation are currently under review, with a top-to-bottom renovation project that is due to start in 2010 and be completed by 2013. The museum is keen to reinvent itself as a modern ethnographical collection that takes a self-critical approach to Belgium's history – and colonialism in general.

The collection occupies the whole of the **ground floor**, and is in fact part ethnographic and part natural history museum, whose old-fashioned painted displays and dioramas are very much part of the museum's charm. Off to the **left of the entrance hall**, various cases cover many aspects of domestic Congolese life – clothing, furniture, tools and musical instruments, an impressive array of dope pipes, and a superb 60m-long dugout canoe that is some 300 hundred years old. The galleries beyond, filling the left-hand wing of the museum, concentrate on animals – stuffed birds, fish and crocodiles, a giraffe set at the centre of a butterfly and insect gallery. Some of them are decorated with images of the Congo – the river, jungle, and the fledgling capital of Leopoldville – that are contemporaneous with the building. At the back there is an impressive, if rather depressing, array of African mammals – lions, leopards, zebra, chimps, rhinos – the lot. The opposite, **right side of the building** gets to grips with Congolese culture and ritual, with nail sculptures, masks, sculptures and busts. Beyond, the museum tells the story of colonization, and the so-called Congo Free State, by means of photos, maps and other documents. There are ancient shots of Stanley, and later ones of Baudouin, the Belgian king, visiting Leopoldville for the independence celebrations before the country descended into violent mayhem. The museum's **grounds** are also well worth a stroll, with the formal gardens set around a series of geometric lakes, flanked by wanderable woods.

The Arboretum Géographique

Though pleasant enough, there's not much to detain you in Tervuren; it's simply an upscale city suburb. But if you follow Pardenmaktstraat, and then take the first left down Pauwstraat, which runs into Arboretumlaan, Tervuren's **Arboretum Géographique** – a fifteen-minute walk or a short drive – gives you the chance to sample the delights of the Forêt de Soignes without going too far out of your way. Originally part of the forest, this wooded area was converted into an arboretum in 1905 on the instructions of Léopold II, and was used to train European officers for the African and Asian colonies. It's still essentially just a planned and extra-protected part of the forest, home to hundreds of different species of trees – redwoods, maples, Scots pines and larches, to name but a few – and covered with paths and walking trails, and as such it makes a great place to explore. There is off-road parking and plenty of circular walks.

Waterloo

WATERLOO, now a run-of-the-mill suburb about 18km south of the centre of Brussels, has a resonance far beyond its size. On June 18, 1815, at this small crossroads town on what was once the main route into Brussels from France, Wellington masterminded the battle that put an end to the imperial ambitions of Napoleon. It turned out to have far more significance than even its generals

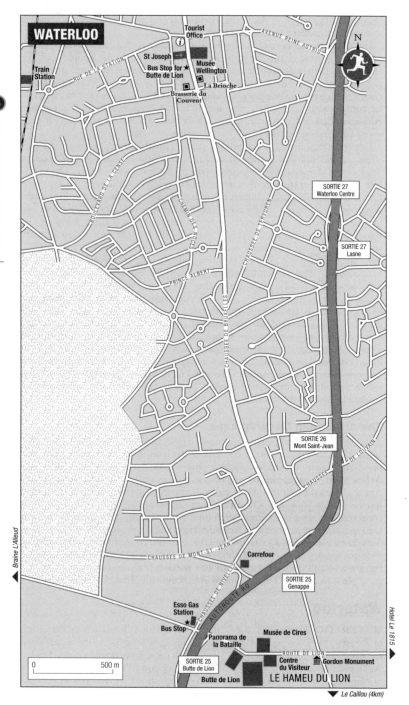

WATERLOO

Train
Station

Tourist
Office

AVENUE REINE ASTRID

N

St Joseph

Bus Stop for ★
Butte de Lion

Musée
Wellington

RUE DE LA STATION

La Brioche

Brasserie du
Couvent

BOULEVARD DE LA CENSE

CHEMIN DES NOTES

PRINCE ALBERT

CHAUSSÉE DE TERVUREN

CHAUSSÉE DE BRUXELLES

SORTIE 27
Waterloo Centre

SORTIE 27
Lasne

SORTIE 26
Mont Saint-Jean

CHAUSSÉE DE LOUVAIN

CHAUSSÉE

Braine L'Alleud

CHAUSSÉE DE MONT-ST.-JEAN

Carrefour

AUTOROUTE RO

CHAUSSÉE DE NIVELLES

SORTIE 25
Genappe

Esso Gas
Station ★

Bus Stop

Panorama de
la Bataille

Musée de Cires

Hôtel Le 1815

SORTIE 25
Butte de Lion

Centre
du Visiteur

ROUTE DE LION

Gordon Monument

Butte de Lion

LE HAMEU DU LION

Le Caillou (4km)

0   500 m

realized, for not only was this the last throw of the dice for the formidable army born of the French Revolution, but it also marked the end of France's prolonged attempts to dominate Europe militarily. Subsequently, however, popular memory refused to vilify Napoleon as the aggressor – and not just in France, but right across Europe, where the Emperor's bust was a common feature of the nineteenth-century drawing room. In part, this was to do with Napoleon's obvious all-round brilliance, but more crucially, he became a symbol of opportunity: in him the emergent middle classes saw a common man becoming greater than the crowned heads of Europe – an almost unique event at the time.

Nevertheless, the historic importance of Waterloo has not saved the **battle-field** from interference – a motorway cuts right across it – and if you do visit you'll need a lively imagination to picture what happened and where – unless, that is, you're around to see either the partial re-enactment they do every year

Practicalities

There are several ways of **getting to Waterloo** and its scattering of sights. By public transport, the most effective is to make a circular loop by train, bus and train. From any of Brussels' three main stations, **trains** take you direct to Waterloo (Mon–Fri 2 hourly, Sat & Sun 1 hourly; 25min; €3). From Waterloo train station, it's an easy fifteen-minute walk – turn right outside the station building and then first left along rue de la Station – to Waterloo tourist office and the Musée Wellington. Or you can take **bus** #W from Brussels' Gare du Midi (every 30min; 45min; day pass €6.30), which stops right on the chaussée de Bruxelles by the museum and tourist office; after you've finished at the museum, take it on again to the Hameau du Lion. The bus stops on the main road by the Gordon monument, about 400m from the Butte de Lion and other buildings, which you can't miss (€1.30 from Waterloo). After visiting the Butte, return to the same bus stop and catch bus #W onto **Braine-l'Alleud train station**, from where there's a fast and frequent service back to Brussels – again to all three main train stations (Mon–Fri 3 hourly, Sat & Sun 2 hourly; 15min; €3.50). Or, to get to Le Caillou, take bus #365 from the Gordon monument; it takes five minutes. Getting to Waterloo **by car**, take junction #27 (Waterloo Centre) off the Mons-Charleroi autoroute to get to the Musee Wellington; to get to the Hameau du Lion, leave the autoroute at junction #25 (Butte du Lion).

Waterloo **tourist office**, the Maison du Tourisme, is handily located in the centre of town, opposite the Musée Wellington at chaussée de Bruxelles 218 (daily: April–Sept 9.30am–6.30pm; Oct–March 10am–5pm; Ⓣize 02 354 99 10, ⓌⓌwww.waterloo.be). They issue free town **maps** and booklets recounting the story of the battle, of which the best is *The Battlefield of Waterloo Step by Step*. They also sell a **combined ticket** (€12; €14.60 including battlefield tours) for all the battle-related attractions, in Waterloo and at the battlefield, which you can also buy at the Hameau du Lion visitor centre, though if you're at all selective (and you may want to be) this doesn't save much – the individual costs are detailed below. If you just want to see the Hameau du Lion attractions and do a battlefield tour, the cost is €8.70. The Brussels Card (see p.34) is valid for most of Waterloo's attractions, too.

There's no compelling reason to stay the night, but Waterloo tourist office does have the details of several **hotels**, both in Waterloo itself and near the Hameau du Lion. For **food**, *La Brioche*, a few doors down from the Wellington museum at chaussée de Bruxelles 161, is a pleasant, modern café serving up a reasonably good line in sandwiches, pancakes and pastries. For something more substantial, try the excellent *Brasserie du Couvent*, rue du Couvent 7, on the other side of the road, down a small alley just past the church from the tourist office, which serves extremely good brasserie fare – steaks, *choucroute*, ribs, pasta – for around €15 for a main course. There are also a couple of places to eat at the Hameau du Lion.

on June 18, or the large-scale re-enactment which takes place every five years; the next one is scheduled for 2010. Otherwise, a visit breaks down into two parts: the **centre of Waterloo**, where the **Musée Wellington** is the pick of the district's museums, and then the **battlefield** itself, 4km to the south, where there are several monuments and memorials, the most satisfying of which is the **Butte de Lion**, a huge earth mound that's part viewpoint and part commemoration, and which is surrounded by several other attractions – a group of buildings that is collectively known as the **Hameau du Lion**.

Musée Wellington

Across the street from the tourist office, at chaussée de Bruxelles 147, is the **Musée Wellington** (daily: April–Sept 9.30am–6.30pm; Oct–March 10.30am–5pm; €5),

▲ Wellingon's headquarters, now the Musée Wellington

The Battle of Waterloo

Napoleon escaped from imprisonment on the Italian island of Elba on February 26, 1815. He landed in Cannes three days later and moved swiftly north, entering Paris on March 20 just as his unpopular replacement – the slothful King Louis XVIII – high-tailed it to Ghent in present-day Belgium. Thousands of Frenchmen rallied to Napoleon's colours and, with little delay, Napoleon marched northeast to fight the two armies that threatened his future. Both were in Belgium. One, an assortment of British and Dutch soldiers and Anglo-allied troops from the Prussian empire, was commanded by the **Duke of Wellington**; the other was a Prussian army led by **Marshal Blücher**. At the start of the campaign, Napoleon's army was about 130,000 strong, larger than each of the opposing armies but not big enough to fight them both at the same time. Napoleon's strategy was, therefore, quite straightforward: he had to stop Wellington and Blücher from joining together – and to this end he crossed the Belgian frontier near Charleroi to launch a quick attack. On June 16, the French hit the Prussians hard, forcing them to retreat and giving Napoleon the opportunity he was looking for. Napoleon detached a force of 30,000 soldiers to harry the retreating Prussians, while he concentrated his main army against Wellington, hoping to deliver a knock-out blow. Meanwhile, Wellington had assembled his troops at Waterloo, on the main road to Brussels.

At **dawn on Sunday June 18**, the two armies faced each other. Wellington had some 68,000 men, about one third of whom were British, and Napoleon around 5,000 more. The armies were deployed just 1500 metres apart, with Wellington on the ridge north of – and uphill from – the enemy. It had rained heavily during the night, so Napoleon delayed his first attack to give the ground a chance to dry. At **11.30am**, the battle began when the French assaulted the fortified farm of Hougoumont, which was crucial for the defence of Wellington's right. The assault failed and at approximately **1pm** there was more bad news for Napoleon when he heard that the Prussians had eluded their pursuers and were closing fast. To gain time he sent 14,000 troops off to impede their progress and at **2pm** he tried to regain the initiative by launching a large-scale infantry attack against Wellington's left. This second French attack also proved inconclusive and so at **4pm** Napoleon's cavalry charged Wellington's centre, where the British infantry formed into squares and just managed to keep the French at bay – a desperate engagement that cost hundreds of lives. By **5.30pm**, the Prussians had begun to reach the battlefield in numbers to the right of the French lines and, at **7.30pm**, with the odds getting longer and longer, Napoleon made a final bid to break Wellington's centre, sending in his Imperial Guard. These were the best soldiers Napoleon had but, slowed down by the mud churned up by their own cavalry, the veterans proved easy targets for the British infantry, and they were beaten back with great loss of life. At **8.15pm**, Wellington, who knew victory was within his grasp, rode down the ranks to encourage his soldiers before ordering the large-scale counterattack that proved decisive. The French were vanquished and Napoleon subsequently abdicated, ending his days in exile on St Helena. He died there in 1821.

which occupies the old inn where Wellington slept the nights before and after the battle. It's an enjoyable museum (the entry price includes a decent audio guide) whose plans and models detail the build-up to – and the course of – the battle, all displayed alongside an engaging hotchpotch of personal effects. Room 4 holds the bed where Alexander Gordon, Wellington's aide-de-camp, was brought to die after losing his leg in the battle, and here also is the artificial leg of Lord Uxbridge, another British commander. Uxbridge is reported to have said during the battle, "I say, I've lost my leg," to which Wellington replied, "By God, sir, so you have!" After the battle, Uxbridge's leg was buried here in Waterloo, but it was returned to London when he died to join the rest of his body; in exchange, his artificial leg was donated to the museum. Neither were the bits and pieces of dead soldiers considered sacrosanct: tooth dealers roamed the battlefields of the Napoleonic Wars, pulling out teeth which were then stuck on two pieces of board with a spring at the back – primitive dentures known in England as "Waterloos".

In Wellington's bedroom, Room 6, there is a model of the great man at his desk compiling his report of the battle, as well as copies of the messages he sent to his commanders during the course of the battle, curiously formal epistles laced with phrases like "Be so kind as to..." and "We ought to...". In spite of this, Wellington had a real knack for the nonchalant turn of phrase: famously, he was at the Duchess of Richmond's ball in Brussels when he heard of Napoleon's rapid advance, prompting the duke to declare, "Napoleon has humbugged me". The museum's last room – Room 14 – occupies a new extension at the back. This reprises, albeit on a slightly larger scale, what has gone before, with more models, plans and military paraphernalia, plus a lucid outline of the historical background.

The Church of Saint Joseph

Across the street from the museum, the **Church of Saint Joseph** is a curious affair, its domed, circular **portico** of 1689 built as part of a larger chapel on the orders of the Habsburg governor in the hope that it would encourage God to grant King Charles II of Spain an heir (see p.43). It didn't, but the plea to God survives in the Latin inscription on the pediment. The portico holds a bust of Wellington and a monument to all those British soldiers who died at Waterloo, and there's an assortment of British **memorial plaques** just inside the door of the chapel beyond. They are, however, a rather jumbled bunch as they were plonked here unceremoniously when the original chapel was demolished in the nineteenth century to be replaced by the substantial building of today. Most of the plaques were paid for by voluntary contributions from the soldiers who survived – in the days when the British Empire rarely coughed up anything for all but the most aristocratic of its veterans.

The battlefield – Le Hameau du Lion

From outside the church of Saint Joseph, pick up bus #W or drive the 4km journey to the **battlefield** – a landscape of rolling farmland interrupted by a couple of main roads and punctuated by the odd copse and whitewashed farmstead. Today, the ridge where Wellington once marshalled his army holds a motley assortment of pleasingly traditional attractions collectively known as **Le Hameau du Lion** (Lion's Hamlet). This comprises four separate sites, beginning with the **Centre du Visiteur** (daily: April–Oct 9.30am–6.30pm; Nov–March 10am–5pm; Ⓦwww.waterloo1815.be), where you can watch an absolutely dire audiovisual display on the battle, and wait for one of the regular truck **tours of the battlefield** (April–Oct daily about every 30min 10.45am–5.30pm; Nov–March Sat & Sun about every hour 10.45am–4.30pm; €5.50; 45min), or just buy souvenirs in the shop.

You're better off heading straight to the adjacent hundred-metre-high **Butte de Lion** (daily: April–Oct 9.30am–6.30pm; Nov–March 10am–5pm; €6; ticket includes Panorama and the Musée de Cire). Built by local women with soil from the battlefield, the Butte marks the spot where Holland's Prince William of Orange – one of Wellington's commanders and later King William II of the Netherlands – was wounded. It was only a nick, so it's anybody's guess how high they would have built it if William had been seriously injured, but even as it is, the mound is a commanding monument, 226 steps high, surmounted by a regal 28-tonne lion atop a stout column. From the viewing platform, there's a panoramic view over the battlefield, and a plan identifies the location of each army.

Right by the base of the Butte is the **Panorama de la Bataille** (same hours and ticket as the Butte de Lion), where a circular, naturalistic painting of the battle, on a canvas 110m in circumference is displayed in a purpose-built, rotunda-like gallery – all to a thundering soundtrack of bugles, snorting horses and cannon fire. Panorama painting was extremely difficult – controlling perspective was always a real problem – but it was very much in vogue when the Parisian artist Louis Dumoulin began the painting in 1912, and this one was particularly highly regarded. Precious few panoramas have survived, and this one is a bit past its best, but even now in its low-tech way it gives you a great sense of the intensity of the battle, as does the churned-up earth and models of dead soldiers and horses just in front.

Back across the street is the final site, the **Musée de Cire** (same hours and ticket as the Butte de Lion) is a wax museum complete with some decent – if dusty – dioramas of the key players in the battle: Ney, in conference with his commanders, a thoughtful Napoleon, both alone and with his bodyguards, and others of Wellington, Blücher and the Prince of Orange.

Le Caillou

Napoleon spent the eve of the battle at **Le Caillou** (daily: April–Oct 10am–6.30pm; Nov–March 1–5pm; €4), a two-storey brick farmhouse about 4km south of the Hameau du Lion further down the chaussée de Bruxelles, and reached from the main road by bus #365. Like Wellington's HQ, it's now a museum, and a memorial to the emperor and his army, but a much less interesting one. Exhibits include Napoleon's camp bed and a bronze of his death mask, a skeleton of a French hussar and tiny dioramas of various battle scenes – for fans of model soldiers only.

7

Day-trips from the city

Almost all of Belgium is within easy striking distance of Brussels, making the list of possible excursions almost endless. In this chapter we've picked out six of the most appealing destinations, none more than an hour's travelling time by train from the capital. To the south of Brussels, deep in the wilds of French-speaking Brabant, lies the Cistercian abbey of **Villers-la-Ville**, perhaps the most beautiful medieval ruins in the country and a popular spot with newlyweds, who go there to have their photo snapped against a romantic backdrop. To the north of the capital, in Flemish Belgium, lies **Mechelen**, with its amiable small-town airs and superb cathedral, and it's north again for the port city of **Antwerp**, which possesses a flourishing nightlife, medieval churches and first-rate museums, as well as an unrivalled collection of the work of its most celebrated son, Pieter Paul Rubens. There's also **Leuven**, just to the east of Brussels, the epitome of the lively university town, with student cafés and bars galore, plus a pair of especially handsome medieval buildings.

The flatlands of Flanders stretch west of Brussels as far as the North Sea. In medieval times, this region was the most prosperous and urbanized part of Europe and its merchants grew rich from the profits of the cloth industry. Those heady days are recalled in the superb architecture and excellent art museums of both **Ghent** and **Bruges**, one of the most perfectly preserved medieval cities in Europe.

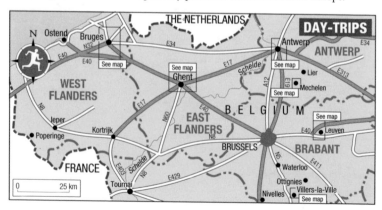

Villers-la-Ville

The ruined Cistercian abbey of Villers-la-Ville (April–Oct daily 10am–6pm; Nov–March Wed–Mon 10am–5pm; €5, audio guide €2; ☎071 88 09 80, ⓦ www.villers.be) nestles in a lovely wooded dell about 30km south of Brussels, and is altogether one of the most haunting and evocative sights in the whole of Belgium. The first monastic community settled here in 1146, consisting of just one abbot and twelve monks. Subsequently the abbey acquired a domain of several thousand acres, with numbers that rose to about a hundred monks and three hundred lay brothers. A healthy annual income funded the construction of an extensive monastic complex, most of which was erected in the thirteenth century, though the less austere structures, such as the Abbot's Palace, went up in a second spurt of activity some four hundred years later. In 1794 French

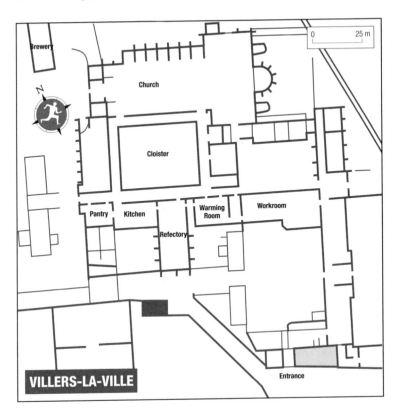

▲ The imposing abbey ruins of Villers-la-Ville

revolutionaries ransacked the monastery, and later on a railway was ploughed through the grounds. Today the site is wild and overgrown and the buildings are all in varying states of decay, but more than enough survives to pick out Romanesque, Gothic and Renaissance features, and to make some kind of mental reconstruction possible.

Arrival and information

To get to Villers-la-Ville from Brussels, take an hourly **train** from any of the capital's three main stations to Ottignies and change; depending on connections, the whole journey takes just over an hour. You can also reach the abbey from Brussels via Charleroi, but the connections tend to be less in synch. The abbey is about a fifteen-minute walk from Villers-la-Ville train station. To get there, follow the road back towards Ottignies and you'll soon spot a small, faded sign to Monticelli; follow the sign and you'll head up and over a little slope until, after about 100m, you reach a T-junction; turn right and follow the road round, and you'll see the ruins ahead. Once there you can take an audio tour, and the abbey sells both an in-depth **guide to the ruins** in English and a booklet (in French) detailing local walks.

The ruins

From the entrance a path crosses the courtyard in front of the Abbot's Palace to reach the **warming room** (*chauffoir*), the only place in the monastery where a fire would have been kept going all winter, and which still has its original chimney. The fire provided a little heat to the adjacent rooms: on one side the monks' **workroom** (*salle des moines*), used for reading and studying; on the other the large Romanesque-Gothic **refectory** (*réfectoire*), lit by ribbed twin windows topped with chunky rose windows. Next door is the **kitchen** (*cuisine*), which contains a few remnants of the drainage system, which once piped waste to the river, and of a central hearth, whose chimney helped air the room. Just behind this lies the **pantry** (*salle des convers*), where a segment of the original vaulting has survived, supported by a single column, and beyond, on the north-western edge of the complex, is the **brewery** (*brasserie*), one of the biggest and oldest buildings in the abbey.

The most impressive building, however, is the **church** (*église*), which fills out the north corner of the complex. It has the dimensions of a cathedral, with pure lines and elegant proportions, and displays the change from Romanesque to Gothic – the transept and choir are the first known examples of Gothic in Brabant. The church is 90m long and 40m wide with a majestic nave whose roof was supported on strong cylindrical columns. An unusual feature is the series of bull's-eye windows which light the transepts. Of the original twelfth-century **cloister** (*cloître*) adjoining the church, a pair of twin windows is pretty much all that remains, though it is flanked by a two-storey section of the old monks' quarters. Around the edge of the cloister are tombstones and the solitary sarcophagus of the Crusader Gobert d'Aspremont.

Mechelen

MECHELEN, midway between Brussels and Antwerp and just twenty minutes by train from the capital, is a lovely little Flemish town with a surprisingly grand history. Now the country's ecclesiastical capital and home of the Primate of Belgium, its Christian heritage dates back to St Rombout, an Irish evangelist who converted the locals in the seventh century. Martyred for his faith, Rombout proved a popular saint and pilgrims flocked here, ensuring Mechelen a steady revenue. The town went on to become one of the most

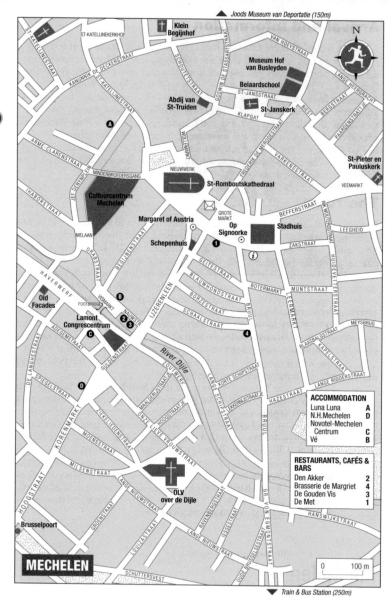

▲ *Joods Museum van Deportatie (150m)*

St-Katelijnekerkhof

Klein
Begijnhof

Museum Hof
van Busleyden

Beiaardschool

ST-JANSSTRAAT

Abdij van
St-Truiden

KLAPGAT

St-Janskerk

N

St-Pieter en
Pauluskerk

VEEMARKT

NIEUWWERK

St-Romboutskathedraal

Cultuurcentrum
Mechelen

Margaret of Austria

GROTE
MARKT

Op
Signoorke

Stadhuis

BEFFERSTRAAT

LEEGHEID

Schepenhuis

ZAKSTRAAT

MELAAN

HAVERWERF

Old
Facades

FOOTBRIDGE

VISMARKT

Lamont
Congrescentrum

River Dijle

OLV
over de Dijle

Brusselpoort

MECHELEN

0   100 m

▼ *Train & Bus Station (250m)*

ACCOMMODATION

Luna Luna	A
N.H.Mechelen	D
Novotel-Mechelen Centrum	C
Vé	B

RESTAURANTS, CAFÉS & BARS

Den Akker	2
Brasserie de Margriet	4
De Gouden Vis	3
De Met	1

powerful in medieval Flanders and entered a brief golden age when, in the 1470s, the dukes of Burgundy moved their court here. The good times lasted just sixty years until, with the Burgundians gone, Mechelen slipped into obscurity, becoming the low-key, laid-back medium-sized town that it still is today. Its pride and joy is the magnificent Gothic **cathedral**, St-Romboutskathedraal, the foremost of several medieval churches here. There's also a sombre **Jewish Deportation Museum** (Joods Museum van Deportatie),

▲ Mechelen's cathedral

recalling the terrible days when the Germans used the town as a transit camp for Jews on their way to the concentration camps. Mechelen is easily explored on a day-trip from Brussels, but spending a night here will allow you give the place the attention it really deserves.

Arrival, information and accommodation

From Mechelen's **train** and adjoining **bus station**, it's a fifteen-minute walk north to the town centre, straight ahead down Hendrik Consciencestraat and its continuation Graaf von Egmontstraat and then Bruul. The **tourist office** is across from the Stadhuis on the east side of the Grote Markt at Hallestraat 2 (April–Sept Mon 9.30am–7pm, Tues–Fri 9.30am–5.30pm, Sat & Sun 10am–4.30pm; Oct–March Mon–Fri 9.30am–4.30pm, Sat & Sun 10.30am–3.30pm; ⊕070 22 28 00, ⓦwww.inenuitmechelen.be). They supply all the usual tourist information on the town, have details of – and sell tickets for – upcoming festivals and events, and can provide a list of all the town's **accommodation**, which they will book for you at no extra charge.

Accommodation

There's rarely any difficulty in finding a room in Mechelen and there are several good choices.

Luna Luna Jef Denynplein 4 ⊕0486 29 67 98, ⓦwww.lunaluna.be. Especially pleasant B&B in a substantial, old town house on a quiet side street, a brief walk from the Grote Markt. There's just one bedroom, but it's a comfortable suite with stripped wood floors and views of the spire of St-Romboutskathedraal. Arrange access before you arrive; no credit cards. €95.

NH Mechelen Korenmarkt 22 ⊕015 42 03 03, ⓦwww.nh-hotels.com. Proficient, modern chain hotel, with three stars and forty-odd comfortable if somewhat ordinary rooms. A brief walk south of the Grote Markt via the Ijzerenleen. Substantial reductions at weekends, otherwise from €120.
Novotel – Mechelen Centrum Van Beethoven-straat 1 ⊕015 40 49 50, ⓦwww.novotel.com.

In a striking modern building, this efficient chain hotel has over one hundred bright but slightly spartan rooms, and a very central location. From €120.

🏃 **Vé Vismarkt 14** ☏ 015 20 07 55, @ www .hotelve.com. Down near the river,

a short walk south of the Grote Markt, this new hotel is an intelligent rework-ing of a 1920s factory building, its forty rooms kitted out in an attractive version of minimalist style with lots of earthy tones. Doubles from €170.

The Town

The centre of town is the **Grote Markt**, a handsome and expansive square flanked on its eastern side by the Stadhuis, whose bizarre and incoherent appearance was the work of the dukes and duchesses of Burgundy. In 1526, they had the left-hand side of the original building demolished and replaced by what you see today, an ornate, arcaded loggia fronting a fluted, angular edifice. The plan was to demolish and rebuild the rest of the building in stages, but after the Burgundians moved out in 1530 the work was simply abandoned, leaving one extravagant wing firmly attached to the plain stonework and simple gables of the earlier, fourteenth-century section on the right.

In front of the Stadhuis is a modern sculpture of **Op Signoorke**, the town's mascot, being tossed in a blanket. Once a generalized symbol of male irresponsi-bility, the eponymous doll and its many forebears enjoyed a variety of names – *vuilen bras* (unfaithful drunkard), *sotscop* (fool) and *vuilen bruidegom* (disloyal bridegroom) – until the events of 1775 redefined its identity. Every year it was customary for a dummy to be paraded through the streets and tossed up and down in a sheet. In 1775, however, a young man from Antwerp attempted to steal it and was badly beaten for his pains – the people of Mechelen were convinced he was part of an Antwerp plot to rob them of their cherished mascot. The two cities were already fierce commercial rivals, and the incident soured relations even further. Indeed, when news of the beating reached Antwerp, there was sporadic rioting and calls for the city burghers to take some sort of revenge. Refusing to be intimidated, the people of Mechelen derisively renamed the doll after their old nickname for the people of Antwerp – "Op Signoorke", from "Signor", a reference to that city's favoured status under earlier Spanish kings. It was sweet revenge for an incident of 1687 that had made Mechelen a laughing stock: staggering home, a drunk had roused the town when he thought he saw a fire in the cathedral. In fact, the "fire" was moonlight, earning the Mechelaars the soubriquet "Maneblussers" (Moondousers).

St-Romboutskathedraal

A little way west of the Grote Markt rises **St-Romboutskathedraal** (April–Oct daily 9am–5.30pm, Nov–March 9am–4.30pm; free), which dominates the town centre just as it was supposed to. It's the cathedral's mighty square **tower** that takes the breath away, a wonderful, almost imperial Gothic structure with soaring, canopied pinnacles and extraordinarily long and slender windows. It's matched down below by the church's heavy-duty buttressing, which supports a superb sequence of high-arched pointed windows that encircle the nave and the choir, rising up to the delicate fluting of a stone balustrade.

The main **entrance** to the cathedral is just off the Grote Markt. Inside, the thirteenth-century **nave** has all the cloistered elegance of the Brabantine Gothic style, although the original lines are spoiled by an unfortunate series of seventeenth-century statues of the apostles. Between the arches lurks an extraordinary Baroque **pulpit**, a playful mass of twisted and curled oak dotted with carefully camouflaged animal carvings – squirrels, frogs and snails, a salamander and a pelican. The main scene shows **St Norbert** being thrown from his horse, a narrow escape which convinced this twelfth-century German prince to give his possessions to the poor and dedicate his life to the church. Moving on, the chapel next to the **north transept** contains the tomb of Mechelen's **Cardinal Mercier**, plus a plaque, presented by the Church of England, commemorating his part in coordinating the Mechelen Conversations. These investigated the possibility of reuniting the two churches and ran from 1921 up to the time of Mercier's death in 1926, but with little result. Across the church in the **south transept** is the cathedral's most distinguished painting, **Anthony van Dyck**'s dramatic *Crucifixion*, which portrays the writhing, muscular bodies of the two thieves in the shadows to either side of Christ, who is bathed in a white light of wonderful clarity. The painting now forms part of a heavy, marble Baroque altarpiece carved for the Guild of Masons, but it was only installed here after the French revolutionary army razed the church where it was originally displayed.

Exhibited in the **aisle of the ambulatory** are twenty-five **panel paintings** relating the legend of St Rombout. Such devotional series were comparatively common in medieval Flanders, but this is one of the few to have survived, painted by several unknown artists between 1480 and 1510. As individual works of art, the panel paintings are not perhaps of the highest order, but the cumulative attention to detail – in the true Flemish tradition – is quite remarkable, with all manner of folksy minutiae illuminating what would otherwise be a predictable tale of sacrifice and sanctity. Many of the panels carry a sombre-looking, kneeling man and woman – these were the donors.

To St-Janskerk

From the north side of the cathedral, Wollemarkt swerves its way past the refuge of the **Abdij van St-Truiden** (no public access), which sits prettily beside an old weed-choked and algae-covered canal, its picturesque gables once home to the destitute. Almost opposite, on Goswin de Stassartstraat, an alley called Klapgat ("gossip") threads through to **St-Janskerk** (Tues–Sun: April–Oct 1.30–5.30pm, Nov–March 1.30–4.30pm; free), whose decaying sandstone exterior belies its richly decorated, immaculately maintained interior. Almost everything is on a grand scale here, from the massive pulpit and the whopping organ through to two large and unusual canons' pews, but it's the Baroque high altarpiece that grabs the attention, a suitably flashy setting for a flashy but wonderful painting – **Rubens**' *Adoration of the Magi*. Painted in 1619, the central panel, after which the triptych is named, is a fine example of the artist's use of variegated lighting – and also features his first wife portrayed as the Virgin. The side panels are occasionally rotated, so on the left hand side you'll see either Jesus baptized by John the Baptist or John the Baptist's head on a platter; to the right it's St John on Patmos or the same saint being dipped in boiling oil.

Joods Museum van Deportatie en Verzet

Heading west from St-Janskerk, turn right along Goswin de Stassartstraat for the five-minute walk to the **Joods Museum van Deportatie en Verzet**, at no.153 (Jewish Museum of Deportation and Resistance; Sun–Thurs 10am–5pm, Fri 10am–1pm; free; ⓦwww.cicb.be). During the German occupation, Nazi officials chose Mechelen as a staging point for Belgian Jews destined for the concentration camps of eastern Europe. Their reasoning was quite straightforward: most of Belgium's Jews were in either Antwerp or Brussels and Mechelen was halfway between the two.

Today's museum occupies one **wing** of the old barracks that were adapted by the Gestapo for use as their principal internment centre. Between 1942 and 1944 over 25,000 Jews passed through its doors; most ended up in Auschwitz and only 1,200 survived the war. In a series of well-conceived, multilingual displays, the museum explores this dreadful episode, beginning with Jewish life in Belgium before the war and continuing with sections on the rise of anti-Semitism, the occupation, the deportations, the concentration camps and liberation. It's designed with older Belgian schoolchildren in mind, so you may share the museum with one or more school parties, but it's still harrowing stuff and some of the exhibits bring a deep chill to the soul, none more so than the pleading postcard thrown from a deportation train. The final section, entitled "Personal Testimonies", is particularly moving, comprising video interviews given by some of the survivors.

The Museum Hof van Busleyden and the Beiaardschool

Doubling back from the Jewish Museum, turn left onto Van Hoeystraat and right at the end to reach the **Museum Hof van Busleyden** (Tues–Sun 10am–5pm; €2), which occupies a handsome High Gothic mansion with Renaissance embellishments, set around a large courtyard that was built for Hieronymus Busleyden, a prominent member of Margaret of Austria's court, in the sixteenth century. Inside, the museum's rambling collection doesn't live up to its setting, but there are a few mildly diverting, mostly unattributed seventeenth-century paintings, as well as a seventeenth-century version of Op Signoorke (see p.146), and examples of the town's traditional crafts, most notably a whole room of the gold-inlaid leather wallpaper for which the town was once famous.

In the same complex, at the corner of St-Janstraat, is Mechelen's internationally renowned **Koninklijke Beiaardschool** (Royal Carillon School; no public access; Ⓦwww.beiaardschool.be), which attracts students from as far away as Japan. Playing the carillon bells is, by all accounts, extremely difficult and the diploma course offered here takes no less than six years to complete.

South of the Grote Markt

The innocuous **statue** of Margaret of Austria on the south side of the Grote Markt dates from 1849, but it was only moved here from the centre of the square a couple of years ago – much to the irritation of many locals, who thought she should have stayed exactly where she was. Behind the statue stands the **Schepenhuis** (Aldermen's House), a good-looking Gothic structure of 1374 that marks the start of the **Ijzerenleen**, the site of one of the region's best Saturday food **markets** (8am–1pm).

At the far end of the Ijzerenleen, just before the bridge, turn right down **Nauwstraat** and keep going past the footbridge to the second bridge along, a quaint little pontoon spanning the River Dijle over to **Haverwerf** (Oats Wharf), which is graced by three old and contrasting facades, each of which has been meticulously restored. On the right is **Het Paradijske** (The Little Paradise), a slender structure with fancy tracery and mullioned windows that takes its name from the Garden of Eden reliefs above the first-floor windows. Next door, the all-timber **De Duiveltjes** (The Little Devils), a rare survivor from the sixteenth century, is also named after its decoration, this time for the carved satyrs above the entrance. Finally, on the left and dating to 1669, is **St-Jozef**, a graceful example of the Baroque merchant's house.

Eating and drinking

Mechelen's **café and restaurant** scene has improved markedly in recent years and, although visitors are hardly overwhelmed with great choices, the town does have a couple of very good and distinctive places. Enjoyable **bars** are thinner on the ground, but there are certainly enough to be getting on with and, while you are here, be sure to try one particular local brew, **Gouden Carolus** (Golden Charles), a delicious dark-brown or blond barley beer once tippled by – so they say – the Emperor Charles V. The town also possesses a brand-new cultural centre, the **Cultuurcentrum Mechelen** (☎015 29 40 00, ⓦwww.cultuurcentrummechelen.be), just off the Grote Markt on Minderbroedersgang, where they put on a varied programme of theatre, dance and debate.

Cafés, restaurants and bars

Den Akker Nauwstraat 11. Laid-back, vaguely New-Age bar with an outside terrace overlooking the river. Mon–Sat from 11.30am, Sun from 3pm till late.

Brasserie de Margriet Bruul 52 ☎015 21 00 17. Popular brasserie in one wing of a former seminary, though it has been revamped in modern style, so only the odd flourish – like the mullioned windows – give a hint as to what went before. The menu covers all the Flemish bases, but there are a few surprises, notably a local delicacy, the "Mechelse Koekoek" (Mechelen Cuckoo) – actually just a (particularly succulent) variety of chicken. Mains €10–18. You can eat on the courtyard in summer. Mon–Sat 9am–10/11pm.

De Gouden Vis Nauwstraat 7. Popular bar with a riverside terrace and antique furnishings and fittings, plus a good beer list. Next door to Den Akker (see above). Mon–Fri from noon, Sat from 10am, Sun from 3pm till late.

De Met Grote Markt 29 ☎015 20 68 81. There are lots of restaurants on the Grote Markt, but this is the pick of the bunch: a bright, modern place offering a good range of seasonal Flemish dishes using, as often as not, local produce. The daily specials are especially tasty. Mains €18–23. Mon–Sat noon–10.30pm.

Antwerp

Belgium's second city, **ANTWERP**, about 50km north of Brussels – and forty minutes by train – is an animated cultural centre which lays fair claim to be the effective capital of Flemish Belgium. The city fans out carelessly from the east bank of the River Scheldt, its centre formed and framed by its enclosing boulevards and the river. It's not an especially handsome city – the terrain is too flat and industry too prevalent for that – but its centre is dotted with some lovely old churches and excellent museums, reminders of its auspicious past as the centre of a large trading empire. In particular, there's the enormous legacy of **Rubens**, whose works adorn Antwerp's galleries and churches, and the presence of a raft of local fashion designers, who gather at exhibitions held in the **MoMu fashion museum**. Add to this a spirited nightlife and a first-rate bar and restaurant scene and you have a city that's well worth an overnight stay.

Arrival and information

Antwerp has two main **train stations**, Berchem and Centraal. A few domestic and international trains pause at Berchem, 4km southeast of the centre, before bypassing Centraal, but the majority call at both. **Centraal Station**, lying about

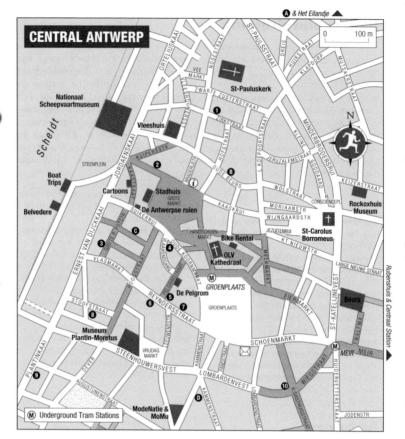

CENTRAL ANTWERP

0   100 m

Nationaal
Scheepvaartmuseum

St-Pauluskerk

Vleeshuis

Boat
Trips

Cartoons   Stadhuis
                  GROTE
Belvedere   MARKT
                  De Antwerpse ruien

Rockoxhuis
Museum

Bike Rental

St-Carolus
Borromeus

OLV
Kathedraal

De Pelgrom   GROENPLAATS

                  GROENPLAATS

Beurs

Museum
Plantin-Moretus

MEIR   MEIR

ModeNatie &
MoMu

Ⓜ Underground Tram Stations

Rubenshuis & Centraal Station

ACCOMMODATION		RESTAURANTS, CAFÉS & BARS					
International Zeemanshuis	A	Den Engel	2	Hungry Henrietta	10	Varelli	9
M0851	D	De Groote Witte Arend	6	De Kleine Zavel	8	Zoute Zoen	1
Matelote	C	De Herk	7	Popoff	4		
Rubens Grote Markt	B	Den Hopsack	3	De Vagant	5		

2km east of the main square, the Grote Markt, is much more convenient for the city centre and most of the major sights. If you do have to change, connections between the two stations are frequent and fast (10 hourly; 4min). **Trams from Centraal Station** to the city centre go underground, departing from the adjacent Diamant underground tram station (#2 or #15 direction Linkeroever; get off at Groenplaats).

The **tourist office** is bang in the centre of the city at Grote Markt 13 (Mon–Sat 9am–5.45pm, Sun 9am–4.45pm; ☏03 232 01 03, Ⓦwww .visitantwerpen.be). They have a comprehensive range of information, most notably a free and very useful guide detailing the city's sights, and an accommodation booklet, covering registered hotels, hostels and B&Bs. They also issue free transport maps and city maps, and this is also a handy spot to pick up the free, fortnightly **Zone 03**, a comprehensive listings magazine, though this is in

Flemish only; *Zone 03* is also available at public news racks across the centre. The tourist office shares its premises with **Info Cultuur** (☎03 203 95 85), who sell tickets for concerts and events.

Accommodation

Finding **accommodation** in Antwerp is rarely difficult, although there are surprisingly few places in the centre, which is by far the best spot to soak up the city's atmosphere. The tourist office issues a free and comprehensive booklet detailing the city's hotels, B&Bs and hostels, and will make last-minute **hotel bookings** on your behalf at no cost, charging only a modest deposit, which is subtracted from your final bill. Antwerp's B&Bs also have their own association, the Gilde der Antwerpse Gastenkamers, whose website provides information on its members (ⓦwww.gastenkamersantwerpen.be).

Internationaal Zeemanshuis Falconrui 21 ☎03 227 54 33, ⓦwww.zeemanshuis.be. A ten-minute walk north of the Grote Markt, out towards the old docks in a lively-verging-on-seedy part of town. The "Seamen's House", set in a substantial, good-looking 1950s block in its own (mini) grounds, has over a hundred modern rooms, all en suite. Despite the name, it's open to landlubbers and women, as well as mariners. €70.

M0851 Nationalestraat 19 ☎03 297 60 66, ⓦwww.m0851.be. The three self-contained suites above the M0851 high-end accessories shop are suitably slick and modern, with painted floorboards and plenty of monochrome. The top suite, right under the eaves (and with air-conditioning), is especially cosy. All three have internet access and kitchen facilities; breakfast is at a nearby café. From €110.

Matelote Haarstraat 11 ☎03 201 88 00, ⓦwww.matelote.be. Decorated in crisp, contemporary style, this small hotel occupies intelligently revamped and remodelled old premises just south of the Grote Markt. The en-suite rooms are large and well-appointed, all wooden floors and primary colours. Breakfast is served in a café next door. From €120.

🏃 **Rubens Grote Markt** Oude Beurs 29 ☎03 222 48 48, ⓦwww.hotelrubensantwerp.be. At probably the most agreeable hotel in town, the public rooms are kitted out in an ornately traditional style, with thirty-six attractively furnished modern rooms beyond. It's in a handy location too, just a couple of minutes' walk north of the Grote Markt. From €145.

The City

The centre of Antwerp is the **Grote Markt**, at the heart of which stands the **Brabo Fountain**, a haphazard pile of roughly sculpted rocks surmounted by a bronze of one Silvius Brabo, depicted flinging the hand of the prostate giant Antigonus into the Scheldt. Legend asserts that Antigonus extracted tolls from all passing ships, cutting off the hands of those who refused to pay. He was eventually beaten by the valiant Brabo, who tore off his hand and threw it into the river, giving the city its name, which literally means "hand-throw". There are more plausible explanations of the city's name, but this is the most colourful, and it certainly reflects Antwerp's early success at freeing the river from the innumerable taxes levied on shipping by local landowners.

Lording it over the Grote Markt, the **Stadhuis** was completed in 1566 to an innovative design by Cornelis Floris. The building's pagoda-like roof gives it a faintly oriental appearance, but apart from the central gable it's quite plain, with a long plastered facade of short and rather shallow Doric and Ionic columns. These, along with the windows, lend it a simple elegance, in contrast to the purely decorative gable (there's no roof behind).

▲ Antwerp's Brabo fountain and Stadhuis

The Onze Lieve Vrouwekathedraal

Just to the southeast of the Grote Markt, the **Onze Lieve Vrouwekathedraal** (Cathedral of Our Lady; Mon–Fri 10am–5pm, Sat 10am–3pm, Sun 1–4pm; €4) is one of the finest Gothic churches in Belgium, a forceful and self-confident structure that mostly dates from the middle of the fifteenth century. Its graceful spire dominated the skyline of the medieval city and was long a favourite with British travellers. Inside, the seven-aisled nave is breathtaking, if only because of its sense of space, an impression reinforced by the bright, light stonework. The religious troubles of the sixteenth century – primarily the Iconoclastic Fury of 1566 – polished off the cathedral's early furnishings and fittings, so what you see today are largely Baroque embellishments, most notably four early paintings by Pieter Paul **Rubens** (1577–1640). Of these, the *Descent from the Cross*, just to the right of the central crossing, is without doubt the most beautiful, a triptych painted after the artist's return from Italy in 1612 that displays an uncharacteristically moving realism, derived from Caravaggio.

The Plantin-Moretus and Nationaal Scheepvaart museums

It takes about five minutes to walk southwest from the cathedral to the **Plantin–Moretus Museum**, which occupies a grand old mansion on Vrijdagmarkt (Tues–Sun 10am–5pm; €6). The mansion was the home and workplace of the printer **Christopher Plantin**, who rose to fame and fortune in the second half of the sixteenth century. One of Antwerp's most interesting museums, it provides a marvellous insight into how Plantin and his family conducted their business, its rabbit-warren rooms holding all sorts of antique books, printers' woodcuts and copper plates, plus several ancient printing presses.

From here it's a brief stroll north to the riverfront **Nationaal Scheepvaartmuseum** (National Maritime Museum: Tues–Sun 10am–5pm; €4), which is situated at the end of Suikerrui and inhabits the Steen, the remaining gatehouse of what was once an impressive medieval fortress. Inside, the cramped rooms feature exhibits on inland navigation, shipbuilding and waterfront life, while the open-air section has a long line of tugs and barges under a rickety corrugated roof.

The Vleeshuis and St-Pauluskerk

Just east of the Maritime Museum rise the tall, turreted gables of the **Vleeshuis** (Tues–Sun 10am–5pm; €5), built for the powerful guild of butchers in 1503. Inside, the cavernous ground floor holds an ambitious, if not entirely successful display on music and dance in the city over the last six hundred years. Headphones handed out at the reception desk enables visitors to listen to a wide range of historic instruments, but somehow it's all too fiddly and a tad tedious. More positively, the museum does hold an excellent range of sixteenth- and seventeenth-century musical instruments, most memorably a platoon of primly decorated **clavichords** and **harpischords**, some of which were produced locally in the Ruckers workshop.

From the Vleeshuis, it's a couple of minutes' walk north to the **Veemarkt** (Cattle Market), where an extravagant Baroque portal leads through to **St-Pauluskerk** (May–Sept daily 2–5pm; free), one of the city's most delightful churches, an airy, dignified late Gothic structure dating from 1517. The Dominicans, for whom the church was built, commissioned a series of paintings to line the wall of the nave's north aisle depicting the *Fifteen Mysteries of the Rosary*. Dating from 1617, the series has survived intact, a remarkable snapshot of Antwerp's artistic talent, with works by the likes of Cornelis De Vos, David Teniers the Elder and van Dyck, but it is **Rubens'** contribution – *The Scourging at the Pillar* – which stands out, a brilliant, brutal canvas showing Jesus clad in a blood-spattered loincloth. There's more Rubens close by – at the far end of the *Mysteries* series – in the *Adoration of the Shepherds* and another, the *Disputation on the Nature of the Holy Sacrament*, in the south transept; both are early works dating back to 1609.

Back outside, in between the Baroque portal and the church, lurks another curiosity in the form of the **Calvarieberg**, an artificial **grotto** begun in 1697 and fifty years in the making. The grotto clings to the buttresses of the south transept, eerily adorned with statues of Christ and other figures of angels, prophets and saints in a tawdry representation of the Crucifixion and Entombment. Writing in the nineteenth century, the traveller Charles Tennant described it as "exhibiting a more striking instance of religious fanaticism than good taste".

The Rockoxhuis Museum

The **Rockoxhuis Museum**, a five- to ten-minute walk southeast of St-Pauluskerk at Keizerstraat 12 (Tues–Sun 10am–5pm; €2.50), occupies the attractively restored seventeenth-century town house of Nicolaas Rockox, friend and patron of Rubens. Inside, a sequence of rooms has been crammed with period furnishings and art works, based on an inventory taken after the owner's death in 1640. Nevertheless, it's far from a re-creation of Rockox's old home, but rather a museum with a small but highly prized collection. **Highlights** include a gentle *Holy Virgin and Child* by Quentin Matsys and a small and romantic Rubens, the *Virgin in Adoration before the sleeping Christ Child*, in which Mary has the features of Rubens' first wife and Jesus is modelled on his son. Finally, Room 6 holds Pieter Bruegel the Younger's (1564–1638) *Proverbs*, an intriguing, folksy work, one of several he did in direct imitation of his father, a frenetic mixture of the observed and imagined set in a Flemish village. The meaning of many of the pictured proverbs has been the subject of long debate, but there's little doubt about the meaning of the central image depicting an old man dressed in the blue-hooded cape of the cuckold at the behest of his young wife.

The Rubenshuis

From either the Grote Markt or the Rockoxhuis, it's a five- to ten-minute walk to the city's most popular tourist attraction, the **Rubenshuis** at Wapper 9 (Tues–Sun 10am–5pm; €6). Not so much a house as a mansion, this was where Rubens lived for most of his adult life, but the building was only acquired by the town in 1937, by which time it was little more than a shell. Skilfully restored, it opened as a museum in 1946. On the right is the classical studio, where Rubens worked and taught; on the left is the traditional, gabled Flemish house, to which is attached Rubens's art gallery, an Italianate chamber where he entertained the artistic and cultural elite of Europe.

Unfortunately, there are only a handful of his less distinguished paintings here, and very little to represent the works of those other artists he collected so avidly throughout his life. The restoration of the rooms is convincing, though, and a clearly arrowed tour begins by twisting its way through the neatly panelled and attractively furnished **domestic interiors** of the Flemish half of the house. Beyond, and in contrast to the cramped living quarters, is the elegant **art gallery**, which, with its pint-sized sculpture gallery, was where Rubens displayed his favourite pieces to a chosen few. The arrows then direct you on into the **great studio**, which is overlooked by a narrow gallery and equipped with a special high door to allow the largest canvases to be brought in and out with ease. Several Rubens paintings are displayed here, including a playful *Adam and Eve*, an early work in which the couple flirt while the serpent slithers back up the tree. Also in the studio is a more characteristic piece, the *Annunciation*, where you can sense the drama of the angel Gabriel's appearance to Mary – both in the preparatory sketch and in the finished article, which are exhibited next to each other.

St-Jacobskerk

Rubens died in 1640 and was buried in **St-Jacobskerk**, just to the north of the Wapper on Lange Nieuwstraat (April–Oct Wed–Mon 2–5pm; €2). Very much the church of the Antwerp nobility, the church is a mighty Gothic structure begun in 1491, but not finished until 1659. This delay means that much of its Gothic splendour is hidden by an overly decorated Baroque interior, the soaring heights of the nave flattened by heavy marble altars and a huge marble rood screen.

Seven chapels radiate out from the ambulatory, including the **Rubens chapel**, directly behind the high altar, where the artist and his immediate family are buried beneath the tombstones in the floor with a lengthy Latin inscription giving details of Rubens' life and honours. The chapel's altar was the gift of Helene Fourment, Rubens' second wife, and shows one of his last works, *Our Lady and the Christ Child surrounded by Saints* (1634), in which he painted himself as St George, his wives as Martha and Mary, and his father as St Jerome.

South to ModeNatie and MOMU

Heading south from Groenplaats along Nationalestraat, it takes about five minutes to reach **ModeNatie** (Ⓦ www.modenatie.com), a lavish and extraordinarily ambitious fashion complex. Spread over several floors, it showcases the work of local fashion designers and incorporates both the fashion department of the Royal Academy of Fine Arts and the Flanders Fashion Institute. As such, it reflects the international success of local designers, beginning in the 1980s with the so-called "**Antwerp Six**" – including Dries van Noten, Dirk Bikkembergs, Marina Yee and Martin Margiela – and continuing with younger designers like Raf Simons and Veronique Branquinho; all are graduates of the academy. Part of the building contains the Mode Museum, or **MoMu** (Tues–Sun 10am–6pm; €6; Ⓦ www.momu.be), whose enterprising and thought-provoking temporary displays cover a lot of ground – everything from the walking stick as fashion statement through to the evolution of the trench coat.

Fashion shopping in Antwerp

The success of Antwerp's **fashion designers** has spawned dozens of excellent designer shops and stores. To help visitors get a grip on it all, the tourist office produces two booklets entitled the *Antwerp Fashion Walk*, a long (€3) and a short version (€1.50), detailing several walks in the city that take you past all the most innovative shops – there is a particular concentration around the ModeNatie complex. Recommended places kick off with the menswear and womenswear of Dries van Noten's **Modepaleis**, Nationalestraat 16 – at the corner of Kammenstraat – and continue with the imported designer clothes of **Alamode**, Nationalestraat 27, and **Veronique Branquinho**'s shop, at Nationalestraat 73. Neighbouring Kammenstraat weighs in with the contemporary jewellery of **Anne Zellien**, at no. 47, and the anarchic club- and streetwear of **Fish & Chips**, at no.36, while Lombardenstraat, just to the east, is home to **Original**, at no. 10, and **Louis**, at no. 2, both of which feature the clothes of many designers, from Hilfiger to Junk de Luxe. There are a couple of **vintage clothes shops** in the area too: women's stuff at **Jutka & Riska**, Nationalestraat 87, and all sorts of interesting gear at **Episode**, Steenhouwersvest 34, just west of Nationalestraat.

Museum voor Schone Kunsten

From ModeNatie, it's a good fifteen-minute walk south – or a quick trip on tram #8 from Groenplaats – to the **Museum voor Schone Kunsten** (Fine Art Museum; Tues–Sun 10am–5pm; €6), which occupies an immense Neoclassical edifice on Leopold de Waelplaats. Inside, the lower level is largely devoted to temporary exhibitions – for which there is usually a supplementary charge – plus the museum's modern art (from the late nineteenth century onwards), but the bulk of the permanent collection is squeezed into the lettered rooms of the upper level. Free plans of the museum are available at reception, and are extremely useful as everything is a little mixed up and the paintings are often rotated. The museum boasts an excellent early Flemish section, featuring paintings by Jan van Eyck, Memling, Rogier van der Weyden and Quentin Matsys, and Rubens has two large rooms to himself. The museum also displays a comprehensive collection of modern Belgian art, with Paul Delvaux and James Ensor leading the charge.

Eating and drinking

Antwerp is an enjoyable and inexpensive place to eat, its busy centre liberally sprinkled with informal **cafés and restaurants**, which excel at combining traditional Flemish dishes with Mediterranean, French and vegetarian cuisines. Antwerp is also a great place to drink, its centre dotted with lots of tiny, dimly lit **bars** that exude a cheerful vitality.

Restaurants and cafés

De Groote Witte Arend Reyndersstraat 18. This eminently appealing café-bar, which occupies one wing and the courtyard of an old mansion, has a great range of beers – including authentic gueuze and kriek – plus delicious Flemish dishes, including stoemp (mashed potato with veg) and stoofvlees (beef cooked in beer) – all to a classical music soundtrack. Mains around €13. Mon–Thurs & Sun 10.30am–midnight, Fri & Sat 10.30am–2am; food served daily 11am–10pm.

Hungry Henrietta Lombardenvest 19 ☏03 232 29 28. Something of a city institution, this family-owned restaurant is decorated in brisk modern style and serves up all the Flemish classics; locals swear by the steaks. Mains average €22, but the daily specials cost half that. Mon–Fri noon–2pm & 6–9pm.

De Kleine Zavel Stoofstraat 2 ☏03 231 96 91. Much-praised, bistro-style restaurant with wood floors and old-style furniture that offers Franco-Belgian cuisine at its tastiest, with a particularly strong line in seafood. On a narrow side street in between the Grote Markt and the river. Mains from €23. Reservations essential. Mon–Fri & Sun noon–2pm & 6.30–10.30pm, Sat 6.30–10.30pm.

Popoff Oude Koornmarkt 18. This tiny café is the place to come for the best desserts, tarts and gateaux in Antwerp. Tues–Sat noon–10.30pm, Sun noon–10pm.

Varelli Plantinkaai 15 ☏03 485 88 82. The best Greek mezze in town are served in this arty, informal restaurant, which occupies the ground floor of an old riverside town house. Main courses €15. Mon–Fri 6–10.30pm, Sat 5–10.30pm, Sun noon–10.30pm.

Zoute Zoen Zirkstraat 15 ☏03 226 92 20. A short walk north of the Grote Markt, this small and polished bistro offers delicious Italian, French and Flemish dishes with main courses around €20, pasta dishes €12–16. Closed Sat lunch and Mon.

Bars

Den Engel Grote Markt 3. Handily located, traditional bar with an easy-going – sometimes verging on anarchic – atmosphere. On the ground floor of a guildhouse on the Grote Markt's northwest corner, it attracts a mixture of business people and locals from the residential enclave round the Vleeshuis, with everyone joining in the dancing later on.

De Herk Reyndersstraat 33. This tiny bar down a narrow alley and set around a courtyard attracts a modish, twenty-something clientele. There's a good range of beers and ales – including an excellent Lindemans gueuze.

Den Hopsack Grote Pieter Potstraat 22. Postmodern bar – all bare wood and spartan fittings – with highbrow conversation, an amenable, low-key atmosphere, and a thirty-something crowd.

De Vagant Reyndersstraat 21. Specialist gin bar serving an extravagant range of Belgian and Dutch jenevers in comfortable, informal surroundings. There's a small pavement terrace too.

Leuven

Less than half an hour by train from Brussels, **LEUVEN** makes for an easy and enjoyable day-trip. The town is home to Belgium's oldest university, nowadays a bastion of Flemish thinking and the wielder of considerable influence over the region's political and economic elite. Leuven's many students give the place a lively, informal air – and sustain lots of inexpensive bars and cafés, especially on and around one of the city's most appealing squares, the **Oude Markt**. What's more, Leuven also boasts a pair of notable medieval buildings, the splendid **Stadhuis** (City Hall) and **St-Pieterskerk**, a late Gothic church that's home to two wonderful early Flemish paintings by Dieric Bouts. Otherwise, the centre is not much more than an undistinguished tangle of streets with a lot of the new and few remnants of the old. Then again, it's something of a miracle that any of Leuven's ancient buildings have survived at all, since the town suffered badly in both world wars. Some 1500 houses were destroyed in World War I, and the university library and main church were gutted, only to suffer further damage in World War II.

Arrival and information

There are at least four trains an hour from Brussels to Leuven, a twenty-minute journey, and it's a gentle ten- to fifteen-minute walk west along Bondgenotenlaan from the train station to the main square, the Grote Markt, where you'll find Leuven's **tourist office** in the Stadhuis, though entered from Naamsestraat (March–Oct daily 10am–5pm; Nov–Feb same hours but closed Sun; ☏016 21 15 39).

The Town

The town centre is marked by two adjacent squares, the more easterly of which is the **Fochplein**, basically just a road junction whose one noteworthy feature is the modern **Font Sapienza**, a wittily cynical fountain depicting a student being literally brainwashed by the book he's reading.

Next door, the wedge-shaped main square, the **Grote Markt**, is Leuven's architectural high spot, dominated by two notable late Gothic buildings – St-Pieterskerk and the Stadhuis. The Stadhuis is the more flamboyant of the two, an extraordinarily light and lacy confection, crowned by soaring pinnacles and a dainty, high-pitched roof studded with dormer windows. It's a beautiful building, though slightly spoiled by the clumsiness of its statues, which were inserted in the nineteenth century and represent everything from important citizens, artists and nobles to virtues, vices and municipal

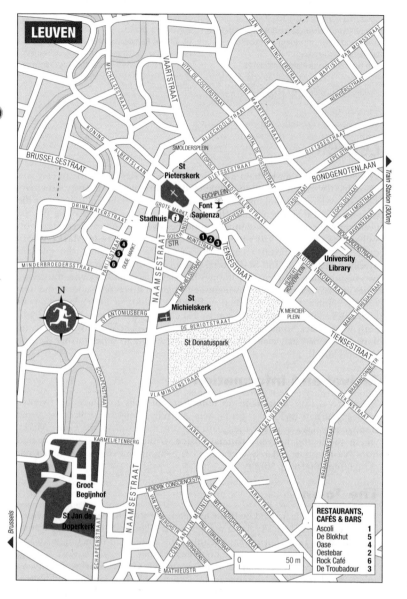

LEUVEN

St Pieterskerk

Font Sapienza

Stadhuis

University Library

St Michielskerk

St Donatuspark

Groot Begijnhof

St Jan de Doperkerk

◀ Train Station (300m)

◀ Brussels

RESTAURANTS, CAFÉS & BARS	
Ascoli	1
De Blokhut	5
Oase	4
Oestebar	2
Rock Café	6
De Troubadour	3

institutions. Until then, the lavishly carved niches stood empty for lack of money. In contrast, the niche bases are exuberantly medieval, depicting biblical subjects in a free, colloquial style and adorned by a panoply of grotesques. The **inside** of the Stadhuis is something of an anticlimax by comparison; guided **tours**, which run from the Naamsestraat tourist office (April–Sept Mon–Fri at 11am & 3pm, Sat & Sun at 3pm; Oct–March daily at

3pm; €2), amble through just a handful of rooms, including overblown salons in the high French style and a neo-Gothic council chamber.

St-Pieterskerk

Across from the Stadhuis, **St-Pieterskerk** (mid-March to mid-Oct Mon–Fri 10am–5pm, Sat 10am–4.30pm & Sun 2–5pm; mid-Oct to mid-March closed Mon; free) is a rambling, heavily buttressed late Gothic pile whose stumpy western facade defeated its architects. Work began on the present church in the 1420s and continued until the start of the sixteenth century when the Roman-esque towers of the west facade, the last remaining part of its predecessor, were pulled down to make way for a grand design by Joos Matsys, the brother of the painter Quentin. It didn't work out – the foundations proved too weak – and finally, another hundred years on, the unfinished second-attempt towers were capped, creating the truncated, asymmetrical versions that rise above the entrance today.

Inside, the church is distinguished by its soaring nave whose enormous pillars frame a fabulous **rood screen**, an intricately carved piece of stonework surmounted by a wooden Christ. The nave's Baroque **pulpit** is also striking – a weighty wooden extravagance which shows St Norbert being thrown off his horse by lightning, a dramatic scene set beneath spiky palm trees. It was this brush with death that persuaded Norbert, a twelfth-century German noble, to abandon his worldly ways and dedicate himself to the Church, on whose behalf he founded a devout religious order, the Premonstratensian Canons, in 1120.

The Schatkamer of St-Pieterskerk

The ambulatory of St-Pieterskerk accommodates the church's **Schatkamer** or **Treasury** (Mon–Fri 10am–5pm, Sat 10am–4.30pm, Sun 2–5pm, mid-March to mid-Oct closed Mon; €2.50), accessible from the Grote Markt, whose three key paintings date from the fifteenth century. There's a copy of Rogier van der Weyden's marvellous triptych, the *Descent from the Cross*, the original of which is now at the Prado in Madrid, and two of the few surviving paintings by Weyden's apprentice **Dieric Bouts** (c.1415–75), who worked for most of his life in Leuven, ultimately becoming the city's official painter. Of the two triptychs on display here, first up is the *Last Supper*, showing Christ and his disciples in a Flemish dining room, with the (half-built) Stadhuis just visible through the left-hand window; the two men standing up and the couple peeping through the service hatch are the rectors of the fraternity who commissioned the work. Dressed in a purple robe, the colour reserved for royalty, Jesus is depicted as taller than his disciples. It was customary for Judas to be portrayed in a yellow robe, the colour of hatred and cowardice, but Bouts broke with tradition and made him almost indistinguishable from the others – he's the one with his face in shadow and his hand on his left hip. In the next chapel along you'll find the second of Bouts' triptychs, the gruesome *Martyrdom of St Erasmus*, which depicts the executioner extracting the saint's entrails with a winch, watched by seemingly regretful court officials.

The University, Oude Markt and Groot Begijnhof

Naamsestraat leads south from the Grote Markt, past the original Gothic **University** building on the right, originally the town's cloth hall, but home to the university since 1432, into the boisterous core of Leuven's student scene, at the centre of which is the **Oude Markt** – a large cobblestoned square surrounded by a fetching ensemble of tall gabled houses that now house some of the liveliest bars in the region. On Naamsestraat itself is the florid Baroque facade of the Jesuit **St-Michielskerk**, restored after wartime damage, but the real prize in this part of town is the wonderfully preserved **Groot Begijnhof** further down Naamsestraat on the right, a labyrinthine sixteenth-century enclave of tall and austere red-brick houses, which was once home to around

▲ Oude Markt, Leuven

three hundred *begijns* – women living as nuns but without taking vows. The Begijnhof was bought by the university in 1962, since when its buildings have been painstakingly restored as student residences. Its cobbled lanes and iron bridges over the bubbling river are truly delightful, and it's rightly been declared a UNESCO world heritage site. You can wander around the complex to your heart's content, but you can't enter any buildings, apart from the fourteenth-century Gothic St-Jan de Doperkerk, whose whitewashed interior is worth a look.

Eating and drinking

The student presence in Leuven means that there is no shortage of cheap **places to eat**, but you have to search carefully to find anywhere halfway decent. Muntstraat, just southeast of the Grote Markt, has a reasonable concentration of cafés and restaurants: *Ascoli* at Muntstraat 17 (☎016 23 93 64; closed Thurs), is a Franco-Italian restaurant with a large and ambitious menu (mains from €13); the *Oesterbar* at no.23 (☎016 20 290 600; closed Sun, Wed & Thurs) is a gourmet restaurant offering what many consider to be the best seafood in town; and the smart and well-appointed, Franco-Belgian *De Troubadour*, next door but one to the *Oesterbar* but with a main entrance at Tiensestraat 32 (☎016 22 50 65; closed Tues all day & Wed lunch time), is especially good for grilled meat and fish, with mains around €18. It also has a small, more informal café and takeaway next door on Tiensestraat that does mussels, pizzas and pasta dishes.

As a university town, Leuven is chock-a-block with lively student **bars**. The best selection – and setting – is down on the Oude Markt, where almost all of the old gabled houses have been turned into drinking holes, most of them offering happy hours and cheap drinks. The best tactic is to wander around until you find somewhere whose decor or music takes your fancy, though in warm weather you'll probably want to join the sea of people sitting out on the square itself. Three good options are *Oase*, in the corner of the square at Oude Markt 53, *De Blokhut* at no. 49, and the *Rock Café* at no. 32, which has live music on Saturdays, and the town's pick of cheap cocktails and drinks deals.

Ghent

Just thirty minutes by train from Brussels, Flemish-speaking **GHENT** is Belgium's third-largest city, a thriving, busy metropolis with an amiable atmosphere, a lively restaurant and bar scene, and an outstanding assortment of medieval buildings. The pick of them is **St-Baafskathedraal**, a handsome Gothic structure which holds one of Europe's most remarkable paintings, the *Adoration of the Mystic Lamb* by Jan van Eyck. Close rivals include an especially dour and surly castle, **Het Gravensteen**, and the late medieval guildhouses of the Graslei quay. Also worth a visit are **S.M.A.K.**, one of the country's finest contemporary art museums, and the **Museum voor Schone Kunsten** (Fine Art Museum). Nonetheless, it is perhaps the general appearance of the city centre that appeals rather than any specific sight, its web of cobbled lanes and alleys overlooked by an enchanting medley of antique terraces and grand mansions, all woven round a tangle of canals.

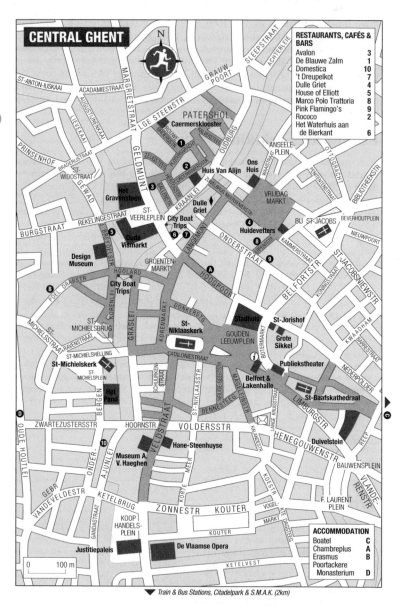

CENTRAL GHENT

RESTAURANTS, CAFÉS & BARS

Avalon	3
De Blauwe Zalm	1
Domestica	10
't Dreupelkot	7
Dulle Griet	4
House of Elliott	5
Marco Polo Trattoria	8
Pink Flamingo's	9
Rococo	2
Het Waterhuis aan de Bierkant	6

ACCOMMODATION

Boatel	C
Chambreplus	A
Erasmus	B
Poortackere Monasterium	D

Train & Bus Stations, Citadelpark & S.M.A.K. (2km)

Arrival, information and accommodation

Trains from Brussels pull into **Ghent St Pieters train station**, which adjoins the **bus station**, some 2km south of the city centre. From the west side of the train station, **tram #1** runs every few minutes to the Korenmarkt, right in the city centre, passing along Kortrijksepoortstraat and Nederkouter. All trams have destination signs and numbers at the front, but if in doubt check with the driver, from whom you can buy your ticket.

Ghent's **tourist office** is right in the centre of the city, in the crypt of the Lakenhalle (daily: April–Oct 9.30am–6.30pm; Nov–March 9.30am–4.30pm; ☎09 266 56 60, ⓦwww.visitgent.be). They dispense a wide range of free city information, including maps and a detailed city guide. The tourist office will make **hotel and B&B reservations** on your behalf at no charge, though they do require a small deposit, which is deducted from the final bill. They also publish a free brochure detailing local accommodation, including hotels and hostels (but not B&Bs), as well as a separate *Bed & Breakfast* leaflet – or check out ⓦwww.bedandbreakfast-gent.be.

Hotels and B&Bs

Boatel Voorhuitkaai 44 ☎09 267 10 30, ⓦwww.theboatel.com. Arguably the most distinctive of the city's hotels, the two-star *Boatel* is, as its name implies, a converted boat – an immaculately refurbished canal barge to be precise. It's moored in one of the city's outer canals, a 10–15min walk east of the centre. The seven bedrooms are stylish and modern, and breakfasts, taken on the poop deck, are first rate. €115.

Chambreplus Hoogpoort 31 ☎09 225 37 75, ⓦwww.chambreplus.be. Charming B&B with three cosy, a/c guest rooms – one decked out like a sultan's room, another the Congo, with the third occupying a self-contained mini-house at the back of the garden. Breakfasts are delicious – as are the home-made chocolates. Unbeatable central location too. €85.

Erasmus Poel 25 ☎09 224 21 95, ⓦwww .erasmushotel.be. A friendly, family-run affair located in an old town house just steps from the Korenlei. Each room has personal touches and is furnished with antiques. Reservations strongly advised in summer. €100–120.

Poortackere Monasterium Oude Houtlei 56 ☎09 269 22 10, ⓦwww.monasterium.be. This unusual hotel-cum-guesthouse, a five-minute walk west of Veldstraat, occupies a rambling and somewhat spartan former monastery dating from the nineteenth century. Guests have a choice between standard en-suite rooms in the hotel, or the more authentic monastic-cell experience in the guesthouse, where some rooms have shared facilities. Breakfast is taken in the old chapterhouse. Hotel doubles from €115; guesthouse singles €60.

The City

The shape and structure of Ghent's city centre reflects ancient class and linguistic divides. The streets to the south of the Korenmarkt, the former

Walking tours and boat trips

Guided **walking tours** are particularly popular in Ghent. The standard walking tour, organized by the tourist office, is a two-hour jaunt round the city centre (Nov–April Sat at 2.30pm, May–Oct daily at 2.30pm; €7); advance booking – at least a few hours ahead of time – is strongly recommended. Alternatively, **horse-drawn carriages** line up outside the Lakenhalle, on St Baafsplein, offering a thirty-minute canter round town for €25 (April–Oct daily 10am–6pm & most winter weekends).

Throughout the year, **boat trips** explore Ghent's inner waterways, departing from the Korenlei and Graslei quays, just near the Korenmarkt, as well as from the Vleeshuis-brug, metres from the Groentenmarkt (March to mid-Nov daily 10am–6pm, mid-Nov to Feb Sat & Sun 11am–4pm; €6). Trips last forty minutes and leave roughly every fifteen minutes, though the wait can be longer as boats often only leave when reasonably full.

▲ Bruges

Corn Market, tend to be straight, wide and lined with elegant old mansions, the former habitations of the wealthier, French-speaking classes, while, to the north, Flemish Ghent is all narrow alleys and low brick houses. They meet at the somewhat confusing sequence of large squares that surrounds the town's principal buildings, spreading out to the immediate east of the Koren-markt, from where most of Ghent's leading attractions are within easy walking distance.

St-Baafskathedraal

The best place to start an exploration of the city is **St-Baafskathedraal** (St Bavo's Cathedral; April–Oct Mon–Sat 8.30am–6pm, Sun 1–6pm; Nov–March Mon–Sat 8.30am–5pm, Sun 1–5pm; free), squeezed into the eastern corner of a tapering square, St-Baafsplein. The third church to be built on this site, and 250 years in the making, the cathedral is a tad lopsided, but there's no denying the imposing beauty of its west tower with its long, elegant windows and perky corner turrets. Some 82m high, the tower was the last major part of the church to be completed, topped off in 1554 – just before the outbreak of the religious wars which were to wrack the country for the next hundred years. Inside, the mighty fifteenth-century nave is supported by tall, slender columns, which give the whole interior a cheerful sense of lightness, though the Baroque marble screen spoils the effect by darkening the choir.

In a small side chapel (April–Oct Mon–Sat 9.30am–5pm, Sun 1–5pm; Nov–March Mon–Sat 10.30am–4pm, Sun 1–4pm; €3) to the left of the cathedral entrance is Ghent's greatest treasure, Jan van Eyck's **Adoration of the Mystic Lamb**. The altarpiece's cover screens display a beautiful Annunciation scene with the archangel Gabriel's wings reaching up to the timbered ceiling of a Flemish house, while below, the donor and his wife kneel piously alongside statues of the saints. The restrained exterior painting is, however, merely a foretaste of what's within – a striking, visionary work of art that would have been revealed only when the shutters were opened on Sundays and feast days. On the upper level sit God the Father, the Virgin and John the Baptist in gleaming clarity; to the right are musician-angels and a nude, pregnant Eve; and on the left is Adam plus a group of singing angels, who strain to read their music. In the lower panel, the Lamb, the symbol of Christ's sacrifice, is approached by bishops, saintly virgins and Old and New Testament figures in a heavenly paradise seen as a sort of idealized Low Countries.

The Lakenhalle and Belfort

Across from the cathedral, on the west side of St-Baafsplein, lurks the **Laken-halle** (Cloth Hall), a dour hunk of a building with an unhappy history. Work began on the hall in the early fifteenth century, but the cloth trade slumped before it was finished and it was only grudgingly completed in 1903. Since then, no one has ever quite worked out what to do with the building, and today it's little more than an empty shell with the city's tourist office tucked away in the basement on the north side.

The first-floor entrance on the south side of the Lakenhalle is the only way to reach the adjoining **Belfort** (Belfry; mid-March to mid-Nov daily 10am–6pm; €3), a much-amended medieval edifice whose soaring spire is topped by a comically corpulent, gilded copper dragon. Once a watchtower-cum-store-house for civic documents, the interior is now almost empty, displaying a few old bells and statues alongside the rusting remains of a couple of old dragons, which formerly perched on top of the spire. The belfry is equipped with a glass-sided lift that climbs up to the roof, where consolation is provided in the form of excellent views over the city centre.

The Stadhuis

Stretching along the west side of the Botermarkt, just to the north of the Lakenhalle, is the striking **Stadhuis** (City Hall), whose main facade comprises two distinct sections. The later section, framing the central stairway, dates from the 1580s and offers a good example of Italian Renaissance architecture, its crisp symmetries faced by a multitude of black-painted columns. In stark contrast are the wild, curling patterns of the section to the immediate north, carved in Flamboyant Gothic style at the turn of the sixteenth century to a design by one of the era's most celebrated architects, **Rombout Keldermans** (1460–1531). The whole of the Stadhuis was originally to have been built by Keldermans, but the money ran out when the wool trade collapsed and the city couldn't afford to finish it off until much later – hence today's discordant facade.

Inside the Stadhuis, **guided tours** (May–Oct Mon–Thurs daily at 2.30pm as the first 45min of the 2hr walking tour organized by the tourist office, see p.163; full 2hr tour €7, Stadhuis only €4) take in a series of halls and chambers, the most interesting being the old Court of Justice or **Pacificatiezaal** (Pacifica-tion Hall), where the Pacification of Ghent treaty was signed in 1576. A plaque commemorates this agreement, which momentarily bound the rebel armies of the Low Countries (today's Belgium and The Netherlands) together against their rulers, the Spanish Habsburgs. The carrot offered by the dominant Protes-tants was the promise of religious freedom, but they failed to deliver and much of the south (present-day Belgium) soon returned to the Spanish fold.

St-Niklaaskerk

Back down the slope from the Stadhuis is the last of this central cluster of buildings, **St-Niklaaskerk** (Mon 2.30–5pm; Tues–Sun 10am–5pm; free), an architectural hybrid dating from the thirteenth century. It's the shape and structure that pleases most, especially the arching buttresses and pencil-thin turrets which, in a classic example of the early Scheldt Gothic style, elegantly attenuate the lines of the nave. Inside, many of the original Baroque furnishings and fittings have been removed and the windows un-bricked, thus returning the church to its early appearance, though unfortunately this does not apply to a clumsy and clichéd set of statues of the apostles. Much better is the giant-sized Baroque **high altar** with its mammoth representation of God glowering down its back, blowing the hot wind of the Last Judgement from his mouth and surrounded by a flock of cherubic angels. The church is sometimes used for temporary art exhibitions, which sometimes charge an admission fee.

The Korenmarkt and St-Michielsbrug

St-Niklaaskerk marks the southern end of the **Korenmarkt** (Corn Market), a long and wide cobbled area where the grain which once kept the city fed was traded after it was unloaded from the boats that anchored on the Graslei dock (see below). The one noteworthy building here is the former **post office**, whose combination of Gothic Revival and neo-Renaissance styles illustrates the eclecticism popular in Belgium at the beginning of the twentieth century. The interior has been turned into a shopping mall.

Behind the post office, the neo-Gothic **St-Michielsbrug** (St Michael's bridge) offers fine views back over the towers and turrets that pierce the Ghent skyline – just as it was meant to: the bridge was built in 1913 to provide visitors with a vantage point from which to admire the city centre. The bridge also overlooks the city's oldest harbour, the **Tussen Bruggen** (Between the Bridges), from whose quays – the **Korenlei** and the **Graslei** – boats leave for trips around the city's canals (see box, p.163).

The guildhouses of the Graslei

Ghent's boatmen and grain-weighers were crucial to the functioning of the medieval city, and they built a row of splendid **guildhouses** along **Graslei**, each gable decorated with an appropriate sign or symbol. Working your way north from St Michielsbrug, the first building of distinction is the **Gildehuis van de Vrije Schippers** (Guildhouse of the Free Boatmen), at no. 14, where the badly weathered sandstone is decorated with scenes of boatmen weighing anchor, plus a delicate carving of a caravel – the type of Mediterranean sailing ship used by Columbus – located above the door. Medieval Ghent had two boatmen guilds: the Free, who could discharge their cargoes within the city, and the Unfree, who could not. The Unfree Boatmen were obliged to unload their goods into the vessels of the Free Boatmen at the edge of the city – an inefficient arrangement by any standards, though typical of the complex regulations governing the guilds.

Next door, at Graslei 12–13, the seventeenth-century **Cooremetershuys** (Corn Measurers' House) was where city officials weighed and graded corn behind a facade graced by cartouches and garlands of fruit. Next to this, at no. 11, stands the quaint **Tolhuisje**, another delightful example of Flemish Renaissance architecture, built to house the customs officers in 1698, while the adjacent limestone **Spijker** (Staple House), at no. 10, boasts a surly Romanesque facade dating from around 1200. It was here that the city stored its grain supply for over five hundred years until a fire gutted the interior. Finally, three doors down at no. 8, the splendid **Den Enghel** takes its name from the angel bearing a banner that decorates the facade; the building was originally the stonemasons' guildhouse, as evidenced by the effigies of the four Roman martyrs who were the guild's patron saints, though they are depicted here in medieval attire, not togas and sandals.

Het Gravensteen

From the north end of Graslei, it's a couple of minutes' walk to **Het Gravensteen** (daily: April–Sept 9am–5 or 6pm; Oct–March 9am–4 or 5pm; €6), the castle of the Counts of Flanders, which looks sinister enough to have been lifted from a Bosch painting. Its cold, dark walls and unyielding turrets were first built in 1180 as much to intimidate the town's unruly citizens as to protect them and, considering the castle has been used for all sorts of purposes since then (it was even used as a cotton mill), it has survived in remarkably good nick. The imposing **gateway** comprises a deep-arched, heavily fortified tunnel leading to the **courtyard**, which is framed by protective battlements complete with wooden flaps, ancient arrow slits and apertures for boiling oil and water.

Overlooking the courtyard stand the castle's two main buildings: the **count's residence** on the left and the **keep** on the right, the latter riddled with narrow, interconnected staircases set within the thickness of the walls. A self-guided tour takes you through this labyrinth, the first highlight being a room full of medieval military hardware, from suits of armour, pikes, swords and daggers through to an exquisitely crafted sixteenth-century crossbow. Beyond is a gruesome collection of instruments of torture; the count's cavernous state rooms; and a particularly dank underground dungeon (*oubliette*). It's also possible to walk along most of the castle's encircling wall, from where there are lovely views over the city centre.

The Patershol

Just east of the castle are the lanes and alleys of the **Patershol**, a tight web of brick terraced houses dating from the seventeenth century. Once the heart of the Flemish working-class city, this thriving residential quarter had, by the 1970s, become a slum threatened with demolition. After much to-ing and fro-ing, the area was saved from the developers and a process of gentrification began, the result being today's gaggle of good bars and excellent restaurants. The process is still underway and the fringes of the Patershol remain a ragbag of decay and restoration, but few Belgian cities can boast a more agreeable restaurant and bar district. One specific sight is the grand old Carmelite Monastery on Vrouwebroersstraat, now the **Provinciaal Cultuurcentrum Caermerskloosster** (☎09 269 29 10, ⓦwww.caermersklooster.be), which showcases temporary exhibitions of contemporary art, photography, design and fashion.

Vrijdagmarkt and Bij St-Jacobs

From the Patershol, it's the briefest of strolls to the **Vrijdagmarkt**, a wide and open square that was long the political centre of Ghent, the site of both public meetings and executions – and sometimes both at the same time. Of the buildings flanking the Vrijdagmarkt, the most appealing is the old headquarters of the trade unions, the whopping **Ons Huis** (Our House), a sterling edifice built in eclectic style at the turn of the twentieth century. Adjoining the Vrijdagmarkt is busy **Bij St-Jacobs**, a sprawling square dotted with antique shops and set around a bruised and battered medieval church. The square hosts the city's biggest and best flea market (*prondelmarkt*) on Fridays, Saturdays and Sundays from 8am to 1pm.

From Bij St-Jacobs, it's about a five-minute walk back to the Korenmarkt.

South of the centre

Veldstraat leads south from the Korenmarkt, running parallel to the River Leie. By and large, it's a very ordinary shopping strip, but the eighteenth-century mansion at no. 82 does hold the modest **Museum Arnold Vander Haeghen** (Mon–Fri 9am–noon & 2–5pm; free), where pride of place goes to the Chinese salon, whose original silk wallpaper has survived intact. Pushing on down Veldstraat, it's a couple of minutes more to a matching pair of grand, Neoclassical nineteenth-century buildings. On the right hand side is the **Justitiepaleis** (Palace of Justice), whose colossal pediment sports a frieze with the figure of Justice in the middle, the accused to one side and the condemned on the other. Opposite stands the recently restored **opera house** – home to De Vlaamse Opera – its facade awash with playfully decorative stone panels.

From the opera house, it's an easy, if dull, ten-minute stroll south to S.M.A.K. and the Museum voor Schone Kunsten via Veldstraat and its continuation Nederkouter, but it's better – and doesn't take much longer – to get there along the banks of the River Leie: turn off Nederkouter at Verlorenkost and then – with the Coupure canal and its dinky swing bridge dead ahead – hang a left along the river.

Citadelpark and S.M.A.K.

Citadelpark, just to the east of Kortrijksepoortstraat, takes its name from the fortress that stood here until the 1870s, when the land was cleared and pretti-fied with a network of leafy footpaths that steer their way past grottoes and ponds, statues and fountains, a waterfall and a bandstand. Later, in the 1940s, a large brick complex was built on the east side of the park and, after many incarnations, part of this now houses **S.M.A.K.** (Municipal Museum of Contemporary Art; Tues–Sun 10am–6pm; €6; ⓦwww.smak.be), one of Belgium's most adventurous modern art galleries. The museum is given over to temporary displays of international standing, and recent exhibitions have displayed the works of Anton Henning and Kendell Geers. These exhibitions are supplemented by a regularly rotated selection of sculptures, paintings and installations distilled from the museum's wide-ranging permanent collection. S.M.A.K has examples of all the major artistic movements since World War II – everything the CoBrA group and Pop Art through to Minimalism and Conceptual Art – as well as their forerunners, most notably René Magritte and Paul Delvaux.

Museum voor Schone Kunsten

Directly opposite S.M.A.K., the recently upgraded **Museum voor Schone Kunsten** (Fine Art Museum; Tues–Sun 10am–6pm; €5; ⓦwww.mskgent.be)

STAM

Founded in the thirteenth century, the old Cistercian **Bijlokeabdij** (Bijloke Abbey) on Godshuizenlaan, just to the west of the River Leie, was savaged by Calvinists on several occasions, but much of the medieval complex has survived, its tidy brown-brick buildings set behind a handsome Baroque portal. The abbey is currently closed to visitors as part of a major redevelopment, which will create **STAM** (ⓦwww.stamgent.be), a museum devoted to the city's heritage. The surrounding grounds are being redeveloped too, with the creation of a concert hall, studios and an academy. The work is scheduled for completion in 2012.

occupies an imposing Neoclassical edifice on the edge of Citadelpark. Inside, the central atrium and connecting rotunda are flanked by a sequence of rooms, with the older paintings exhibited to the right in Rooms 1–8, the bulk of the eighteenth- and nineteenth-century material in Rooms 13–19, and the early twentieth-century works mostly on the left in Rooms A–K. There's not enough space to display all the permanent collection at any one time, so there's some rotation, but **highlights** of the collection include paintings by Rogier van der Weyden, Hieronymus Bosch, Anthony van Dyck, Jacob Jordaens, and an especially powerful *St Francis* by Rubens. There are also two harrowing studies by Ostend's Leon Spilliaert and, among a wide selection of works by James Ensor, his famous *Self-Portrait with Flower Hat*.

Eating and drinking

Ghent's numerous **restaurants and cafés** offer the very best of Flemish and French cuisines with a sprinkling of Italian, Chinese and Arab places for variety. There is a concentration of deluxe restaurants in and around the narrow lanes of the Patershol and another, with less expensive options, on and around the Korenmarkt. Ghent also has a first-rate range of **bars**, from old-world drinking dens with nicotine-stained ceilings through to slick, modern places with slick furnishings.

Restaurants and cafés

Avalon Geldmunt 32 ☎09 224 37 24. The key draw at this vegetarian restaurant is the daily lunch time specials, which cost about €9. Eat at one of the many rooms inside or on the terrace out back in the summer. Mon–Thurs 11.30am–2.30pm, Fri & Sat 11.30am–2.30pm & 6–9pm.

De Blauwe Zalm Vrouwebroersstraat 2 ☎09 224 08 52. This outstanding seafood restaurant is the best in town, serving up everything from cod, salmon, monkfish and haddock through to anemone, sea bass, turbot and John Dory. The decor, with fish tanks for the crustacea, has a distinctly maritime feel – though it's all done in impeccably cool style. Main courses from €20. Reservations recommended. Mon & Sat 7–9.30pm, Tues–Fri noon–2pm & 7–9.30pm.

Domestica Onderbergen 27 ☎09 223 53 00. Smart and chic brasserie-restaurant serving up an excellent range of nouvelle Belgian dishes – both French and Flemish – with main courses from €20. There's a garden terrace too. Mon & Sat 6.30–10.30pm, Tues–Fri noon-2.30pm & 6.30–10.30pm.

House of Eliott Jan Breydelstraat 36 ☎09 225 21 28. Idiosyncratic, spilt-level restaurant strewn with Edwardian bric-a-brac and offering a limited, but well-chosen menu of meat and fish dishes, with mains at €20–25 – all freshly prepared and very tasty. The window tables overlook a canal and

you can eat on the pontoon at the back in fine weather. Mon & Thurs–Sun noon–2pm & 6–10pm.

Marco Polo Trattoria Serpentstraat 11 ☎09 225 04 20. This simple, rustic restaurant is part of the Italian "slow food" movement, in which the emphasis is on organic, seasonal ingredients prepared in a traditional manner. The menu is small, but all the dishes are freshly prepared and delicious. Mains from €13. Tues–Fri noon–2.30pm & 6–10pm, Sat & Sun 6–10pm.

Bars

't Dreupelkot Groentenmarkt 12. Cosy bar specializing in jenever (Belgian gin), of which it stocks more than 215 brands, all kept at icy temperatures – the vanilla flavour is particularly delicious. It's down a little alley leading off the Groentenmarkt – and next door to Het Waterhuis (see p.170). Daily: July & Aug from 6pm until late; Sept–June from 4pm until late.

Dulle Griet Vrijdagmarkt 50. Long, dark and atmospheric bar with all manner of incidental *objets d'art* – and an especially wide range of beers. Mon 4.30pm–1am, Tues–Sat noon–1am & Sun noon–7.30pm.

Pink Flamingo's Onderstraat 55, ☎09 233 47 18, ⓦwww.pinkflamingos.be. The interior of this weird and wonderful place is the height of kitsch, with plastic statues of film stars, tacky religious icons and Barbie dolls. Its great aperitifs and cocktails draw a trendy crowd. Mon–Wed noon–midnight, Thurs & Fri noon–3am, Sat 2pm–3am, Sun 2pm–midnight.

Rococo Corduwaniersstraat 57. This intimate café-bar attracts a cool, diverse clientele and is a perfect place to relax on a cold winter evening, with candles flickering and the fire roaring. Stocks a good range of wines and beers, as well as home-made cakes. Tues–Sun from 10pm until late.

Het Waterhuis aan de Bierkant
Groentenmarkt 9. More than a hundred types of beer are available in this engaging, canalside bar, popular with tourists and locals alike. Stropken (literally "noose") is a delicious local brew named after the time in 1453 when Philip the Good compelled the rebellious city burghers to parade outside the town gate with ropes around their necks. Daily from 11am until late.

Bruges

BRUGES is one of the most beautifully preserved medieval – or, in parts at least, ersatz medieval – cities in western Europe and it draws visitors in their thousands. Inevitably, the crowds tend to overwhelm the town's charms, but as a day-trip destination from Brussels – it's just an hour away by train – Bruges is hard to resist: its museums hold some of the country's finest collections of Flemish art and its intimate streets, woven around a pattern of narrow canals, live up to even the most inflated tourist hype. Indeed, many visitors choose to spend several days here rather than day-tripping in from Brussels – if you plan to do the same, you may want to take a look at the Rough Guides' *Bruges Directions* before you go.

Bruges came to prominence in the thirteenth century when it shared effective control of the cloth trade with its great rival, Ghent (see pp.161–170), turning high-quality English wool into clothing that was exported all over the known world. It was an immensely profitable business, and it made the city a centre of international trade. By the end of the fifteenth century, however, Bruges was in decline, principally because the River Zwin – the city's vital link to the North Sea – was silting up. By the 1530s, the town's sea trade had collapsed completely, and Bruges simply withered away. Frozen in time, Bruges escaped damage in both world wars to emerge the perfect tourist attraction.

Arrival and information

Bruges' train station adjoins the bus station, 2km southwest of the town centre. If the twenty-minute walk into the centre doesn't appeal, you can get a local bus from outside the train station: most head off either to the Biekorf or the neighbouring Markt, right in the centre of town; the single fare costs €1.50 from the driver, €1.20 in advance from the De Lijn information kiosk outside the train station.

There is a **tourist information desk** (Tues–Sat 9.30am–12.30pm & 1–5pm) at the train station, but this is a very modest affair compared with the main **tourist office**, in the Concertgebouw (Concert Hall) complex, on the west side of the city centre on 't Zand (Fri–Wed 10am–6pm, Thurs 10am–8pm; ☎050 44 46 46, ⊛www.brugge.be). The latter offers an **accommodation-booking service**, which is free, though you do have to pay a small deposit, which is deducted from the final bill. Buses from the train station usually pause on 't Zand on their way to the Markt.

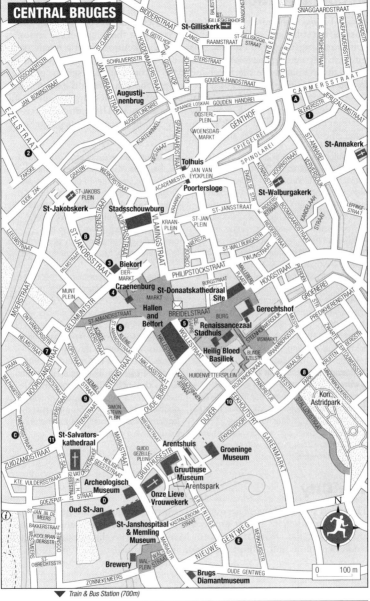

CENTRAL BRUGES

Train & Bus Station (700m)

ACCOMMODATION		RESTAURANTS, CAFÉS & BARS					
Adornes	A	De Belegde Boterham	6	Den Dyver	10	Oud Vlissinghe	1
Alegria	B	Het Brugs Beertje	9	L'Estaminet	8	Wijnbar Est	7
De Goezeput	D	Cafedraal	11	De Garre	5	In den	
Montanus	E	Café de Medici	4	Kok au Vin	2	Wittekop	3
Passage hotel & hostel	C						

Accommodation

Bruges has over a hundred **hotels**, dozens of **B&Bs** and several unofficial **youth hostels**, but still can't accommodate all its visitors at the height of the season. If you're arriving in July or August, be sure to book ahead or, at a pinch, make sure you get here in the morning before all the rooms have gone. Given the crush, many visitors use the hotel and B&B accommodation service provided by the tourist office (see p.170) – it's efficient and can save you endless hassle. At other times of the year, things are usually much less pressing, though it's still a good idea to reserve ahead, especially if you are picky. The tourist office issues a free **accommodation booklet** providing comprehensive listings including hotel photographs, websites and a city map.

Adornes St Annarei 26 ☏ 050 34 13 36, ⓦ www.adornes.be. Set in a tastefully converted old Flemish town-house, with a plain, high-gabled facade, at the junction of two canals near the east end of Spiegelrei. Both the public areas and the comfortable bedrooms are decorated in clean neutrals, which emphasize the antique charm of the place. The breakfasts are delicious and the hotel is very child-friendly. €110–140.

Alegria Sint Jakobsstraat 34 ☏ 050 33 09 37, ⓦ www.alegria-hotel.com. Formerly a B&B, this appealing, family-run hotel has just six well-appointed rooms, each decorated in fresh, pared-down pastels. The rooms at the back overlooking the garden are the quietest, and it's just a brief stroll from the Markt. Doubles €90.

De Goezeput Goezeputstraat 29 ☏ 050 34 26 94, ⓦ www.hotelgoezeput.be. Set in a charming location on a quiet street near the cathedral, this outstanding hotel occupies an immaculately refurbished eighteenth-century convent, complete with wooden beams and oodles of antiques. A snip, with en-suite doubles from €80.

Montanus Nieuwe Gentweg 78 ☏ 050 33 11 76, ⓦ www.montanus.be. Smart hotel in a substantial seventeenth-century mansion, elegantly furnished – although most of the rooms are at the back, in chalet-style accommodation at the far end of an attractive garden. There's also an especially appealing room in what amounts to a (particularly luxurious) garden shed. From €135.

Passage Hostel Dweersstraat 26 ☏ 050 34 02 32, ⓦ www.passagebruges.com. The most agreeable hostel in Bruges, accommodating fifty people in ten dormitories, all with shared bathrooms. The location – in an old and interesting part of town, about ten minutes' walk west of the Markt – is a bonus. Rates from €14 for a dorm bed; breakfast €5 extra. The hostel is attached to a budget hotel – the *Passage Hotel* (same contact details) – where en-suite doubles cost just €65, €50 with shared facilities. There's a busy bar too, serving inexpensive meals.

The City

The oldest part of Bruges fans out from two central squares, the Markt and the Burg. From either, it's a short stroll south to the city's premier museums, which line up along the Dijver and adjacent Mariastraat, with the impossibly picturesque Begijnhof and Minnewater beckoning beyond.

The Markt

The larger of the Bruges' two central squares is the **Markt**, an expansive open area edged on three sides by nineteenth-century gabled buildings and on the south side by the city's most famous edifice, the **Belfort** (Belfry; daily 9.30am–5pm; €5), which was built in the thirteenth century when the town was at its richest. Inside, the belfry staircase passes the room where the town charters

Half-hour **boat trips** around the city's central canals leave from a number of jetties south of the Burg (March–Nov daily 10am–6pm; €6.50). Boats depart every few minutes, but long queues still build up during high season, with few visitors seemingly concerned by the canned commentary. In wintertime (Dec–Feb), there's a spasmodic service at weekends only.

were locked for safekeeping, and an eighteenth-century carillon, before emerging onto the roof, from where there are wonderful views over the city centre. At the foot of the belfry, the quadrangular **Hallen** is a much-restored edifice dating from the thirteenth century, its arcaded galleries built to facilitate the cloth trade.

The Burg

From the Markt, Breidelstraat leads through to the **Burg**, whose southern half is fringed by the city's finest group of buildings. One of the best of these is the **Heilig Bloed Basiliek** (Basilica of the Holy Blood; April–Sept daily 9.30–11.50am & 2–5.50pm; Oct–March Mon, Tues & Thurs–Sun 10–11.50am & 2–3.50pm, Wed 10–11.50am; free), named after the holy relic that found its way here in 1150. The basilica divides into two parts. Tucked away in the corner, the **lower chapel** is a shadowy, crypt-like affair, originally built at the beginning of the twelfth century to shelter another relic, that of St Basil, one of the great figures of the early Greek Church. Next door, approached up a wide staircase, the **upper chapel** was built at the same time, but it's impossible to make out the original structure behind the excessive nineteenth-century decoration. The phial containing the Holy Blood is stored here, within a magnificent silver **tabernacle**, the gift of the Habsburg governors Albert and Isabella of Spain in 1611. One of the holiest relics in medieval

▲ Bruges' canals

Europe, the phial supposedly contains a few drops of blood and water washed from the body of Christ by Joseph of Arimathea. The Holy Blood is still venerated in the upper chapel on Fridays, and reverence for it remains strong, not least on Ascension Day when it is carried through the town in a colourful but solemn procession.

To the left of the basilica, the **Stadhuis** (town hall) is graced by a beautiful, turreted sandstone facade from 1376, though its statues of the counts and countesses of Flanders are much more recent. Inside, the magnificent **Gothic Hall** (daily 9.30am–5pm; €2.50) boasts fancy vault-keys depicting New Testament scenes and romantic paintings commissioned in 1895 to illustrate the history of the town.

The Groeninge Museum

From the arch beside the Stadhuis, Blinde Ezelstraat ("Blind Donkey Street") leads south across the canal to the huddle of picturesque houses crimping the **Huidenvettersplein**, the old tanners' quarter that now holds some of the busiest drinking and eating places in town. Nearby, Dijver follows the canal to the **Groeninge Museum**, Dijver 12 (Tues–Sun 9.30am–5pm; €8), which boasts an outstanding collection of early Flemish paintings. Among them are several works by Jan van Eyck, who lived and worked in Bruges from 1430 until his death eleven years later. Featured also are works by Rogier van der Weyden, Hugo van der Goes, Hans Memling, Gerard David and Hieronymus Bosch, whose paintings are crammed with mysterious beasts, microscopic mutants and scenes of awful cruelty. The museum's selection of late sixteenth- and seventeenth-century paintings is far more modest, though highlights here include canvases by Pieter Bruegel the Younger and Pieter Pourbus. The modern paintings are distinguished by the spooky Surrealism of Paul Delvaux and by Constant Permeke, noted for his dark and earthy representations of Belgian peasant life.

The Arentshuis and Gruuthuse museums

Also on the Dijver, in a big old mansion just west of the Groeninge, is the **Arentshuis Museum** (Tues–Sun 9.30am–5pm; €2.50), whose ground floor is given over to temporary exhibitions, usually of fine art. The floor above displays the moody etchings, lithographs, studies and paintings of the much-travelled artist **Frank Brangwyn** (1867–1956). Born in Bruges, of Welsh parents, Brangwyn donated this sample of his work to his native town in 1936. Apprenticed to William Morris in the early 1880s and an official UK war artist in World War I, Brangwyn was a versatile artist who turned his hand to several different media, though his drawings are much more appealing than his paintings, which often slide into sentimentality.

Close by, at Dijver 17, the **Gruuthuse Museum** (Tues–Sun 9.30am–5pm; €6) occupies a large, sprawling mansion that dates from the fifteenth century. Distributed amongst the many rooms is a hotchpotch of Flemish fine, applied and decorative arts, mostly dating from the medieval and early modern period, plus paintings and sculptures, silverware, lace, ceramics and musical instruments, while antique furniture crops up just about everywhere. The museum's strongest suit is its superb collection of **tapestries**, mostly woven in Brussels or Bruges and dating from the sixteenth and seventeenth centuries. Most intriguing of all, however, is the 1472 oak-panelled **oratory**, which, very unusually, juts out from the first floor of the museum to overlook the high altar of the adjacent Onze Lieve Vrouwekerk (see p.175).

The Onze Lieve Vrouwekerk

Beyond the Gruuthuse, the **Onze Lieve Vrouwekerk** (Mon–Sat 9.30am–4.45pm, Sun 1.30–4.45pm; free) is a rambling shambles of a church, a clamour of different dates and different styles, whose brick spire is – at 122m – one of the tallest in Belgium. The **nave** was three hundred years in the making, an architecturally discordant affair, whose thirteenth-century, grey-stone central aisle, with its precise blind arcading, is the oldest part of the church. At the east end of the south aisle is the church's most celebrated work, a delicate marble *Madonna and Child* by Michelangelo. Otherwise, the most interesting of the church's accumulated treasures are situated in the **chancel** (€2.50), where the mausoleums of Charles the Bold and his daughter Mary of Burgundy are exquisite examples of Renaissance carving, their side panels decorated with coats of arms connected by the most intricate of floral designs. In the 1970s, archeologists dug beneath the mausoleums; the hole was never filled in and today mirrors reflect Mary's coffin along with the burial vaults of several unknown medieval dignitaries, three of which have now been moved to the Lanchals Chapel just across the ambulatory. Plastered with lime mortar, the inside walls of the three vaults sport brightly coloured **grave frescoes**, an art that flourished hereabouts from the late thirteenth to the middle of the fifteenth century.

St-Janshospitaal and the Hospitaalmuseum

Opposite the entrance to the Onze Lieve Vrouwekerk is **St-Janshospitaal**, a sprawling complex which sheltered the sick of mind and body until well into the nineteenth century. The oldest part of the hospital is at the front, behind two church-like gable ends, and this has been turned into a slick **museum** (Tues–Sun 9.30am–5pm; €8), with one large section – in the former ward – exploring the hospital's historical background by means of documents, paintings and religious *objets d'art*. A second, smaller but much more alluring section, sited in the old hospital chapel, is dedicated to the paintings of **Hans Memling** (1433–94). Born near Frankfurt, Memling spent most of his working life in Bruges, where he stuck to the detailed symbolism of his contemporaries, but suffused his figures with a velvet-like gracefulness that greatly appealed to the city's burghers. Indeed, their enthusiasm made Memling a rich man – in 1480 he was listed among the town's major moneylenders. Of the six works on display, Memling's *Reliquary of St Ursula* of 1489 is the most unusual, a lovely piece of craftsmanship comprising a miniature wooden Gothic church painted with the story of St Ursula.

St-Salvatorskathedraal

From St-Janshospitaal, it's a couple of minutes' walk north to **St-Salvator-skathedraal** (Holy Saviour's Cathedral; Mon 2–5.30pm, Tues–Fri 9am–noon & 2–5.30pm, Sat 9am–noon & 2–3.30pm, Sun 9–10am & 2–5pm; free), a bulky Gothic edifice that mostly dates from the late thirteenth century, though the Flamboyant Gothic ambulatory was added some two centuries later. Nearing the end of a long-term refurbishment, the cathedral's **nave** has recently emerged from centuries of accumulated grime, but it remains a cheerless, cavernous affair. The star turn is the **set of eight paintings** by Jan van Orley displayed in the transepts. Commissioned in the 1730s, the paintings were used for the manufacture of a matching set of **tapestries** from a Brussels workshop, and, remarkably enough, these too have survived and hang in sequence in the choir and nave. Each of the eight scenes is a fluent, dramatic composition featuring a familiar episode from the life of Christ – from the Nativity to the Resurrection – complete with a handful of animals, including a remarkably determined Palm Sunday donkey. The tapestries are actually mirror images of the paintings because the weavers worked with the rear of the tapestries uppermost on their looms; to further assist them, the weavers also had cartoon copies of the tapestry paintings – but not the originals as they were too valuable to be kept beside the looms.

Entered from the nave, the cathedral **treasury** (daily except Sat 2–5pm; €2.50) occupies the adjoining neo-Gothic chapterhouse, whose nine rooms are packed with ecclesiastical tackle, from religious paintings and statues through to an assortment of reliquaries, vestments and croziers. The labelling is poor, however, so it's a good idea to pick up the English-language guide at the entrance. Room B holds the treasury's finest painting, a gruesome, oak-panel triptych, *The Martyrdom of St Hippolytus*, by Dieric Bouts (1410–75) and Hugo van der Goes (d.1482).

The Begijnhof

Heading south from St-Janshospitaal, it's a short stroll to **Wijngaardstraat**, whose antique terrace houses are crammed with souvenir shops, bars and restaurants, but there's relief near at hand in the much more appealing, if just as over-visited, **Begijnhof** (daily 9am–6.30pm or sunset; free), where a rough circle of old and infinitely pretty whitewashed houses surrounds a central green. The best time to visit is in spring, when a carpet of daffodils pushes up between the wispy elms, creating one of the most photographed scenes in Bruges. There were once *begijnhofs* all over Belgium, and this is one of the few to have survived in good nick. They date back to the twelfth century, when an influential Liège priest encouraged widows and unmarried women to live in communities, the better to do pious acts. These communities were different from convents in so far as the inhabitants – the **beguines** (*begijns*) – did not have to take conventual vows and had the right to return to the secular world if they wished. Margaret, Countess of Flanders, founded Bruges' *begijnhof* in 1245 and, although most of the houses now standing date from the eighteenth century, the medieval layout has survived intact, preserving the impression of the *begijnhof* as a self-contained village, with access controlled through two large gates.

The Minnewater

Metres from the more southerly of the *begijnhof*'s two gates is the **Minnewater**, often hyped as the city's "Lake of Love". The tag certainly gets the canoodlers going, but in fact the lake – more a large pond – started life as a city harbour. The distinctive stone **lock house** at the head of the Minnewater recalls its earlier function, though it's actually a very fanciful nineteenth-century recon-struction of the medieval original. The **Poertoren**, on the west bank at the far end of the lake, is more authentic, its brown brickwork dating from 1398 and once part of the city wall. This is where the city kept its gunpowder – hence the name, "powder tower".

Beside the Poertoren, a footbridge spans the southern end of the Minnewater to reach the leafy expanse of **Minnewaterpark**, which trails north back towards the *begijnhof*.

Eating and drinking

In Bruges, most of the **restaurants and cafés** – and there are scores of them – are geared up for the tourist trade. Standards are variable, with a whole slew of places churning out some pretty mediocre stuff, but there are, of course, lots of exceptions – including the places we recommend below. Few would describe Bruges' **bars** as cutting-edge, but neither are they staid and dull – far from it if you know where to go. Indeed, drinking in the city can be a real pleasure and one of the potential highlights of any visit.

Cafés and restaurants

De Belegde Boterham, **De Kleine St Amandsstraat 5.** Most of the cafés in and around the Markt are firmly tourist-oriented, but this bright and breezy little place, in attractively renovated old premises, has a local following on account of its fresh sandwiches (€7–10) and tasty salads (€10–12). Mon–Sat noon–4pm.

Café de Medici Geldmuntstraat 9. An enjoyable antidote to the plain modernism of many of its rivals, this café boasts an extravagantly ornate interior, complete with a huge mirror and spindly, curving staircase. The best range of coffees in town, not to mention mouthwatering cakes and tarts. Sandwiches and salads are served too. Mon–Sat 9am–6pm.

Cafedraal Zilverstraat 38 ☎050 34 08 45, ⊛www.cafedraal.be. Fashionable and justifiably popular restaurant decked out in ersatz medieval style, with wood panelling, a big open fire in winter and a garden terrace in summer. The menu runs the gamut of French and Flemish dishes, but it's hard to beat the North Sea bouillabaisse or the lobster and veal cooked in mustard. Mains around €20–25. Mon–Sat noon–3pm & 6–11pm.

Den Dyver Dijver 5 ☎050 33 60 69. Top-flight restaurant popular with an older clientele, specializing in traditional Flemish dishes cooked in beer – the quail and rabbit are delicious, though the seafood comes a close second. The decor is plush and antique, with tapestries on the wall beneath an ancient wood-beamed ceiling. The only real negative is the tiresome muzak. Reservations advised. Mains around €25. Mon, Tues & Fri–Sun noon–2pm & 6.30–9pm, Wed & Thurs 6.30–9pm.

Kok au Vin Ezelstraat 19 ☎050 33 95 21. Swish restaurant in tastefully modernized old premises on the north side of the city centre. An ambitious menu covers all the Franco-Belgian bases and then some, with mains averaging around €25, though lunch is half that. Fri–Tues noon–2pm & 6.30–10pm.

In Den Wittekop St-Jakobstraat 14 ☎050 33 20 59. This small and intimate, split-level restaurant is one of the most appealing in town, its decor a fetching mix of the tasteful and the kitsch. There's smooth jazz as background music, plus good Flemish food, including the local speciality of pork and beef stewed in Trappist beer. Mains average around €18. Tues–Sat noon–2pm & 6–9.30pm.

Bars

Het Brugs Beertje Kemelstraat 5. This small and friendly speciality beer bar claims a stock of three hundred beers, which aficionados reckon is one of the best selections in Belgium. There are tasty snacks too – cheeses and salads – but note that the place is very much on the (backpacker) tourist trail. Thurs–Mon 4pm–1am.

L'Estaminet Park 5. Groovy café-bar with a laid-back, neighbourhood feel and (for Bruges) a diverse and cosmopolitan clientele. Rickety furniture both inside and on the large terrace adds to the flavour of the place, as does the world music in the background, while the first-rate beer menu skilfully picks its way through Belgium's myriad beers. Tues–Sun 11.30am–1am or later, but Thurs from 4pm.

De Garre De Garre 1. Down a narrow alley off Breidelstraat between the Markt and the Burg, this cramped but charming estaminet (tavern) has an outstanding range of Belgian beers and snacks, while classical music adds to the relaxed air. Mon–Fri noon–midnight, Sat & Sun 5pm–1am.

Oud Vlissinghe Blekersstraat 2. With its wood panelling, antique paintings and long wooden tables, this is one of the oldest and most distinctive bars in Bruges, thought to date from 1515. The atmosphere is easy-going, with the emphasis on quiet conversation – there are no juke boxes here. There's a pleasant garden terrace too. Wed–Sat 11am–midnight, Sun 11am–7pm.

Wijnbar Est Noordzandstraat 34 ⊕ 050 33 38 **39.** The best wine bar in town, with a friendly atmosphere, an extensive cellar and over twenty-five different wines available by the glass every day – it's especially strong on New World vintages, and also serves a selection of cheeses in the evening. There's live (free) jazz, blues and folk music every Sun from 8pm to 10.30pm. Mon, Thurs & Sun 5pm–midnight, Fri 5pm–1am & Sat 3pm–1am.

Listings

Listings

Accommodation

With over seventy hotels and several hostels dotted within its central ring of boulevards, Brussels has no shortage of **places to stay**. Some of the most opulent places – as well as some of the most basic – are scattered amongst the cobbled lanes on and around the **Grand-Place** and there's another equally convenient cluster round the **Bourse**. Nearby, the trendy **Ste-Catherine** district weighs in with a good selection of low- to mid-range hotels, or you can venture south of the Lower Town, to the smart chain hotels of **avenue Louise**. Nevertheless, despite the number and variety of hotels and hostels, finding accommodation can still prove difficult, particularly in the **spring and autumn** when the capital enjoys what amounts to its **high seasons** – July and August are much slacker as the business trade dips when the EU all but closes down for its summer recess.

We have selected around forty hotels and hostels in this chapter, and given their prices and contact details, but if you want to view all of the city's (registered) accommodation, consult the **TIB** (Brussels tourist office) website on Ⓦ www.brusselsinternational.be. All the accommodation listed below is marked on the colour **maps** at the end of the book.

Hotels

The capital's **hotels** are ranked according to a five-star system used across the whole of Belgium, though note that stars are allocated on amenities – 24-hour reception, en-suite rooms, etc – and never on aesthetics or atmosphere, and therefore tend to favour chain (as distinct from family) hotels. Generally speaking, standards in Belgian hotels are fairly high and you can expect your room to be well maintained and in good order.

Brussels has quite a competitive hotel market, and **prices** are keen. It's also more of a business than a tourist city, which means that rates come down hugely at **weekends** – and usually, the swankier the hotel, the larger the discount; indeed it's not uncommon to pay half the midweek rates on weekends at the city's larger and more upscale options. Most hotels include **breakfast** in the overnight rate; it is included in the rates of the hotels listed below, except where noted. An increasing number of hotels will accommodate **children** for free if they stay in their parents' room; others require you to pay the cost of an extra bed.

Whatever the time of year, it's a good idea to reserve a room ahead of time at least for your first night, either by contacting the hotel or hostel direct – language is rarely a problem as most receptionists speak at least some English – or via the TIB (Brussels tourist office) website, Ⓦ www.brusselsinternational.be.

Our hotel **listings** are divided into the following areas: the Grand-Place and around (p.182); the Lower Town (p.183); the Upper Town (p.185); St Gilles, avenue Louise and Ixelles (p.186); and the EU Quarter and Faround (p.187).

The TIB also publishes a free and comprehensive **hotel booklet**, which can be ordered via their website or picked up in person at any of their offices in Brussels (see p.34). Alternatively, contact **Resotel** (℡02 779 39 39 ⓦwww .belgium-hospitality.com), Belgium's central reservation agency, who operate an efficient hotel booking service, seeking out the best deals and discounts. If you arrive in the city with nowhere to stay, the TIB office on the Grand-Place (see p.34) offers a same-night hotel booking service – they don't make advance reservations. The service is provided free – you just pay a percentage of the room rate as a deposit, which is then subtracted from your final hotel bill.

The Grand-Place and around

The listings below are marked on the "Grand-Place & around" colour **map** at the back of the book.

Amigo rue de l'Amigo 1–3 ℡02 547 47 47, ⓦwww.roccofortehotels.com or www.hotelamigo.com. This lavish, five-star hotel is Brussels' finest, boasting impeccable service, a central location, just around the corner from the Grand-Place, and supremely elegant furnishings, from Flemish tapestries and paintings to oriental rugs. The building itself mostly dates back to the 1950s, though the stone flagging of the public areas is much earlier, inherited from the time when this was the site of the town prison, where Karl Marx was briefly incarcerated in 1848. The 173 rooms are decorated in tasteful, contemporary style, all natural hues with splashes of red, blue and green. The "Classic" rooms are the least expensive

option, the suites the priciest. Prices begin at €200 for a double room at weekends. Prémétro Bourse or Métro Gare Centrale.

Aris rue du Marché aux Herbes 78 ℡02 514 43 00, ⓦwww.arishotel.be. This 70-room hotel couldn't be more convenient, and its relatively bland rooms are large and well appointed, though there's a bit of noise from the street outside. Facilities include TV, a/c and wheelchair access, and doubles go for around €150 midweek, almost half that at weekends; breakfast is €8. Wi-fi access extra. Prémétro Bourse or Métro Gare Centrale.

Le Dixseptième rue de la Madeleine 25 ℡02 517 17 17, ⓦwww.ledixseptieme .be. Just a couple of minutes' walk from the Grand-Place on the way to Gare Centrale, this place does its best to be central Brussels' most elegant boutique hotel, with just 24 deluxe rooms and suites. Half of the rooms are in the tastefully renovated seventeenth-century mansion at the front (named after old Flemish masters), the remainder in the contemporary extension at the back (named after modern artists). There's a lovely downstairs sitting-room and bar with comfy sofas to sink into, and the rooms themselves have a grand yet homely feel – all very soothing, and a real antidote to the mayhem outside. There are just four standard rooms for €200; the rest are mainly suites ranging from €250 to a wallet-draining €430, but weekend discounts are possible. Métro Gare Centrale.

La Légende rue du Lombard 35 ℡02 512 82 90, ⓦwww.hotellalegende.com. Very centrally located hotel, two minutes from the Grand-Place, but with a pleasant, tucked-away feel, in an old mansion set around a small

▲ Hotel Amigo

courtyard. All of the hotel's 26 bedrooms have en-suite facilities, TVs and telephone, and room sizes are reasonable (you pay more for the larger rooms), but the decor is pretty bland and characterless. Doubles €85–125. Prémétro Bourse.

La Madeleine rue de la Montagne 22 ⊕02 513 29 73, ⓦwww.hotel-la-madeleine.be. In a handy location – just down the hill from the Gare Centrale and metres from the Grand-Place – this small hotel has 55 routine, modern rooms, most of which come with en-suite bathroom. The smaller rooms (€112 for a double) are a bit poky, but the larger ones (€127) are fine and have TV and reasonable bathrooms, some with bathtub. There are triples and quads too, and wi-fi access (extra) in some rooms. Métro Gare Centrale.

Le Méridien carrefour de l'Europe 3 ⊕02 548 42 11, ⓦwww.starwoodhotels.com/lemeridien. This modern and expansive 224-room, five-star chain hotel is conveniently situated two minutes from the Grand-Place. It's not overloaded with character, but the rooms are large and pleasant with all mod cons. Midweek rates start at around €350 (not including breakfast) for a double room, less than half that at the weekend. Right across the road from Gare Centrale.

Mozart rue Marché aux Fromages 23 ⊕02 502 66 61, ⓦwww.hotel-mozart.be. Right in the heart of Brussels' kebab quarter, literally around the corner from the Grand-Place, this hotel is a warren-like conversion of three seventeenth-century town houses, tiled in Moorish style and with walls lined with ranks of old masters. Its 54 rooms can't possibly live up to the ornateness of the lobby, but all have private bathroom (with showers only) and TV, and include breakfast, although some can be a bit dark and poky, so ask to see a selection. Doubles and twins go for €100, the larger executive rooms for around €150; there are triples and quads too. Métro Gare Centrale.

Royal Windsor rue Duquesnoy 5 ⊕02 505 55 55, ⓦwww.royalwindsorbrussels.com. Five minutes from both the Grand-Place and the Upper Town, this stalwart of the Brussels high-end hotel scene has 200-odd rooms, which are well – if not particularly imaginatively – furnished, and have all mod cons, including satellite TV and 24hr room service. If you want something a bit different you can opt for one of their "fashion rooms", each

conceived by a top Belgian designer. Doubles start at about €170, but you can expect big discounts at weekends. Métro Gare Centrale.

Saint-Michel Grand-Place 15 ⊕02 511 09 56, ⓕ02 511 46 00. Only in Belgium could one of the cheapest places in town have one of the best views. This hotel sits above the *'t Kelderke* restaurant on the Grand-Place, and for around €140 you can have a large double room with bath overlooking one of the finest city squares in the world. The rooms are fairly spartan, but clean and equipped with TV. You may be kept awake by drunken revellers or woken by street cleaners at the crack of dawn, but that's a small price to pay. And if you want something quieter, the rooms at the back are cheaper – around €120. Breakfast is taken downstairs at the *'t Kelderke* café or at café *La Brouette* across the square – both of which are part of the hotel. Prémétro Bourse.

La Vieille Lanterne rue des Grands Carmes 29 ⊕02 512 74 94, ⓦwww.lavieillelanterne.be. A tiny, family-run pension tucked away above a souvenir shop overlooking the Manneken Pis, the briefest of strolls from the Grand-Place. There are six boxy but perfectly adequate rooms, simply furnished and each with shower and TV; breakfast is brought up to your room. Advance booking advisable. Doubles cost around €80, triples around €100, making this is one of the cheapest options in the heart of town. Prémétro Bourse.

The Lower Town

The listings below are marked on the "Lower & Upper Town" colour **map** at the back of the book.

West of the Grand-Place

Astrid place du Samedi 11 ⊕02 219 31 19, ⓦwww.astridhotel.be. A bit characterless, but for once the rooms are nicer than the soulless lobby – good-sized, many of them recently refurbished and with wi-fi access (extra). The 100 or so rooms go for around €130, plus €8 for breakfast, much less at weekends, but you choose this hotel more for its location or size than for any degree of atmosphere. Métro Ste-Catherine.

Atlas rue du Vieux Marché-aux-Grains 30 ⊕02 502 60 06, ⓦwww.atlas-hotel.be. Behind the handsome stone facade of this nineteenth-century mansion lies a rather bland modern hotel. Still, it's in the heart of the Ste-Catherine district, and a 5min walk or so from the Grand-Place, and although it feels a bit like a chain, its 88 rooms are a cut above the average chain offerings, and it's wheelchair accessible. Doubles cost €130, dropping to €85 at weekends. Métro Ste-Catherine.

Brussels Welcome Hotel quai au Bois à Brûler 23 ☎ 02 219 95 46, ⓦ www .brusselshotel.travel. Truly one of the most welcoming hotels in Brussels, and perhaps its most unique, this friendly, family-run hotel is well positioned in the heart of the Ste-Catherine district and has 17 country-themed rooms, all with bathrooms inspired by the owners' travels and furnished with the plunder of their trips. Smaller standard rooms go for €115, and the larger deluxe ones for €140, or you can splurge on the sumptuous Silk Road or Egyptian suites for €210. Wi-fi access throughout, Jacuzzis in the deluxe rooms and a free internet connection on the ground floor. Métro Ste-Catherine.

Noga rue du Béguinage 38 ☎ 02 218 67 63, ⓦ www.nogahotel.com. Tucked away among the peaceful streets around St-Jean Baptiste au Béguinage, this is not the grandest of the city's hotels by a long chalk, but it's a good budget option, with a cosy reception and 19 rooms for €110 a double. The rooms, all en suite, are variable: a couple have baths, most have just showers, but all are good value at this price, and some have been recently refurbished. There's a pool table and a bar, and a library for guests' use. All in all, a very friendly and accommodating option. Métro Ste-Catherine.

Orts rue Auguste Orts 38–40 ☎ 02 517 07 17, ⓦ www.hotelorts.com. Situated above its café-restaurant, the *Orts* is a relative newcomer to the Brussels hotel scene, and it's a welcome one, with 14 impeccably furnished rooms decked out in soothing neutrals for €130–140 a night, and free wi-fi access too. It can get a bit noisy at night, but the location, between the Bourse and Ste-Catherine, is excellent. There's also a lovely suite for €250 a night. Métro Ste-Catherine.

South of the Grand-Place

A La Grande Cloche place Rouppe 10 ☎ 02 512 61 40, ⓦ www.hotelgrandecloche.com.

A 10min walk from the Grand-Place and not much more from the Gare du Midi, this hotel has 36 large, classically decorated double rooms, all with bathrooms, and most of them recently renovated and very spick-and-span. Doubles cost €90; you might want to spend what you saved by staying here at the swanky Michelin-starred *Comme Chez Soi* opposite. Métro Anneessens.

Be Manos Square de l'Aviation 23–27 ☎ 02 520 65 65, ⓦ www.bemanos.com. The latest addition to this small, family-owned Brussels chain is a boutique hotel 5min walk from Gare du Midi. Not the most picturesque location, but it's undeniably convenient for Eurostar, and only 10min walk from the Grand-Place. The rooms, set around a slender internal courtyard, are sleek and spacious affairs – the schist-tiled bathrooms are lovely and there's free wi-fi access throughout. There's also a "wellness" centre, with steam room and sauna, and a pleasant upstairs bar with terrace – though the views across the rooftops are not the city's most alluring. Doubles start at around €300, but at weekends you can pay less than half this. Métro Gare du Midi.

▲ Be Manos

Floris Avenue av de Stalingrad 25–31 ☎ 02 548 98 38, ⓦ www.florishotels.com. Midway between the Gare du Midi and the Grand-Place, and less than ten minutes' walk from each, this hotel is ideally placed if you're travelling by Eurostar. It has a pleasant modern lobby and breakfast room, and very large and bright rooms furnished in modern style that are good value too, costing around €160 a night midweek, and much less at weekends. Métro Lemonnier or Anneessens.

North of the Grand-Place

Comfort Art Hotel Siru place Rogier 1 ☎ 02 203 35 80, ⓦ www.comforthotelsiru.com.

This 101-room hotel was conceived in the late 1980s, when a team of Belgian art students was given carte blanche to decorate the hotel's corridors and bedrooms. Their work is still here, and although the hotel, now part of the Comfort chain, is looking a little tired these days, some of the rooms are still strikingly original (even if others are very ordinary). Official rates are hugely overpriced but you're likely to be able to pick up a room here for around €100 midweek, less at weekends. It's very handy for the Gare du Nord, too. Métro Rogier.

Floris Arlequin rue de la Fourche 17–19 ⊕02 514 16 15, ⓦ www.florishotels.com. Don't be deterred by the grotty approach to the hotel: its large, sleek lobby can't help but impress. The 92 rooms are pleasant enough, and fully renovated with flat-screen TVs and wi-fi access (extra). And it's right in the thick of the downtown action, with a seventh-floor breakfast room that offers amazing views of the Hôtel de Ville. Doubles go for around €180 midweek, but expect big reductions at the weekend. Prémétro Bourse.

Métropole place de Brouckère 31 ⊕02 217 23 00, ⓦ www.metropolehotel.com. Dating from 1895, this grand hotel, one of Brussels' finest, boasts exquisite Empire and Art Nouveau decor in its public areas. The rooms vary quite a lot though: some are nothing special, while others are very spacious and retain their original fittings – don't be afraid to ask for something else if your room isn't to your taste. The classic Art Nouveau bar remains a popular meeting point for tourists and locals alike. Rates start just short of €400 for a double, half this at the weekend, and various weekend packages are always available. Métro De Brouckère.

▲ The Métropole

NH Atlanta blvd Adolphe Max 7 ⊕02 217 01 20, ⓦ www.nh-hotels.com. The pick of the NH chain's hotels in Brussels, decorated in the chain's trademark style of classy modern furnishings and fittings matched by pastel-painted walls. It's deliberately unexciting, but the rooms are well appointed, although those at the front, overlooking the boulevard, can be a tad noisy. Standard doubles go for €180 midweek, €195 for a larger deluxe, while at weekends you can get a standard room for €85, a deluxe for €100; breakfast not included. Métro De Brouckère.

Radisson SAS rue Fosse-aux-Loups 47 ⊕02 219 28 28, ⓦ www.radissonsas.com. This large hotel is one of the best of the city centre chains, with an enormous glass-roofed atrium at its centre. It's in a handy location, about five minutes' walk north of the Grand-Place, its rooms have every mod con, including free wi-fi, and it boasts a good bar and the highly regarded *Sea Grill* restaurant. Standard doubles start at about €200; at weekends they are one of the city's best bargains at €125 for a standard double – around €200 for a junior suite. Métro Gare Centrale.

🏃 **The Dominican rue Léopold 9** ⊕02 203 08 08, ⓦ www.thedominican.be. This new hotel occupies a prime location a brief stroll from the Grand-Place. All 150 rooms here are stylishly kitted out with wooden floors and earthy tones. There is free internet and a spacious foyer, plus a generous buffet-breakfast. The hotel also boasts a claim to fame: part of the building occupies the mansion where the painter Jacques-Louis David drew his last breath in 1825 – hence the plaque on the facade. Doubles from €150–400; weekend discounts. Prémétro De Brouckère or Métro Gare Centrale.

The Upper Town

The listings below are marked on the "Lower & Upper Town" colour **map** at the back of the book.

Bloom! rue Royale 250 ⊕02 220 66 11, ⓦ www .hotelbloom.com. It may be hard to warm to a hotel that insists on adding an exclamation mark to its name, but there's no denying the panache that went into designing the interior – from the hanging bubble chairs and coffered ceiling of the enormous foyer through to the sharp modern decor of the guest rooms. The best rooms overlook the lovely gardens of Le Botanique (see p.60), but otherwise the location is a tad dreary and the exterior does the place few favours – the hotel occupies a big bruiser of a modern block. Doubles €100–370, often with substantial discounts at weekends. Métro Botanique.

Du Congrès rue du Congrès 38–44 ☎ 02 217 18 90, ⊛ **www.hotelducongres.be.** This pleasant hotel occupies a set of attractive late nineteenth-century town houses in an especially good-looking corner of the Lower Town, a survivor from the 1890s with a network of mini-boulevards interrupted by leafy little squares. The hotel's seventy-odd en-suite rooms are spacious, airy and decorated in plain, modern style. Doubles €100–200. Métro Madou.

NH Hotel du Grand Sablon rue Bodenbroeck 2–4 ☎ 02 518 11 00, ⊛ **www.nh-hotels.com.** Rooms at this 200-room hotel are decorated in a rather fusty, traditional style – though a revamp is in the air. More positively, the hotel overlooks the place du Grand Sablon, one of the city's most appealing squares with its terraced cafés and designer shops. Doubles begin at a very reasonable €80. A 5-10min walk from Métro Louise.

Sabina rue du Nord 78 ☎ 02 218 26 37, ⊛ www .hotelsabina.be. Basic hotel in an attractive late nineteenth-century town house with 24 workaday, en-suite rooms. It's located in an appealing residential area that was once a favourite haunt of the city's nineteenth-century bourgeoisie. Doubles cost from as little as €60. A 5-10min walk from Métro Madou.

St Gilles, avenue Louise and Ixelles

The listings below are marked on the "St Gilles, avenue Louise & Ixelles" colour **map** at the back of the book.

Argus rue Capitaine Crespel 6 ☎ 02 514 07 70, ⊛ **www.hotel-argus.be.** Just to the south of the boulevards of the petit ring, a 5min walk from place Louise. The hotel's forty modern and modest rooms are a bit on the small side, but they're cosy enough and there's free wi-fi. The service is impeccable, too. A nice alternative to the gargantuan – and expensive – hotels that pepper this district. Doubles €65–160. Métro Louise.

Les Bluets rue Berckmans 124 ☎ 02 534 39 83, ⊛ **www.geocities.com/les_bluets.** Charming, family-run hotel with just ten en-suite rooms in a large, handsome old stone terrace house. The rich fin-de-siècle-style decor is a pleasant change from the blander feel of many of the chains. Doubles €68–81. One block south of the petit ring and Métro Hôtel des Monnaies.

Conrad Brussels av Louise 71 ☎ 02 542 42 42, ⊛ **www.conradhotels.com.** One of the capital's top five-star hotels, the Conrad was former US president Clinton's choice when in town. Housed in a tower block with all sorts of retro flourishes, the hotel boasts over 250 large and lavish rooms, comprehensive facilities and ultra-attentive service. Doubles from €230. It's situated near the north end of the avenue, a 5min walk from Métro Louise.

Manos Premier Chaussée de Charleroi 100–106 ☎ 02 537 96 82, ⊛ **www.manoshotel.com.** Close to avenue Louise, this elegant five-star offers a real taste of antique luxury with its eighteenth-century-style furniture and fittings – all marble and chandeliers. There's also an oasis of a garden and an on-site restaurant, *Kolya*, serving up French and Mediterranean cuisine. Doubles €350. Métro Louise.

Manos Stephanie Chaussée de Charleroi 28 ☎ 02 539 02 50, ⊛ **www.manoshotel.com.** Comparable with its cousin *Manos Premier* just along the street, this four-star hotel has every convenience and is also kitted out in ornate eighteenth-century style. Doubles €320. Métro Louise.

Rembrandt rue de la Concorde 42 ☎ 02 512 71 39, ⊛ **www.hotel-rembrandt.be.** This quiet, pension-style hotel on a dispiriting side street just off avenue Louise has twelve clean and comfortable double rooms. Half the rooms are en suite, half are not. En-suite doubles €90–100, doubles with shared facilities €90; breakfast included. Tram #94 from place Louise or av de la Régence.

The White Hotel av Louise 212 ☎ 02 644 29 29, ⊛ **www.thewhitehotel.be.** Distinctive designer hotel, where – you guessed it – the walls and the drapes, the duvets and the chairs are (nearly) all white. Adding flair are the rooms in which Belgian designers have been given a free hand to make their mark – and sometimes it's really great stuff too. Free wi-fi. Prices for the 53 doubles begin at a very reasonable €85. Tram #94 from place Louise or av de la Régence.

Warwick Barsey av Louise 381–383 ☎02 649 98 00, ⓦwww.warwickbarsey.com. Chic, recently revamped chain hotel whose public areas are decorated in an eclectic version of Victorian style down to (or up as far as) the ersatz Greek friezes. The hotel's 99 bedrooms eschew uniformity, but many of them continue with the neo-Victoriana, a star feature being the fancily-tiled bathrooms. Doubles €170–350. Popular with business travellers, the hotel is located at the south end of avenue Louise, near the Musée Constantin Meunier; tram #94 from place Louise or av de la Régence.

The EU Quarter and around

The listings below are marked on the "EU Quarter & around" colour **map** at the back of the book.

Leopold rue du Luxembourg 35 ☎02 511 18 28, ⓦwww.hotel-leopold.be. If you're staying in the EU Quarter, it's easy to get stuck beside a thundering boulevard, but this smart, four-star hotel has a first-rate location – on a quiet(ish) side street, a brief walk from place du Luxembourg. Has over one hundred rooms, all kitted out in typical modern chain-hotel style. The official rate for a double is €270, but discounts are common. Métro Trône.

Monty Small Design Hotel blvd Brand Whitlock 101 ☎02 734 56 36, ⓦwww.monty-hotel.be. Well-regarded, pocket-sized boutique hotel with a commitment to modern design: it's crammed with designer touches, with every fixture and fitting painstakingly chosen to fit. Each of the eighteen guest rooms is imaginatively furnished too – no chain-hotel blandness here. Doubles €95–215. Prémétro Georges-Henri.

Stanhope rue du Commerce 9 ☎02 506 91 11, ⓦwww.stanhope.be. Prestigious, five-star hotel whose humdrum location – on an unremarkable side street near the EU Parliament building – belies its studied elegance. The interior is modelled on a nineteenth-century mansion and great care has been taken with the decor: there are Neoclassical columns rising from gleaming marble floors; a courtyard garden; pendulous chandeliers and a full-scale library adjoining the bar. At the weekend doubles start at about €130, but normally you can expect to pay €200–400. Métro Trône.

B&Bs

Staying at a **B&B** can prove a cheaper alternative to a hotel, and the standard of accommodation can be just as good. Rooms are often comfortable, although location is sometimes a problem – don't expect to be in the centre of things.

The tourist office on the Grand-Place can make reservations for free; alternatively, you could try contacting one of the city's **budget accommodation agencies**. Bed & Brussels (rue Kindermans 9 ☎02 646 07 37, ⓦwww .BnB-Brussels.be) has a good reputation and the standard of rooms is usually high, with doubles within reasonable striking distance of the city centre for around €75–100; you pay less for staying further out and for longer. Taxistop (Mon–Fri 10am–5.30pm; rue du Fossé-aux-Loups 28 ☎070 222 292, ⓦwww .taxistop.be) is a non-profit organization that aims to foster the informal exchange of goods and services – from carpools to home exchange and B&B. It has a wide range of budget accommodation (doubles €70–100), all on the website, and bookings are (usually) made direct with the host.

L'Art de la Fugue rue de Suède 38 ☎0478 69 59 44, ⓦwww.lartdelafugue.com. At just 2min walk from the Eurostar terminal, it's a shame this fabulous B&B doesn't have more rooms. Each room has its theme – "Laurence of Arabia" with an African flavour, "Indochina" with a collection of antique Buddhas, and lavish, opera-themed "Farinelli"; a 1960s design is planned. There's plenty of space to relax and enjoy the books and art of the owners, as well as an excellent continental breakfast. Book ahead as it quickly fills up. Doubles €97. Métro Gare du Midi. For location, see "St Gilles, avenue Louise & Ixelles" map at the back of the book.

Chambres en Ville rue de Londres 19 ☎02 512 9290, ⓦwww.chambresenville.be. The four

Self-catering

Brussels' hotels are undeniably expensive, and it can be cheaper to rent a furnished **apartment** for a few days, especially if you're travelling as a family, when self-catering might be preferable. There are a number of agencies who rent out apartments on short-term lets, one of the best of which is Aedifica-Rue Souveraine, avenue Louise 331 (☎02 626 0884, ⓦwww.ruesouveraine.com), who rent furnished apartments for anything from a few nights to six months in Ixelles, mostly in buildings on rue Souveraine itself, which runs between place Fernand Cocq and avenue Louise. Prices range from about €125 to €150 per night for a one- or two-bedroom place (for a week you can expect to pay around €900), plus a deposit for the telephone. The apartments are clean and excellently serviced, with phone and internet access.

Another option is the Citadines Apart Hotel (ⓦwww.citadines.com), which has branches in the Ste-Catherine district, a short stroll northwest of the Grand-Place at quai au Bois à Brûler 51 (Métro Ste-Catherine), or at avenue de la Toison d'Or 61–63 – on the petit ring, near avenue Louise (Métro Louise): both good locations. Their cheerfully decorated apartments come in two sizes: for 1–4 people, with one double and one sofabed, and studios (for 1–2 people, with a sofabed); all are well equipped and come with a fridge, hob, microwave and toaster. You can reckon on paying €90–130 a night, depending on how long you're staying.

▲ L'Art de la Fugue

large and airy, en-suite rooms in this distinguished, nineteenth-century Ixelles town house just off rue du Trône are decorated in a clever amalgam of traditional and modern styles. Each room is different, with boutique-hotel-style touches such as freestanding baths and original art on the walls. Doubles €100. Métro Trône. For location, see "The EU Quarter & around" map at the back of the book.

Ursule la Libellule chaussée de Vleurgat 165 ☎0475 715 705, ⓦwww.ursule.be. Two cosy, en-suite rooms, decorated in pretty, country-cottage style, set in the garden of an old Ixelles town house. Guests are invited to help themselves to breakfast (included) from the fridge in the breakfast room, or there are plenty of cafés nearby; Doubles €80; minimum two nights stay. Tram #94 from place Louise or av de la Régence. For location, see "St Gilles, avenue Louise & Ixelles map" at the back of the book.

Hostels

If you don't like communal living or the idea of a complete stranger snoring in your ear all night, don't panic – Brussels has its fair share of **hostels** offering cheap, modern and private accommodation. Practically all the hostels in the capital eschew large dorms in favour of singles, doubles and rooms for four. **Prices** vary, but generally speaking a single costs around €32, a double €22 and a quad €19 per person. Most hostels are located either within the petit ring or just outside it and are close to the Metro – Métro Botanique in particular has two good hostels within easy striking distance. The majority provide disabled access and are well worth contacting for special offers for groups or for longer stays. Official **IYHF** hostels will charge an extra €3 per night if you don't have a membership card. If you're planning several nights in an IYHF hostel, either join the IYHF in your home country or collect the stamps issued by every Belgian IYHF hostel when you pay the €3 surcharge: these are affixed to a guest card and, when you have six stamps, you become a member.

Bruegel rue du Saint-Esprit 2 ☏02 511 04 36, Ⓦwww.vjh.be. This is Brussels' official Flemish youth hostel, and is very centrally situated right by the church of Notre-Dame de la Chapelle, close to the Marolles and the Sablon districts. Housed in a functional modern building, it has 135 beds and prices include a basic breakfast – as well as the hire of sheets; doubles cost €22.80 per person; a bed in a four-bed dorm will set you back €18.60. Dinner costs an extra €9.10 and you can request a packed lunch for €5.60. It's clean and well run, and in a great position; the only drawback is the 1am curfew. Check-in 10am–1pm & 2–4pm. Métro Gare Centrale. For location, see "Lower & Upper Town" map at the back of the book.

Le Centre Vincent Van Gogh rue Traversière 8 ☏02 217 01 58, Ⓦwww.chab.be. A rambling 200-bed hostel with a good reputation and friendly staff, though it can all seem a bit chaotic. Prices are fairly standard – singles €34, doubles and triples €27 and quads €22 per person – but its main advantage is that there's no curfew. Breakfast is included and there are sinks in all rooms. Launderette and kitchen facilities available. Métro Botanique. For location, see "Lower & Upper Town" map at the back of the book.

Génération Europe rue de l'Eléphant 4 ☏02 410 38 58, Ⓦwww.laj.be. This IYHF hostel is located in a modern, barracks-like building in Molenbeek, an inner-city industrial district that is slowly being revived. Molenbeek lies just to the west of the centre, across the canal de Charleroi, a

15min walk from the Grand Place – and the hostel is 500m from the Comte de Flandre Métro station. Prices for IYHF members, including breakfast and sheets, are €32 for singles, €22.80 for doubles, and €18.50 for quads per person. Check-in is from 7am to 2pm and there's no curfew. Métro Comte de Flandre.

Jacques Brel rue de la Sablonnière 30 ☏02 218 01 87, Ⓦwww.laj.be. This official IYHF hostel is modern and comfortable, with a hotel-like atmosphere – and rivals some of the city's cheaper hotels for comfort too. Breakfast is included in the price: €32 for singles, €22.80 for doubles and €18.50 for quads per person. There's no curfew (you get a key), and cheap meals can be bought on the premises. Check-in 7.30am–1am. Métro Madou or Métro Botanique. For location, see "Lower & Upper Town" map at the back of the book.

Sleep Well rue du Damier 23 ☏02 218 50 50, Ⓦwww.sleepwell.be. Bright and breezy hostel close to the city centre and only a 5min walk from place Rogier. Hotel-style facilities include a bar-cum-restaurant, which serves traditional Belgian beers and well-priced local dishes. There's also an excellent information point for tourists, internet access, and no curfew. Prices, including breakfast, are €18.50 a night in an 8-bed dorm, €20.50 in a six-bed dorm, €22 in a quad, while double or triple rooms go for €27 per person – and prices are about 20 percent lower for subsequent nights. Métro Rogier. For location, see "Lower & Upper Town" map at the back of the book.

ACCOMMODATION | Hostels

Eating and drinking

Brussels has a deserved reputation for the quality of its food. Even at the dowdiest snack bar, you'll almost always find that the food is well prepared, and the city's **restaurants** are the equal of anywhere in Europe. Traditional Bruxellois dishes feature on many restaurant menus too, canny amalgamations of Walloon and Flemish ingredients and cooking styles – whether it be rabbit cooked in beer, steamed pigs' feet or **waterzooi** (see the *Belgian food* colour insert for more culinary specialities). In the Lower Town, you can sample magnificent fish and seafood, especially in and around the appealing Ste-Catherine quarter; enjoy the fashionable restaurants dotted along rue Antoine Dansaert; or venture south to the burgeoning restaurant scene in the Marolles. Elsewhere, there are slim but occasionally exquisite gastronomic pickings in the Upper Town and a raft of great places in both St Gilles and Ixelles, where you will rarely see a tourist. The only negatives apply to the Lower Town's well-known rue des Bouchers, where a gaggle of restaurants attracts tourists in their droves, despite the excessive prices and – for the most part at least – uninspired food. Brussels is also among Europe's best cities for sampling a wide range of different cuisines – from ubiquitous Italian places and the Turkish restaurants of St Josse, through to Spanish, Vietnamese, Japanese and vegetarian places.

Opening times are pretty standard but restaurants only tend to open for relatively short hours – a couple of hours at lunch, usually noon to 2pm or 2.30pm, and again in the evening from 7pm to around 10pm or 11pm. Our restaurant listings detail opening hours as well as phone numbers: advance reservations are rarely essential, but they are usually a good idea in more popular spots, especially at the weekend. For the most part, eating out is rarely inexpensive, but the **prices** are almost universally justified by the quality. As a general rule, the less formal the restaurant, the less expensive the meal, although price is no indicator of the quality of the food; indeed it's sometimes hard to

---

The listings in this chapter are divided as follows:

Restaurants: Grand-Place and around (p.191); Lower Town (p.192); Upper Town (p.196); St Gilles, avenue Louise and Ixelles (p.197); EU Quarter and around (p.201); Outlying districts (p.201).

Cafés: Grand-Place and around (p.202); Lower Town (p.203); Upper Town (p.203); St Gilles, avenue Louise and Ixelles (p.204); EU Quarter and around (p.205); Outlying districts (p.205).

Bars: Grand-Place and around (p.206); Lower Town (p.207); Upper Town (p.209); St Gilles, avenue Louise and Ixelles (p.209); EU Quarter and around (p.211); Outlying districts (p.211).

distinguish between the less expensive restaurants and the city's **cafés**, which provide some of the tastiest food in town. Many bars also serve food – often just spaghetti, sandwiches and *croques monsieurs*, though some offer a much more ambitious spread. A **service charge** is often included in the bill in restaurants, but otherwise a ten to fifteen percent tip is the norm. A basic **menu reader** is provided on pp.280–282.

Drinking in Brussels, as in the rest of Belgium, is a joy. The city has an enormous variety of **bars** and **café-bars**, from swanky, Parisian-style terrace cafés and Art Nouveau extravagances to traditional drinking dens with ceilings stained by a century's smoke. Many of the city's most enjoyable bars are concentrated in the Lower Town around the Grand-Place, the Bourse and the place St-Géry, though some of the most fashionable and arty are located in St Gilles and Ixelles. The drinking scene in the Upper Town is more restrained, and the EU Quarter only musters up a handful of good expat places, mostly within comfortable walking distance of Métro Schuman. **Bar opening hours** are fairly elastic, but the majority close around 2am, sometimes later at the weekend. **Prices** for drinks can vary hugely depending on where you are, but as a general rule you pay over the odds for the privilege of drinking on the Grand-Place, though not necessarily in the streets around it. Beer is cheap: a glass of draught Belgian beer costs around €3; spirits are relatively expensive, and a gin and tonic can cost you between €4 and €6, though the measures are often generous. There's also a good selection of reasonably priced wines (especially white and red Burgundy) available by the bottle or glass. But the main event is the **beer**, as it is everywhere in Belgium: almost every bar has a choice of at least a dozen brews, and the more specialized places have beer menus that can list several hundred. For our recommendations, see the *Belgian beer* colour insert.

Restaurants

The Grand-Place and around

See the "Grand-Place & around" **map** at the back of this book.

Brasserie de la Roue d'Or rue des Chapeliers 26 T 02 514 25 54. This old and eminently appealing brasserie, with Art Nouveau panelling, stained glass and brass fittings, serves generous portions of Belgian regional specialities, such as *anguilles au vert* (eels in fresh herb sauce) for around €20–30. Also recommended are the roasted *magret de canard* (rosted duck breast) and the *jambonneau caramélisé* (caramelized pork) with endive salad. Daily noon–midnight; closed for one month in the summer, usually July. Métro Gare Centrale.

't Kelderke Grand-Place 15 T 02 513 73 44. You can't get more Belgian than this well-known restaurant, housed in an ancient cellar right on the Grand-Place. Dishes include all the old Belgian favourites (see the *Belgian food* colour section), such as *moules*, *stoemp*, *carbonnade flamande à la bière* and *waterzooi*; prices range from €9 to €16.50 for a main dish, with mussels, in season,

▲ 't Kelderke

between €18.50 and €22. The lunch time *plat du jour* is a very reasonable €8.50. Daily noon–2am. Métro Gare Centrale.

Kokob rue des Grandes Carmes 10 ☏ 02 511 19 50. New kid on the gastronomic block, this Ethiopian restaurant is an excellent place for a large group of friends to share the spicy *wot* – dishes such as lentils in a mild pea sauce (€7.90), or fish with rosemary and lemon (€11.90), served on large pancakes called *injera*. All the meat served is halal. Menus cost from €18 to €30. Tues–Sat noon–3pm & 6.30–10.30pm. Prémétro Bourse.

La Mirante Plattesteen 13 ☏ 02 511 15 80. Arguably the best pizza in Brussels is served in this jam-packed restaurant with a pizza oven in the back. The imaginative menu includes the "Pavarotti" (with spinach and ricotta cheese), and the "Dante" (with aubergine and fennel seeds); all pizzas and pastas cost around €10; seafood risotto is €15. Booking recommended. Mon–Sat noon–2.30pm & 6–11.30pm, Sun 6–11.30pm. Closed Aug & last week Dec. Prémétro Bourse.

Tapas Locas rue du Marché au Charbon 74 ☏ 02 502 12 68. A lively tapas bar popular with a youthful crowd who grab a bite to eat before hitting the town. They serve a wide range of cheap tapas at €3.50 per portion (minimum order of three tapas per person). Standards such as tortilla, calamares and chorizo are on the menu, plus there's a changing selection of more unusual dishes chalked up on the blackboards. Spanish wine and sangria available by the jug. No credit cards. Wed–Sat 7pm–1am. Prémétro Bourse.

The Lower Town

See the "Lower & Upper Town" **map** at the back of this book.

West of the Grand-Place

L'Achepot place Ste-Catherine 1 ☏ 02 511 62 21. This welcoming, family-run restaurant in the appealing Ste-Catherine district specializes – unlike most of its neighbours – in meat rather than fish. The menu is traditional Belgian and French, with mains at €12–22.50: try the spicy black pudding with sweet onion compote and mashed potatoes with apple (€17.50). Dishes come with heaps of fresh vegetables. Mon–Sat noon–2.30pm & 6.30–10.30pm. Métro Ste-Catherine.

Ateliers de la Grande Ile rue de la Grande Ile 31–33 ☏ 02 512 81 90. Only a couple of minutes' walk from place St-Géry, located in a converted nineteenth-century foundry, this winding, candlelit, Russian restaurant serves large and hearty meat dishes, and all the vodkas you can think of and then some. Traditional dishes from all over Eastern Europe include goulash for €15.50 and beef stroganoff with mashed potatoes and gherkins for €20.50. With Magyar musicians attacking their violins for hours on end, it's worth paying a visit simply for the joyous – if slightly eccentric – atmosphere. Tues–Sat 8pm–1am. Prémétro Bourse.

Bar Bik – Brussels International Kitchen quai aux Pierres de Taille 3 ☏ 02 219 75 00. Next door to the newly renovated KVS (Royal Flemish Theatre; see p.218) is the colourful oasis of the *Brussels International Kitchen*. There's no fixed menu, just a board which changes all the time. A lunch dish of the day could be rabbit with endive salad (€10), or in the evening, red tuna with noodles, mango and coconut (€20); vegetarian options are always available. Mon–Fri 11.30am–10.30pm. Métro Yser.

La Belle Maraichère place Ste-Catherine 11 ☏ 02 512 97 59. Smart, bistro-style restaurant with acres of wood panelling and waiters hovering as you tuck into the excellent seafood; main courses will set you back €21–55. Lobster (€60 for two) is a house speciality; a more reasonable option is the three-course lunch menu for €36. Fri–Tues noon–2.30pm & 6–9.30pm; closed most of July. Métro Ste-Catherine.

Bij den Boer quai aux Briques 60 ☏ 02 512 61 22. There are no pretentions in this good old neighbourhood café-restaurant with its tiled floor and bygones on the walls. They serve up a wide range of tasty seafood, with main courses averaging around €25–35, plus a first-class range of daily specials that cost much less. A great place for either a drink or a meal. Mon–Sat noon–2.30pm, 6–11pm. Métro Ste-Catherine.

Au Bon Bol rue Paul Devaux 9 ☏ 02 513 16 88. Opposite the Bourse, this place is as cheap as it gets – yet the noodles are made in front of you and the vegetables are fresh. The setting is all clean functionality, while the food is basically Chinese with hints of Thai spices – try the huge bowl of noodle soup with beef, duck or seafood for €7.50.

Mains are all under €8.50. Daily noon–2.30pm & 7–10.30pm. Prémétro Bourse.

Bonsoir Clara rue Antoine Dansaert 22 ☎ 02 502 09 90. One of the capital's trendiest restaurants, on arguably the hippest street in town. Moody, atmospheric lighting, 1970s geometrically mirrored walls and zinc-topped tables set the tone. Expect to find a menu full of Mediterranean, French and Belgian classics, all excellent (though expensive) – make sure you reserve. Mon–Fri noon–2.30pm & 7–11.30pm, Sat 7–11.30pm. Prémétro Bourse.

Domaine de Lintillac rue de Flandre 25 ☎ 02 511 51 23. Delicious cuisine from the southwest of France is served up at this warm, easy-going restaurant. The prices are ridiculously cheap for what might just be some of the best *foie d'oie* and *foie gras* in Brussels (€9.60–14.20). Down-to-earth and full of character, the relaxed atmosphere (and clientele) make it perfect for family outings. Tues–Sat noon–2pm & 7.30–10pm. Métro Ste-Catherine.

Le Fourneau place Ste-Catherine 8 ☎ 02 513 10 02. This tapas bar-meets-Parisian brasserie is a buzzing addition to the Ste-Catherine scene. The kitchen is in the centre of the restaurant, and you can eat at the bar and watch the chefs work up a head of steam. Asparagus *à la flamande* and cappuccino of lobster with herbs are just a couple of the options. Dishes are about €7 each, with meat and fish ordered by weight. Don't be deceived by the low prices, though – portions are small and the bill can easily add up to €40 per head, without wine. Tues–Sat noon–2.30pm & 7–10pm. Métro Ste-Catherine.

François quai aux Briques 2 ☎ 02 511 60 89. Smart, long-established, bistro-style seafood restaurant with crisp white tablecloths and a tasteful mishmash of nautical bygones dotted about the place. Lobster and oysters are the house speciality, but there's always a catch of the day, and the fish soup is excellent. Main courses range from €20 to €35. Tues–Sat noon–2.30pm & 6.30–10.30pm. Métro Ste-Catherine.

Jaloa place Ste-Catherine 5–7 ☎ 02 512 18 31. This refined newcomer to the Ste-Catherine restaurant scene serves gourmet takes on traditional Belgian and French food and has an intriguing claim to fame: Van Gogh is reputed to have lived upstairs. The ultra-short menu – a few meat dishes, a fish of

the day and a handful of inventive starters – makes it easy to choose. Starters and mains go for €25–30 – no more than you might expect for a restaurant of this calibre – but the two-course lunch menu, at €16, is quite a bargain. At the other extreme, there's a six-course tasting menu (€65), which in summer you can enjoy in the garden out back. Mon–Sat noon–2.30pm & 7–11pm. Métro Ste-Catherine.

Kasbah rue Antoine Dansaert 20 ☎ 02 502 40 26. Popular with a youthful, trendy crowd, this Moroccan restaurant is famous for its enormous portions of couscous and other North African specialities. It's run by the same people as *Bonsoir Clara* next door (see p.193), and although equally hip, the lantern-lit decor makes it seem slightly less fashion-conscious and more welcoming. Main dishes (€14–18) may be on the expensive side for this type of food – a lamb and prune tajine costs €16 – but there's no denying the quality. Reservations necessary. Thurs–Sat 7pm–midnight, Sun–Fri noon–2.30pm & 7pm–midnight. Prémétro Bourse.

La Manufacture rue Notre-Dame du Sommeil 12–20 ☎ 02 502 25 25. A good 10min walk from the Bourse down rue du Chartreux, this converted factory makes an impressive setting for an evening out. There are high ceilings and industrial architecture inside and a grassy courtyard for outdoor dining on balmier evenings. The menu offers variations on a range of Belgian staples and prices range from €14–25 for main courses such as risotto with crayfish or grilled lamb chops with cardamom butter. Especially good for groups; menus on offer from €32. Mon–Fri noon–2pm & 7–11pm, Sat 7–11pm. Prémétro Bourse.

▲ Le Pré Salé

La Marée rue de Flandre 99 ☎02 511 00 40. A pint-sized bistro specializing in fish and mussels located a short walk up rue de Flandre, in the Ste-Catherine district. The decor is pretty basic, but the restaurant still manages to feel cosy and the food is reasonably priced. Fresh fish is delivered twice daily and the menu includes eight different variations on the classic *moules* from €13, and lobster from €20. Wed–Sat noon–1.45pm & 6.30–9.45pm. Métro Ste-Catherine.

La Paix rue Ropsy-Chaudron 49 ☎02 523 09 58. It's worth taking a trip to this restaurant on the edge of the city centre if you appreciate more unusual meat dishes, but be sure to book first. Young chef David Martin has won prizes for his dedication to pig's trotters and offal at this restaurant, strategically placed opposite the abattoir. Try the much-lauded Basque hot black pudding (€16), or Belgian pork cheek with Colonnata bacon, vegetables and truffles (€25.50). Mon–Thurs noon–2.30pm, Fri noon–2.30pm & 7–11.30pm, Sat 7–11.30pm. Métro Clemenceau.

La Papaye Verte rue Antoine Dansaert 53 ☎02 502 70 82. Tasty and inexpensive Thai and Vietnamese food served up in smart surroundings. Main courses are very reasonably priced with, for example, fried ravioli with vegetables, pork and prawns at €5, and grilled chicken with coconut and lemongrass at €10; good range of vegetarian options too. Mon–Sat noon–2.30pm & 6–11.30pm, Sun 6–11.30pm; closed one month in summer. Prémétro Bourse.

🏃 **Le Pré Salé rue de Flandre 16** ☎02 513 43 23. Friendly, old-fashioned, typically Bruxellois neighbourhood restaurant located just off place Ste-Catherine and providing an appealing alternative to the swankier restaurants in the area. The cream tiled interior dates from the days it used to be a chip shop, but now the menu offers great mussels (€21), fish dishes (*anguilles au vert* €13) and other Belgian specialities. Wed–Sun noon–2.30pm & 6.30–10.30pm. Métro Ste-Catherine.

Rugantino blvd Anspach 184–186 ☎02 511 21 95. Reminiscent of the set of *The Godfather*, this long-established Italian restaurant has the classics on the regular menu, but the blackboards tempt you with their fresh pasta dishes – perhaps ravioli with squid and fresh peas or *porchetta alla romana*, both €15. With wine by the carafe, it makes for a reasonably priced meal – but leave space for one of the classic Italian desserts. Mon–Fri noon–3pm & 6–11pm, Sat 6–11pm. Prémétro Anneessens.

In 't Spinnekopke place du Jardin aux Fleurs 1 ☎02 511 86 95. This long-standing restaurant with outside seating is only 10min walk from the Grand-Place, but feels like an old *estaminet* in a provincial Belgian town. It's famous for its extensive beer list and traditional dishes, many of which are cooked in beer – on which the owner has written a cookbook. It's not posh by any means, and the service can be a bit hit-and-miss, but the food is good and hearty. Mon–Fri 11am–11pm, Sat 6–11pm. Métro Ste-Catherine.

North of the Grand-Place

Aux Armes de Bruxelles rue des Bouchers 13 ☎02 511 55 50. Right in the heart of restaurant central, but you'll find no hawkers trying to entice you in here; this place survives on reputation alone. It's not hip, and it's far from cutting-edge, but if you want an old-fashioned restaurant which serves all the Belgian classics at reasonable prices, then it's hard to better this old-style brasserie. On the menu are great steaks, oysters, carbonades, *waterzooi*, eels in green sauce – but leave room for dessert. Tues–Sun noon–11pm. Prémétro Bourse.

Belga Queen rue Fossé aux Loups 32 ☎02 217 21 87. There's no grander setting for a restaurant in the whole of Brussels: the deluxe *Belga Queen* occupies the former headquarters of the Crédit du Nord bank, a nineteenth-century building with a high and mighty, curved and vaulted stained-glass ceiling, and an army of Greek columns, stucco griffins and coats of arms. The revamp has added a clutch of modern sculptures and sleek modern furnishings, and the waiters are stylish in slick tabards,

▲ Belga Queen

perfectly in tune with the housey backtrack. The food doesn't quite live up to the setting, but the restaurant is strong on seafood (dishes €20–45). Mains also include smoked pork ribs with prunes and juniper, and unlike many other restaurants of this standing, vegetarians are catered for too. Business lunches are also available, with a starter and main course for just €15. Daily noon–2.30pm & 7pm–midnight. Métro De Brouckère.

Brasserie Horta rue des Sables 20 ☏ 02 217 72 71. Part of the Bande Dessinée museum (see p.59), this place is carved out of a corner of the impressive Art Nouveau Maison Wacquez, and is almost worth a visit for the setting alone. It serves salads, pasta dishes and some Belgian classics like *blanquette de veau*, vol au vents and *carbonnades*. Main courses €12–15. Métro De Brouckère.

Café Bota rue Royale 236 ☏ 02 219 20 65. This restaurant in the Botanique arts centre has a good, if small, menu of Italian dishes, including pasta for around €9 and classic meat dishes like *saltimbocca alla romana* and escalope *milanese* for around €12. Good value, and with an outside terrace in summer that overlooks the gardens – and, admittedly, the petit ring skyscrapers. Sun–Wed noon–2.30pm, Thurs–Sat noon–2.30pm & 6.30–11pm. Métro Botanique.

 L'Ogenblik Galerie des Princes 1 ☏ 02 511 61 51. In the Galeries St-Hubert, bang in the centre of town, this outstanding restaurant is kitted out in antique bistro style, right down to the ancient cash till. The well-judged, wide-ranging menu begins with the basics – steak and chips with wild mushrooms – but soon climbs to greater gastronomic heights, such as pigeon in a truffle *jus*. Main courses are €25–35; look out also for the daily specials. Reservations advised. Mon–Sat noon–2.30pm & 7–11.30pm. Prémétro Bourse.

Vincent rue des Dominicains 8–10 ☏ 02 511 26 07. The entrance to this lively restaurant is through the kitchen, which gives customers a good view of the culinary action. The restaurant beyond specializes in Belgo-French cuisine, with meat and seafood dishes both prominent. The dashing waiters in their long aprons will flambée at your table – an entertainment in itself. Steak flambéed in a cream and pepper sauce with chips costs €23. Well worth the extra

minute's walk to get off the depressingly touristy rue des Bouchers. Daily noon–2.45pm, 6.30–11.30pm. Closed beginning Jan and first two weeks Aug. Métro De Brouckère.

South of the Grand-Place

Bleu de Toi rue des Alexiens 73 ☏ 02 502 43 71. The name means "Crazy about you", but this charming restaurant near place de la Chapelle is just crazy about spuds: never has the humble baked potato been offered with so many exotic fillings. While downstairs is given over to potatoes, upstairs lobster is the speciality. The lunch menu – starter and main – costs €13.50 and main dishes begin at €13 but can reach €65 if you like your spud with caviar. Mon–Fri noon–2pm & 7–11pm, Sat 7–11pm. Prémétro Anneessens.

Les Brigittines aux Marchés de la Chapelle place de la Chapelle 5 ☏ 02 512 68 91. This large and well-established restaurant behind the church of Notre-Dame de la Chapelle is popular for its Art Nouveau furnishings and fittings, from the fancy lighting to the dark-green walls. The place may lack intimacy, but the quality of the food more than compensates, with a choice selection of meat and seafood dishes prepared in the French style, but without an over-reliance on heavy, creamy sauces. The *croustillant de cabillaud danois* (Danish cod in filo pastry) is particularly tasty at €22. Mon–Fri noon–2.30pm & 7–10.30pm, Sat 7–11pm; closed Sun, public holidays and two weeks in summer. Prémétro Anneessens.

La Cantina rue du Jardin des Olives 13–15 ☏ 02 513 42 76. All the warmth and exuberance of Brazil awaits in this colourful restaurant just west of the Grand-Place. The menu offers a variety of exotic dishes and there are one or two cocktails to soup things up too. A buffet is available at lunch time, when you pay by weight; otherwise, a typical main is chicken with mango and okra for €13.50. Mon–Fri noon–2.30pm & 7–11pm, Sat 7–11pm. Prémétro Bourse.

Comme Chez Soi place Rouppe 23 ☏ 02 512 29 21. Tucked away in the corner of place Rouppe, *Comme Chez Soi* is something of a gastronomic legend. The restaurant's successful blending of new and more traditional French cuisine has cemented the loyalty of a varied clientele, who come for such tasty creations as spring chicken with crayfish Béarnaise sauce. There are three fixed, seasonal menus and these are the most "cost-effective" way to dine: three courses for €76, six courses for €147 or seven for €190. Reservations are necessary weeks in advance. Tues & Thurs–Sat noon–1.30pm & 7–9.30pm, Wed 7–9.30pm; closed throughout July and over the New Year period. Prémétro Anneessens.

Easy Tempo rue Haute 146 ☎ **02 513 54 40.** Bustling, popular Italian restaurant, where the service can be less than upbeat, but the antipasti selection is second to none. A two-course meal will set you back €15–25. Reservations essential. Tues–Sat noon–2.30pm & 6.30–10.30pm, Sun noon–2.30pm. Métro Louise or Porte de Hal; bus #27, #48.

La Grande Porte rue Notre Seigneur 9 ☎ **02 512 89 98.** On the northern edge of the Marolles, up near Notre-Dame de la Chapelle (and some distance from the Metro), this is a narrow and cosy old café-restaurant, whose walls are plastered with ancient posters and photos. The food could carry the Belgian flag: *stoemp*, mussels, *carbonnades à la flamande* and *waterzooi* all make an appearance, and prices are very competitive – mains cost €10–16. It can get very crowded, though. Mon–Fri noon–3pm & 6pm–2am, Sat 6pm–2am. Prémétro Anneessens.

🏃 **Orphyse Chaussette rue Charles Hanssens 5** ☎ **02 502 75 81.** Chef and owner Philippe Renoux prides himself on creating simple dishes with quality ingredients and, despite the French inspiration, vegetarians are catered for too. The setting is candle-it and intimate, and the staff willing to help you navigate your way through the extensive Tour de France wine menu. Main dishes €12–25. Tues–Sat noon–2.30pm, 7–10.30pm. Bus #27, #48, #95.

🏃 **Ploegmans rue Haute 148** ☎ **02 503 21 24.** Right in the heart of the Marolles, this is surely a contender for the title of Brussels' most authentic old brasserie, serving solid Belgian main courses for €11–16, beautifully cooked and presented, in a chatty and unpretentious environment. Mon–Thurs noon–2.30pm & 6–9.30pm, Fri & Sat noon–2.30pm & 6–10.30pm, Sun noon–3pm. Métro Porte de Hal.

Resource rue du Midi 164 ☎ **02 514 32 23.** This creative restaurant adheres to the slow food movement, and a four-course set menu,

guaranteed to last a few hours, will set you back a very competitive €53. Portions are on the small side – very nouvelle – but the quality of the ingredients, all prepared in the French manner, is second to none. Examples include turbot on a bed of laurel leaves and hind bacon with fresh herbs. Be prepared to take your time – it's a restaurant to relax in. Lunch menu €20. Tues–Sat noon–2.30pm & 7–10pm. Prémétro Anneessens.

Restobières rue des Renards 32 ☎ **02 502 72 51.** The decor may reflect the nearby flea market, with crowded walls of old musical instruments, coffee grinders and cheese graters, but what's on offer is quite simply beer. Beer in all guises, including a full range of bottles, drafts and, more originally, beer in every dish: goat's cheese salad with Kriek (€9), a casserole of mussels with Chouffe (€19) and even chocolate mousse with Hercule (€3). If the beer list is too much to take in, for €15 the selection is made for you: four beers served with dinner and a coffee at the end of your meal. Tues–Sun noon–2.30pm & 6–11pm. Métro Louise or Porte de Hal.

🏃 **Soul Food rue de la Samaritaine 20** ☎ **02 513 52 13.** An evening at *Soul Food* is both a pleasure and an education. The menu is based on the idea that we are what we eat, but there's nothing ascetic about the food, with mainly organic dishes such as sesame-encrusted salmon and quinoa with brie, courgette and seaweed. There's also a mood menu of the week – aphrodisiac or low-cholesterol, for example – for €25. Wed–Sun 7–11pm. Métro Louise or Porte de Hal; bus #48.

The Upper Town

See the "Lower & Upper Town" **map** at the back of this book.

Aux Bons Enfants place du Grand Sablon 49 ☎ **02 512 40 95.** Popular and amenable old Italian place, housed in a seventeenth-century building on the attractive place du Grand Sablon. Rustic-style decor, classical music and a menu of simple but tasty Italian dishes – steaks, pasta, hearty soups and pizza – at very reasonable prices (€8–12 for pasta, €14 for *saltimbocca* and €15 for *ossobuco*). Tues 6.30–10.15pm, Thurs–Mon noon–3pm & 6.30–10.15pm. Bus #95; tram #92, #94.

L'Ecailler du Palais Royal rue Bodenbroeck ☏ 02 521 87 51. This ultra smart and formal restaurant – there's even a dress code (no shorts or sandals) – offers perhaps the finest seafood in Brussels, with particularly wonderful lobster, but it comes at a price, with main courses kicking off at around €35. The decor is classically elegant, the atmosphere hushed and the service immaculate. Mon–Sat noon–2.30pm & 7–10.30pm; closed Aug. Métro Louise.

Et qui va promener le chein? rue de Rollebeek 2 ☏ 02 503 23 04. Situated on the pedestrianized street at the base of the Sablon, this curiously named restaurant – "And who's going to walk the dog?" – offers a mix of African, Asian, Latin American and Mediterranean dishes. At lunch, the *plat du jour* will set you back €10; a three-course evening menu €29. A la carte, dishes include chicken and mango curry (€14) and meat and seafood paella (€17). Daily noon–3pm & 6–11pm. Bus #95; tram #92, #94.

Point Bar rue du Pépin 39 ☏ 02 503 04 03. In a side street off boulevard Waterloo, this chic, contemporary restaurant has an open kitchen so you can watch the chefs as they assemble various "tastes", served in glass vessels – reminiscent of a chemistry lab. Three "tastes" at €26 might include a salad, a pasta dish and a chef's special, such as red snapper with aniseed. Nothing clinical about the final dishes – they are veritable works of art. Mon–Fri noon–2pm & 7–9.30pm, Sat 7–9.30pm. Métro Porte du Namur.

Au Stekerlapatte rue des Prêtres 4 ☏ 02 512 86 81. This famous old brasserie on a side street tucked away behind the Palais de Justice is frequented by a crowd who come for the Franco-Belgian cuisine and the friendly atmosphere, with the early-twentieth-century bistro decor an added bonus. Try the roasted pork (€18) or the

poulet à la Bruxelles (€15); there's also a daily vegetarian option. The lunch time three-course menu will set you back €12.50. The smoking bar on the first floor evades anti-smoking legislation. Tues–Fri noon–3pm & 7pm–11pm, Sat 7pm–midnight. Métro Hôtel des Monnaies.

St Gilles, avenue Louise and Ixelles

See the "St Gilles, avenue Louise & Ixelles" **map** at the back of this book.

Casa Dario av Fonsny 10 ☏ 02 539 16 42. Still standing even though many of its neighbours have been pulled down to make way for office blocks, *Casa Dario's* Spanish regulars cluster at the bar, drinking aperitifs and wolfing down tapas. The house speciality is paella (€15 per person for a minimum of two, or €22 with lobster), but meat such as roast lamb (€15) is also on offer. Tues–Fri noon–2pm & 7.30–10.30pm, Sat 7.30–10.30pm. Métro Gare du Midi.

Chez Marie rue Alphonse de Witte 40 ☏ 02 644 30 31. This long-established bistro serves impressive, mostly French cuisine in lavish but never snobbish surroundings. You can get a lovely two-course lunch for a very reasonable €16.50, but prices are a lot steeper in the evening. Mains include sea bass with olives and roast lamb with an aubergine and goat's cheese filo parcel (both €28). There's also an extensive wine list. Booking necessary. Tues–Fri noon–2pm & 7.30–10.30pm, Sat 7.30–10.30pm. Tram #81; bus #71.

Chez Oki rue Lesbroussart 62 ☏ 02 644 45 76. Japanese chef Oki Haruki has created a fusion of French and Japanese cuisine at *Chez Oki* – sushi with foie gras (€15) may sound bizarre, but it works well. The setting is pure, minimalist Zen, so there's nothing to distract you from the chef's creations. At lunch time you can order a main dish and coffee for €9, while in the evening there are several menu choices, including Oki's surprise, based on the day's offerings in the market for €30–50. Tues–Fri noon–2.30pm & 7–10pm, Mon & Sat 7–10pm. Tram #81, #94.

Citizen place St-Boniface 4 ☏ 02 502 00 08. How hot can you go? The handy guide of one, two or three chillies on the menu gives you a good idea of what to expect. This new kid on the St-Boniface block offers Thai and Vietnamese food served up by friendly

▲ Au Stekerlapatte

staff. Decor is black on black, but with a rather distracting big screen, running a classic film throughout the evening – fine if the conversation is not up to much. Rice, noodles and coconut curries with vegetables, fish, duck, pork or beef for €10–14. Mon–Fri noon–2.30pm & 7–11pm, Sat 7–11pm. Métro Porte de Namur.

Coimbra rue Jean Volders 54 ℡02 538 65 35. Renowned Portuguese restaurant specializing in fish dishes, including the sublime *caldeirada de peixe* (fish casserole with onions, potatoes and tomatoes; €18), as well as *bacalao* (salted cod) in many guises. Usually full of Portuguese locals, who also come for the excellent wine selection provided by wine merchant Alambique, whose shop is a bit higher up in St Gilles at av des Villas 5. Thurs–Mon noon–2.30pm & 7–10pm, Tues noon–2.30pm. Closed Aug. Métro Porte de Hal.

Convivio rue de l'Aqueduc 76 ℡02 539 32 99. This bright, wedge-shaped wine and pasta shop doubles up as a restaurant and is a great place for a spot of lunch or an evening meal. The menu offers a choice of four antipasti, *primi*, *secondi* and desserts – all mouth-wateringly fresh. Spinach *gnocchi* with butter and sage costs €12.50, and *ossobuco* €15; the wine list covers all of Italy's regions. There's an upbeat, convivial atmosphere, and the restaurant is child-friendly. Tues–Sat noon–2.30pm & 7–10.30pm. Bus #54; tram #81.

Dolma chaussée d'Ixelles 329–331 ℡02 649 89 81. This new-agey veggie joint, popular with locals, serves a €15 buffet lunch and a €18 buffet dinner, including quiche, soups and salads. As vegetarian cuisine goes, the dishes here aren't particularly refined – but for a refuelling carb-feast it's good value. Mon–Sat noon–2pm & 7–9.30pm. Bus #71.

L'Elément Terre chaussée de Waterloo 465 ℡02 649 37 27. One of the few entirely vegetarian restaurants left in Brussels, serving imaginative food from a creative menu. Dishes combine local vegetables with sauces and spices from around the world – enough to seduce the most determined carnivore. Main courses are themed by country or region – for example, Japanese triangles of marinated tofu with spring onions, leeks and shiitake mushrooms (€17). Friendly staff will help you distinguish tofu from tempeh, and mung beans from chickpeas. There's also a

lovely garden, open as weather permits. Tues–Fri noon–2.30pm & 7–10.30pm, Sat 7–10.30pm. Bus #54, #60, tram #92.

Le Fils de Jules rue du Page 37 ℡02 534 00 57. Basque chefs serve up first-class cuisine from southwestern France at this small and chic restaurant, in the swankiest part of Ixelles. Dishes include *cassoulet maison* – a traditional casserole with sausage, duck and beans – for €17.20. A two-course lunch with coffee is €12.80; Sunday special menu with three courses for €25. Reservations usually necessary, particularly at weekends. Tues–Fri noon–2.30pm & 7–11pm, Sat & Sun 7pm–midnight. Tram #81, bus #54.

Le Grain de Sel chaussée de Vleurgat 9 ℡02 648 18 58. French cuisine is the order of the day at this amenable restaurant, but Mediterranean influences also nose their way onto the menu; ingredients in all dishes are fresh and seasonal. A set three-course menu is a very affordable €18, with five choices of starter and main course – offerings include sea bass with courgette and fresh tomato sauce, and pork stuffed with cabbage and foie gras. Tues–Fri noon–2pm & 7.30–10pm, Sat 7.30–10pm. Bus #38, #60, #71.

L'Horloge du Sud rue du Trône 141 ℡02 512 18 64. Senegalese and Congolese specialities at highly affordable prices. Plantain, yucca and spices go into many of the daily specials and there's always a vegetarian dish of the day (€11). The three-course menu (from €20) includes dishes such as chicken marinated in lime, onions and pepper; the zingy *jus sauvage* ("wild juice"), a mix of ginger and baobab, is a great accompaniment. Among the original desserts is banana flambéed in rum from the Antilles. Mon–Fri 11am–1am, Sat & Sun 6pm–1am. Métro Trône; bus #34, #80, #95.

Leonor av de la Porte de Hal 19 ℡02 537 51 56. This well-established tapas restaurant, with a pleasant view out onto the old Porte de Hal gateway, has been going strong for thirty years. The ground floor doubles as a bar, while upstairs the wooden tables and warm lighting make for a more intimate dining space. Tapas are mainly fish-based and include plenty of octopus and Coquilles Saint-Jacques (from €5). Main dishes include veal cheek with peas and mashed potatoes for €17. A two-course lunch costs a remarkable €8. No credit cards. Mon–Sat

noon–3pm & 6.30–10pm, Sun noon–3pm.
Métro Porte de Hal.

La Medina av de la Couronne 2 ☎02 640 43 28.
Popular Moroccan restaurant kitted out in
traditional North African style. The tajines
and couscous are known for the freshness
of their ingredients and the delicacy of their
spices. The *tajine de kefta* is €12.50 and
meaty couscous, €17.50. Belly-dancing
shows at weekends. Daily noon–3pm &
6–11pm. Bus #38, #60, #95.

La Meilleure Jeunesse rue de l'Aurore 58 ☎02
640 23 94. Hidden away near the Abbaye de
la Cambre (see p.101), this chic, polished
restaurant is decorated in an idiosyncratic
version of Baroque. The food is a real exotic
mix – African, Asian and European – though
service can be slow, perhaps a trick to lure
you into drinking the fruity house cocktails.
Two-course lunch €13.50; Victoria sea bass
in a spicy African sauce €24. Mon–Fri
noon–3pm & 7pm–midnight, Sat & Sun
7pm–midnight. Tram #94.

Mille et une nuits rue Mouscou 7 ☎02 537 41
27. There's a host of Moroccan restaurants
on rue Mouscou, just off the Parvis de St
Gilles, and the competition keeps prices low
and standards high. The luxuriant decor of
this particular restaurant (the "1001 Nights")
is inviting – try the couscous *maison*
(€16.90) or the tajine with chicken, sesame
and honey (€14.90). Second helpings of
couscous are available too. Mon–Sat noon–
2.30pm & 6–11pm. Métro Porte de Hal.

La Mirabelle chaussée de Boondael 459 ☎02
649 51 73. Up near the university, at the
southern end of Ixelles, this Belgian
brasserie serves up mostly meaty dishes,
with some – like rabbit *à la gueuze* (€13.70)
– cooked in beer. The interior is simple, with
bare brick walls, and there's a conservatory
and a large terrace at the back. Daily noon–
3pm & 6pm–2.30am. Bus #71, #95.

Mont Liban rue de Livourne 30–32 ☎02 537 71
31. A combination of Lebanese restaurant
and snack bar, where the food is excellent
at both, though prices at the snack bar are
– as you might expect – considerably
cheaper. The houmous is especially tasty,
and there's a wide choice of *mezze*. Fixed
four-course menu €20 (minimum two
people); main courses include fried baby
octopus for €12.50 and grilled or fried sea
bream for €37.50/kilo. Sunday brunch €25
for adults, half-price for children. The restaurant gets lively at weekends when the

belly-dancers turn up. Snack bar: daily
11am–11pm; restaurant daily noon–3pm &
7–11pm. Tram #92, #94.

Notos rue de Livourne 154 ☎02 513 29 59.
Owner and chef Constantin Erinkoglou
takes great pride in serving up the freshest
and tastiest of ingredients in all his dishes,
beating the usual Greek *mezze* by a mile.
Try the duck with figs and pear at €26, the
leg of lamb with courgette and coriander at
€24 or the vegetarian special at €20.
Two-course lunch €18. Reservations
recommended. Tues–Fri noon–2pm &
7–11pm, Sat 7–11pm. Tram #81, #94.

O-Chinoise-Riz rue de l'Aqueduc 94 ☎02 534
91 08. This small restaurant, just round the
corner from place du Châtelain, is where the
Chinese come to eat Chinese food. The
food is excellent, and almost as much as a
draw is the spectacle of seeing the cooks
boiling and sizzling your meal in the open-
plan kitchen. Get your chopstick skills up to
scratch as no cutlery is available. It's
remarkably cheap by Brussels standards – a
three-course lunch is €10 and Peking duck
pancake €13.50, as well as the usual
noodle combos for around €9.50. Tues–Fri
noon–2.30pm & 6–11pm, Sat & Sun
6–11pm. Bus #54; tram #81.

Le Pavillon rue Defacqz 64 ☎02 538 02 15.
This appealing restaurant, with the
atmosphere of a cosy bistro, offers no-frills
cuisine such as roast shoulder of lamb (€12)
and *roulades au chicon* (endive rolls). The
menu is strictly seasonal and uses local
suppliers. No credit cards. Mon–Fri
noon–11.30pm. Bus #54; tram #81.

**Premier Comptoir Noi chaussée de Charleroi
39** ☎02 537 44 47. Don't be put off by the
bright-yellow facade – behind it is a simple
and welcoming Thai restaurant where the
service is exemplary. Amongst many
inexpensive dishes, there's very spicy raw
scampi and red pepper and bamboo
chicken. Also on the menu is *tom yam
khung* (lemongrass soup with prawns;
€14.90), and duck in red curry with
coconut milk (€16.50). You can eat on the
terrace out back when weather permits.
Vegetarian menu available on request.
Mon, Tues & Sat 7–10.30pm, Wed–Fri
noon–2pm & 7–10.30pm. Closed Aug.
Tram #92, #94.

La Quincaillerie rue du Page 45 ☎02 533 98 33.
A stylish, well-heeled clientele frequent this
restaurant, occupying an imaginatively

▲ La Quincaillerie

revamped old hardware shop in the fashionable Châtelain area. It's well known for its delicious Belgian and French cuisine, with fish and fowl specialities, often prepared in imaginative ways. A two-course set lunch costs as little as €13, while a three-course dinner weighs in at either €26 or €30. The menu might include sole with lobster sauce or rack of lamb with courgette purée and rosemary. There's also an enormous seafood platter for €28. Mon–Fri noon–2.30pm & 7pm–midnight, Sat & Sun 7pm–midnight. Bus #54; tram #81.

Shanti av Adolphe Buyl 68 ☎02 649 40 96. Vegetarian and fish restaurant with an ornate interior littered with plants. Elaborately presented dishes include vegetable korma with tofu croquettes (€17) and the "Pleasures of Neptune" – fish and seafood platter (€14). Be sure to leave room for the chocolate cake. Tues–Sat noon–2pm & 7–10pm. Bus #71; tram #94.

Tan rue de l'Aqueduc 95 ☎02 537 87 87. Walk through the wholefoods shop and up the stairs to the restaurant at the back – all wood and natural tones. Ultra-healthy dishes made using local, organic produce and cooked in such a way as to preserve all the nutritional benefits. The menu is divided into vegan dishes and those that contain cheese, fish or meat. Tues–Fri noon–3pm & 7–11pm, Sat 7–11pm. Bus #54; tram #81.

Tom Yam chaussée de Boondael 341 ☎02 646 50 13. Out by the university, this popular Thai restaurant has a warm and welcoming feel. The menu is large, but based on a handful of key ingredients and sauces, with plenty of vegetarian options. A two-course lunch with tea/coffee is €10.50; evening mains include the very spicy chicken with Thai basil at €10 and green, red or yellow vegetable curries for €9.85. Mon–Fri

noon–2pm & 6.30–10.30pm, Sat 6.30–10.30pm. Bus #71; tram #94.

Toucan av Louis Lepoutre 1 ☎02 345 30 17. The name of this brasserie may come from the tropical bird, but the decorative theme is more about clocks – there's a massive clockwork sculpture on the wall and a projected image of a clock behind the bar. The food is excellent, with a varied menu of meat, fish and vegetarian dishes, and there's a very good wine list too. Mains include red tuna in filo pastry with leeks for €16.50 and spinach and ricotta *ravioles* in a sage sauce for €12.60. Save space for the desserts, which include crème brûlée with acacia honey and saffron. Reservations advised. Daily noon–2.30pm & 7–11pm. Bus #60 from Gare Centrale; tram #92.

Volle Gas place Fernand Cocq 21 ☎02 502 89 17. This traditional, wood-panelled bar-brasserie serves classic Belgian cuisine in a friendly, family atmosphere. The Brussels specialities on offer include the delicious *carbonnades de boeuf à la gueuze* (€12.50) and *lapin à la kriek* (€13.50) – beef or rabbit cooked in beer – but pasta and salads are also available. Mon–Sat noon–3pm & 6pm–midnight, Sun 6pm–midnight. Bus #54, #71.

Yamato rue Francart 11 ☎02 502 28 93. This tiny and busy Japanese noodle bar with minimalist decor just round the corner from rue St-Boniface is not the place for a leisurely lunch – it's eat and go. This is authentic Japanese food at affordable prices, with mains for as little as €8. Vegetarians must not be fooled by the noodles with vegetables – there's a big bone simmering in the pot. Tues, Wed & Fri–Sat noon–2pm & 7–10pm. Métro Porte de Namur.

Yamayu Santatsu chaussée d'Ixelles 141 ☎02 513 53 12. This well-established sushi and sashimi restaurant is one of the finest in Brussels and, despite its reputation for the rudeness of its staff, is popular with Belgians and Japanese alike. Ask to sit downstairs, where the sushi bar is the centre of the action. It's usually packed, so you need to be snappy with your orders and settle down with some cold *sake* for what can be a considerable wait. Lunch – including sushi and grilled fish or meat – is €10, otherwise sushi is €14–25. Reservations essential. Tues–Sat noon–2pm & 7–10pm. Bus #54, #71.

EU Quarter and around

See the "EU Quarter and around" **map** at the back of this book.

L'Ancienne Poissonerie rue du Trône 65 ⊕ **02 502 75 05.** A small, flashy Italian restaurant in a cleverly reworked old fish shop – the Art Nouveau trimmings on the outside have been kept, but everything within is stylishly modern. The food is very nouvelle, so if you're really hungry you're probably better off elsewhere. *Linguine alla puttanesca* will set you back €12, sea bream with white wine and tomatoes €18. Mon–Fri noon–3pm & 7–11pm, Sat 7–11pm. Métro Trône.

L'Atelier rue Franklin 28 ⊕ **02 734 91 40.** Set back behind a peaceful courtyard, this French-Belgian restaurant has a light, airy feel, and serves good food at reasonable prices – for example *waterzooi* for €17. Outside seating in summer. Mon–Fri noon–2.30pm & 7–10pm. Métro Schuman.

La Bodeguilla rue Archimède 65–67 ⊕ **02 736 34 49.** This simple Spanish tapas bar in a basement is popular with legions of Spanish expats, who are attracted by the home cooking and inexpensive prices – the daily special costs just €9.50. A particular favourite is the tortilla, gambas and garlic mushrooms. A good place for a quick snack before hitting the town. Mon–Sat noon–midnight. Métro Schuman.

Chou place de Londres 4 ⊕ **02 511 92 38.** Chef Dominque Aubrey has taken a bit of a gamble by investing in this restaurant on a pretty but really rather run-down square on the edge of the EU Quarter. The welcome, however, is second to none, and the French cuisine is exemplary. Try the fresh herb salad and mackerel starter (€14), and the cod with vegetables as a main (€24). Mon–Fri noon–2.30pm & 7–10.30pm. Métro Porte de Namur.

Enoteria av des Celtes 8 ⊕ **02 735 01 50.** The *Enoteria* has a first-rate wine cellar and offers a tasty range of broadly Italian dishes as accompaniment. Main dishes include *tagliatelle* with asparagus, scampi and goat's cheese (€13), or veal liver with sun-dried tomatoes and coriander (€18). Two-course lunch menu €14.50. Mon–Fri noon–2.30pm & 7–10.30pm. Métro Mérode.

Mi Tango rue de Spa 31 ⊕ **02 230 99 95.** This tiny restaurant brings together Italian and Argentinian cuisine in giant-sized portions. Home-made ravioli stuffed with ricotta, saffron and lemon (€12) and Argentinian steak with heaps of vegetables (€17.50) – followed by tiramisù – are just some of the delights on offer. Mon–Fri noon–2.30pm & 7–10.30pm, Sat 7–10.30pm. Métro Arts-Loi.

Slovenian House chaussée de Wavre 402 ⊕ **02 646 63 91.** Just off place Jourdan, this restaurant specializes in everything Slovenian, a cuisine which combines the polenta of northern Italy, southern European vegetables, and mouthwatering pastries and strudels. The excellent lunch-time buffet is a snip at €15; evenings are à la carte. Mon–Fri noon–3pm & 7–10.30pm, Sat 7–10.30pm. Métro Schuman.

Outlying Districts

For restaurants in Waterloo, see p.135.

Atomium Restaurant Sphere Lola Bobesco (Heysel) ⊕ **02 479 58 50.** Moderately priced considering the location, although you have to get a €3 ticket to ride the elevator to get up here, and you may have to queue. This objection aside, the food is pretty good, with the emphasis on seasonal Belgian cooking and produce. There are several set menus, including a monthly three-course menu for €25, and a tasting menu for €35. Good cooking, attentive service in an informal environment, and great views over the whole of Brussels. Daily 10am–6pm. Métro Heysel.

La Cueva de Castilla place Colignon 14 (Schaerbeek) 14 ⊕ **02 241 81 80.** Spanish brothers Roberto in the restaurant and Javier in the kitchen offer a menu that brings together the creative and the traditional. Don't be put off by the kitsch decor, with a painted wine cellar on the wall, as the food is superlative; grilled swordfish with garlic, Spanish peppers and almonds is a typical offering. The dish of the day is chalked up

▲ Turkish restaurants in St Josse

on the board, and there's also a three-course menu (€39), as well as a tapas menu. Mon, Tues, Thurs, Fri & Sun noon–2.30pm & 6.30–10.30pm, Sat 6.30–10.30pm. Tram #92.

Has chaussée de Haecht 15; no phone (Schaarbeek). A Turkish restaurant with great wood-oven-cooked *pide* bread – long and thin, with a variety of toppings, and washed down with Turkish tea for around €6. The *etli ekmek* – *pide* with minced lamb, herbs and chilli – is a popular choice. Very kid-friendly, like all the places along this stretch. Métro Botanique, then tram #92 or #94.

Sahbaz chaussée de Haecht 102–104 (Schaarbeek) ☎ 02 217 02 77. Undoubtedly one of the best Turkish restaurants in the capital. The food is cheap and delicious, the staff friendly and attentive, and a cheerful atmosphere prevails. Favourites include the Turkish pizzas (€5–8), and the mixed grill (€12), accompanied by a glass of *ayran*, a delicious yoghurt drink. Thurs–Tues 11.30am–3pm & 6pm–midnight. Métro Botanique, then tram #92 or #94.

Senza Nome rue Royale Sainte-Marie 22 (Schaarbeek) ☎ 02 223 16 17. The distressed terracotta walls and faded frescoes at this Michelin-starred restaurant next to the Halles de Schaerbeek make it a perfect spot for a dinner for two. Try the veal escalopes fried with sage, parma ham and *taleggio* cheese and glazed with white wine – great cuisine that doesn't come cheap: expect to pay around €30 for a main course. Mon–Fri noon–2.30pm & 7–11pm, Sat 7–11pm. Closed mid-July to mid-Aug. Tram #92, #94.

Cafés

See the "Grand-Place & around" **map** at the back of this book.

The Grand-Place and around

🏃 **L'Arrière Cuisine rue des Grands Carmes 11.** Delicious quiches and cakes, an all-day breakfast for late-risers, and over forty varieties of tea. Wed–Sat 11.30am–7pm, Tues & Sun 9.30am–7pm. Prémétro Anneessens.

Café Vaudeville Galerie de la Reine. A good place to rest your weary legs and watch the world go by in the Galeries St-Hubert. They do a great hot chocolate, cocktails in the evening, and decent food (salads, Belgian specialities such as steak tartare and *waterzooi*, and great fish dishes) – very moderately priced and served all day. Mon–Sat 10am–10pm, Sun 10am–8pm. Métro De Brouckère or Gare Centrale.

L'Express Quality rue des Chapeliers 8. Lebanese specialities – pitta with meat or falafel, houmous, halloumi and the like – are on offer here. You can either eat in the cushion-filled basement, or take away. Mon–Fri noon–3pm & 6pm–1am, Sat & Sun 1pm–1am. Prémétro Bourse.

Le Falstaff rue Henri Maus 19. Something of an institution, this venerable café-cum-restaurant is much lauded for its Art Nouveau decoration. It attracts a mixed

▲ Le Falstaff

bag of tourists, eurocrats and bourgeois Bruxellois, and is a great place to sit back and soak up the atmosphere. There's a predictable choice of Belgian food on offer, including a mouthwatering selection of cakes and tarts. The waiters can be startlingly brusque, though. Daily 10am–2am. Prémétro Bourse.

🏃 **Senne rue du Bon Secours 4.** Named after the river that used to run through Brussels, but was covered over in the mid-nineteenth century, this modern snack-bar provides simple, fresh and healthy food at reasonable prices. It's both a shop selling tempting Italian delicacies and a café serving home-made quiches, pastas, soups and cakes (€8.50–13.50). You can take away, but the funky music and lively atmosphere make it an ideal place to eat in.

Just off blvd Anspach. Tues–Sat 10am–6pm. Prémétro Anneessens.

The Lower Town

See the "Lower & Upper Town" **map** at the back of this book.

West of the Grand-Place

Le Cirio rue de la Bourse 18. This is one of Brussels' oldest café-bars, originally opened in 1886 as a shop-cum-restaurant by Francesco Cirio, a pioneer of canned fruit and vegetables. Although the elaborate Art Nouveau decor is now somewhat frayed round the edges, it remains one of the most attractive places in town. Once frequented, they say, by Jacques Brel, it appeals mostly to an older clientele, many of whom come here specially for their "half-and-half", made up of champagne and white wine – a drink the house claims to have invented. Prémétro Bourse.

Comus & Gasterea quai aux Briques 86. Truly divine ice cream in an amazing variety of flavours, including the likes of curry and ginger – but in winter try a hot chocolate with 70 percent real chocolate and no added sugar. Tues–Fri 11am–6pm, Sat 9am–11am, Sun, Mon & public holidays 2–6pm. Métro Ste-Catherine.

Côté Soleil rue van Artevelde 93–95. Shop and tasting-house for a cooperative of farmers from the Pajottenland district southwest of Brussels. The food and drinks are full of flavour and, of course, very fresh. Fetch your own drinks from the fridge and order breakfast, veggie tapas, quiche and sandwiches at the counter. Mon–Sat 11am–11pm, Sun 11am–6pm. Métro Bourse.

Eetcafé de Markten place du Vieux Marché aux Grains 5. This Flemish café, with long wooden tables and friendly staff, buzzes with chatter and activity, and offers no-nonsense, good-quality salads and pastas at very reasonable prices. Mon–Sat 11am–11pm, Sun 11am–6pm. Métro Ste-Catherine.

Noordzee place Ste-Catherine 1. A fish shop really, but at lunch-time it's also a stand-up joint that serves oysters and whelks, soup and other fishy snacks, washed down with chilled white wine, to a crowd of very appreciative regulars. Mon–Fri noon–2pm. Métro Ste-Catherine.

North of the Grand-Place

Arcadi rue d'Arenberg 1b. At the northern end of the Galeries St-Hubert, this hard-to-beat café is a perfect spot for lunch, afternoon tea or just a snack. Decorated in brisk, functional style, it's something of a warren, with three small areas: two on the ground floor and a mezzanine up above. The menu offers plenty of choice, but the salads, quiches and fruit tarts are particularly delicious and very reasonably priced. It can get a little too crowded for comfort at lunchtimes, but at least the service is turbo-charged. Daily 7/8am–11pm. Métro De Brouckère or Gare Centrale.

South of the Grand-Place

Het Warm Water rue des Renards 25. At the top of this cobbled side street, which is lined with galleries and shops, "Warm Water" is a typical, down-to-earth Marolles café. One evening a week there's also a political debate when you're bound to hear a spot of Brusselse Sproek, the local lingo. The food is simple – quiche, salad, pasta – and it's one of the few Belgian originals that's great for veggies. Mon, Tues & Sun 8am–7pm, Thurs–Sat 8am–10pm. Métro Louise or Porte de Hal; bus #27, #48.

Jeux de Bols rue Blaes 163. Inspired by his mother, who used to make Lebanese-style soup for the shoppers at the flea market, Salah Jalkh has set up this lively café on the corner of place du Jeu de Balle at the heart of the Marolles district. Salah has even brought the market inside, as all the bric-a-brac is for sale. Tues–Sun 7am–4pm. Métro Porte de Hal; bus #27, #48.

Novo place de la Vieille Halles aux Blés 37. Friendly café with excellent local cuisine, including daily specials for around €11. There's a terrace out front as well as a sunny courtyard at the back, making it a great place to while away a few hours – and they provide the newspapers. Mon–Sat 10am–2am, Sun 6pm–2am. Bus #48, #95.

The Upper Town

See the "Lower & Upper Town" **map** at the back of this book.

Artipasta place de la Liberté 1. Real Italian home-made pasta – much, much more than the usual suspects – is served in this corner café that, as the name suggests, doubles up as an art gallery. There's a great variety of antipasti on offer too, and both the menu and the art change regularly. Mon–Thurs 11am–4pm, Fri 11am–4pm & 7pm–midnight. Métro Madou.

Crêperie L'Herbaudière place de la Liberté 9. Cheerful, neighbourhood pancake place in a pleasant corner of the Upper Town. Agreeable, low-key atmosphere and a great range of crepes from €8. Mon–Fri 10am–7pm. Métro Madou.

L'Orangerie du Parc d'Egmont parc d'Egmont. Hidden away near the Palais de Justice, the parc d'Egmont features on few itineraries, but it's a pleasant slice of greenery and an enjoyable setting for the *Orangerie*, which makes the most of its location with a large terrace. Soups and quiches, as well as more substantial main dishes, are available, but it's also ideal for tea and cakes on a sunny afternoon. Sun–Fri 10.30am–6pm. Métro Louise.

Le Pain Quotidien rue des Sablons 11. One of a successful chain of bakery-cafés serving simple but good-quality home-baked food – bread, croissants, quiches and pastries. The decor – all natural colours and plain wood – is livened up by the range of goodies on sale: chocolate cookies, home-made jams and coffee. The atmosphere's relaxed too. Mon–Fri 7.30am–7pm, Sat & Sun 8am–7pm. Métro Louise. Also at rue Antoine Dansaert 22 (Métro Ste-Catherine).

Le Perroquet rue Watteau 31. This small, semicircular café-bar, a 2min walk from place du Grand Sablon, has stained-glass windows and original Art Nouveau decor. Young and old rub shoulders over cheap salads and pittas, whilst those of a more dipsomaniacal disposition work their way through the long list of speciality beers. Although it's often difficult to get a seat no matter when you turn up, it's worth the hassle. Daily noon–1am. Bus #48, #95.

St Gilles, avenue Louise and Ixelles

See the "St Gilles, avenue Louise & Ixelles" **map** at the back of this book.

BHV place Van Meenen 33. In the shadow of the Maison Communale in St Gilles, the cheekily named *BHV* is a classic Belgian pun: at one level, it stands for *Buffet de l'Hôtel de Ville*, on another Brussels-Hal-Vilvorde, an ongoing political sticking point between the country's Flemish- and French-speakers (see p.263). Joking aside,

the place offers excellent lunches with plenty of fresh vegetables and organic products. Mon–Fri 11am–3pm. Prémétro Horta.

Café Belga place Flagey 18. With its terrace overlooking the étangs d'Ixelles (see p.105), this big, modern café-bar is an ideal spot for breakfast, lunch or dinner – or just a drink or two – before or after visiting the place Flagey market or the film and concert hall next door. Another Nicolay classic (see *Zebra*, p.208). Sun–Thurs 8am–2am, Fri & Sat 8am–3am. Bus #71; tram #81.

The Coffee Shop rue de Stassart 131. It's open during the week for breakfast and lunch, but one of the main attractions of this bright café is its Sunday brunch, with a full English breakfast for just €9.50. Just off place Stéphanie, opposite Nicola's Bookshop (see p.224). Mon–Fri 7.30am–3.30pm, Sat & Sun 10am–6pm. Métro Louise.

Comptoir Florian rue Saint-Boniface 17. A well-known figure hereabouts, Vincent Perpète has been buying, testing and selling teas and coffees for over six years. His café lends itself to intimate conversation – mobile phones are forbidden – and this is not the place for anyone in a hurry: a good cup of tea takes (and deserves) time. Ask for advice on the best blends. Tues–Sat 11am–8pm. Métro Porte de Namur.

Les Deux Paons rue d'Albanie 77. "The Two Peacocks" offers coffee, tea and hot chocolate with cinnamon or orange in an exquisite 1903 Art Nouveau house – designed by architect Frank Arendsoet. It's also the perfect spot for a weekend aperitif. Sat & Sun 2–7pm. Prémétro Horta.

L'Epicerie rue Keyenveld 56. You can enjoy a tasty lunch or grab a bite to eat before the cinema at this grocery shop-cum-café, among the assorted shelves, counters and scales. On the menu is Thai curry, as well as salads and quiches. Mon–Sat 10am–3pm & 5–8pm. Métro Porte de Namur.

Friterie Flagey place Flagey. Everyone has their favourite *friterie* and some claim this one to be the best in Brussels – it's certainly always busy. Buy your *frites* and eat them by the Ixelles ponds across the street. Bus #70; tram #81.

Passiflore rue du Bailli 97. Overlooking the church of Ste-Trinité, this trendy but relaxing café serves light lunches, including home-made salmon and spinach quiche, crepes and salads. It's usually packed on

Sunday mornings, when hordes of pasty-faced late-twenty-somethings attempt to cure their hangovers with one of the good-value continental breakfasts. Mon–Fri 8am–7pm, Sat & Sun 9am–7.30pm. Bus #54; tram #81.

SiSiSi chaussée de Charleroi 174. This popular, late-opening café enjoys a loyal, local following of hip young things. The large windows allow you to watch the world drift by, and it's a particularly good spot for lunch, with good panini, salads and pastas. Daily 11am–4am (kitchen closes at midnight). Tram #81, #92, #97.

Sucré Salé place Fernand Cocq 10. Great spot for a sweet or savoury bite to eat, with generous salads and delicious cakes, temptingly displayed in the Art Nouveau window. Mon–Fri 7am–6.30pm, Sat 8am–7pm. Métro Porte de Namur.

Tartisan rue de la Paix 27. Well-established café and takeaway that's famous for its quiches – with fillings such as goat's cheese and spinach or ratatouille, served with a large salad. Leave room for dessert – the chocolate log melts in the mouth. Mon–Sat 10am–11pm. Métro Porte de Namur.

L'Ultime Atome rue St-Boniface 14. A large selection of beers and wines, simple but tasty cuisine and late opening hours make this funky café-bar a hit with the trendy Ixelles crowd on weekdays and weekends alike. Its location, on rue St-Boniface, also makes it a great place to sit outside with a newspaper in the summer. Daily 8.30am–12.30am. Métro Porte de Namur.

EU Quarter and around

See the "EU Quarter & around" **map** at the back of the book.

El Vergel rue du Trône 39. This colourful café brings a burst of Latino sun to Brussels' grey skies. The Mexican enchiladas, fair-trade products and inexpensive daily specials are all draws, though portions are on the small side. Mon–Wed & Fri 7.30am–3pm, Thurs 7.30am–3pm & 6–10.30pm. Métro Trône.

Kafeneio rue Stevin 134. Behind the Berlay-mont, this Greek-themed café and ouzeri does good coffee and Greek cakes, as well as ouzo and retsina, and cold *mezze*, as well as more substantial fare. Daily 8am–1am. Métro Schuman.

Maison Antoine place Jourdan. Not a café at all, but generally regarded as the best *frites* stand in the city. Apparently the secret is in the double-frying – first the potatoes are blanched at a low temperature and then, after ordering, finished to a crispy golden brown. A good dollop of mayonnaise – or one of the host of other toppings – will finish it off a treat. If it's raining, you can tuck into your *frites* at any one of the bars around the square, as long as you buy a drink (see *Chez Bernard*, p.211). Daily 11.30am–2am. Métro Schuman.

Le Midi Cinquante parc du Cinquantenaire 10. On the right of the arc de triomphe as you enter Le Cinquantenaire park from Métro Schuman, the light and airy café of the Royal Museum of Art and History (see p.114) is worth a visit in its own right. In the summer there's a lovely terrace overlooking the park. Tues–Sun 9.30am–5pm. Métro Schuman.

Mi Figue-Mi Raisin rue Archimede 71. Organic breakfasts and lunches – tortilla, quiche, pasta, salad – are served in the tiled café, or in the garden when the elements permit. It's also a pleasant spot for afternoon tea. Mon–Fri 8am–7pm. Métro Schuman.

Le Petit Village rue Froissart 87. You'll find steamy windows and a warm welcome at this tiny restaurant, where the menu is solidly Middle Eastern. Most people visit the kitchen to see what's cooking before they make their choice. Mon–Fri noon–3pm. Métro Schuman.

Le Thé au Harem d'Archi Ahmed chaussée de Louvain 52–54. Belgians like to play with words and the name of this Art Nouveau café is a great example – "Archi Ahmed's Harem" or "Archimedes's Theorem" – whichever way you want to read it, though it's probably the former, judging by the fancy decoration. Great for a fresh mint tea break during a shopping trip, and simple Belgian food and salads are also served until 4.30pm. Mon–Sat 11.30am–7pm. Métro Madou.

Outlying Districts

Chez Martin place St Josse (St Josse). A favourite Brussels *friterie*, whose excellent chips you can enjoy in one of the nearby bars provided you buy a drink. Daily 11.30am–2.30pm & 6.30–9pm. Bus #63 from place de Brouckère.

Bars

The Grand-Place and around

See the "Grand-Place & around" **map** at the back of this book.

La Bécasse rue de Tabora 11 ⊕ **02 511 00 06.** Down a short and inconsequential-looking alley, this unreconstructed, nineteenth-century bar, with its long wooden benches, stained panelling and draped curtains, has an excellent beer menu and the atmosphere of a community hall. It's one of the few places in Belgium where you can drink authentic lambic and gueuze (see the *Belgian beer* colour section), served in earthenware jugs that can hold up to 15 litres. Located just to the northwest of the Grand-Place, and metres from St-Nicolas. Métro De Brouckère or Prémétro Bourse.

Au Bon Vieux Temps rue du Marché aux Herbes 12 ⊕ **02 217 26 26.** Tucked away down an alley and only a minute's walk from the Grand-Place, this is a small, intimate and wonderfully cosy place with tile-inlaid tables and a big wooden bar, attracting a convivial, older crowd. The building dates back to 1695 and the stained-glass window, depicting the Virgin Mary and St Michael, was originally in a local parish church. Popular with British servicemen just after the end of World War II, the bar still has ancient signs advertising Mackenzie's Port and Bass pale ale. Métro De Brouckère or Prémétro Bourse.

La Brouette Grand-Place 2–3 ⊕ **02 511 54 94.** Arguably the pick of the many café-bars lining the Grand-Place, *La Brouette* is comfortably decked out, and there's a splendid open fireplace and an upstairs section whose window seats offer a charming view over the main square. A tasty range of snacks, salads, cakes and pancakes are on offer, and the service is usually rapid, which can't be said for many of its neighbours. Prémétro Bourse.

Café Fontainas rue du Marché au Charbon 91 ⊕ **02 503 31 12.** The epitome of cool Brussels, this old favourite still manages to draw a trendy crowd to its rather cramped interior and outside tables. DJs at weekends. Prémétro Bourse.

Le Cercle des Voyagers rue des Grandes Carmes 18 ⊕ **02 514 39 49.** This colonial-style lounge bar with deep leather chairs and atmospheric lighting is the perfect place to plan your next holiday. Browse through the brochures on the tables or pop next door to the travel bookshop. Prémétro Bourse.

Dolle Mol rue des Éperonniers 52. In the Sixties *Dolle Mol* was home to a band of anarcho-artistic regulars. The bar eventually closed and the building was abandoned until Jan Bucquoy – artist and political activist – came along and squatted in the building until he could convince the Flemish community to buy it as an item of local heritage. Now reopened, the walls sport the café's archives and the tables and chairs have been provided by supporters of the cause. The beer is very cheap and there's (anarchic) entertainment on a regular basis. Métro Gare Centrale.

Goupil Le Fol rue de la Violette 22 ⊕ **02 511 13 96.** This unusual bar, between the Grand-Place and the Manneken Pis, should not be missed, especially if you're keen on traditional French singing from the likes of Edith Piaf or Belgium's own Jacques Brel (see p.64). Every surface is covered with *chanson française* memorabilia and the decor holds reminders of the building's previous incarnation as a brothel, with three floors of cosy corners, sofas to sink into, and dimmed red lights. A house speciality is the delicious and extremely potent fruit wine, which comes in all manner of combinations. Métro Gare Centrale.

A l'Imaige de Nostre-Dame rue du Marché aux Herbes 6 ⊕ **02 219 42 49.** A quirky little bar with two small rooms and rough plaster walls, situated at the end of a long, narrow alley. Wooden benches propel strangers into conversation, as do the bar staff, at least one of whom loves letting rip with his *chansons*. There's also a good range of speciality beers including Saint Feuillien and dark Affligem. Prémétro Bourse.

El Metteko blvd Anspach 88 ⊕ **02 512 46 48.** The noise of the traffic on the main road does nothing to dissuade an eclectic, youthful clientele from gathering on *El Metteko*'s terrace. There's frequent live music at the weekends – expect to hear anything from *klezmer* to salsa. They also serve food – mainly pasta, salads and tapas. Next door to the Bourse. Prémétro Bourse.

Ommegang rue Charles Buls 2 ☎ 02 511 82 44.
Surprisingly enough, this venerable establishment, attached to the posh *Maison du Cygne* restaurant just off the Grand-Place, was once Karl Marx's local. Marx knew it as the *Cygne Café*, and it was here that he polished and buffed the *Communist Manifesto* at meetings of exilèd German socialists. There's nothing to commemorate Marx's visits, but there is a plaque on the wall celebrating the founding of the Belgian Socialist Party here in April 1885. The café serves great food and is a good spot for a quiet drink, though poor old Karl would doubtless find it all a bit bourgeois. Prémétro Bourse.

O'Reilly's place de la Bourse 1 ☎ 02 552 04 80.
This large Irish theme bar directly opposite the Bourse is the venue of choice for Irish supporters when there's a rugby or football game on. It's also the only bar in the centre which screens live English premiership football. Although nothing to write home about, it's a handy enough meeting place, except on Fri and Sat nights when the bar is mobbed with drunken revellers. Food (fries, baked potatoes, Irish stew, chicken) is available from 11am–10pm. Prémétro Bourse.

Plattesteen rue du Marche au Charbon 41 ☎ 02 512 82 03. Though right in the heart of gay Brussels, there is no bar more mixed or more convivial than this old-timer. It's also unintentionally famous as it features in every photo you see of the famous Frank Pé mural right next door. Prémétro Bourse.

Le Roi d'Espagne Grand-Place 1 ☎ 02 513 08 07. A well-known, supremely touristy café-bar housed in one of the Grand-Place's handsome guildhouses. Inside, a collection of marionettes and inflated animal bladders is suspended from the ceiling, and there are naff imitation pikes in the boys' toilet. To its credit, you do get a fine view of the Grand-Place from the room upstairs, as well as from the pavement-terrace, but frankly *La Brouette* (see p.206), just along the square, is a much better bet. Prémétro Bourse.

🏃 **Au Soleil rue du Marché au Charbon 86 ☎ 02 512 34 30.** Formerly a men's clothing shop, this cramped and popular bar attracts a mixed, bohemian crowd. Bar snacks are served, as well as a good range of beers at very competitive prices. There's an appealingly laid-back atmosphere, but

it's often difficult to get a seat come nightfall. A brief walk southwest of the Grand-Place, at the corner of rue des Grands Carmes. Prémétro Bourse.

🏃 **Toone Impasse Schuddeveld 6 ☎ 02 513 54 86.** The ancient bar belonging to the Toone puppet theatre (see p.57) comprises two small rooms with old posters on rough plaster walls, plus a small (and really rather uninviting) outside terrace. It has a reasonably priced beer list, a modest selection of snacks, and a soundtrack of classical and jazz, making it one of the centre's more congenial watering holes. There are two alley-entrances, one on Petite rue des Bouchers, the other on rue du Marché aux Herbes, opposite rue des Harengs. Métro Gare Centrale.

The Lower Town

See the "Lower & Upper Town" **map** at the back of this book.

West of the Grand-Place

Le Greenwich rue des Chartreux 7 ☎ 02 511 41 67. An oasis of calm in a commercial storm, this smoky, traditional chess bar has long been patronized by chess and back-gammon enthusiasts, including – locals say – Magritte, no less. Although a little down-at-heel, it was recently immort alized in

▲ La Fleur en Papier Doré

Francois Ozon's film *Paradise*, starring Charlotte Rampling. Prémétro Bourse.

Le Java rue St-Géry 31 ☏ **02 512 37 16.** Close to the attractive place St-Géry, this small triangular bar seems perpetually thronged with city slickers and funksters living it up on schnapps and cocktails. If you like Gaudí-inspired decor, groovy music and a kicking atmosphere, look no further. Prémétro Bourse.

Kafka rue de la Vierge Noire 6 ☏ **02 513 54 89.** No prizes for guessing the theme of this bar – though it's certainly not as surreal as its Czech namesake. It's dark and smoky, even on the sunniest of days, but the place does have its own particular charm. Métro De Brouckère.

Mappa Mundo rue du Pont de la Carpe 2 ☏ **02 514 35 55.** People come to this oak-lined pub, another Frédéric Nicolay adventure (see *Zebra*, p.208), for some serious drinking. To soak it all up, try one of their copious all-morning breakfasts or the Sunday brunch (for which reservations are essential). The rest of the menu consists of bagels, pittas, salads and soups, served 11am–3pm and 6pm–1am. Prémétro Bourse.

Monk rue Ste-Catherine 42 ☏ **02 503 08 80.** With its high ceilings and dark wooden panelling, this large, popular, mostly Flemish bar is named after the jazz musician Thelonious Monk. Appropriately, a grand piano takes pride of place. Unusually for Brussels, service is at the bar. Just off place Ste-Catherine. Métro Ste-Catherine.

🏃 **Walvis rue Dansaert 209** ☏ **02 219 95 32.** Frédéric Nicolay (see *Zebra*, below) strikes again, attracting a hip young crowd to this lively, modern canalside café-bar, a 10min walk from place Ste-Catherine. DJs often do a turn on Thurs and Fri evenings. Métro Ste-Catherine; tram #81.

Zebra place St-Géry 33–35 ☏ **02 511 19 01.** This small, fashionable bar on the corner of place St-Géry was the first venture of Frédéric Nicolay, the Belgian entrepreneur who went on to reinvigorate the city's nightlife with *Bonsoir Clara* (see p.193), *Belga* (see p.194), *Mappa Mundo* (see above) and *Walvis* (see above). It remains the chicest of locations – anyone who's anyone has been here at some point – and attracts a young, trendy crowd who come for the upbeat atmosphere and groovy

music. It's also hugely popular in summer when people come in their droves to read their newspapers on the large terrace. Prémétro Bourse.

North of the Grand-Place

Café Métropole place de Brouckère 31 ☏ **02 219 23 84.** This ritzy café, belonging to an equally opulent hotel (see p.59), boasts sumptuous fin-de-siècle decoration – an appealing blast of frilly mirrors, gilded woodwork, stained-glass windows and ornate candelabras. Surprisingly, many people prefer to sit outside, presumably for a view of the flashing ads and zipping traffic of place de Brouckère, rather than enjoying the unhurried charms of the interior. If you've got cash to spare, indulge in a brunch of smoked salmon or caviar. Métro De Brouckère.

🏃 **A la Mort Subite rue Montagne aux Herbes Potagères 7** ☏ **02 513 13 18.** This famous/infamous 1920s bar loaned its name to a popular bottled beer. A long, narrow room with nicotine-stained walls, long tables and lots of mirrors, on a good night it's frequented by a dissolute, arty clientele, but on others by large groups of young, college-aged tourists. Snacks are served, or just order a plate of cheese cubes to accompany your beer. Just northeast of the Grand-Place opposite the far end of the Galeries St-Hubert. Métro Gare Centrale.

Les Postiers rue du Fossé aux Loups 14 ☏ **02 219 07 15.** This bar has been here forever (its name derives from the fact that the employees from the nearby post office spent so much time in here), and its marble-topped tables and wood panels are a welcome respite from soulless place de la Monnaie and rue Neuve. They serve sandwiches, omelettes and other snacks – and there's free wi-fi too. Daily 8am–1am. Métro De Brouckère.

South of the Grand-Place

La Brocante rue Blaes 170 ☏ **02 512 13 43.** This neighbourhood hangout on the corner of the place du Jeu de Balle is one of the busiest and best of the bars around the square – big and relaxed, with old folk playing chess and pets ambling about, and occasional live music. Some simple food is served too: soup, sandwiches, omelettes with ham and sausage, and sausage and

Belgian food

Food is perhaps the perfect reason for visiting Brussels. Whether you want to eat traditional Belgian cuisine – which some say rivals that of France – or sample the dishes of some of the immigrant communities that live here, there are few better European capitals in which to break bread. The variety of restaurants is huge, and there are plenty of places to try classic Belgian staples at all prices. And with appetizing street food such as the celebrated frites, plus – of course – world-class chocolate, Brussels truly does have something for every palate.

Frites served in a cone with mayonnaise ▲

Mussels on a market stall ▼

Frites

They may be known almost everywhere as French fries, but **frites** are in fact a Belgian invention; you can find *friteries* all over the city, but there are one or two extra-special places to try them (see Chapter 9 for our recommendations). To be truly authentic, Belgian *frites* must be made with home-grown potatoes and parboiled before being deep-fried. They're also not quite the same unless you eat them with a wooden fork out of a large paper cone, preferably with a dollop of mayonnaise on top – or one of the many different toppings available, ranging from curry sauce to goulash.

Moules

The Belgian national dish is, of course, *moules frites* or **mussels** and chips, which you can eat year-round, though strictly speaking, May to August is not mussels season and during this time the most authentic places won't serve them. They're best eaten the traditional way, served in a vast pot with chips and mayonnaise on the side, either *à la marinière* (steamed with white wine, shallots and parsley or celery) or *à la crème* (as above, but thickened with cream and flour). Discard the shells in the pot lid or scoop up the juices with them, and accompany the whole thing with lashings of crusty bread. The other way to eat mussels – though less fun and not nearly as satisfying – is baked, with a variety of sauces.

Other Belgian specialities

There are many other **traditional Belgian dishes** you should try. Meat-based favourites include *carbonnade à la flamande* (*stoofvlees* in Flemish), a rich beef stew made with beer and accompanied by mashed potato with cabbage or other diced root vegetables (stoemp); and *waterzooi*, a creamy Flemish stew native to Ghent, made with chicken or white fish, leek and boiled potatoes. More adventurous carnivores might like to try *filet américaine* (raw minced steak served with chopped onion) and *andouilette* (a coarse sausage made with sweetbreads). Food **cooked in beer** is predictably popular – try *lapin* (rabbit) served *à la gueuze* (in the local beer of Brussels) or *à la kriek* (in cherry beer), or *poulet* (chicken) served *à la framboise* (in raspberry beer) or *à la Bruxelles* (stuffed with cheese and basted in beer). Fresh **seafood** is widely available, with *crevettes* (shrimps) often used in salads, and *anguilles au vert* (eels in green sauce) staples of many a restaurant menu. On the **vegetable** front, chicory or endive is served in a variety of ways, most often *gratinée* (with cheese). Traditional **snacks** include *kip-kap* – jellied meat often sold in bars – and *croque monsieur*, a toasted ham and cheese sandwich.

▲ Traditional Belgian waterzooi

▼ Chocolates at Wittamer

Chocolate

The Belgians have a notoriously sweet tooth, and this is manifest in the country's obsession with **chocolate**. Belgium produces a massive 172,000 tonnes of the world's favourite confectionery every year, sold through two thousand chocolate shops – and it sometimes feels as if most of them are around the Grand-Place. Certainly you could be forgiven for being sick of the sight and smell of the stuff by the time you leave Brussels, but it's worth remembering that Belgian chocolates are a lot cheaper in Belgium, even at the Brussels headquarters of international brands Godiva, on the Grand-Place itself,

and Neuhaus, in the Galeries St-Hubert. Leonidas, the country's most widespread mid-range brand, has quite a few city-centre outlets too, though you should also try to seek out some of the best independent suppliers; see p.225 for our pick of the city's chocolatiers.

Waffles

The **waffle** or *gaufre* is Belgium's other favourite snack – a mixture of butter, flour, eggs and sugar, grilled on deep-ridged waffle irons and sold on the street. There are two types: you'll most likely come across the Brussels waffle, a grid-like slab of yeasty batter dusted with sugar and served with whipped cream, ice cream, chocolate or fruit. Its rival – the so-called Liège waffle – is a smaller and more intensely sweet affair, cooked with a sugar coating and more usually available from bakeries than street stands.

Freshly baked waffles ▲

Great Belgian cuisine at the Brasserie de la Roue d'Or ▼

Brussels' best...

▸▸ **moules-frites** *Le Pré Salé*, see p.194.

▸▸ **street food** *Noordzee*, see p.203.

▸▸ **frites** *Maison Antoine*, see p.205.

▸▸ **Belgian cuisine** *Brasserie de la Roue d'Or*, see p.191.

▸▸ **fish** *Bij den Boer*, see p.192.

▸▸ **ethnic food** *Has*, see p.202.

▸▸ **expense-account meal** *Jaloa*, see p.193.

▸▸ **brasserie experience** *Ploegmans*, see p.196.

▸▸ **cheap meal** *La Brocante*, see p.208.

▸▸ **ice cream** *Comus et Gasterea*, see p.203.

▸▸ **chocolate** *Frederic Blondeel*, see p.225.

▸▸ **outdoor dining** *La Manufacture*, see p.193.

▸▸ **views** *Atomium Restaurant*, see p.201.

stoemp: very Old Brussels. Bus #48 from rue du Lombard.

Chaff place du Jeu de Balle 21 ☎ 02 502 58 48. There's no better place to take in the hustle and bustle of the city's biggest and best flea market (see p.230) than this amenable café-bar-restaurant, where the food is delicious and very French. There are some real bargains at lunch time – fresh tuna with coriander, for example, at just €9 – and the menu is chalked on a board. In the evening, you can pop in just for a drink or have a full meal. Métro Porte de Hal.

La Fleur en Papier Doré rue des Alexiens 53 ☎ 02 511 16 59. This cosy locals' bar went bust in 2006, but a group of enthusiasts rallied round to save this intriguing slice of Brussels heritage. Cluttered with antique bygones, its walls covered with doodles, *La Fleur* was once one of the chosen watering holes of René Magritte, and the novelist Hugo Claus (see p.264 & p.274) apparently held his second wedding reception here. The cooperative which now owns the place hopes to restore *La Fleur*'s literary-artistic credentials, stocking the shelves with great beers (including several gueuzes), excellent house wine, strong coffee and exclusive chocolates. Only 5min from the Grand-Place. Métro Gare Centrale or Prémétro Anneessens.

Poechenellekelder rue du Chene 5 ☎ 02 511 92 62. This highly atmospheric bar, whose ceiling is hung with puppets, is right opposite the Manneken Pis and has one of the city centre's best beer menus, including an excellent choice of *Gueuze*. The enthusiastic staff will advise as to what's on the menu – usually platters of cold meats and cheeses, plus some more substantial options. Prémétro Bourse.

La Porte Noire rue des Alexiens 67 ☎ 02 511 78 37. This basement bar is a busy and friendly place most nights, with a great selection of different beers, including plenty on tap, and live music later on. Mon–Fri 5pm–3am, Sat 5pm–4am. Bus #48 from rue du Lombard.

Recyclart rue des Ursulines 25 ☎ 02 289 00 59, ⓦ www.recyclart.be. This small café under the arches of La Chapelle railway station is part of the wider Recyclart arts project, and its slightly ramshackle but convivial interior is good for both drinks and food, with well-priced mains – pasta, chicken and fish dishes, *carbonnades* – for under €10. Prémétro Anneessens.

The Upper Town

See the "Lower & Upper Town" **map** at the back of this book.

The Flat rue de la Reinette 12 ☎ 02 502 74 34. The prices of drinks are based on the market at this chichi temple to capitalism – so get in a quick round when the stocks crash. Its other quirk is that it's kitted out like a real flat, even down to the bathroom. Métro Porte du Namur.

De Ultième Hallucinatie rue Royale 316 ☎ 02 217 06 14. This well-known and fancifully ornate Art Nouveau bar is done up like an old 1920s train car, its middle room inspired by Charles Rennie Mackintosh. It offers a good choice of beers and reasonably priced food – such as omelettes and lasagne – and there's a lavishly decorated restaurant here too, serving up Franco-Belgian cuisine. Tram #92, #94.

▲ De Ultième Hallucinatie

St Gilles, avenue Louise and Ixelles

See the "St Gilles, avenue Louise & Ixelles" **map** at the back of this book.

L'Amour Fou chaussée d'Ixelles 185 ☎ 02 514 27 09. An upbeat café-bar off place Fernand Cocq, where you can drink a delicious selection of vodkas, mescal and tequila while checking your email (there's a wi-fi connection) and taking in the contemporary art that decorates the walls. The spacious central room has a cool, modern feel and the back room with couches is now given over to smokers. The food – sandwiches, omelettes and the like – is decent and the kitchen is open from 11am till 1am, but service can be erratic. Bus #54, #71.

Bar Parallèle place Fernand Cocq 27 ☎ 02 512 30 41. Next to the Maison Communale of Ixelles, this simple café gets the balance of good-value food, relaxed atmosphere and

▲ L'Amour Fou

cool music just right. It even offers a few no-smoking tables. The outdoor terrace is a good spot to enjoy sunny afternoons with a chilled beer. Bus #54, #71.

Belladone rue Moris 17a ☎0479 48 46 63. The menu at this Eastern European bar sports all sorts of interesting information – "Belladone" is, for instance, the plant used by women to bring about success in love or business, or bad luck to an enemy. There's Pilsner Urquell on tap and available by the litre, as well as flavoured vodkas, specialist teas, including Hot Attila – tea with schnapps – and sweet and savoury bites. Tram #81, #92, #97.

Brasserie Verschueren Parvis de Saint Gilles 11–13 ☎02 539 40 68. Vaguely Art Deco neighbourhood bar with a laid-back atmosphere and old wooden panels displaying football league results on the wall – essential in the days before television. You can buy your croissant in the bakery opposite and just come in for a coffee to dip it in. There's a good range of Belgian beers too. Prémétro Parvis de St Gilles.

Café des Spores chaussée d'Alsemberg 103 ☎02 534 13 03. Dedicated to mushrooms of all shapes and sizes, this wine bar is great for an aperitif, but they also serve more substantial dishes – all with mushrooms of course. If you want to eat, it's best to phone in advance. Wine ranges from €5 a glass to €250 for the best bottle in the cellar. Prémétro Horta; bus #48, #54.

Chez Moeder Lambic rue de Savoie 68 ☎02 535 14 19. This small bar in upper St Gilles, just behind the *commune*'s Hôtel de Ville, stocks over a thousand beers, including five hundred Belgian varieties. It can get very busy (and smoky). Prémétro Horta; tram #81.

La Maison du Peuple 39 Parvis de Saint-Gilles ☎02 850 09 08. One of the last remaining socialist "houses of the people" in Brussels – built in 1905 for the education and entertainment of the workers. It has recently been renovated and now pulls in the crowds, who are drawn by its spacious interior and buzzing terrace. Eminent leftists like Lenin and Paul-Henri Spaak once spoke here, and it was this history that prevented the *maison* from being turned into a super-market like some of its cousins. From a breakfast stop with the newspapers during the Parvis market, to dancing the night away with visiting DJs and live music, there's something for everyone. Prémétro Parvis de St-Gilles.

Le Pantin chaussée d'Ixelles 355 ☎02 502 42 76. Laid-back café-bar, where you can lose yourself in a game of chess or join the regular crowd rolling a cigarette and putting the world to rights by candlelight – daylight is always excluded. Bus #71, tram #81.

La Porteuse d'Eau av Jean Volders 48a ☎02 537 66 46. In the heart of St Gilles, on the corner of rue Vanderschrick, this Art Nouveau bar has a delightfully ornate interior – well worth the price of a beer. Métro Porte de Hal.

Roxi rue du Bailli 82 ☎02 646 17 92. Trendy corner café-bar with large windows that open out to the street and a vibrant crowd spilling out over the pavement at weekends. There's more space – and a terrace – on the upper floor. Food – cheese and ham platters, pasta and salads – is available from noon to midnight, and breakfast is served earlier in the day. Daily 8am–1am. Bus #54; tram #81.

Les Salons de l'Atalaïde chaussée de Charleroi 89 ☎02 537 21 54. There are mixed reports about the restaurant here, but the bar is good fun and its terrace is used for a variety of events, the current craze being the afternoon tea dance held on the last Sun of each month (2–10pm), with brunch included until 4pm. Métro Porte de Hal.

Supra Bailly rue de Bailli 77 ☎02 534 09 01. Situated in the mini-hub of Ixelles bars, this is the unpretentious alternative to *Roxi* and *The Bank* across the street – smoky and relaxed, and serving decent pub food too. Bus #54, tram #81.

The Bank rue du Bailli 79 ☎02 537 52 65. Recently taken over by the owners of *Roxi* (see p.210), the food on offer is no longer staple Irish grub, but more tapas, toasts and typical brasserie fare. But it's still a pub, with Champions League and international football on Sat afternoons, live music on Thurs evenings, and rugby on Sun afternoons, with or without a pint of Guinness. Bus #54; tram #81.

EU Quarter and around

See the "EU Quarter & around" **map** at the back of this book.

Chez Bernard place Jourdan 47 ☎02 230 22 38. Pleasant and very authentically Belgian bar that – like most of the places around here – lets you sit and eat your *frites* from *Maison Antoine* (see p.205) right opposite. Just a few minutes from rue de la Loi. Métro Schuman.

La Galia rue Jacques Lalaing 22 ☎02 230 24 27. Quite a rarity in this part of town, this unpretentious neighbourhood bar is full of locals, with barely a eurocrat in sight, making it the perfect place to escape the most de-humanized part of the EU Quarter. Sandwiches and other snacks at lunch-time make it an option for lunch too. Métro Belliard.

Hairy Canary rue Archimède 12. This Victorian pub in the heart of the EU area has a daily happy hour (5–7pm), and on Sun mornings they offer the full, heart-stopping English/ Irish breakfast. Métro Schuman.

Kitty O'Shea's blvd Charlemagne 42 ☎02 230 78 75. This large Irish bar behind the Berlaymont building, part of an international chain, is a popular place to come for Irish food and draught Guinness. Although it gets a bit rowdy when there's a football or rugby international on, it's one of the more palatable bars in the area. Métro Schuman.

Le Pullman place Luxembourg 12 ☎02 230 15 82. This very basic bar a stone's throw from the glass wall of the European Parliament does cheap lunches from around €10 – steak *frites*, pasta, omelettes and the like. Métro Trône.

La Terrasse av Des Celtes 1 ☎02 732 28 51. Hidden away behind a holly-and-ivy hedge, this cosy bar decked out in wood and red leather makes a pleasant retreat form the Cinquantenaire museums, just five minutes' walk away. It also serves good, reasonably priced food and a wide range of beers, including all the Trappist specials. Outside seating in summer. Métro Merode.

Outlying Districts

Ane Fou rue Royale Ste-Marie 19 (Schaarbeek) ☎02 218 86 62. Bistro-bar just opposite the Halles de Schaerbeek – a perfect spot for a pre-concert drink or to sit in the curved Art Deco windows and watch St Josse stroll by. Pasta is available by the cone to take away – beats the late-night chip shop by a long chalk. Tram #92, #94.

Clubs and live music

Brussels boasts any number of established **clubs**, playing anything from acid and techno beats to deep house, best known of which is the throbbing *Fuse* (see p.213), with its regular line-up of big-name DJs. Perhaps even better, the city also has an active underground scene of parties and club nights – Los Niños, Bulex and Strictly Niceness, to name but three – in venues all over the city, though you'll need to keep your eyes open to find out what's on and where. Your best bet is to check out Ⓦwww.noctis .com – going since 1994 and still keeping its finger firmly on the pulse of the underground nights that often don't get advertised anywhere else – or Ⓦwww .brusselssucks.be. In the summer, the parties move outdoors with the not-to-be-missed Soirées Gazon, held every Saturday night during August (weather permitting) – see Ⓦwww.legazon.be.

Entry prices to clubs are usually around €10, although some places have free or lower priced entry early on. Clubs are mainly **open** Thursday to Saturday from 11pm until dawn, but it's possible to go clubbing every night of the week. The **cost of drinks** varies depending on where you are, although shorts and cocktails are expensive across the board. If you're on a limited budget it's worth remembering that there are a number of bars which morph into clubs (see **club-bars** below) at the weekend, such as *Beursschouwburg* (see p.214) and *Café Central* (see p.215). Entry is free and drinks tend to be cheaper than in ordinary clubs. In a few cases, where there are bouncers on the door, men may be asked to tip them a nominal fee (€1 or so) on the way out.

As for **live music**, Brussels has a vibrant **jazz** scene, with many bars, both in the centre and on the outskirts, playing host to local and international acts. Live jazz has been popular in Brussels since the 1920s – a tradition kept alive today by small, atmospheric venues such as Sounds (see p.216) and L'Archiduc (see p.215), and by the annual Audi Jazz Festival and the Jazz Marathon (see pp.246–250). The same cannot be said of the local **rock** and **indie** scene, though the annual Les Nuits Botanique festival in May (see p.248) is a great time to catch new bands of all genres. The good news for mainstream **gig-goers** is that Brussels is a regular stop on the European tours of major artists. The biggest gigs are held in Forest National (see p.216), although for a more intimate perform-ance Le Botanique (see p.216), Cirque Royal (see p.216) and Ancienne Belgique (see p.215) are good-to-great venues. It's also worth considering one of the **music festivals** (see "Festivals", pp.246–250) held regularly in and around Brussels; these usually attract decent line-ups with Couleur Café (see p.248), held in late June, being the trendiest and most exotic.

Getting around by **public transport** late at night is much easier now the city has introduced night buses (see p.25). Twenty lines operate on Friday and Saturday from midnight to 3am, even getting out to the newer venues of

Tour & Taxis (see box, p.217) and *Ancienne Ecole de la Batellerie* (see below). Tickets cost €3 for one trip or €21 for ten.

The free, trilingual *Agenda* has the most comprehensive **listings** of concerts and events. Published every Thursday, it can be picked up in all main Metro stations, plus some bars and cafés. Tickets for most concerts are available from Caroline Music (see p.231), Fnac in the City 2 complex on rue Neuve (see p.231), or directly from the venues' websites. For up-to-date information on clubs and parties see the websites listed above.

Clubs

All clubs listed below are marked on the colour **maps** at the back of the book.

The Grand-Place and around

Montecristo rue Henri Maus 25. Just next door to *Le Falstaff* (see p.202), the *Montecristo* is well known as a salsa venue. Wednesday night is pure salsa night, while at weekends, a mix of Latin beats and mainstream music attracts a mixed crowd, with lots of hip gyrating going on. Entrance is free on Wed, up to €5 other days. Wed 10.30pm–2am, Thurs–Sat 10.30pm–5am. Prémétro Bourse.

Le You rue du Duquesnoy 18 ⓦ www.leyou.be. *Le You*'s interior design is by Miguel Cancio Martins, the man behind the *Buddha Bar* in Paris. Not surprisingly then, this two-level establishment, with comfy couches in the bar-lounge, claims to be much more than just a club, but rather a design concept – and they're looking for punters to match. There are visiting DJs, a wide musical repertoire – from funk and disco to electro and house – and gay tea dances on Sun. Check the website for programme details. Entry (with one or two drinks included) is €6 for the tea dance, €10 other nights. Thurs 11pm–5am, Fri & Sat 11.30pm–6am, Sun 8pm–2am. Métro Gare Centrale.

The Lower Town

Ancienne Ecole de la Batellerie rue Claessens 10. Novices once learned how to steer boats here, but nowadays the moves are all on the dance floor, with regular parties such as the popular Bulex (ⓦ www.bulexasbl.be) – at €5, a cheap night's grooving. They also organize a techno night, Nemo Underground Adventures (ⓦ www.undergroundadventures.be). Close to Tour & Taxis: Métro Pannenhuis or Yser; bus #57 or #88.

Le Bazaar rue des Capucins 63, just off rue Haute, down from the Palais de Justice ☏ 02 511 26 00, ⓦ www.bazaarresto.be. Gaze at the decor in the upstairs bar-restaurant – with its air balloon and huge mirrors – as you sample some of the restaurant's international cuisine, before descending to the cellar-like club below for a mixture of funk, soul, rock and indie. Tues–Thurs 7.30pm–midnight, Fri & Sat 7.30pm–4am. Métro Porte de Hal or Louise.

La Bodega rue de Birmingham 30 ☏ 02 410 04 49, ⓦ www.la-bodega.be. Impressive venue with various club nights, located in Molenbeek, a gritty inner-city suburb immediately to the west of – and across the Charleroi canal from – the Lower Town. Downstairs is a tapas bar, while the rooms upstairs and at the back are where the dancing takes place. Parties hosted here include the monthly Strictly Niceness, with an emphasis on funk and soul. Entry €6–8. Métro Gare de l'Ouest or Delacroix.

The Fuse rue Blaes 208 ⓦ www.fuse.be. Widely recognized as the finest techno club in Belgium, this pulsating dance club has played host to some of the best DJs in the world, including Dave Clarke, Miss Kittin, Carl Cox, Ken Ishii and Laurent Garnier. Three floors of techno, house, jungle and occasional hip-hop, as well as the usual staples of chill-out rooms and visuals. Entrance is €5 before midnight, €10 thereafter; the price goes up if there's a big name spinning the discs. On other evenings, when *The Fuse* is closed, the venue hosts other parties and events. Sat 11pm–7am. Métro Porte de Hal.

Havana rue de l'Epée 4, at the foot of the lift from the Palais de Justice, or about halfway down rue Haute ⓦ www.havana-brussels.com.

A Latino club very popular with the thirty-something expat crowd. Punters mostly start early with a bite to eat, then schmooze the night away on mojitos and margaritas before dancing till dawn to hot Latin beats. Free entry. Tues–Thurs 7pm–3am, Fri & Sat 7pm–7am, Sun 2pm–2am. Métro Louise or Porte de Hal; bus #27, #49.

K-nal ave du Port 1 ⓦ www.k-nal.be. Bringing life to the Brussels canal, this former warehouse has been renovated into an impressive venue with a terrace overlooking the water. Host to numerous nights including Anarchic (ⓦ www.anarchic.be); see website for details. Métro Yser.

Recyclart rue des Ursulines 25 ⓦ www .recyclart.be. *Recyclart* puts on a whole host of underground parties and happenings in the old station building of Gare de la Chapelle, complete with the old ticket booth (now a bar) and friendly station café. It's a hub of urban art and social activity, bringing together young creative minds to put on some of the most memorable nights in Brussels. Look out for the organic nights – "where nature meets neon" – of Los Niños (ⓦ www.losninos.be). Opening times vary – check the website. Prémétro Anneessens; bus #27 and #48 to Chapelle.

St Gilles, avenue Louise and Ixelles

Louise Gallery Galerie Louise, ave Louise ⓦ www.louisegallery.com. Kitsch temple to all things bling where wall-to-wall fake-tanned bodies writhe to R&B. Recent stars on show include Eric Cantona and David Copperfield, but it's more likely to feature DJs from the Côte d'Azur. Sun is gay cabaret night. Admission €11. Fri–Sun 11pm–7am. Métro Louise.

EU Quarter

Mirano Continental chaussée de Louvain 38 ⓦ www.mirano.be. Two major club nights – Dirty Dancing every Sat night and @Seven on Thurs. Dirty Dancing offers resident DJs as well as occasional guests such as Matthew Herbert, Tiefschwarz and Justice; dress to impress or you won't get in. @Seven is the Thursday Euro-networking night, with a concept borrowed from New York. The suits come together at 7pm and, before long, ties get slackened and the dancing begins. Sat 11pm–7am; admission around €10, and generally free before midnight. Thurs 7pm–1am; admission €5 membership plus €7 entrance. Métro Madou.

Club-bars

All club-bars listed below are marked on the colour **maps** at the back of the book.

The Grand-Place and around

Canoa Quebrada rue du Marché au Charbon 53. This lively Latin American bar, close to *Au Soleil* (see p.207), mutates into a club at weekends. It's popular with the post-party crowd and other drunken revellers who come to salsa and samba the night away on the (compact) dance floor. If it gets too hectic, head for the small bar at the back to sample the delicious caipirinhas. No admission charge, but cocktails cost around €8. Thurs–Sat 10pm–late. Prémétro Bourse.

Dalí's Bar petite rue des Bouchers 35 ⓦ www .myspace.com/dalisbar. As the name suggests, this bar's decor is suitably surreal, with Dalí prints, weird and wonderful furniture and bright colours. Impromptu percussion and didgeridoo concerts provide

a contrast to the trip-hop, house and funk DJs on Thurs, Fri and Sat nights. The comfortable space and equally relaxed crowd ensure this is a chill-out rather than heat-up venue. Thurs–Sat 10pm–5am. Prémétro Bourse.

Soixante rue du Marché au Charbon 60 ☏0477 704 156 ⓦ www.bar-60.be. As well as a lively programme of DJs playing everything from retro-house to electro from Thur through to Sat evenings, there's a Saturday morning "party continuation" groove from 8am. Thurs–Sat 10pm–9am. Prémétro Bourse.

The Lower Town

Beursschouwburg rue Auguste Orts 22 ☏02 550 03 50, ⓦ www.beursschouwburg.be. Occupying a handsomely restored building dating from 1885, this is a fine venue that makes the most of its different spaces, from the cellar to the stairs, the theatre to the café. Great place to go in the evening to listen to DJs of all genres and have a dance, with just about every musical taste catered for. Thurs–Sat 7pm–late; free. Prémétro Bourse.

Café Central rue Borgval 14 ☏ 0486 72 26 24, ⊛ www.lecafecentral.com. Cool bar just off Place St-Géry with D-Geranium (yes, named after the flower) as the excellent DJ in residence. There's often an English-style battle at the bar but it's worth it for the great atmosphere and clientele. Regular film screenings too; see website for details. Fri & Sat 4pm–4am, Sun–Thurs 4pm–1am. Prémétro Bourse.

Coasters rue des Riches Claires 28. This cosy, two-roomed bar is where students come to play table football and take advantage of the very generous happy hour (8–11pm). In the early hours, however, especially at weekends, the place becomes a pulsating mass of gyrating bodies. Daily 8pm–6am. Prémétro Bourse.

MP3 Disco Bar rue du Pont de la Carpe 17 ☏ 0476 73 72 25, ⊛ www.mp3discobarbrussels .be. Lively DJ bar just off place St-Géry, with disco sounds and a bar that spontaneously ignites. Thurs to Sat afternoons are a

chance for young DJs to try spinning some discs, staying on for the evening if they prove their worth. Happy hour Mon–Wed 6–10pm. Open Mon–Sat 5pm–3/4am. Prémétro Bourse.

The Wax Club blvd Anspach 66 ☏ 02 503 22 32, ⊛ www.thewaxclub.com. With plenty of mirrors to make the place look bigger than its actual capacity, the *Wax Club* is a fish bowl on the first floor, providing views over the city's main traffic thoroughfare. DJs with a smooth and ambient touch, plus some more boisterous nights. Wed–Sat 9pm–3/4am. Prémétro Bourse.

St Gilles, avenue Louise and Ixelles

Le Tavernier chaussée de Boendael 445, southern periphery of Ixelles ☏ 02 640 71 91, ⊛ www.le-tavernier.be. A cool bar, filled with students and young clubbers, so who else could be behind it but Fred Nicolay (see *Zebra*, p.208)? It's all here: a great outdoor terrace, exposed brick and slightly scruffy furnishings, DJs, concerts – including the Jazzbreak sessions on Wed – and movies projected onto giant screens. Sun–Thurs 10am–2am, Fri & Sat 10am–4am. Tram #95, #96; bus #71.

Live music venues

The Lower Town

Ancienne Belgique blvd Anspach 110 ☏ 02 548 24 24, ⊛ www.abconcerts.be. The capital's premier rock and indie venue with a standing capacity of 2000 (seated 700) and a reputation for showcasing both local bands and international acts who perform either in the main auditorium or the smaller AB Club on the first floor. There are usually around four gigs a week; visiting artists to the AB have included Jools Holland, dEUS, Roni Size and Massive Attack. Concert tickets cost around €20–30 and are available online or at the ticket shop on nearby rue des Pierres 23 (Mon–Fri 11am–6pm). Closed July & Aug. Prémétro Bourse.

L'Archiduc rue Antoine Dansaert 6 ☏ 02 512 06 52, ⊛ www.archiduc.net. A famous and fabulous Art Deco jazz café, full of thirty-somethings tapping their fingers and wiggling their toes to Blue Note and post-1960s

sounds. Legend has it that Nat King Cole once played here, and the quality of the acts is still very high. Live local jazz musicians can be heard every Sat from 5pm in Jazz Après Shopping (free) and Sun evenings is Round About Five, a couple of hours of live jazz. Daily 4pm–5am. Prémétro Bourse.

Halles de Schaerbeek rue Royale Ste-Marie 22a ☏ 02 218 21 07, ⊛ www.halles.be. In the Schaerbeek neighbourhood, just to the north of the Lower Town, this magnificent wrought-iron building dates from 1865 and started life as an indoor market. Now it's a venue for an eclectic programme of contemporary and international productions, featuring some excellent, if lesser known, artists of many genres. Tram #92, #94.

Magasin 4 rue du Magasin 4 ☏ 02 223 34 74, ⊛ www.magasin4.be. This small converted warehouse is a good place to catch the latest in punk, ska, indie, rap and hip-hop – it has something of a reputation for featuring "the next big thing". Entrance usually around €10. A 5-10min walk from Métro Yser – head south from the station and turn left along rue des Commerçants. Métro Yser; tram #18; bus #47.

The Music Village rue des Pierres 50 ☎02 513 13 45, ⓦwww.themusicvillage.com. Jazz venue showcasing live music on most Wed, Thurs, Fri and Sat. The line-up includes swing jazz, jam sessions, Cuban jazz and plenty of singers. Reservations – highly recommended – can be made via the website, which also has the performance schedule. Entrance requires an initial annual membership fee of €10 plus a concert fee, usually between €7.50 and €20, although there is an option for a one-off visit which adds €2 to the concert price. Prémétro Bourse.

▲ Live jazz at The Music Village

La Tentation rue de Laeken 28 ☎02 223 22 75, ⓦwww.latentation.org. Galician cultural centre in an impressive building. Most of the week is taken up with flamenco and Galician dance lessons, but it also hosts folk concerts. Métro De Brouckère.

De Vaartkapoen (VK) rue de l'Ecole 76 ☎02 414 29 07, ⓦwww.vaartkapoen.be. One of the best alternative venues in the capital, VK regularly features top-class hip-hop, ragga, rock and indie acts, and puts on the odd punk band. One word of caution: it's not the best area to hang around after the gig, so try to clear off quickly. In the inner-city suburb of Molenbeek, to the west of the Lower Town, across the Charleroi canal. Tickets around €6–10. Métro Compte de Flandre.

The Upper Town

Le Botanique rue Royale 236 ☎02 218 37 32, ⓦwww.botanique.be. Housed in the nineteenth-century conservatory of the Parc du Jardin Botanique – and including an art gallery, two theatres and a small cinema –

the recently refurbished *Café Bota* offers some decent Italian food, plus the "*Café Bota* Stereo" nights on Fri and Sat, with DJs and dancing. Frequent rock and pop concerts, and some good, mostly contemporary, theatre. Les Nuits Botanique (see p.248) have become one of the highlights of the Brussels musical calendar. Tickets €10–20. Métro Botanique.

Bozar rue Ravenstein 23 ☎02 507 82 00, ⓦwww.bozar.be. With a stunning Art Deco concert hall holding around 2000, as well as some smaller theatres, the Bozar is used for anything from contemporary dance to Tom Jones, though the majority of performances are of classical music – the place is home to the Orchestre National de Belgique (see p.220). Métro Gare Centrale.

Cirque Royal rue de l'Enseignement 81 ☎02 218 20 15, ⓦwww.cirque-royal.org. Formerly an indoor circus, this impressive venue has been host to the likes of David Byrne and Lou Reed, and more recently The Divine Comedy and Morcheeba. Gigs are fairly frequent and it's also the venue for the larger bands during Les Nuits Botanique (see p.248). Métro Madou.

St Gilles, avenue Louise and Ixelles

Le Grain d'Orge chaussée de Wavre 142 ☎02 511 26 47. Belgian brown café that hosts regular (and free) rock and blues concerts, generally on a Fri or Sat night. It also has pinball-style machines and a happy hour between 7pm and 8pm. Open Mon–Fri 11am–3am, Sat & Sun 6pm–3am. Métro Porte de Namur.

Sounds rue de la Tulipe 28, near pl Fernand Cocq ☎02 512 92 50, ⓦwww.soundsjazzclub .be. Atmospheric jazz café, which has showcased both local and internationally renowned jazz acts every night for the last twenty years or so. The bigger names mostly appear at the weekend. Concerts usually start at 10pm, but food is served from 8pm and admission costs €10–12. Mon–Sat 8pm–1am. Bus #54 or #71.

Outlying Districts

Forest National ave du Globe 36, Forest ☎0900 69 500, ⓦwww.forestnational.be. Brussels' main arena for big-name international concerts, holding around 11,000. Recent names have included Michael Jackson, B.B. King, Portishead and Katie Melua. Tram #18; bus #54.

The performing arts and cinema

The more time you spend in Brussels, the more you discover the quality and diversity of its **cultural scene**, which is characteristically discrete and unshowy. Domestic talent flourishes, particularly in the **theatre**, with acclaim for a new generation of playwrights, such as Philippe Blasband and Jean-Marie Piemme, and in **contemporary dance**, now one of Belgium's biggest exports, with home-grown talent on show in Tokyo, Moscow and New York. The city also scores well when it comes to **opera** and **classical music**, with the Orchestre National de Belgique continuing to thrive, and Belgian **cinema** has received a welcome fillip from the success of the social reality films of the Dardenne brothers from Liège. Indeed, the city that produced Jean-Claude van Damme, aka the "Muscles from Brussels", is full of avid cinema-goers, and both mainstream and art-house films are screened throughout the city.

Listings of theatre and dance performances, concert recitals and film showings are published in the free, tri lingual *Agenda* published every Thursday and available in all main Metro stations, plus several bars and cafés, and in the "What's On" section of the weekly English-language magazine *The Bulletin*. These two magazines also cover events at a host of local **centres culturels**, which have sprung up in every district of the city: the central Les Riches Claires (rue des Riches-Claires 24 ℡02 548 25 70), St–Gilles' Jacques Franck (chaussée de Waterloo 94 ℡02 538 90 20) and Etterbeek's Espace Senghor (chaussée de Wavre 366 ℡02 230 31 40) are arguably three of the best places in the city to catch a film or performance.

Tour & Taxis

The obscurely named Tour & Taxis (ⓦwww.tourtaxis.be) is a new work of urban regeneration in the northwest of the city. Designed as a "trade palace" at the beginning of the twentieth century, the buildings were originally used as warehouses to store mechandise arriving and departing from the Port of Brussels. The Thurn und Taxis family, founders of the European postal service and owners of the site when it was used as grazing land for horses, gave the complex its name.

The warehouses ceased to be used in 1987, and were left derelict for a decade before the redevelopers moved in. The newly revamped red brick and slate buildings attract hordes of people to its exhibitions, concerts, shops and bars, as well as to some well-known festivals such as Couleur Café (see p.248).

Tour & Taxis is a ten-minute walk from Métros Yser and Ribaucourt.

For **tickets** and information, either go to the appropriate website or visit the tourist office on the Grand-Place (see p.34). Discounted **last-minute** tickets for same-day performances at many venues are available from Tuesday to Saturday, from 12.30pm to 5.30pm, from Arsène50 (ⓦ www.arsene50.be), in the Cinéma Arenberg (see p.221) and the Flagey arts centre (see p.221). Tickets can only be bought directly at these outlets, not via phone or internet; a list of what is available is published weekly in the *Agenda*.

Theatre, dance and comedy

Despite some underfunding, the Brussels **theatre** scene remains strong. The city currently has more than thirty theatres staging a variety of productions, ranging from Shakespeare to Stoppard. Most theatre is performed in French or Flemish, but it is not unusual for a production in one language to be subtitled in the other. There are also a number of high-quality, amateur theatre groups of American, Irish and British extraction. Being at the centre of Europe, Brussels is also a **tour stop-off point** for many international dance and theatre groups – including the RSC and the Comédie Française – and it's quite common for the capital's theatres to stage joint productions with other European theatre companies.

Brussels' **dance** tradition has been impressing visitors ever since Maurice Béjart brought his classical Twentieth Century Ballet here in 1959. The innovative legacy of Béjart lives on with his old company (now called Rosas and led by Anne-Theresa de Keersmaeker) regularly performing at La Monnaie and KVS.

The **comedy** scene – mainly in French or Flemish – is fairly lacklustre, though the monthly Anglophone comedy club "Stand up world" at Théâtre 140 (see p.219) is a notable exception.

Ticket prices vary with the venue, but a good seat at most places costs around €15–30.

Bozar rue Ravenstein 23 ☎02 507 82 00, ⓦ www.bozar.be & www.rideaudebruxelles.be. Housed in the Palais des Beaux Arts, the Bozar resident theatre company – Rideau de Bruxelles – has been putting on modern theatre productions since its inception in 1943. Performances are in French, and playwrights to have had their work performed here include David Hare, Paul Willems and Jean Sigrid, as well as Brecht and Lorca. It's also an excellent venue for modern dance and classical ballet, and is often one of the first ports of call for touring dance companies, though tickets can rise to €50 for these perfor-mances. Métro Parc.

Cirque Royal rue de l'Enseignement 81 ☎02 218 20 15, ⓦ www.cirque-royal.org. This former indoor circus offers one of the city's most eclectic performing arts programmes. It's best known for dance, classical music, rock concerts and operettas, but has also staged acts ranging from Riverdance to the Chippendales. Métro Madou.

Halles de Schaerbeek rue Royale Sainte-Marie 22b ☎02 218 21 07, ⓦ www.halles.be. In the steel and glass structure of the former covered market of Sainte Marie, Les Halles offers an eclectic international programme, with everything from circus performances and theatre to music and plenty of dance, alongside fun shows for the kids. Métro Botanique, tram #92 and #94, or bus #65 and #66.

Kaai Theater square Sainctelettes 20 ☎02 201 59 59, ⓦ www.kaaitheater.be. This beautiful Art Deco theatre on the banks of the Charleroi canal, run by the Flemish community, is one of the city's best venues for dance, but the programme also includes theatre from local and visiting companies. Performances are mainly in Flemish but shows in English are occasion-ally put on too. Tickets cost around €12.50. Métro Yser.

Koninklijke Vlaamse Schouwberg (KVS) quai aux Pierres de Taille 7 ☎02 210 11 00, ⓦ www.kvs.be. There are now two adjacent venues

THE PERFORMING ARTS AND CINEMA | Theatre, dance and comedy

for this Dutch-language theatre – the original Flemish neo-Renaissance building which underwent major renovations and re opened in 2006, called the BOL (rue de Laeken 146), and a new studio which was opened to host the theatre during renovations, called the BOX. The KVS has an excellent reputation for showcasing the works of up-and-coming young playwrights, as well as staging modern classics by the likes of Chekhov, Pinget and Beckett. *Café Congo* in the BOX is open at lunch times and before performances for a very reasonable bite to eat. Métro Yser.

Théâtre 140 rue Eugène Plasky 140, Schaerbeek Ⓣ 02 733 97 08, ⓌＷwww.theatre140.be. Théâtre 140, or "Le 140", has been offering an international outlook on the world of performing arts through music, variety theatre, dance and visual theatre for over forty years. It's also the venue for regular English-language comedy nights ("Stand Up World") featuring some talented comedians from the UK and USA. Tickets for the comedy nights (best booked in advance) are €22, but allow an extra €9 to tuck into the Indian buffet before the show. For programme details see Ⓦwww .standupworld.com. Métro Diamant, bus #21, #29 and #63, or tram #23 and #25.

Théâtre National blvd Emile Jacqmain 111–115 Ⓣ02 203 41 55, Ⓦwww.theatrenational.be. Opened in 2004, this plush venue was built to accommodate the national theatre. Performances, invariably in French, are highly polished productions of everything from the classics – Molière and so forth – to cabaret. There's also an excellent café with an all-you-can-eat exotic buffet before perfomances for a very reasonable €14. Métro Rogier.

Théâtre de Poche chemin du Gymnase 1A Ⓣ02 649 17 27, Ⓦwww.poche.be. Politically engaged Francophone theatre to the south of the city centre, in the middle of the Bois de la Cambre. The programme here covers a variety of social issues, such as immigration and religion, and reveals many international influences. Performances often combine movement and music, making them enjoyable even if you're not fluent in French. The theatre bar is a fun place to hang around, with lots of activity and artists presenting their work. Tram #23, #24 and #94, or bus #38.

Théâtre Royal du Parc rue de la Loi 3 Ⓣ02 512 23 39, Ⓦwww.theatreduparc.be. Stage productions are in French only, but even if you don't fancy a performance it's worth visiting this glorious theatre for the beautiful architecture alone – the building dates back to 1782. The programme consists mainly of French burlesques and twentieth-century classics – Ionesco, Brecht, Camus – and performances tend to be classical, verging on staid. Métro Parc.

The Warehouse rue Waelham 69a, Schaerbeek Ⓣ02 203 53 03, Ⓦhttp://theatreinbrussels.com /ecc/. In 1994 the American Theatre Company, the English Comedy Club and the Irish Theatre Group clubbed together to buy a performance complex now known as The Warehouse. If you're looking for English-language theatre this is where you'll find it, but it's a fair old trek north from the centre to Schaerbeek. Tram #23, #55.

Classical music and opera

The **classical music** scene in Brussels is impressive. The main venue is the Bozar, while the Conservatoire Royal de Bruxelles has an excellent reputation for its programme of chamber music and song recitals. **Annual events** include the recently established Ars Musica (see p.247), held in April, the summer lunch time concerts of Midis Minimes (see p.220), and the prestigious Concours International Musical Reine Elisabeth de Belgique (see p.247), a competition for piano, violin or voice held in May and numbering among its prize-winners Vladimir Ashkenazy, David Oistrakh and Marie-Nicole Lemieux.

Opera-lovers need go no further than the beautiful and historic Théâtre de la Monnaie, which has enjoyed something of a renaissance of late, first under the direction of Bernard Foccroule, but more recently with the inspired conductor Kazushi Ono. **Tickets** for concerts and the opera start from as little as €15, but can zoom up to as much as €180 for a first night at La Monnaie.

Bozar rue Ravenstein 23 ⊤**02 507 82 00,**
Ⓦ**www.bozar.be.** The epicentre of the
capital's classical music scene, the Bozar is
not only the home of Belgium's national
orchestra (Ⓦwww.nob.be), but also stages
an eclectic programme of world music,
themed festivals and visiting orchestras.
The revamping of the Bozar's image and
the re-invention of its programme in 2005
has turned the venue into one of the
most popular venues in town, attracting a
wide and cosmopolitan audience and
hosting in excess of 350 concerts each
year. Métro Parc.

**Conservatoire Royal de Bruxelles rue de la
Régence 30** ⊤**02 511 04 27,** Ⓦ**www
.conservatoire.be.** Although the main venue is
getting a tad shabby, the acoustics at the
Conservatoire are second to none and
there is an impressive – at times highly
innovative – programme interspersed with
the early rounds of the Concours Musical
International Reine Elisabeth de Belgique
competition (see p.247). On Thurs and
Fri lunch times in July and Aug, the
Conservatoire hosts the mini-concerts of
Midis Minimes (€4; on Mon–Wed, the
concerts are held in the Eglise des Minimes,
rue des Minimes 62; Ⓦwww.midis-minimes
.be). Métro Louise.

Théâtre de la Monnaie place de la Monnaie
⊤**070 23 39 39,** Ⓦ**www.lamonnaie.be.**
Belgium's premier opera house is
renowned for its adventurous repertoire
and production style, and has earned itself
glowing reviews over the years, whilst its
policy of nurturing promising singers –

▲ The lavish interior of the Théâtre de la Monnaie

rather than casting the more established
stars – makes it a great place to spot
newcomers. Book well in advance: tickets
are always difficult to obtain as the house
contains only 1200 seats. The building
itself is also of considerable significance:
during a performance of Auber's *The Mute
Girl of Portici* in 1830, a nationalistic libretto
sent the audience charging out into the
street, where they promptly started a
rebellion that was soon to lead to the
establishment of an independent Belgium
(see p.257). Métro De Brouckère.

Cinema

Belgium's contribution to world **cinema** may be modest – *The Sexual Life of the Belgians*, *Man Bites Dog* and *Ma Vie en Rose* spring to mind – but its profile received a welcome boost in 2005 when the Dardenne brothers were awarded the Palme d'Or for *L'Enfant* (The Child).

Brussels is also a good spot for cinema-goers: beyond the usual chain cinemas showing Hollywood blockbusters – notably UGC De Brouckère and Heysel's Kinepolis – the city boasts a decent flush of art-house cinemas and *centres culturels* (see p.217), with screenings of offbeat independent films, as well as the classics. Look out also for the highly recommended, annual **film festivals**, the Brussels Festival of European Film (see p.248) and the bizarre, but wonderful, Brussels Festival of Fantasy Film, Science Fiction and Thrillers (see p.246).

Except for films targeted at children, the vast majority of films shown in Brussels' cinemas are in English (coded "VO" or "version originale"), and **subtitled** in French and/or Flemish as appropriate. *The Bulletin* and *Agenda* (free magazine available in bars and Metro stations) are the best sources for **listings** of the week's movies. Cinemas usually change their programmes on Wednesdays. **Ticket prices** depend on the venue: at the large commercial cinemas they are €9.20, while the smaller art-house venues charge between €6 and €8. In the cheaper independent cinemas also expect to be asked to tip the person who takes your ticket – €0.50 will do fine.

Actors' Studio petite rue des Bouchers 16 ☎02 512 16 96. This small cinema is probably the best place in the centre to catch art-house and independent films. It's also cheaper than its more commercial rivals, with the added advantage that you can buy a beer or a coffee and take it in with you. Easy to miss, as it's hidden away in an arcade just off the petite rue des Bouchers. Prémétro Bourse or métro Gare Centrale.

Cinéma Arenberg galerie de la Reine 26 ☎02 512 80 63, ⓦwww.arenberg.be. Set in a good-looking Art Deco building converted from a theatre, the Arenberg Galleries is best known for its "Ecran Total", a programme of classic and art-house films shown over the summer months, with occasional polls to gauge the audience's reaction to the film. An adventurous variety of world cinema is also screened. Métro Gare Centrale.

Flagey place Sainte-Croix 5, Ixelles ☎02 641 10 20, ⓦwww.flagey.be. Part of the Art Deco cultural centre situated on place Eugene Flagey, this studio cinema showcases an impressive range of classic films, usually focusing on a particular genre or director. The whole building becomes a haven for film-lovers once a year when it plays host to the Brussels Festival of European Film (see p.248). Bus #71 from Métro Porte de Namur or tram #81 from Gare du Midi.

Kinepolis blvd du Centenaire 20 ☎0900 00 555. A hi-tech cinema complex with 27 auditoriums and one of the largest IMAX screens in Europe. The line-up is purely commercial, but the choice of mainstream films is unrivalled. A word of warning, though: films are more likely to be dubbed here than anywhere else. Métro Heysel.

Movy Club rue des Moines 21, Forest ☎02 537 69 54. An Art Deco delight and one of a dying breed of local cinemas, this is a good place to catch the best of the new films that have just come off the main cinema circuit. Dress warmly, though, as there's not much

in the way of heating. Tram #81, or bus #49 or #50.

Musée du Cinéma rue Baron Horta 8 ☎02 507 83 70, ⓦwww.cinematheque.be. This small museum-cum-cinema has now reopened after renovation in 2008. It's popular with film buffs, who come to watch an excellent selection of films, including old silent movies with piano accompaniment. The small museum is pretty interesting too, especially displays on the early attempts at moving pictures such as the "mutoscope" and "kinetoscope". Not many seats, so you need to get there early; prices are amazingly low at just €2. Children under 16 not admitted. Métro Gare Centrale.

Nova rue d'Arenberg 3 ☎02 511 27 74, ⓦwww .nova-cinema.com. There's no regular programme at the Nova, so check the website for upcoming screenings. A young crowd of film fanatics keep the venue going, and it's a great place to catch new and local cinematic talent. They also host a number of special events, festivals and political debates. Métro De Brouckère.

Styx rue de l'Arbre Bénit 72 ☎0900 27 854. A tiny, recently renovated, two-screen repertory cinema showing a selection of old and new films, always in the original language, as well as midnight screenings. A ten-minute walk from Métro Porte de Namur, or bus #71.

UGC De Brouckère place de Brouckère 38 ☎0900 10 440. A ten-screen cinema showing mainstream and Hollywood block-buster fare. Be sure to enter the right auditorium, as they often show two versions of the same film, one in the original version and one dubbed. Métro De Brouckère.

Vendôme chaussée de Wavre 18 ☎02 502 37 00. Well known for showing a wide selection of arty films, plus some more mainstream stuff. They also offer a multiple ticket valid for three months – six films for €30.30 – which is very good value. Métro Porte de Namur.

Shopping

Brussels isn't up there with Paris or London when it comes to **shopping**. It has all the big mainstream names, and all of the major designers too; and of course it excels when it comes to Belgium's shopping trinity of beer, chocolate and the comic strip ("*bande dessinée*", or just BD) – outlets for which it has in spades. But what the city is really good for is small **designer and specialist shops** selling everything from handmade hats to gloves and umbrellas, many of which still occupy prime spots around the city centre. Brussels is also easy to navigate, with different kinds of shops located in different neighbourhoods. In the city centre, pedestrianized **rue Neuve** is the main source of the mainstream chains and clothing outlets, though to be honest you could be anywhere in Europe here and the real charm of shopping in Brussels lies elsewhere. Behind the Bourse, **rue Antoine Dansaert** is lined with quality fashion shops of both established and up-and-coming designers, many from Belgium, and this is starting to spill over into the nearby streets of rue des Chartreux and rue de Flandre, and to the narrow streets around **place St–Géry** which hold a clutch of inventive streetwear shops. Nearby, rue du Midi is the home of camera shops and musical instrument outlets, while boulevards Anspach, Adolphe-Max and Lemonnier hold a number of comic stores. The wallet-crunching designer stores – Armani, Versace and so forth – are on the other side of the city centre, on **avenue Louise** and the petit ring at **place Louise**. For something a little easier on the budget, head south along avenue Louise to **rue du Bailli** and **place du Châtelain**, a compact shopping spot dotted with cafés. The city's most expensive antique shops are on and around **place du Grand Sablon**, with another, slightly less pricey, group strung along the more northerly part of rue Blaes and rue Haute in the **Marolles**.

Central Brussels is also liberally sprinkled with **galeries** and **passages** – sheltered shopping arcades. These range from the illustrious **Galeries St–Hubert**, near the Grand-Place, with good chocolate shops and chic clothing and furniture stores, and the attractive old bookstores of the **Galerie Bortier**, close to the Gare Centrale, to the **Galerie Agora**, just off the Grand-Place, whose shops peddle cheap leather jackets, incense, jewellery and ethnic goods. Other *galeries* around place Louise are good for mainstream clothing. Another of the city's strengths is its open-air **markets**, two key targets being the weekend **antiques market** held on the place du Grand Sablon and the sprawling **flea market** that takes place daily on the place du Jeu de Balle in the Marolles district.

The **shops** recommended in this chapter have been divided into the following **categories**: art, antiques and design p.223; books and comics p.224; chocolate p.225; department stores and *galeries* p.226; fashion and secondhand clothes p.227; food, drink and cookware p.228; lace p.229; markets p.230; music p.231; and toys and games p.231.

Opening hours

Shops are generally **open** from Monday to Saturday, 10am to 6pm or 7pm, though the more tourist-orientated places, especially on and around the Grand-Place, are usually open on Sundays too. On Fridays, department stores typically stay open until 8pm. In most districts there are also **night shops** – mainly selling booze, cigarettes and food – and these stay open till 1am or 2am, sometimes later in the city centre. Sundays, when most shops are closed, see many of the city's open-air markets at their busiest and best.

Art, antiques and design

Alice Gallery & Shop rue Antoine Dansaert 182 (Lower Town) ☎02 513 33 07, ⊛www.alicebxl .com. Contemporary gallery specializing in graphic design and including textiles. Up-and-coming artists exhibit here and the shop sells books and more affordable designer T-shirts. Tues–Sat 11am–7pm. Métro Ste-Catherine.

Art Deco 1920–1940 ave Adolphe Demeur 16 (St Gilles) ☎02 534 70 25, ⊛www .artdecoannebastin.be. As you might guess from the name, Anne Bastin's shop is a shrine to Art Deco. Walk by in the evening to see the beautifully lit windows, or drop in during the day to explore her collection of lamps, furniture and jewellery. Mon 11am–1pm, Wed–Sat 11am–6.30pm, Sun 11.30am–6.30pm. Prémétro Horta.

Costermans place du Grand Sablon 5 (Upper Town) ☎02 512 21 33. Famous Grand Sablon antiques shop, established in 1839 and now run by Marc-Henri Jaspar-Costermans. Its speciality is eighteenth-century furniture and *objets d'art* as well as old paintings and beautifully crafted clocks. There's an impressive range of antique fireplaces and wrought ironwork too. Prices are mostly prohibitive, but it's a lovely place to look around nonetheless. Tues–Sat 10am–6pm. Métro Louise.

D Plus Design rue Blaes 83–87, Marolles (Lower Town) ☎02 512 44 04. D Plus specializes in twentieth-century design and decorative arts, with collections of items designed by great Italian designers like Ettore Sottsass, Gio Ponti, Ico Parisi and Castiglioni. You can also find modern designs from Scandinavia (somewhat classier and pricier than their Ikea equivalents). Mon, Tues, Thurs–Sat 11am–6pm, Sun 10am–4pm. Métro Porte de Hal.

Espace Bizarre rue des Chartreux 17 & 19 (Lower Town) ☎02 514 52 56. Contemporary furniture and accessories, including Italian firms like Mobileffe, Gervasoni and Casamilano. Tues–Sat 10am–7pm. Prémétro Bourse.

L'Instant Présent rue Blaes 136, Marolles (Lower Town) ☎02 513 28 91. Photographer Nicolas Springael opens his shop at weekends to sell his stunning black-and-white photos of Brussels, including unusual shots capturing the backstreets of the Marolles district as well as more classic takes of the Musical Instrument Museum and the Grand-Place. A keen traveller, he also has selections from trips to India and Africa. Fri & Sun 10.30am–4pm, Sat 10.30am–6pm. Métro Porte de Hal.

De Leye rue Lebeau 16 (Upper Town) ☎02 514 34 77, ⊛www.orfevrerie.be. Bruxellois Bernard De Leye's shop specializes in high-quality seventeenth- and eighteenth-century silverware with everything from silver candlesticks to serving ladles, mirrors, statuettes, teapots and gravy boats. Excellent selection and competitive prices. Tues–Sat 10.30am–12.30pm & 2.30–6.30pm. Just off place du Grand Sablon; Métro Louise.

Passage 125 Blaes rue Blaes 125, Marolles (Lower Town) ☎02 503 10 27. Thirty antique dealers occupy the four floors and 1200 square metres of this shop in the Marolles district. Retro, Art Deco, lamps, jewellery and piles of other stuff – what they don't have hanging from some ceiling or other in this labyrinth is really not worth having. Mon, Wed & Fri 10am–5pm, Tues, Thurs and Sat 10am–6pm, Sun 10am–5.30pm. Métro Porte de Hal.

Books and comics

See also Galerie Bortier (p.226) and Galeries St–Hubert (p.226).

La Boutique Tintin rue de la Colline 13 (just off the Grand-Place) ☎02 514 51 52, ⓦwww.tintin .com. Set up, no doubt, by someone with an unhealthy obsession with Hergé's quiffed hero. Expect to find anything and everything to do with Tintin – comic books, postcards, stationery, figurines, T-shirts and sweaters – and all Hergé's other cartoon creations, such as Quick & Flupke. Mon–Sat 10am–6pm, Sun 11am–5pm. Prémétro Bourse.

Brüsel blvd Anspach 100 (near the Grand-Place) ☎02 511 08 09, ⓦwww.brusel.com. This well-known comic shop stocks more than eight thousand new issues and specializes in French underground editions – *Association*, *Amok* and *Bill* to name but three. You'll also find the complete works of the famous Belgian comic-book artist Schuiten, best known for his controversial comic *Brüsel*, which depicts the destruction of a city (guess which one) in the 1960s. Calvin and Hobbes make an appearance, as does Tintin, in a babel of languages. The shop is particularly worth visiting when it hosts a pop art or comic-book exhibition. Mon–Sat 10.30am–6.30pm, Sun noon–6.30pm. Prémétro Bourse.

▲ Shopping for comics at Brüsel

Espace BD place Fernand Coq 2 (Ixelles) ☎02 512 68 69. Selling principally adult-themed comics, Espace BD features a beautiful gallery displaying a host of prints and sketches from all sorts of artists, including Dany, Gimenez, Berthet and Alice. Immaculately organized and a pleasant place to spend an afternoon browsing. Tues & Thurs–Sat 11am–6.30pm. Bus #71, #54.

Filigranes ave des Arts 39–40 (Upper Town) ☎02 511 90 15. Open 365 days a year.

Novels are mainly French-language, but there's a good range of travel and art books in English, as well as magazines. English-language novels have been relegated to a dim cellar down the steps on the right of the entrance. Mon–Fri 8am–8pm, Sat 10am–7.30pm, Sun and public holidays 10am–7pm. Métro Arts-Loi.

Librairie du Rome rue Jean Stas 16A (Upper Town) ☎02 511 79 37. A stone's throw from place Louise, every surface of this bustling little shop is filled with a comprehensive collection of international newspapers and magazines. Daily 8.30am–8pm. Métro Louise.

Librairie St Hubert Galerie du Roi 2 (Lower Town) ☎02 511 24 12, ⓦwww .librairie-saint-hubert.com. Right in the heart of things in the Galeries St-Hubert, this is the city's most attractive art bookstore, peaceful and elegant, with an exhibition room upstairs. Gare Centrale.

Maison de la Bande Dessinée blvd de l'Impératrice 1 (Lower Town) ☎02 502 94 68, ⓦwww.jije.org. In part this is a small museum, dedicated to the art of *Spirou* magazine and in particular that of the comic book artist Jijé. But it's also one of the city's best comic stores, with a great selection of strips from Belgium and around the world. Tues–Sun 10am–6pm. Métro De Brouckère.

Nicola's Bookshop rue de Stassart 106 (Ixelles) ☎02 513 94 00, ⓦwww .nicolasbookshop.com. A haven for book-lovers, this independent English-language bookshop offers an excellent selection of books from around the world, in the relaxed and friendly environment created by owner Nicola Lennon. Regular events include readings, signings and a book club – check the website for details. Mon–Sat 11am–7pm. Métro Louise.

Nine City blvd Reyers 32 (Schaerbeek) ☎02 705 57 09, ⓦwww.ninecity.be. Just off chaussée de Louvain, this is Brussels' largest comic strip location – a store, exhibition space, museum, bar and auction house for rare items all rolled into one. Mon–Sat 10.30am–7pm. Bus #63 from De Brouckère.

Passa Porta rue Dansaert 46 (Lower Town) ☎02 502 94 60, ⓦwww.passaportabookshop.be.

International bookshop with about ten percent of the total stock in English, but also good selections of German, Italian, Spanish and Portuguese literature. Regular events in all languages and an easy-going atmosphere with a free tea or coffee thrown in. Manager Ludovic Bekaert has the theory that you wouldn't buy clothes without trying them on – the same goes for books. Mon–Sat 11am–7pm, Sun noon–6pm. Prémétro Bourse.

Pêle-Mêle blvd Maurice Lemonnier 55–59 (Lower Town) ☏02 548 78 00. A maze-like shop with a jumble of secondhand books stacked up against the walls. Thrillers, classics, comics, magazines and even CDs retail at some of the lowest prices in Brussels: a Balzac or a Camus will cost around €0.50 and there's a whole wall devoted to English-language titles selling at €1–1.50. It's also a good place to unload any unwanted books as they also buy. Mon–Sat 10am–6.30pm. Prémétro Anneessens.

Slumberland rue des Sables 20 (Lower Town) ☏02 219 19 80. This bookstore, inside the Centre Belge de la Bande Dessinée

(see p.59), is definitely worth a visit even if you haven't been to the museum, as it contains a wide range of new comics. Tues–Sun 10am–6pm. Métro Botanique or Rogier.

Sterling Books rue du Fossé aux Loups 38 (Lower Town) ☏02 223 78 35, ⊛www .sterlingbooks.be. This large English-language bookshop has more than 50,000 UK and US titles, including a large selection of magazines, and is much cheaper than Waterstone's – they sell books at the cover price, converted at the day's exchange rate, plus six percent VAT. There's also a children's corner with a small play area. Mon–Sat 10am–7pm, Sun noon–6.30pm. Métro De Brouckère.

Waterstone's blvd Adolphe Max 71–75 (Lower Town) ☏02 219 27 08, ⊛www.waterstones.be. The Brussels branch of the British parent company stocks over 70,000 English-language titles. The premises are a bit cramped, making it far from ideal for browsing, but there's an excellent selection of books and magazines and a good ordering service. Mon–Sat 9am–7pm, Sun 10.30am–6pm. Métro De Brouckère or Rogier.

Chocolate

Frederic Blondeel quai aux Briques 24 (Lower Town) ☏02 502 21 31. Just behind place Ste-Catherine, this is *the* place for chocolate connoisseurs, with the chocolate made on site, and recipes including aromatic infusions of mint, basil and coriander. It's all beautifully presented and reasonably priced, considering the quality (250g for €14). The small café serves mouthwatering hot chocolate and, in summer, Madagascan chocolate with Tahitian vanilla ice cream. Mon–Fri 10.30am–6.30pm, Sat 10.30am–9.30pm, Sun 1–7.30pm. Métro Ste-Catherine.

Galler rue au Beurre 44 (near the Grand-Place) ☏02 502 02 66. Chocolatier to the King as the holder of the Royal Warrant. Less well-known than many of its rivals, unless you're Belgian royalty of course, and not often seen outside Belgium, so a good choice for a special present. Excellent dark chocolate; 250g will set you back €13.90. Daily 10am–9.30pm. Prémétro Bourse.

Godiva place du Grand Sablon 47/48 (Upper Town) ☏02 502 99 06. This popular chain

chocolatier definitely holds its own against the best of the rest. Jealously guarded recipes and seasonal, handcrafted packaging ensure customers keep coming back for more. €15 for 250g. Daily 9am–7pm. Métro Louise.

Léonidas blvd Anspach 46 (Lower Town) ☏02 218 03 63. One reason for Léonidas's popularity is the competitive price of its chocolates and pralines (€4.35 for 250g), though this is production-line stuff and their confections tend to be rather sugary and sickly-sweet, especially in comparison with those of their (more expensive) rivals. Mon–Fri 9am–6.30pm, Sun 10am–6pm. Prémétro Bourse.

Neuhaus Galerie de la Reine 25–27 ☏02 512 63 59; Grand-Place 27 ☏02 514 28 50. The Galerie de la Reine location was the first Neuhaus store, and for some is the home of the praline – indeed the chocolates here are really quite special, even for Belgium. For a rich treat try the Caprices – pralines stuffed with crispy nougat, fresh cream and soft-centred chocolate – or the delicious Manons – white chocolates with fresh cream, vanilla or coffee fillings. Prices are €12.50 for 250g. Daily 9am–10.15pm. Métro Gare Centrale, or Prémétro Bourse for the Grand-Place branch.

Pierre Marcolini place du Grand Sablon 39 (Upper Town) ☎02 514 12 06. Considered by many to be the world's premier chocolatier, Pierre Marcolini sells simply wonderful chocolates – try his spice- and tea-filled chocs to get you started. Classy service and beautiful packaging, plus chocolate cakes to die for. Expect to pay for the quality, with 250g costing €17.50. Wed–Fri & Sun 10am–7pm, Sat 10am–6pm. Branch at ave Louise 75 (☎02 538 42 24). Métro Louise for both branches.

Planete Chocolat rue du Lombard 24 ☎02 511 07 55 (near the Grand-Place). This shop is right at the heart of Chocolate Central, and as well as selling the world's favourite confectionery in all sorts of fancy shapes and sizes, it also offers chocolate-making demonstrations and other events, including Sunday afternoon tea dances. You can get better chocolate at other places, but it's decent enough, and the events can be fun. Mon–Sat 10.30am–6.30pm, Sun 11am–6.30pm. Prémétro Bourse.

Wittamer place du Grand Sablon 6 (Upper Town) ☎02 512 37 42. Brussels' most famous patisserie and chocolate shop, established in 1910 and still run by the Wittamer family, who sell gorgeous (if expensive) light pastries, cakes, mousses and chocolates. They also serve speciality teas and coffees in their tearoom just along the street at no. 12. Mon 8am–6pm, Tues–Sat 7am–7pm, Sun 7am–6pm. Métro Louise.

Department stores and galeries

City 2 rue Neuve 123 (Lower Town) ☎02 219 18 76. A whopping shopping mall, easily the biggest in the city centre, with a superabundance of multinational shops, plus the INNO department store (see below) and the massive Fnac music shop (see p.231). Mon–Sat 10am–7pm, Fri until 7.30pm. Métro Rogier.

Galerie Agora off rue des Eperonniers (near the Grand-Place). Large and central *galerie* where the emphasis is on the cheap and quasi-exotic, from ethnic clothes and incense through to tattooists and ear-piercers. Mon–Sat 10am–7pm. Métro Gare Centrale.

Galerie Bortier off rue de la Madeleine (near the Grand-Place). This cloistered shopping arcade, with its glass roof and wood-panelled shops, dates back to the middle of the nineteenth century. It's known for its new and second-hand bookshops. Métro Gare Centrale.

Galeries St-Hubert between place Espagne and rue de l'Ecuyer (near the Grand-Place). Dating back to the 1840s, this splendid glass-roofed *galerie* divides up into three subsections – the Galerie de la Reine, the Galerie du Roi and, at right angles to the other two, the Galerie des Princes. It holds several bookshops, a cinema, numerous shops dedicated to the best in bags, gloves and umbrellas, as well as a good scattering of chocolate shops, cafés and restaurants. Métro Gare Centrale.

▲ The Galeries St-Hubert

INNO rue Neuve 111–123 (Lower Town) ☎02 211 21 11. Brussels' largest department store has five floors selling goods ranging from perfume and lingerie to home furnishings, clothing and shoes. Prices vary from the high-rise to the bargain basement. Another branch on ave Louise. Mon–Thurs & Sat 9.30am–7pm, Fri 9.30am–8pm. Métro De Brouckère or Rogier.

Fashion and secondhand clothes

Bellerose rue des Chartreux 19 (Lower Town) ☎ 02 539 44 76. City-centre branch of this popular Belgian chain, which does affordable fashion for men, women and kids. Mon–Fri 10.30am–6.30pm, Sat 10.30am–7pm. Prémétro Bourse.

La Boutique Rouge chaussée de Waterloo 203 (St Gilles) ☎ 02 534 90 74. Distinctive designs on colourful T-shirts under the in-house Sambalou label, as well as hippie-style trousers, African jewellery and a few musical instruments to boot. There's also a branch just for Sambalou at rue de la Madeleine 13, just off the Grand-Place. Tues–Sat 10am–7pm. Prémétro Horta.

Cora Kemperman rue du Marché aux Herbes 16 (near the Grand-Place) ☎ 02 223 69 74, ⊛ www .corakemperman.nl. This well-known Dutch designer is popular amongst Belgian women for her unique but accessible designs and natural colours and fabrics. Mon–Sat 10am–6pm. Prémétro Bourse.

Ethic Wear rue des Chartreux 25 (Lower Town) ☎ 02 514 78 08. The clothes here are made of organic cotton, their production respects the environment and they are fair trade. In addition, shop owner and designer of the collection Marie Cabanac has found a conveniently central spot to promote her clothes and values. Not cheap – but this kind of quality never is. Mon–Sat 11am–7pm. Prémétro Bourse.

Gabriele Vintage rue des Chartreux 27 (Lower Town) ☎ 02 512 67 43. Gabriele Wolf presents her stylish secondhand clothes from the 1920s to the 1980s, from bowler hats to ball gowns, flares to platform shoes. Tues–Fri 11am–6.30pm, Sat 1–6.30pm. Prémétro Bourse.

Idiz Bogam Antoine Dansaert 76 (Lower Town) ☎ 02 512 10 32. This pricey vintage clothing is a real treasure trove of one-off pieces, including newer designs from Idiz's own collection such as well-cut dresses in colourful prints. Excellent range of new vintage-look shoes and leather boots as well as a wide selection of leather handbags. Mon–Sat 11am–7pm. Métro Ste Catherine.

Mais il est où le soleil? place du Châtelain 18 (Ixelles) ☎ 02 538 82 77. This Belgian label specializes in women's linen and cotton clothing in natural colours, for both summer and winter. Mon 2–6.30pm, Tues–Sat 11–6.30pm. Tram #81 or 94, bus #54.

Mr Ego rue des Pierres 29 (near the Grand-Place) ☎ 02 502 47 87. Large, airy store with hip labels such as Carhartt, Kangol and Boxfresh for men and women, with an art gallery set in the middle. Regular in-store events and *vernissage* evenings bring in the trendiest of punters. Watch out for the signs in the changing rooms. Mon–Sat 11am–6.30pm. Métro De Brouckère or Prémétro Bourse.

Olivier Strelli ave Louise 72 (Ixelles) ☎ 02 512 56 07, ⊛ www.strelli.be. One of Belgium's most celebrated designers, Olivier Strelli has been creating simple, classic and very modern clothes for many years, often with a splash of colour – the rainbow scarves for women are very popular. Prices are on the high side. Mon–Sat 10am–6.30pm. Métro Louise.

Pax rue de la Paix 8 (Ixelles) ☎ 02 502 52 31. One of several streetwear shops on rue de la Paix, this one is just that little bit different, stocking shoes to undies, as well as coats and a good selection of T-shirts. Brands include Carhartt, Camper and Hardcore Session. Mon–Sat 10.30am–7pm. Métro Porte de Namur.

Privejoke rue du Marché au Charbon 76 (near the Grand-Place) ☎ 02 502 63 67. A very cool clothing store whose selection of fun, casual fashion is equally good for men as it is for women. Mon–Sat 11am–7pm, Sun 2–7pm. Prémétro Bourse.

Stijl rue A. Dansaert 74 (Lower Town) ☎ 02 512 03 13. This sleek store has covetable clothes by the top Belgian designers, all under one roof, with prices to match. Métro Ste-Catherine.

Underwear rue Antoine Dansaert 47 (Lower Town) ☎ 02 514 27 31. For those who want to take fashion right down to the bare essentials, this place is worth a visit, with designer undies at designer prices: a La Fille d'O set for women rings in at €107. Mon–Sat 10.30am–6.30pm. Métro Ste-Catherine.

Waffles rue A Dansaert 189 (Lower Town) ☎ 02 219 05 75. The city centre's best trainer and casual shoe store attracts a suitably hip clientele. Tues–Sat 11.30am–6pm. Métro Ste-Catherine.

Y-Dress rue Antoine Dansaert 102 (Lower Town) ☎ 02 502 69 81, ⊛ www.ydress.com. Polish-born Aleksandra Paszkowska came to Brussels via a tour of Europe, eventually bringing her distinctive, cute yet practical

Clothing and shoe sizes

Women's dresses and skirts

American	4	6	8	10	12	14	16	18
British	8	10	12	14	16	18	20	22
Continental	38	40	42	44	46	48	50	52

Women's blouses and sweaters

American	6	8	10	12	14	16	18
British	30	32	34	36	38	40	42
Continental	40	42	44	46	48	50	52

Women's shoes

American	5	6	7	8	9	10	11
British	3	4	5	6	7	8	9
Continental	36	37	38	39	40	41	42

Men's suits

American	34	36	38	40	42	44	46	48
British	34	36	38	40	42	44	46	48
Continental	44	46	48	50	52	54	56	58

Men's shirts

American	14	15	15.5	16	16.5	17	17.5	18
British	14	15	15.5	16	16.5	17	17.5	18
Continental	36	38	39	41	42	43	44	45

Men's shoes

American	7	7.5	8	8.5	9.5	10	10.5	11	11.5
British	6	7	7.5	8	9	9.5	10	11	12
Continental	39	40	41	42	43	44	44	45	46

designs to the city's key fashion street. Garments that can be worn upside down or packed to take up next to no space in a bag are just some of the many innovations of her clothes. Tues–Sat 11am–7pm. Métro Ste-Catherine.

Food, drink and cookware

Beer Mania chaussée de Wavre 174–176 (Ixelles) ☎02 512 17 88, ⊛www .beermania.be. Perhaps the city's best beer shop, stocking more than 400 different types of beer, with a good selection of both well-known and more obscure brands. Prices are competitive and you can even buy the correct glass in which to serve your favourite tipple. Tables at the back of the shop allow you to take the weight off your feet and enjoy your purchases. There's a website for home delivery, and they have regular tasting sessions (some given in English). Mon–Sat 11am–8pm. Métro Porte de Namur.

Beer Planet rue de la Fourche 45 (near the Grand-Place) ☎0484 955 350, ⊛www .beerplanet.eu. This well-stocked beer shop is bang in the centre, just a few minutes from the Grand-Place, and is guaranteed to stock all your Belgian favourites. Tues–Fri 1–9pm, Sat & Sun 11am–9pm. Prémétro Bourse.

Le Caprice des Lieux rue du Bois de Linthout 3 (EU Quarter) ☎02 773 17 99. A cheese lover's heaven, with hundreds of immaculately presented cheeses set amid tasteful decor. You can also purchase entire cheese platters. Tues–Sat 9am–7pm, Sun 9am–12.30pm. Métro Georges Henri.

Dandoy rue au Beurre 31 (near the Grand-Place) ☎02 511 03 26. This famous shop has been making biscuits since 1829, so it's no surprise that they have it down to a fine art. Their main speciality is known locally as "*speculoos*", a kind of hard gingerbread biscuit, which is something of an acquired taste. They also sell some extremely large

▲ Window-shopping at Dandoy

biscuits, the size of small children and costing as much as €50: they arrive in a weird variety of shapes – the most unappetizing being a life-size Manneken Pis. Dandoy also operates a tearoom just off the Grand-Place at rue Charles Buls 14. Mon–Sun 10am–7pm. Prémétro Bourse.

Délices et Caprices rue des Bouchers 68 (near the Grand-Place) ☎ 02 512 14 51. This is perhaps the city centre's best beer store, not because of its range, which is probably not as great as its rivals, but because Pierre the owner goes to great lengths to stock really special beers, some of which you won't find anywhere else. He also runs beer-tasting sessions on a regular basis for groups of three people or more, laying on local cheeses, hams and patés to go with your beer for around €25 a head. Thurs–Mon noon–8pm. Prémétro Bourse.

Den Teepot rue des Chartreux 66 (Lower Town) ☎ 02 511 94 02. Vegetarian store packed with organic and macrobiotic produce and a cool room full of fruit and vegetables. The upstairs café specializes in macrobiotic vegan cuisine. Mon–Sat 8.30am–7pm. Prémétro Bourse.

Desmecht place Ste-Catherine 10 (Lower Town) ☎ 02 511 29 59, ⊛ www.desmecht.com. This is the place where the city's top chefs congregate, and for anyone searching for that elusive ingredient to spice up a special dish,

it's a godsend. Whether it's Sélim peppers from West Africa, Tasmanian peppercorns or other rare aromatics, the team of herbalists can help you out. Tues–Fri 9.30am–6pm, Sat 9.30am–5pm. Métro Ste-Catherine.

Jack O'Shea's rue le Titien 30 (EU Quarter) ☎ 02 732 53 51, ⊛ www.jackoshea.com. With shops in Knightsbridge as well as Brussels, this Irish butchers, on the corner of rue Franklin, is renowned for the superb quality of their beef and free-range poultry, as well as home-made sausages and meat pies – but be prepared to pay the price. Mon–Fri 9am–7pm, Sat 9am–6pm. Just north of the Parc du Cinquantenaire; Métro Schuman.

Lauffer rue des Bouchers 59 (near the Grand-Place) ☎ 02 511 15 92, ⊛ www.lauffer.be. This fantastic shop, right in the heart of Brussels' restaurant district, has been in these premises since 1871. It's a treasure trove of cookware, stocking everything from gleaming pans to professional spatulas. Prémétro Bourse.

La Maison du Miel rue du Midi 121 (Lower Town) ☎ 02 512 32 50. As the name suggests, this tiny, family-run shop is all about honey, and has been trading from these premises since the late nineteenth century. It's filled to the rafters with jar upon jar of the sticky stuff and its by-products, from soap and candles to sweets and face creams, plus a number of curious honey pots and receptacles. Also has a branch at rue du Marché aux Herbes 11. Mon–Sat 9.30am–6pm. Prémétro Anneessens.

La Maison du Thé Plattesteen 11 (near the Grand-Place) ☎ 02 512 32 26. This shop is dedicated to tea, but not your average English brew – rather the whole world of teas: smell them, read about them, taste them. Pots, cups, strainers and all other tea paraphernalia are on sale too. Tues–Sat 9am–6pm. Prémétro Bourse.

Lace

Louise Verschueren rue Watteeu 16 (Upper Town) ☎ 02 511 04 44, ⊛ www.belgian-lace.com. There are four generations of lace-makers in the Verschueren family and the shop aims to keep the spirit of that long-standing tradition alive. No cheap imitations here – they guarantee craftsmanship and authenticity and thereby contribute to the survival of this most traditional of Belgian industries. Mail order also available on their website. Daily 9am–6pm. Métro Louise.

Lace

Renowned for the fineness of its thread and beautiful motifs, Belgian lace is famous the world over. Flanders lace, as it was formerly known, was once worn in the courts of Brussels, Paris, Madrid and London – Queen Elizabeth I of England is said to have had no fewer than three thousand lace dresses – and across Europe the ruffs of the royal courtiers were also made in Flanders and Brussels. Indeed, the Bruxellois helped their own commercial cause by first using starch to keep the ruffs stiff. Lace reached the peak of its popularity in the late nineteenth century, when an estimated ten thousand women and girls worked as lacemakers in the capital, though by then much of it was produced by machine. The industry collapsed after World War I when lace, a symbol of an old and discredited order, suddenly had no place in the wardrobe of most women. An excellent sample of old lace, both hand- and machine-made, is displayed at Brussels' Musée du Costume et de la Dentelle (see p.62), but if you're keen to buy, be warned that most of the lace on sale in the capital today is actually made in China.

The authentic handmade stuff can be very pricey, particularly in the much-hyped lace shops in and around the Grand-Place. Your best bet is to head for the flea market at place du Jeu de Balle, in the Marolles district (see below), where you can usually pick up far nicer pieces for much less money, or try the (more expensive) lace shops listed on pp.229–230.

Manufacture Belge de Dentelle Galerie de la Reine 6–8, in the Galeries St-Hubert (near the Grand-Place) ☏ **02 511 44 77,** ⓦ **www.mbd.be**. The city's largest lace merchant, in business since 1810. Sells a wide variety of modern and antique lace at fairly reasonable prices. The service is helpful and appealingly old-fashioned too. Mon–Sat 9.30am–6pm, Sun 10am–4pm. Métro Gare Centrale.

Markets

One of the special charms of Brussels has to be its plethora of **open-air markets**. The Grand-Place's **flower and plant market** wins the prize for the most picturesque (March–Oct Tues–Sun 8am–6pm), whilst the swankiest is the **antiques and collectibles** market, held at the **place du Grand Sablon** (Sat 9am–6pm, Sun 9am–2pm). But the real bargains can be found at the flea market on the **place du Jeu de Balle** in the Marolles quarter. It's held every morning from 7am to 2pm, but it's at its biggest at weekends, when the eccentric muddle of colonial spoils, quirky odds and ends, and domestic and ecclesiastical bric-a-brac give the flavour of a century of bourgeois fads and fashions. Sunday is the main day for **food** markets, including the largest and most colourful at the **Gare du Midi** (6am–1pm), a bazaar-like affair, with traders crammed under the railway bridge and spilling out into the surrounding streets. Stands sell pitta, olives, spices, herbs, pulses, vegetables cheap clothes and North African *raï* CDs. Place Flagey, the parvis de St-Gilles and just about every square in the nineteen boroughs of the city have markets at the weekend. There's also a chic but pricier food market at **place du Châtelain** every Wednesday (2–7pm), jam-packed with tiny stalls selling fresh vegetables, cheeses, cakes and pastries, as well as locals enjoying the perfect spot for an aperitif.

Music

Arlequin rue de L'Athenée 7 & 8 (Ixelles) ☎02 512 15 86. Small, beat-up secondhand record and CD shop offering decent collections of almost every type of music you can imagine and then some. The vinyl is in good shape – with some sealed copies around – and the service amiable. There's another branch near the Manneken Pis at rue du Chêne 7. Daily 11am–7pm. Métro Porte de Namur.

La Boîte à Musique Coudenberg 74 (Upper Town) ☎02 513 09 65. Supplier

▲ Kitsch souvenirs

to the Belgian court, owner Bertrand de Wauters is a veritable encyclopedia of classical music. Not only can he describe differing interpretations of classical works, he can also advise you on the quality of the recordings. Mon–Sat 9.30am–6.30pm. Métro Gare Centrale.

Le Bonheur rue Antoine Dansaert 196 (Lower Town) ☎02 511 64 14. At the top end of rue Dansaert, this record shop-cum-épicerie offers a great range including lounge, electro and funk, as well as some tasty treats. Mon–Sat 11am–7pm, Sun 1.30–7pm. Métro Ste-Catherine.

Caroline Music Passage St-Honoré 20, off rue du Marché aux Poulets (Lower Town) ☎02 217 07 31. One of the best shops in the city for general rock and new releases. Also sells concert tickets for many of the city's venues. Mon–Sat 10am–6.30pm. Métro De Brouckère.

Fnac City 2, rue Neuve 123 (Lower Town) ☎02 275 11 11. A large, mainstream store with a fairly wide selection of French and English CDs, along with DVDs, books and newspapers. It also sells tickets for mainstream gigs and concerts. Mon–Thurs & Sat 10am–7pm, Fri 10am–8pm. Métro Rogier.

Lost in Music Plattesteen 3 (near the Grand-Place) ☎02 514 42 24. The vinyl hanging in the window gives you a taste of the wide spectrum of secondhand grooves on offer – Michael Jackson cheek-to-cheek with Carl Craig. Tues–Sat noon–6.30pm. Prémétro Bourse.

Toys and games

The Grasshopper rue du Marché aux Herbes 39–43 (near the Grand-Place) ☎02 511 96 22, ⊛www.thegrasshopper.be. A great toy store just steps from the Grand-Place. Lots of traditional dolls and soft toys, as well as games, puzzles and puppets. It's great for indulging post-Toone inspiration – the famous puppet theatre (see p.242) is

almost opposite. Daily 10am–7pm. Métro Bourse.

Serneels ave Louise 69 (St Gilles) ☎02 538 30 66, ⊛www.serneels.be. A beautiful and quite traditional toyshop, with lots of great, if pricey, stuff for kids – cuddly toys, wooden toys, puppets, puzzles and more. Mon–Sat 9.30am–6.30pm. Métro Louise.

Sports and activities

Cycling and football are the nation's top sports, though Belgium has tennis to thank for its most recent international successes. Francophone Justine Henin, ranked world number one in early 2007, has won five Grand Slam titles, three against her Flemish rival Kim Clijsters, who has her fair share of singles victories in her own right. Belgians also have an ongoing love affair with motorsports, be it motocross or amateur rallying; the country is also home to the world-famous Spa-Francorchamps grand prix track.

Perhaps the most common sports in Brussels itself are the extremely strenuous "kicker" (table football), and many versions of bar billiards. Pétanque is also making a comeback with the young, and on sunny days, hours can be whiled away with a set of boules on the Vieux Marché aux Grains or les étangs d'Ixelles. More surreally, there's the traditional sport of tir à l'arc found in big parks like the Parc Josaphat, in which contestants shoot down feathers from the top of a very tall pole with a bow and arrow.

Athletics

The major event dominating the city's athletics calendar is the Ivo van Damme Memorial IAHF Grand Prix – one of the International Athletic Federation meets that's held yearly (late Aug/early Sept) in the Stade Roi Baudouin. Named after the Belgian 800m silver-medallist of the 1976 Olympics in Montréal, it attracts many star athletes. Call ☏02 479 36 54 or see ⓦwww .memorialvandamme.be for tickets and details.

There's also the popular Brussels 20km, which takes place during the last weekend in May, and usually attracts a field of twenty thousand runners. Although it consists of mostly serious runners, there are lots of festivities along the way and some people semi-walk it. The course takes participants halfway round the city near the EU Quarter, the Palais Royale, avenue Louise, the Bois de la Cambre and through the tunnels of the Brussels inner ring road. It starts and finishes under the grandiose arch of the Esplanade du Cinquantenaire, and participants are charged €15 for the privilege of running their socks off. Call ☏02 511 90 00 or see ⓦwww.20kmdebruxelles .be for details.

Less popular is the ING Brussels Marathon, which takes place in October. The course is the same as the Brussels 20km, except it adds a long straight stretch out to Tervuren and then back again – perhaps not the most inspiring of city marathon routes. There's also a half-marathon option and a kids' run on the same day. For more information check ⓦwww.sport.be/brusselsmarathon.

SPORTS AND ACTIVITIES | Athletics

Cycling

Cycling is immensely popular in Belgium, both as a sport and as a hobby, with the sheer flatness of much of the country being very much to the cyclist's advantage. For spectators, Brussels plays host to many national cycling meets and has also been a stop-off point for the Tour de France. Top of the list is the **Eddy Merckx Grand Prix**, named in honour of the great Belgian cyclist and held on the last Sunday in August; it's a timed event attracting top professionals (call ☎02 349 19 11 for information). For those who would rather cycle than watch, highlights include the **European Car-Free Day** (third Sun in Sept, ⓦwww.mobilityweek.eu), when cyclists take over the entire city centre. The **Dring Dring cycling week** (ⓦwww.dringdring.be), held in May, kicks off with a bike festival in the Parc du Cinquantenaire, where you can pick up an old bike, learn how to become a bike mechanic or take tours of the city on two wheels.

For **bike rental**, the city council offers a **public bike scheme** (ⓦwww.cyclocity.be) in which sturdy city bikes can be picked up from any one of twenty-four locations around the city centre and returned to another after use. The website provides information on rates and the various options available (see also "Basics", p.26). For longer rental, or a more sporty bike, head to Provelo at rue de Londres 15 (April–Oct Mon–Sun 10am–6pm, Nov–March Mon–Fri 10am–5pm; ☎02 502 73 55, ⓦwww.provelo.org; Métro Trône). They speak English and can also organize English-language **guided bike tours** of Brussels and its environs. The tours are usually themed – "Art Nouveau Brussels" and "Comic Strips and Cafés", for example. Bike rental itself costs from €4 for an hour to €72 for a week. Alternatively, check out Belgian Railways' **Train-plus-Vélo** scheme (☎02 555 25 25), in which bike rental is thrown in with the price of a train ticket to eight selected destinations; you pick the bike up on arrival. Those who already have their own bike can take it on the train for a minimal fee for a single journey, or anywhere in the country during one day for €8. Keen cyclists can also contact the Fédération Belge du Cyclotourisme (ave du

▲ Cycling is one of Belgium's most popular sports

Eddy Merckx

One of a handful of cyclists to win the Tour de France five times, many cycling aficio-nados agree that Belgium's own **Eddy Merckx** was the greatest all-round cyclist of all time.

In his very first Tour, in 1969, Eddy finished eighteen minutes in front of the runner-up (this in a race in which five minutes is a big gap), destroying the field in a style that was to earn him the nickname "The Cannibal". As strong on mountain climbs as in races against the clock (he set a world record for the greatest distance covered in an hour), Merckx amassed a tally of titles that no rider is ever likely to equal: five victories in the Giro d'Italia (Tour of Italy); three-times winner of the Paris–Nice race; three-times World Road Champion; five-times winner of the Liège–Bastogne–Liège race; three-times winner of the Paris–Roubaix (the so-called "Hell of the North"); seven-times winner of the Milan–San Remo … the list goes on. In the 1974 season, he managed to win the tours of Italy and France, then the World Championship – a Grand Slam that only Stephen Roche has matched. Indeed, so complete was his dominance that a disconsolate rival once observed: "If Merckx has decided he wants to win today, then he will."

Merckx retired in 1978, having racked up 525 victories, and has since divided his time between punditry and running his own bike factory (⊛ www.eddymerckx.be). His son **Axel** made some brave attempts to follow in his father's wheel-tracks, but retired in 2007 without coming close. However, like his dad, he continues to nurture the up-and-coming stars of the sport and runs cycling tours both in his native Belgium and in his new home in Canada (⊛ www.axelmerckx.com).

Limbourg 34 ☎ 02 521 86 40, ⊛ www.cyclo.be), which organizes some six hundred cycle rides every year throughout Belgium.

Football

After jointly hosting **Euro2000** with the Netherlands, Belgium failed to qualify for the European cup in both 2004 and 2008. Despite this lack of success, however, thousands of Belgians remain ardent supporters of their national team. In **league football**, there are four national divisions and Brussels has long been dominated by one of the top-flight clubs, **Royal Sporting Club Anderlecht**, who have won the Belgian league twenty-nine times, the Belgian cup eight times and five European titles. Most of the city's other clubs have either folded, migrated or merged to help form the city's much less substantial **FC Brussels** (formerly Racing White Daring Molenbeek, or RWDM). Anderlecht's facilities and resources put other Belgian clubs in the shade, but this difference is all the more marked in Brussels, as FC Brussels attracts only a few thousand fans. A third city club, **Union Saint-Gilloise**, was a significant Brussels club until its relegation in 1973. The stadium has a real neighbourhood feel, and the sardonic Bruxellois humour can still be heard in the club bar. In 2004 it managed to claw its way back into division two, giving its few fans, who still shuffle up religiously to the rue du Stade, a ray of hope.

Royal Sporting Club Anderlecht

Stade Constant Vanden Stock ave Théo

Verbeeck 2 ☎ 02 529 40 67, ⊛ www.rsca.be. **Métro St-Guidon.** Founded in 1908, Ander-lecht only won its first title in 1947. Two years later, an England ex-goalie by the name of Bill Gormlie was appointed first team coach, ushering in a decade of seven titles that established Anderlecht as the country's biggest club.

Still lingering in the Belgian memory, the **Heysel disaster** is synonymous with football violence. Built in 1930 in the Parc des Expositions in northwest Brussels, the Heysel stadium hosted the 1985 **European Cup Final** between Liverpool FC and Juventus. Liverpool fans had started drinking early in the day, and were probably joined by neo-Nazi elements in the stands, as seems manifest from the pamphlets later found near the seats. Shortly before kick-off, a group of Liverpool fans charged through the supposedly neutral block Z, and 39 supporters (mainly Italian) were crushed to death when the sector wall collapsed. The match was played out to avoid further pandemonium, resulting in a win for Juventus. English clubs were banned from Europe for five years.

The stadium obviously had to be refurbished, and after various arguments, the Belgian FA agreed to foot the bill. The Stade du Roi Baudouin was built in its place, although some of the original Heysel infrastructure remains. The stadium, with a capacity of fifty thousand, all seated, boasts its own new Metro station at the end of the 1A line. The stadium ticket office, marked Kartenverkoop/Vente Tickets, along avenue du Marathon by Tribune no. 1, sells tickets in four different colour-coded price brackets. Call ☏02 477 12 11 for details.

In the early 1960s Real Madrid, CDNA Sofia and Bologna were all beaten by Anderlecht, while at home it won five titles in a row. In 1964, the Belgian team that beat Holland 1–0 was composed entirely of Anderlecht players. All of Anderlecht's three European successes came during the late 1970s and early 1980s, the club's golden period. After that, the money needed to convert the club's stadium meant that there was less to spend on players. The Mauves (so-called because of their strip) have thus under-achieved in Europe since the 1990s – the only highlight being an appearance in the 1990 Cup Winners' Cup Final, which it went on to lose to Sampdoria.

The Vanden Stock Stadium is located within the Parc Astrid in Anderlecht, five minutes' walk from Métro Saint-Guidon, though plans are afoot to build a new stadium on the city's outskirts.

FC Brussels

Stade Edmond Machtens rue Charles Malis 61 ☏02 411 69 86, Ⓦwww.fc-brussels.be. **Métro Beekkant.** FC Brussels started life as RWDM, which itself was formed by the merging of two Brussels football clubs, Daring and Racing White, in 1973. Only two years later, a goal from international Jacques Teugels against Anderlecht won the club its first and only title. Though the club was unable to keep its title, the team remained in the top six, and in 1977 it was only one goal away from a UEFA Cup Final against Juventus.

The club was rebranded in 2004, adopting its present name, FC Brussels, and is currently clinging onto its first division slot.

To get to the stadium from Métro Beekkant, take bus #85 or tram #82 to Meenekens, or walk 10min down rue Jules Vieujant, then turn left down rue Osseghem, then right onto rue de la Fraicheur. Rue Charles Malis is a continuation of this road – beyond rue van Kalck.

Union Saint-Gilloise

Stade Joseph Marien chaussée de Bruxelles 223 ☏02 544 03 16, Ⓦwww.rusg.be. **Prémétro Horta.** A more romantic ground would be difficult to imagine. The Stade Joseph Marien, named after a former club president, is bordered by the forest of Parc Duden on one side and by a wonderful old club bar on the other. Founded in 1897, people banked up the hillside in their thousands to see Union in its golden prewar days, when it was the biggest club in Belgium. The last decent Union side, that of the late 1950s and early 1960s, made occasional forays into the Fairs' Cup, even beating Roma and Olympique Marseille.

Union continues to fight mergers and resist being swallowed by Anderlecht, with fans proudly flying banners proclaiming "We will not be mauved" – in reference to the Anderlecht strip. They are currently hanging on for dear life in division two. To get to the stadium, take tram #97 from Louise or #82 from Gare du Midi, getting off at Union, from where it's a 2min walk up rue du Stade.

Go-karting

Given the Belgians' infatuation with motorsports, it comes as no surprise that **go-karting** is a very popular pastime. There's a track at City Kart, square des grées du Loû 5A, in Forest (€15 for 15min; ☎02 332 36 96, ⓦ www.citykart .com), or you can head for the Brussels Formula One indoor carting centre, petite rue de Cerf 45, in Anderlecht (€14 for 15min or €26 for 30min; ☎02 332 37 37, ⓦ www.brusselsformula1.be).

Golf

Most **golf** courses are outside Brussels; the Fédération Royale Belge de Golf, chausée de la Hulpe 110 (☎02 672 23 89, ⓦ www.golfbelgium.be), can provide information on full-size golf courses in Belgium. The best 18-hole course in Brussels itself is the Royal Amicale Anderlecht Golf Club, rue Scholle 1 (☎02 521 16 87, ⓦ www.golf-anderlecht.com), which has training and driving ranges and is well laid out in wooded surroundings with lakes. Brabantse Golf at Steenwagenstraat 11, Melsbroek (☎02 751 82 05, ⓦ www.brabantsegolf.be), near the airport, is a pleasant full practice course, just 5km long. The Golf de l'Empereur, near Waterloo (☎067 77 15 71, ⓦ www.golfempereur.com), is both challenging and beautiful, with the clubhouse set in an old farmhouse, and both nine- and eighteen-hole courses. Virtual golf is available at the Royal La Rasante gym in Woluwé-Saint-Lambert (☎02 609 19 06, ⓦ www.aspria.be), where you can take your pick from fifty courses and also choose the perfect weather conditions. An hour's session costs €30.

Skating

Fans of **ice-skating** will delight in the whimsical atmosphere surrounding the rink on place Ste-Catherine in December. The Patinoire de Forest Nationale, avenue du Globe 36 (☎02 345 16 11), is another public rink, open from September to May. **Skateboarders** meet at the skatepark at square des Ursulines, near the old Gare de la Chapelle, and the association Brusk (ⓦ www .brusk.be) organizes events and skateboard lessons for kids at the park.

Spa-Francorchamps

Two and a half hours from Brussels, in the heart of the Ardennes forest, is **Spa-Francorchamps**, generally considered to be one of the most challenging racetracks in the world on account of its hilly and twisty course. The track's recent history has been fraught: there have been several serious accidents and, in late 2005, the organizer of the Belgian Grand Prix went bankrupt and Spa was dropped from the Formula 1 calendar in 2006. Controversially, the Wallonia government stepped in to provide the necessary funds and the track was renovated in 2007 at a cost of €19 million.

The annual **Belgian Grand Prix** takes place in August or September (☎087 27 51 38, ⓦ www.spa-francorchamps.be), but there are plenty of other opportunities to watch motorbikes and cars blast their way around the track. To get there from Brussels, take the train to Spa (hourly; 2hr), then bus #4 or #4A to the track.

Rollerbladers are in seventh heaven on Fridays between June and September for the Roller Parade (Ⓦwww.belgiumrollers.com). It starts at the Palais de Justice and roads are closed to give the rollers right of way. Rollerblades are available for rent and there's usually an early start for beginners. On a smaller scale, the Bois de la Cambre is a favourite spot for rollerbladers on Sundays in summer, when the roads are closed to traffic.

Sports centres and gyms

Brussels offers a good choice of **sports centres** and **gyms**, and several of the major hotels have gym facilities, such as the *Conrad* on avenue Louise (see p.186). Admission to the majority of gyms is by membership only, but those listed below are open to all, for a daily admission fee.

Winner's, at rue Bonneel 13 (Ⓣ02 280 02 70, Ⓦwww.winnersclub.be; entry €12), has an inside climbing wall, as well as squash courts and a gym. Terres Neuves, at rue Terre Neuve 28 in the city centre (Ⓣ02 512 18 15, Ⓦwww .terresneuves.be, entry €8), is the best option for indoor climbing, with the highest wall at 18 metres, and equipment and courses available. The Golden Club at place du Châtelain 33 (Ⓣ02 538 19 06, Ⓦwww.goldenclub.be; entry €15) is a beefcake haven since the spectacular rise of Belgium's own Jean-Claude van Damme, who started off here. It has two thousand square metres of muscle-honing machinery, plus saunas and sunbeds, and runs classes in everything from aerobics to martial arts. The American Gym at boulevard Général Jacques 144 (Ⓣ02 640 59 92, Ⓦwww.americangym.be; entry €10) has similar facilities, plus top-notch boxing, kickboxing and kung-fu.

A number of **yoga**, pilates and T'ai chi classes are available around the city; for one-off, personalized classes, try Serendip Spa on place Stephanie (Ⓣ02 503 55 04, Ⓦwww.serendip-spa.com). Yantra near place Flagey, at Rue de la Cuve 16b (Ⓣ02 646 25 64, Ⓦwww.aca-yantra.be), offers daytime and evening **dance** classes and courses, from ballet to belly-dancing.

Skiing and **snowboarding** are available on the artificial slopes of the Parc de Neerpede's Yeti Ski and Snowboard venue, dreve Olympique 11 (Ⓣ02 520 77 57, Ⓦwww.yetiski.be). You can book lessons and rent all the equipment you need; note that gloves are obligatory.

Swimming pools

The city has a number of **swimming pools** in its sports centres, including an Olympic-sized version at Sportcity in suburban Woluwé-Saint-Pierre (Mon–Thurs & Sat 8am–7pm, Fri 8am–8pm; Ⓣ02 773 18 20, Ⓦwww.sportcity-woluwe .be; €3). Elsewhere, the St Gilles swimming pool, at rue de la Perche 38 (Mon,

Tenpin bowling

The city has a number of **bowling alleys**. The biggest and most centrally located is Crosly Super Bowling, at boulevard de l'Empereur 36 (Mon–Sat 2pm–1am, Sun 10am–midnight; Ⓣ02 512 08 74, Ⓦwww.crosly.be; €3), which has twenty lanes and a late bar.

Tues, Thurs & Fri 8am–7pm, Wed 2–7pm, Sat 9am–6pm; €3), comes complete with a **Turkish steam room** (☎02 539 06 15; €18), and Poséidon, out in Woluwe-Saint-Lambert at avenue des Vaillants 2 (daily 8am–7.30pm), has a **sauna** and a separate **children's pool**, but can get mighty crowded at weekends. More central is the Bains de la ville de Bruxelles (Mon–Fri 7.30am–7.30pm, Sat 7.30am–5pm; ☎02 511 24 68; €3), at rue du Chevreuil 28, near place du Jeu de Balle in the Marolles. Housed on the top floor of a listed Art Deco building, the pool affords a pleasant view of the city too. Finally, both Aqualibi and the Océade water park (see "Kids' Brussels", p.239) are great places to go for water slides, wave-making machines and other aquatic havoc.

Kids' Brussels

nevitably, many of the main monuments and museums in Brussels will hold little of interest for all but the most studious of children, but in fact the city can be a very child-friendly place overall. In the centre, the comic strips of the **Centre Belge de la Bande Dessiné** and the puppets of the **Théâtre de Toone** are the main attractions for younger and older children alike. Elsewhere, the **Musée des Sciences Naturelles**, host to an impressive display of dinosaur skeletons, is ideal for pre-teens, whereas the **Musée du Jouet**, with its huge collection of toys throughout the ages, is a hit with visitors of all ages.

Out of the centre, Heysel sometimes feels as if it was specifically designed for the under-12s – it's home to **Bruparck**, and specifically **Mini-Europe** and the **Océade water park**, as well as the excellent **Planétarium** and the recently renovated landmark **Atomium**. Further afield, the **Walibi** amusement park and attached **Aqualibi** waterpark offer enough roller coasters, amusement rides and water slides to make a day of it. Most of the city's **parks** have playgrounds – the most popular one is at the lovely Bois de la Cambre – and the city also has a summer funfair – **Foire du Midi** – which is held near the Gare du Midi from mid-July to mid-August. Here you'll find the usual riot of candy floss, amusement arcades and rides, including a large Ferris wheel.

Full listings of children's exhibitions, shows and fairs can be found in the "Jeunes Publics" section of Wednesday's *Le Soir* newspaper.

Activities

City Kart square des Grées du Loû 5a, Forest ☎02 332 36 96, ⓦwww.citykart.com. Kids will have a great time tearing around the track at these children-only sessions under adult supervision. Karts can reach speeds of up to 60kph, so you'd better make sure your nerves are up to it first. Children's sessions (ages 4–16) are on Wed afternoons (12.30–5pm) and on Sat & Sun mornings (9.30am–2pm), and cost €15 per 15min, plus €3 for an obligatory membership card valid for a year. Reservations not necessary. Tram #32 from Bourse, or #82 from the Gare du Midi.

Océade Bruparck, blvd du Centenaire 20 ☎02 478 43 20, ⓦwww.oceade.be. Year-round water park with attractions including high-speed slides, wave pools, whirlpools, solariums and saunas. Four hours of splashing costs €15.50 for adults and children over 1.3m tall, €12.50 for children between 1.15m and 1.3m; children under 1.15m go free. A special combination ticket for Mini-Europe (see p.240) and Océade

---

See p.231 for details of toy shops and other **shops** that may be of interest to kids and their parents.

costs €23.50 for adults and €17.50 for children. Open July & Aug daily 10am–9pm; Sept–March Wed–Fri 10am–6pm, Sat & Sun 10am–9pm; April–June Tues–Fri 10am–6pm, Sat & Sun 10am–9pm. Métro Heysel. **Walibi and Aqualibi** ☎010 42 15 00, ⊛www.walibi.be. A little way southeast of Brussels and relatively easy to reach, the Walibi theme park sports around fifty rides, including an original wooden rollercoaster, the Dalton Tower, which drops you from a height of nearly 80m, as well as gentler attractions such as traditional Ferris wheels. Tickets cost €31 for adults, €27 for children under 11 – kids under 3 go free. Open end March–April Fri, Sat & Sun 11am–6pm, May to mid-June Mon & Wed–Sun 10am–6pm, mid-June to July & Sept daily 10am–6pm, Aug daily 10am–7pm.

The attached water park, Aqualibi ☎010 42 16 00, ⊛www.aqualibi.be. Has two 140-metre-long water slides, a wild river journey through the jungle, and all the usual aquatic offerings. It costs quite a lot less – €16 per person, children under 5 go free – and is open end March–April Wed, Fri & Sat 2–10pm, Sun 10am–10pm, May to mid-June Wed–Sat 2–10pm, Sun 10am–10pm, mid- to end June Mon–Fri 2–10pm, Sat & Sun 10am–10pm, July & Aug daily 10am–10pm, Sept & Oct Wed, Fri & Sat 2–10pm, Sun 10am–10pm.

You can get to the parks by train via Leuven or Ottignies – the station (Walibi-Bierges) is just 150m from the entrance; by car, take either exit 6 or exit 9 off the A4 autoroute for Namur.

Museums and sights

Centre Belge de la Bande Dessinée rue des Sables 20 ☎02 219 19 80, ⊛www.cbbd.be. As popular with adults as it is with children, the Belgian Comic Strip Centre documents the illustrious history of the Belgian comic book with numerous displays ranging from Tintin and the Smurfs to comic-book production. The bookshop is one of the city's best comic shops, and there's a kid-friendly restaurant too. Adults €7.50. Open Tues–Sun 10am–6pm. Métro Botanique or Rogier. **Mini-Europe blvd du Centenaire 20** ☎02 478 05 50, ⊛www.minieurope.com. Mini-Europe is pure tack, but children love it. All the historic European sights are reproduced in miniature – there are three hundred in all – and you can even re-enact the eruption of Vesuvius and the fall of the Berlin Wall. Fireworks displays are held on Sat at 10.30pm during July and Aug. Adults €12.40, children €9.40; a combination ticket for Mini-Europe and Océade (see p.239) costs €23.50 for adults and €17.50 for children. Open mid-March–June & Sept daily 9.30am–6pm; July & Aug 9am–8pm; mid-July to mid-Aug Sat till midnight; Sept 9.30am–6pm; Oct–early Jan 10am–6pm. Métro Heysel. **Musée des Enfants rue du Bourgmestre 15** ☎02 640 01 07, ⊛www.museedesenfants.be. Not far from the Ixelles ponds, this is a great museum aimed at children (mostly under-11s), and – like Scientastic (p.241) – its strong point is that it's almost entirely

interactive, with lots of buttons to press and knobs to turn. There are exhibits, but children can also paint, cook, have a go at basic woodwork or even participate in a play. Because it's aimed mainly at school groups, most of the year it's only open to the general public on Wed, Sat & Sun 2.30–5pm; during most of July it's open Mon–Fri 2.30–5.30pm, but it's closed altogether from the end of July until the beginning of Sept. Adults and children €6.85. Bus #71; tram #90, #23.

Musée du Jouet rue de l'Association 24 ☎02 219 61 68, ⊛www.museedujouet.eu. Three floors of toys, ancient and modern, stacked up in every corner and filling dusty cabinets to overflowing. There's virtually no labelling, and the museum actively encourages kids to hurtle around from one battered object to the next. It's most suitable for 5- to 12-year-olds, but even if you don't have children, it's an opportunity to take in the chipped and faded interior of one of these large central Brussels nineteenth-century town houses. Adults €5.50, children €.50. Open daily 10am–noon and 2–6pm. Métro Botanique or Madou, or a short walk from the Gare Centrale.

Musée des Sciences Naturelles rue Vautier 29 ☎02 627 42 38, ⊛www.sciencesnaturelles.be. Kids will love the fantastic new dinosaur gallery with its impressive collection of scary 65-million-year old iguanodon skeletons

▲ Iguanodons at the Muséum des Sciences Naturelles

the end of the equally entertaining insect gallery), with its tanks of weird and wonderful live creatures like tarantulas, stick insects, crickets and albino frogs. There's also a small aquarium. Adults €7, children aged 6–17 €4.50, under-6s free. Open Tues–Fri 9.30am–4.45pm, Sat & Sun 10am–6pm. Métro Trône.

Planétarium av de Bouchout 10 ☏ **02 474 70 50,** ⓦ **www.planetarium.be.** A great place for children to take time out and look skyward. There's a small museum of astronomy on the ground floor, with displays on rockets, satellites and astronomical instruments, as well as regular star shows, some of which are in English. Adults €4, children €3. Open Mon–Fri 9am–4.30pm, Sun 1.30–4pm. Métro Heysel.

Scientastic Level –1, Prémétro Bourse station ☏ **02 732 13 36,** ⓦ **www.scientastic.be.** Down in the echoey halls of the Metro system, both younger and older children love the hands-on nature of this small science museum. There are around 100 interactive exhibits including visual illusions such as an "impossible box", and sensory games like smelling your way out of a maze, changing your voice, or fusing your image with that of a friend. Adults €7.30, under-26s and over-65s €4.90. Open Mon, Tues, Thurs & Fri 10.30am–5.30pm, Wed, Sat & Sun 2–5.30pm. Prémétro Bourse.

(unearthed in southern Belgium in 1878), and numerous interactive exhibits, including a sandpit where kids can uncover a dinosaur skeleton for themselves. Other highlights include the extensive mammal exhibits – a veritable Noah's Ark of stuffed creatures, from polar bears to lions to porcupines – and the fascinating vivarium (at

Parks and city farms

Bois de la Cambre At the intersection of av Louise and blvd de la Cambre. The capital's largest and most popular inner-city park. Dotted with lakes and woodland, there's plenty of room for the kids to go crazy, and when they get bored of that, you can take them to the Halle du Bois – a giant playground in the middle of the park equipped with a bouncy castle and toboggan run. It's open on school holidays and weekends 2–6pm and costs €2.50 per child. Tram #94 from rue de la Régence.

Ferme du Parc-Maximilien quai de Batelage 21. Incongruously hemmed in by high-rise

apartment blocks and the petit ring, this is an oddly bucolic interlude in one of Brussels' least attractive corners – a city farm that's just a five-minute walk from the Gare du Nord. It's really a facility for local kids but you can wander in freely, and there are sheep, goats, chickens and donkeys grazing the few patches of grass around a small pond and a handful of farm buildings. You can feed the animals and even help out if you want, and although it's not the greatest city farm you'll ever see, it's certainly the most urban. Open Tues 1–6pm, Wed–Sat 10am–6pm. Métro Yser.

Other **sights and museums** that may be of particular interest to – but are not specifically geared up for – children include the Atomium (p.127), Autoworld (p.116) and the Musée des Instruments de Musique (p.77).

Theatre

▲ Curtain up at the Toone puppet theatre

Théâtre Royal de Toone impasse Ste-Petronille, rue Marché aux Herbes 66 ☎02 511 71 37, ⓦ www.toone.be. This world-famous puppet theatre is housed in a seventeenth-century building a few steps from the Grand-Place, and is perhaps the city centre's most unique night out. The repertoire ranges from *The*

Three Musketeers and *The Hunchback of Notre Dame* to classics like *Faust* and *Hamlet* and *The Passion* at Easter – plus there's a puppet museum which can be visited free of charge during the intermission. It is suitable for children, who love the puppets, and adults, who appreciate the sly references to recent news, politicians and other salacious titbits – though of course for tourists who don't speak Brussels-dialect French, much of the humour is lost. Shows are held on Thurs, Fri and Sat nights at 8.30pm, and there's a matinee on Sat at 4pm; shows last for around two hours with an interval. Check the website for programme details, and make a reservation if you can – it can get pretty packed. Adults €10, children €7; no credit cards. Métro Bourse or Gare Centrale.

Gay and lesbian Brussels

Brussels seems to lag behind the times when it comes to **gay politics** – the city's first pride event, for example, wasn't held until 1996. Nevertheless, the **gay scene** is itself reasonably well developed, with a decent selection of bars, clubs and restaurants. The area just south of the Bourse remains the centre of the action, particularly in the triangle between rue des Pierres, rue du Marché au Charbon, and rue St-Géry, which is the closest the capital has to a designated **gay quarter**, though even here few of the bars are specifically gay as such. The **lesbian scene**, on the other hand, is less developed. A few venues welcome both gays and lesbians equally, but there are very few lesbian-only nightspots.

The scene changes fast and the first port of call for anyone visiting Brussels should be the **listings** provided by the gay and lesbian associations mentioned below.

Gay and lesbian associations

Among the city's many **gay associations**, Rainbow House, at rue du Marché au Charbon 42 (☎02 503 59 90, ⓦwww.rainbowhouse.be), is a good starting point for gays and lesbians and hosts regular events. The student equivalent, Cercle Homosexuel Etudiant (☎02 650 47 27, ⓦwww.che-ulb.be) organizes regular nights out and gay activities. The main English-speaking group for gays and lesbians is the EGG (ⓦwww.geocities.com/eggbrussels), which operates an informative website, with events and listings, and holds a regular Sunday afternoon meeting, followed by an optional dinner, to help people to meet. There's also BGS (Brussels Gay Sports; ⓦwww.bgs.org), which arranges events and tournaments, and even a hiking group (☎02 649 58 49). The main provider of information is Tels Quels (see "Information Services" below), which caters for both gays and lesbians and coordinates a number of leading events, notably the Gay and Lesbian Film Festival held every January at Le Botanique (ⓦwww.fglb.org). There are also monthly film screenings organized by Genres d'à Côté (ⓦwww.gdac.org) who also provide listings of other events. For something a little different, *Smouss Café*, rue Marché au Charbon 122, hosts Sunday Tea Dances from 4pm to 10pm, complete with cake and cheesy pop classics. Those with the staying power then head off to *Le You* (see p.213) for the Sunday night continuation – popular with younger lesbians and a gay and straight crowd. As regards **lesbian associations**, Tels Quels organizes a meeting every Monday evening at the Tels Quels café–bar (see below) and are probably the most active, but also worth checking out are Genres d'à Côté (see 243) and ⓦ www.lezz78.net for the latest news.

Many of the city's gay associations also provide sexual health education and support people with **HIV/AIDS**. The most high-profile organizations are Aide Info Sida (ⓣ 02 514 29 65, ⓦ www.aideinfosida.be) and Act Up (ⓣ 02 512 02 02), which also aims to inform government policy. Act Together, at rue d'Artois 5 (ⓣ 02 512 05 05), provides support for the families of AIDS sufferers, and has an English-speaking helpline.

The **age of consent** for gay men and women is 16.

Information Services

Tels Quels rue Marché au Charbon 81 ⓣ 02 512 45 87, ⓦ www.telsquels.be. Gay and lesbian meeting place just round the corner from *Chez Maman* (see p.245). Although there's a small café, it's best known for its documentation centre, which has information on gay and lesbian rights and forthcoming events. It also hosts occasional art exhibitions and group discussions. Its monthly French-language publication includes political reports and a full gay and lesbian listings section for bars, clubs and restaurants, as well as hairdressers, saunas and sex shops. Sun–Tues & Thurs 5pm–2am, Wed 2pm–2am, Fri & Sat 5pm–4am. Métro Bourse.

Gay restaurants

Le Boys Boudoir rue du Marché au Charbon 25 (near the Grand-Place) ⓣ 02 502 09 18, ⓦ www.leboysboudoir.be. Good French cuisine often served up with musical accompaniment, in relatively chic surroundings. Also has a lively bar (see below). Wed–Sun 7–11pm. Métro Bourse.
El Papagayo place Rouppe 6 (Lower Town) ⓣ 02 514 50 83. Busy, and gets packed out at weekends when you can expect to wait for a table. The decor is a flush of colour, there's a small dance floor (salsa music nightly) and the Latin American food is spicy and inexpensive. A healthy blend of people and styles ensures it's never dull. Mon–Thurs & Sun 4pm–2am, Fri & Sat 6pm–2am. Métro Anneessens.

Gay bars and clubs

Le Belgica rue du Marché au Charbon 32 (near the Grand-Place) ⓦ www.lebelgica.be. A respected fixture of the Brussels gay scene, *Le Belgica* is arguably the capital's most popular gay bar and pick-up joint. It's a tad run-down, with formica tables and dilapidated chairs that have seen better days, but if you're out for a lively, friendly atmosphere, you could hardly do better. Come at the weekend when the place is heaving – all are welcome, whether male, female, gay or straight – and be sure to sample the house speciality, lemon-vodka "Belgica" shots. Thurs–Sat 10pm–3am, Sun 8pm–3am. Métro Bourse.

Bitchy Butch Barrio, place de la Chapelle 6 (Lower Town) ⓦ www.bitchybutch.be. Second Sat of the month. A mixed lesbian, gay and straight night. The music is electro pop and the crowd is a bit alternative – an easygoing, fun night out.
Box rue des Riches Claires 7 (Lower Town) ⓣ 02 512 63 43. A mainly gay nightclub that's open every night of the week, the three-level *Box* is regularly heaving on the weekends with mostly younger men dancing to house and dance tracks. Daily 11pm–6am; admission free. Métro Bourse.
Le Boys Boudoir rue du Marché au Charbon 25 (near the Grand-Place) ⓦ www.leboysboudoir.be.

Trendy bar attached to restaurant (see p.244) attracting a wide age range with its pumping electronica. Daily 6pm-4am. Métro Bourse.

Chez Maman rue des Grands Carmes 7 (near the Grand-Place). This tiny bar has achieved almost cult-like status in Brussels, mainly because of the supremely flamboyant proprietor, "Maman", and his hugely popular half-hour transvestite shows. People flock from all corners of the city to see him, and his protégés strut up and down the bar – which serves as an impromptu stage – singing their hearts out, Marlene Dietrich-style. Jam-packed every weekend. Fri & Sat midnight till dawn. Métro Bourse.

La Démence The Fuse, rue Blaes 208 (Lower Town) ☎ 02 538 99 31, ⓦ www.lademence.com. The city's most popular gay club night, is held monthly on three floors in *The Fuse* (see p.213), and plays cutting-edge techno. Busloads of guys from Amsterdam, Cologne and Paris make the crowd difficult to pigeonhole – expect to find a hybrid mix of muscle men, transsexuals, the chic and fashionable, and out-and-out ravers. Back rooms available. Entrance €18, cheaper before 11pm. Sun 10pm–7am only. Métro Porte de Hal.

Le Duquesnoy rue Duquesnoy 12 (near the Grand-Place). Known simply as *Le Duq* to its regulars, this bar-cum-club is open every night and on Sun afternoons from 3pm, when there's a themed party. The late-night dress code is leather, rubber, latex, uniform or naked – no suits or ties. Mon–Thurs 9pm–3am, Fri & Sat 9pm–5am, Sun 3pm–3am. Free except Sun, when it's €5. Métro Bourse.

Handz' Up Café Bota, at Le Botanique, rue Royale 236 (Lower Town) ⓦ www.septantesept .be/handzup/menu.html. First Sat of the month; closed Jan. A club night with fun music and a bit of sunshine, open to all persuasions. Music is funk, breakbeat, r'n'b, hip hop, latino, disco: "groovy rhythms to pleasure your ears and make your feet move!" Plus – admission is free.

L'Homo Erectus rue des Pierres 57 (near the Grand-Place) ☎ 02 514 74 93. It's a tight squeeze in this brazenly named gay bar, but the atmosphere is cosy and there's an intimate dance floor, complete with obliga-tory disco balls. Music ranges from house to disco. Daily 11am–late. Métro Bourse.

Lesbian bars and clubs

Girly Mondays Argane Café, rue du Marché au Charbon 94 (near the Grand-Place) ⓦ www .moonday.org. A regular lesbian night with DJ and girly performances throughout the evening, and a drink and dish of the day available for €9. Mon 8pm–2am; admission free. Prémétro Bourse.

Les Jeudis d'Amélie Chez Maman (see above). "Amélie's Thursdays" at the famous cabaret club are a fun mix of DJs and dancing with a slice of live performance thrown in. Thurs 9pm–2am.

Festivals and events

M usic and film feature most prominently in the Brussels calendar of annual **festivals**, although flower lovers, theatre-goers and fine art devotees will not be disappointed. The more traditional festivals – the medieval-style **Ommegang** and the **Planting of the Meyboom** (May tree) – centre on the Grand-Place, while most of the modern ones, like the **jazz** and **film** festivals, take place in venues around the city, bringing the whole of the capital to life. The main annual events are listed below, but for information on the dozens of mini-festivals held in Brussels throughout the year, check the widely available English-language city magazine *The Bulletin*, or pick up the *Agenda*, a free trilingual (French, Dutch & English) magazine out every Thursday and available in all main Metro stations, as well as bars and cafés; the tourist office (see p.34) also issues a programme of upcoming events. It's well worth taking a train to one of the many festivals held in the towns outside the capital, primarily Bruges, Ghent or Namur.

January

Antiques fair (last two weeks; ☏ 02 513 48 31, ⓦ www.antiques-fair.be). This annual event is a meeting point for all dedicated antique dealers, international as well as Belgian, who display their choicest pieces at the Tour & Taxis exhibition centre (see p.217). There's everything here from blunderbusses to African and Oriental art, silverware, jewellery, furniture, *objets d'art*, paintings, sculptures, carpets, tapestries and books – and the quality is tightly controlled by experts. Ave du Port 86, northwest of the centre, about fifteen minutes' walk from Métro Yser, or take bus #14 or #57 from Gare du Nord, or bus #88 from Bourse. Entrance €20.

February

Anima – Animation and Cartoon Festival (early Feb; ☏ 02 534 41 25, ⓦ www.awn.com /folioscope). After years of being hidden away in a poky cinema in an old shopping arcade, this little-known animation festival is attracting more attention in its new prestigious venue, the Flagey arts centre. There are more than twenty categories, including feature-length animation, shorts, student prizes, video clips and advertising. Tram #81 from Gare du Midi or bus #71 from De Brouckère.

March

Night of Brussels Museums (first Sat night in March; ☏ 02 512 77 80, ⓦ www .museumnightfever.be). Launched in 2008, this is an opportunity to experience many of the city's museums like never before. From 7pm until 1am the Fine Art Museum (see pp.78–85), the Musical Instrument Museum (see p.77) and the Comic Strip Museum (see p.59), among many others, are open to the public, with lots of extra activities including DJs, VJs and special guided tours. The night ends with a party at the Bozar (see p.75).

Brussels International Festival of Fantasy Film, Science Fiction and Thrillers (last week March & first week April; ☏ 02 201 17 13, ⓦ www.bifff .org). This well-established festival is a favourite with cult-film lovers, and has become the place to see all those entertainingly dreadful B-movies, as well as more recent sci-fi flicks, thrillers and fantasy epics.

The venue changed in 2007 to the restored warehouses of the Tour & Taxis exhibition centre on ave du Port, where the cellars make an appropriately spooky backdrop to the Vampire's Ball on the last night of the festival – dress the part or you won't get in. Entrance €15. Métro Yser; bus #14 or #57 from Gare du Nord or #88 from Bourse.

April

Ars Musica (all month; ℡02 219 26 60, ⓦwww .arsmusica.be). This contemporary classical music festival with an impressive international reputation regularly features well-known composers such as Argentina's Mauricio Kagel and France's Pascal Dusapin. The festival organizers are keen to promote interaction between the audience and the musicians, and it's often possible to have a chat with the artists. Performances are held in numerous venues around the city.

The Royal Glasshouses in Laeken (ten days late April to early May; ℡02 513 89 40). For ten days every year, the Royal Glasshouses, or *Serres Royales*, at the palace in Laeken (see p.125) are open to the public. The handsome glass and iron greenhouses shelter an abundance of colourful blooms, both indigenous and tropical, all towered over by mighty palm trees: a popular attraction that draws thousands of visitors, so expect long queues. Métro Bockstael, then bus #53 to the Serres Royales stop.

May

Kunsten Festival des Arts (all month; ℡02 219 07 07, ⓦwww.kfda.be). Contemporary and interdisciplinary festival that brings together over 130 new creations in twenty venues all over the city – from the Théâtre Nationale (see p.219) to the Beursschouwburg (see p.214). Performances are in different languages and the festival's forte is the showcasing of new theatrical talent. There are several ticket options; a festival pass to see everything costs €125 and includes a reduced price ticket for the person accompanying the holder.

Brussels Jazz Marathon (three days in May; ℡02 456 04 94, ⓦwww.brusselsjazzmarathon .be). Hip cats can listen to non-stop jazz around the city for three whole days (which change each year – check the website), and although most of the sixty-plus bands are perhaps less familiar names, the quality is

usually very high. The festival is paid for by its sponsors, so there are over 125 free concerts around the city, plus free buses to transport you between the venues and open-air stages. Too good to be missed.

Zinneke Parade (one Sat in May every two years; ℡02 214 20 04, ⓦwww.zinneke.org). Municipal tinkering at its very best, the Zinneke is an ambitious and inventive attempt to boost local neighbourhoods by encouraging them into a veritable frenzy of artistic activity. The end result is a remarkably lively and diverse parade-cum-carnival, which overwhelms the city centre for one day every two years (2010 is the next). Anything goes, except for the combustion engine and amplified music, both of which are banned.

Heilig Bloedprocessie, Bruges (Procession of the Holy Blood; Ascension Day, forty days after Easter; ℡05 044 86 86). One of Christendom's holiest relics, the phial of the Holy Blood, believed to contain a few drops of the blood of Christ, is carried through the centre of Bruges every year on Ascension Day. Nowadays, the procession is as much a tourist attraction as a religious ceremony, but it remains a prominent event for many Bruggelingen (citizens of Bruges). Grandstand tickets (€5–11) are sold at the Concertgebouw ticket office on 't Zand (℡070 22 33 02, ⓦwww.tinck.be).

Namur en Mai, Namur (early May; ℡081 22 20 42, ⓦwww.namurenmai.be). This four-day festival packs the streets of Wallonia's capital with jugglers, stilt-walkers and circus acts of all kinds, showcasing the talents of some internationally acclaimed street performers.

Concours Musical International Reine Elisabeth de Belgique (two weeks in May; ℡02 213 40 50, ⓦwww.concours-reine-elisabeth .be). A world-famous classical music competition founded over fifty years ago by Belgium's violin-playing Queen Elisabeth. The categories change annually, rotating piano, voice and violin, and the winners perform live in the Grand-Place in July. Tickets for the competition can be difficult to get hold of and can cost as much as €50, but the venues do include the splendid Palais des Beaux Arts (see Bozar p.218) and the Conservatoire Royal de Musique (see p.220).

Dring Dring (early May; ℡02 502 73 55, ⓦwww.dringdring.be). This week-long bike festival in Brussels kicks off with bike mania in the Parc du Cinquantenaire, with maintenance classes, tours of the city and a host of other activities on two wheels. Between métros Schuman and Merode.

Les Nuits Botanique (mid-May; ☎ 02 218 37 32, ⓦ www.botanique.be). For one week during May, Le Botanique (the Botanical gardens, see p.216) and the Cirque Royal (see p.218) open their doors to a host of electro, pop and rock bands. There are plenty of new sounds to be discovered and it's always a good opportunity to catch future stars. Food and drink stalls in the park provide a real festival atmosphere. Tickets cost around €8–26. Métro Botanique; tram #92 or #94.

June

Festival van Vlaanderen (Flanders Festival; June–Oct; ☎ 070 70 00 00, ⓦ www.festival -van-vlaanderen.be). Begun in 1958, the year of the World Expo in Brussels, the Flanders Festival has provided over four decades of classical music in churches, castles and other impressive venues in over sixty Flemish towns. The festival comprises more than 120 concerts and features international symphony and philharmonic orchestras. Each of the big Flemish-speaking towns – including Antwerp, Ghent and Bruges – gets a fair crack of the cultural whip with the festival celebrated for about two weeks in each city before it moves on to the next. Most of the festival's international symphony orchestras perform in Brussels; in the past these have included the London Symphony Orchestra, the Los Angeles Philharmonic, the Chicago Symphony Orchestra and the Vienna Philharmonic.

Couleur Café (last weekend of June; ☎ 0900 260 25, ⓦ www.couleurcafe.be). A fashionable, three-day live music festival held in tents on the site of the Tour & Taxis exhibition centre, on ave du Port. Heralding the start of summer, the festival offers a mix of African rhythms, acid jazz and world music, as well as reggae, dub and hip-hop. There are also plenty of stands selling food, clothes and ornaments from around the world, as well as a fair bit of political activity. Métro Yser or bus #14 or #57 from Gare du Nord or #88 from Bourse. Late-night bus service available after the last concert.

July

Ommegang (first Tues and Thurs of July; ☎ 02 513 89 40, ⓦ www.ommegang.be). One of the capital's best-known annual events, the Ommegang is essentially a grand procession that cuts a colourful course from place du Grand Sablon to the Grand-Place. It began in the fourteenth century as a religious event, celebrating the arrival of a miracle-working statue of the Virgin from Antwerp, but nowadays it's almost entirely secular, with a gaggle of locals dressed up in period costume. It all finishes up with a traditional dance on the Grand-Place and has proved so popular that it's now held twice. If you want a ticket for a seat on the Grand-Place for the finale, you'll need to reserve at the tourist office (see p.34) at least six months ahead.

▲ Guards at the Ommegang Festival

Brussels Festival of European Film (first two weeks of July; ☎ 02 533 34 20, ⓦ www.fffb.be). Promoting young film directors from the 45 countries of the Council of Europe, this may not be one of Europe's better-known film festivals, but it's a great opportunity to catch up on some of the best but least-distributed new European films. The festival takes place at the Flagey arts centre (see p.221). Tram #81 or bus #71.

Brosella Folk and Jazz Festival (second weekend of July; ☎02 270 98 56, ⓦwww .brosella.be). A small, long-established jazz and folk festival held at the Théâtre de Verdure, Parc d'Osseghem. The surrounding chaos (things rarely start on time) somehow adds to the attraction, and the bands – mostly Belgian but occasionally international – offer good-quality, free entertainment. Métro Heysel, bus #88 from Bourse or tram #23, #81.

Cactusfestival, Bruges (three days over the second weekend of July; ☎050 33 20 14, ⓦwww.cactusmusic.be). Going strong for over twenty years, the Cactusfestival is something of a classic. Known for its amiable atmosphere, it proudly pushes against the musical mainstream with rock, reggae, rap, folk and r'n'b all rolling along together. Both domestic and foreign artists are featured – recent show-stoppers have included Elvis Costello, Patti Smith and Richard Thompson. It's held in Bruges' city centre, in the park beside the Minnewater.

Gentse Feesten, Ghent (Ghent Festival; mid- to late July, but always including July 21; ⓦwww .gentsefeesten.be). For ten days every July, Ghent gets partying in a big way, pretty much round the clock. Local bands perform free open-air gigs throughout the city and street performers turn up all over the place – fire-eaters, buskers, comedians, actors, puppeteers and so forth. There's also an outdoor market selling everything from jenever (gin) to handmade crafts.

Bruxelles Les Bains (late July to late Aug; ⓦwww.bruxelleslesbains.be). Inspired by the artificial urban beach created in Paris, Brussels took its first sandy steps in 2003 – and it proved to be a great success with beach volleyball, pétanque, seafood stalls, and plain and simple sunbathing by the Charleroi canal. To get there, go to Métro Yser and follow the buckets and spades. Opening hours are Tues–Thurs 11am–8pm & Fri–Sun 11am–10pm.

Rock Werchter Festival, Werchter (last weekend of July; ☎01 660 04 06, ⓦwww.rockwerchter .be). Belgium's premier mainstream rock and pop festival, and one of the largest open-air music festivals in Europe. In recent years the all-star line-up has included the likes of Massive Attack, Nick Cave and the Bad Seeds, Faithless, Björk, Sonic Youth and Tricky, but prices have rocketed since a multinational concert organizer has taken it

over. To reach Werchter from Brussels, take the train to Leuven (25min), after which a festival bus will take you to the site.

August

Planting of the Meyboom (Aug 9; ⓦwww .meyboom.be). An annual event in which a *meyboom* (May tree) is planted at the corner of rue des Sables and rue du Marais, involving a procession accompanied by much boozing, feasting and general partying. The story goes that in 1213 a wedding party was celebrating outside the city's gates when it was attacked by a street gang from Leuven. They were beaten off (with the help of a group of archers who happened to be passing by), and in thanks, the duke gave them permission to plant a May tree (also known as the tree of joy) on the eve of their patron saint's feast day.

Tapis de Fleurs (one weekend mid-Aug every two years; ⓦwww.flowercarpet.be). If you like flowers, head down to the Grand-Place in mid-August, where the cobblestones are covered with a lovely floral carpet made up of over 700,000 begonias from Ghent. The event takes place every two years (2010 is next).

Marktrock, Leuven (three days mid-Aug; ⓦwww.marktrock.be). Leuven's lively Marktrock ("Market Square Rock") is an extremely popular city-centre event showcasing local rock groups and solo artists with a handful of foreign acts thrown in for good measure. Train from Brussels to Leuven (25min).

October

Audi Jazz Festival (Oct & Nov; ☎02 456 04 85, ⓦwww.audijazz.be) A two-month-long jazz extravaganza, featuring a wide range of local and international acts which in the past have included Courtney Pine, Steve Coleman and Ray Charles. Like the Jazz Marathon (see p.247), concerts are held in many live music venues around the city, but the difference is you have to cough up €10–25 per concert.

Europalia (mid-Oct to mid-Jan; ☎02 507 85 95, ⓦwww.europalia.be). Since 1969, the Europalia festival has focused on a different EU country each year. In 2007–08, however, in celebration of the fiftieth anniversary of the signing of the Treaty of Rome which launched the EU, all 27 Member States had a go at contributing something artistic to Brussels. The festival comprises paintings and exhibitions, as well as theatre, dance and live music. The Bozar (see p.218) is the hub of the festival, but other venues across the city are also pressed into service.

Ghent: Ghent Film Festival (12 days mid-Oct; ℡ 09 242 80 60, ⓦ www.filmfestival.be). The Ghent Film Festival has developed into one of Europe's foremost cinematic events. Every year, the city's art-house cinemas combine to present a total of around two hundred feature films and a hundred shorts from all over the world, screening Belgian films and the best of world cinema well before they hit the international circuit. There's also a special focus on music in film.

November

Ghent: Zesdaagse an Vlaanderen (The Six days of Flanders cycling event; mid-Nov; ⓦ www .zesdaagse.be). This annual cycling adrenalin-charger takes place in the velodrome at the Citadelpark, 15min walk from Ghent St Peters train station. Cyclists from all over Europe thrash around for dear life in six days of high-speed racing. You may need to ask an enthusiast to explain the rules, but once you understand what's going on it's a great night out, complete with beer and hot-dogs.

December

Le Marché de Noël (mid-Dec; ℡ 02 513 89 40, ⓦ www.plaisirsdhiver.be). The capital's traditional Christmas market and fair, held on and around the Bourse and place Ste-Catherine in the weeks leading up to Christmas, features food, drink and various wares from EU countries. The piped Christmas muzak is rather tacky, but the fair still manages to instil the Christmas spirit into the most cynical of humbugs. Festivities include a skating rink on place Ste-Catherine and a light show on the Grand-Place.

Contexts

Contexts

A history of Brussels

Early settlement to the sixteenth century

Brussels takes its name from "Broekzele", or "village of the marsh", referring to the community which grew up beside the wide and shallow River Senne in the sixth century, reputedly around a chapel built here by St Géry, a French bishop sent to convert the pagans. A tiny and insignificant part of Charlemagne's empire at the end of the eighth century, it was subsequently inherited by the **dukes of Lower Lorraine** (or Lotharingia – roughly Wallonia and northeast France), who constructed a fortress here in 979; the first city walls were added a few decades later. Its inhabitants protected, the village began to benefit from its position on the trade route between Cologne and the burgeoning cloth towns of Bruges and Ghent, and soon became a significant trading centre in its own right. The surrounding marshes were drained to allow for further expansion, and by the end of the twelfth century Brussels had a population of around thirty thousand.

In 1229 the city was granted its first charter by the **dukes of Brabant**, the new feudal overlords who controlled things here, on and off, for around two hundred years, governing through seven *échevins*, or **aldermen**, each of whom represented one of the patrician families that monopolized the administration. This self-regarding oligarchy was deeply unpopular with the skilled workers who made up the **guilds**, the only real counterweight to the aristocrats. The guildsmen rose in rebellion in 1302 and again in 1356, when the Count of Flanders, Louis de Maele, occupied Brussels during his dispute with Jeanne, the Duchess of Brabant. Putting past disputes behind them, the guildsmen rallied to the Brabantine cause under the leadership of **Everard 't Serclaes** and, after ejecting the count's garrison, exacted terms from the returning duchess. Jeanne was obliged to swear an oath – the *Joyeuse Entrée* – which stipulated the rights and responsibilities of the ruler and the ruled, effectively a charter of liberties, which also recognized the guilds and gave them more political power. This deal between the duchess and her craftsmen led to a period of rapid expansion and it was at this time that a second town wall was constructed, an eight-kilometre pentagon whose lines are followed by the boulevards of today's **petit ring**.

The early decades of the fifteenth century proved difficult: the cloth industry began its long decline and there was more trouble between the guildsmen and the patricians. Temporary solutions were, however, found to both these problems. The craftsmen started making luxury goods for the royal courts of Europe, while the city's governing council was modified to contain seven aristocrats, six guildsmen and two aldermen – a municipal compromise that was to last until the late eighteenth century. There was a change of overlord too, when, in 1430, marriage merged the territories of the duchy of Brabant with those of Burgundy. Initially, this worked against the interests of the city as the first Burgundian rulers – Philip the Good and his son Charles the Bold – paid little regard to Brussels, and indeed Charles' ceaseless warmongering resulted in a steep increase in taxation. But when Charles' daughter, **Mary of**

Burgundy, established her court in Brussels, the city gained political stature and its guildsmen found a ready market for the luxury goods they were already making – everything from gold jewellery and silverware through to tapestries and illuminated books. Painters were drawn to Mary's court, too, and Rogier van der Weyden was appointed the city's first official artist.

Mary married **Maximilian**, a **Habsburg** prince and future Holy Roman Emperor in 1477. She died in a riding accident five years later and her territories passed to her husband, who ruled until 1519. Thus Brussels – along with the whole of present-day Belgium and Holland – was incorporated into the Habsburg Empire. A sharp operator, Maximilian whittled away at the power of the Brabantine and Flemish cities and despite the odd miscalculation – he was imprisoned by the burghers of Bruges in 1488 – had to all intents and purposes brought them to heel by the end of the century. Maximilian was succeeded by his grandson **Charles V**, whose vast kingdom included Spain, the Low Countries and large parts of Germany and Italy. By necessity, Charles was something of a peripatetic monarch, but he favoured Brussels, his home town, more than any other residence, running his empire from here for a little over twelve years, which made the city wealthy and politically important in equal measure. Just like his grandfather, Charles kept the city's guilds firmly under control.

The Reformation and the revolt against Spain

The **Reformation** was a religious revolt that stood sixteenth-century Europe on its head. The first stirrings were in the welter of debate that spread across much of western Europe under the auspices of theologians like **Erasmus** (see p.121), who wished to cleanse the Catholic church of its corruptions and extravagant ceremony; only later did some of these same thinkers – principally Martin Luther – decide to support a breakaway church. The seeds of this **Protestantism** fell on fertile ground among the merchants of Brussels, whose wealth and independence had never been happily accommodated within a rigid caste society. Similarly, their employees, the guildsmen and their apprentices, who had a long history of opposing arbitrary authority, were easily convinced of the need for reform. In 1555, **Charles V abdicated**, transferring his German lands to his brother Ferdinand, and his Italian, Spanish and Low Countries territories to his son, the fervently Catholic **Philip II**. In the short term, the scene was set for a bitter confrontation between Catholics and Protestants, while the dynastic ramifications of the division of the Habsburg Empire were to complicate European affairs for centuries.

After his father's abdication, Philip II decided to teach his heretical subjects a lesson. He garrisoned Brussels and the other towns of the Low Countries with Spanish mercenaries, imported the Inquisition and passed a series of anti-Protestant edicts. However, other pressures on the Habsburg Empire forced him into a tactical withdrawal and he transferred control to his sister, **Margaret of Parma**, in 1559. Based in Brussels, the equally resolute Margaret implemented the policies of her brother with gusto. Initially, the repression worked, but in 1565 the Protestant workers struck back. In Brussels and most of the other big cities hereabouts they ran amok, sacking the churches and destroying their rich decoration in the **Iconoclastic Fury**.

Protestantism had infiltrated the nobility, but the ferocity of the rioting shocked the upper classes into renewed support for Spain. Philip was keen to capitalize on the increase in support and, in 1567, he dispatched the **Duke of Albe**, with an army of ten thousand men, to the Low Countries to suppress his religious opponents absolutely. Margaret was not at all pleased by Philip's decision and, when Albe arrived in Brussels, she resigned in a huff, initiating a long period of what was, in effect, military rule. One of Albe's first acts in the capital was to set up the Commission of Civil Unrest, which was soon nicknamed the "**Council of Blood**" after its habit of executing those it examined. No fewer than 12,000 citizens went to the block, most famously the counts of **Egmont** and **Hoorn** (see p.88), who were beheaded on the Grand-Place in June 1568.

Once again, the repression backfired. The region's greatest landowner, Prince William of Orange-Nassau, known as **William the Silent** (1533–84), raised the Low Countries against the Habsburgs and swept all before him, making a triumphant entrance into Brussels, where he installed a Calvinist administration. Momentarily, it seemed possible for the whole of the Low Countries to unite behind William and all signed the **Union of Brussels**, which demanded the departure of foreign troops as a condition for accepting a diluted Habsburg sovereignty. But Philip was not inclined to compromise. In 1578, he gathered together another army which he dispatched to the Low Countries under the command of Alessandro Farnese, the **Duke of Parma**. Initially, Parma was successful, recapturing most of modern Belgium including Brussels and finally Antwerp in 1585. He was, however, unable to advance any further north and the Low Countries were divided into two – the **Spanish Netherlands** and the **United Provinces** – beginning a separation that would lead, after many changes, to the creation of Belgium and the Netherlands.

The Spanish Netherlands

Parma was surprisingly generous in victory, but the city's weavers, apprentices and skilled workers – the bedrock of Calvinism – still fled north to escape the new Catholic regime, fuelling an economic boom in the province of Holland. The migration badly dented the economy of the **Spanish Netherlands** as a whole, but Brussels – the capital – was relatively immune, its economy buoyed by the Habsburg elite, whose conspicuous consumption fostered luxury industries like silk weaving, diamond processing and lace making. The city's industries also benefited from the digging of the Willebroek canal, which linked Brussels to the sea for the first time. This commercial restructuring underpinned a brief flourishing of artistic life both here and, in comparable circumstances, in Antwerp, where it was centred on **Rubens** and his circle, principally Anthony van Dyck and Jacob Jordaens.

Meanwhile, months before his death in 1598, Philip II had granted control of the Spanish Netherlands to his daughter and her husband, appointing them the **Archdukes Isabella** and **Albert**. Failing to learn from experience, the ducal couple continued to prosecute the war against the Protestant north, but with so little success that they were obliged to make peace – the **Twelve Year Truce** – in 1609. When the truce ended, the new Spanish king, Philip IV, stubbornly resumed the campaign against the Protestants, this time as part of a general and even more devastating conflict, the **Thirty Years' War** (1618–48), a largely religious-based conflict between Catholic and Protestant countries that involved most of western Europe. Finally, the Habsburgs were compelled to accept the humiliating terms of the **Peace of Westphalia**, a general treaty whose terms formally recognized the independence of the United Provinces and closed the Scheldt estuary, thereby crippling Antwerp. By these means, the commercial pre-eminence of Amsterdam was assured and its Golden Age began.

The Thirty Years' War had devastated the Spanish Netherlands, but the peace was perhaps as bad. Politically dependent on a decaying Spain, economically ruined and deprived of most of its more independent-minded citizens, the country turned in on itself, sustained by the fanatical Catholicism of the **Counter-Reformation**. Literature disappeared, the sciences vegetated and religious orders multiplied to an extraordinary degree. In **painting**, artists – such as Rubens – were used to confirm the ecclesiastical orthodoxies, their canvases full of muscular saints and angels, reflecting a religious faith of mystery and hierarchy; others, such as David Teniers, retreated into minutely observed realism.

The Peace of Westphalia had also freed the king of France from fear of Germany, and the political and military history of the Spanish Netherlands after 1648 was dominated by the efforts of **Louis XIV** to add the country to his territories. Fearful of an over-powerful France, the United Provinces and England, among others, determinedly resisted French designs and, to preserve the balance of power, fought a long series of campaigns beginning in the 1660s. It was during one of these wars, the **War of the Grand Alliance**, that Louis XIV's artillery destroyed much of medieval Brussels, a disaster that led to the construction of the lavish Grand-Place that survives today.

The **War of the Spanish Succession** – the final conflict of the series – was sparked by the death in 1700 of **Charles II**, the last of the Spanish Habsburgs, who had willed his territories to the grandson of Louis XIV. An anti-French coalition refused to accept the settlement and there ensued a haphazard series of campaigns that dragged on for eleven years. Eventually, with the **Treaty of Utrecht** of 1713, the French abandoned their attempt to conquer the Spanish Netherlands, which now passed under the control of the Austrian Habsburgs in the figure of the Emperor Charles VI.

The Austrian Netherlands

The transfer of the country from Spanish to **Austrian control** made little appreciable difference: a remote imperial authority continued to operate through an appointed governor in Brussels and the country as a whole remained poor and backward. This sorry state of affairs only began to change in the middle of the eighteenth century when the Austrian oligarchy came under the influence of the **Enlightenment**, that belief in reason and progress – as opposed to authority and tradition – that had first been proselytized by French philosophers. In 1753, the arrival of a progressive governor, the **Count of Cobenzl**, signified a transformation of Habsburg policy. Cobenzl initiated an ambitious programme of public works and set about changing the face of Brussels – which had become an urbanized eyesore – by pushing through the grand Neoclassical boulevards and avenues which still characterize the Upper Town.

In 1780, the **Emperor Joseph II** came to the throne, determined to "root out silly old prejudices", as he put it – but his reforms were opposed on all sides. The liberal-minded **Vonckists** demanded a radical, republican constitution, while their enemies, the conservative **Statists**, insisted on the Catholic status quo. There was pandemonium and, in 1789, the Habsburgs dispatched an army to restore order. Against all expectations, the two political groups combined and defeated the Austrians near Antwerp in what became known as the **Brabant Revolution**. In January 1790, the rebels announced the formation of the United States of Belgium, but the country remained in turmoil and when Emperor Joseph died in 1790, his successor, **Léopold**, quickly withdrew the reforming acts and sent in his troops to restore imperial authority.

French occupation and the Kingdom of the Netherlands

The new and repressive Habsburg regime was short-lived. French Republican armies brushed the imperial forces aside in 1794, and the Austrian Netherlands were annexed by France the following year, a state of affairs that was to last until 1814. The **French** imposed radical reforms: the Catholic Church was stripped of much of its worldly wealth, feudal privileges were abolished and, most unpopular of all, conscription was introduced. The invaders were deeply resented and French authority had largely evaporated long before **Napoleon**'s final defeat just outside Brussels at the **battle of Waterloo** (see pp.133–139) in 1815.

At the **Congress of Vienna**, called to settle Europe at the end of the Napoleonic Wars, the main concern of the great powers – including Great Britain and Prussia – was to bolster the Low Countries against France. With scant regard to the feelings of those affected, they therefore decided to establish the **Kingdom of the Netherlands**, which incorporated both the old United Provinces and the Austrian Netherlands, and on the throne they placed Frederick William of Orange, appointed **King William I**. From the very beginning, the union proved problematic – there were even two capital cities, Brussels and The Hague – and William simply wasn't wily enough to hold things together. Nonetheless, the union struggled on until August 25, 1830, when the singing of a duet, *Amour sacré de la Patrie*, in the Brussels opera house hit a nationalist nerve. The audience poured out onto the streets to raise the flag of Brabant in defiance of King William, thereby initiating a countrywide **revolution**. William sent in his troops, but Great Britain and France quickly intervened to stop hostilities. In January of the following year, at the **Conference of London**, the great powers recognized Belgium's independence, with the caveat that the country be classified a "neutral" state – that is one outside any other's sphere of influence. To bolster this new nation, they dug out the uncle of Queen Victoria, Prince Léopold of Saxe-Coburg, to present with the crown.

Independent Belgium: 1830–1900

Shrewd and capable, **Léopold I** was careful both to maintain his country's neutrality and encourage an industrial boom that saw coal mines developed, iron foundries established and the rapid expansion of the railway system. Meanwhile, the country's political representatives, who were elected on a strictly limited franchise, divided into two loose groups, the one attempting to undermine Catholic influence and control over such areas as education, the other

Léopold I (1831–65) Foisted on Belgium by the great powers, Léopold, the first King of the Belgians, was imported from Germany, where he was the prince of Saxe-Coburg – and the uncle of Queen Victoria. Despite lacking a popular mandate, Léopold made a fairly good fist of things, keeping the country neutral as the great powers had ordained.

Léopold II (1865–1909) Energetic and forceful, Léopold II – son of Léopold I – encouraged the urbanization of his country and promoted its importance as a major industrial power. He was also the man responsible for landing Brussels with such pompous monuments as the Palais de Justice and for the imposition of a particularly barbaric colonial regime on the peoples of the Belgian Congo – now the Republic of Congo.

Albert I (1909–34) Easily the most popular of the dynasty, Albert's determined resistance to the German invasion of World War I, when the Germans occupied almost all of the country, made the king a national hero whose untimely death, in a climbing accident, traumatized the nation. Albert was the nephew of Léopold II and the father of Léopold III.

Léopold III (1934–51) In contrast to his father, Léopold III had the dubious honour of becoming one of Europe's least popular monarchs. His first wife died in a suspicious car crash; he nearly lost his kingdom by remarrying (anathema in a Roman Catholic country); and he was badly compromised during the German occupation of World War II. For the first four years of the occupation, Léopold remained in Belgium rather than face exile, fuelling rumours that he was a Nazi collaborator – though his supporters maintained that he prevented thousands of Belgians from being deported. In 1944, the retreating Germans moved Léopold east into the Reich, but after the war finished precious few Belgians wanted their king back and Léopold moved to Switzerland. After several years of heated postwar debate about exactly what to do with the king, the issue of his return was finally put to a referendum in 1950. Just over half the population voted in Léopold's favour, but there was a clear French/Flemish divide, with opposition to the king concentrated in French-speaking Wallonia. Fortunately for Belgium, Léopold abdicated in 1951 in favour of his son, Baudouin.

Baudouin I (1951–93) A softly spoken family man, Baudouin did much to restore the popularity of the monarchy, not least because he was generally thought to be even-handed in his treatment of the French- and Flemish-speaking communities. He also hit the headlines in April 1990 by standing down for a day so that an abortion bill (which he as a Catholic had refused to sign) could be passed. Childless, he was succeeded by his brother.

Albert II (post-1993) Born in 1934, the present king, Baudouin's younger brother, is impeccably royal, from his Swiss finishing school to his aristocratic Italian wife, Queen Paola. Albert is a steady chap who looks like an avuncular bank manager, though (horror, scandal) his wife was the first Belgian royal to be photographed in a swimming costume – and even worse, it was a bikini. Albert has proved to be a safe pair of hands, becoming a national figurehead in the manner of his predecessor and steering a delicate diplomatic course through the shoals of Flemish–Wallonian antagonisms. The royal family is one of Belgium's few unifying forces and any slip off the linguistic/inter-community tightrope is always blown out of all proportion, like the (admittedly ill-advised) comments criticizing the Flemish nationalists made by Albert's son Crown Prince Philippe in late 2004.

profoundly conservative in its desire to maintain the status quo. Progressive elements within this bourgeoisie coalesced in the Liberal Party, which was free-trade and urban in outlook, whereas their opponents, the Catholic party, promised to protect Belgian agriculture with tariffs. The political twist was that the Catholic Party, in its retreat from the industrialized and radicalized cities, began to identify with the plight of rural Dutch-speaking Belgians – rather than the French-speaking ruling and managerial classes.

His successor, **Léopold II**, further boosted industry and supervised the emergence of Belgium as a major industrial power. The king and the reforming Brussels burgomaster (mayor) Anspach also set about modernizing Brussels. New boulevards were built; the free university was founded; many slum areas were cleared; the Senne – which by then had become an open sewer – was covered over in the city centre; and a series of grandiose buildings was erected, the most unpopular of which was the Palais de Justice (see p.90), whose construction involved the forced eviction of hundreds of workers. To round the whole thing off – and turn Brussels into a city deserving of its king – Léopold held the golden jubilee exhibition celebrating the founding of the Belgian state in the newly inaugurated Le Cinquantenaire (see pp.114–117), a mammoth edifice he had built just to the east of the old city centre. The flip side of all this royal posturing was a good deal less pleasant. Determined to cut an international figure, Léopold II had decided to build up a colonial empire. The unfortunate recipients of his ambition were the Africans of the Congo River basin, who were effectively given to him by a conference of European powers in 1885. Ruling the Congo as a personal fiefdom, Léopold established an extraordinarily cruel colonial regime – so cruel in fact that even the other colonial powers were appalled and the Belgian state was obliged to end the embarrassment by taking over the region – as the Belgian Congo – in 1908.

The first fly in the royal ointment came in the 1860s and 1870s with the first significant stirrings of a type of **Flemish nationalism** which felt little enthusiasm for the unitary status of Belgium, divided as it was between the French-speakers in the south of the country – the Walloons – and the Dutch-speakers in the north – the Flemings. The Catholic party ensured that, under the Equality Law of 1898, Dutch was ratified as an official language, equal in status to French – the forerunner of many long and difficult debates. In 1893, the **franchise** was extended to all men over the age of 25.

The twentieth century to 1939

At the beginning of the twentieth century, Belgium was an industrial powerhouse with a booming economy and a rapidly increasing workforce – 934,000 in 1896, 1,176,000 in 1910. It was also determined to keep on good terms with all the great powers, but could not prevent getting caught up in **World War I**. Indifferent to Belgium's proclaimed neutrality, the Germans had decided as early as 1908 that the best way to attack France was via Belgium, and this is precisely what they did in 1914. They captured almost all of the country, the exception being a narrow strip of territory around De Panne. Undaunted, King **Albert I** and the Belgian army bravely manned the northern part of the Allied line, and it made the king a national hero. The trenches ran through western Flanders and all the towns and villages lying close to them – principally Ieper (Ypres) – were simply obliterated by artillery fire. The destruction was, however, confined to a narrow strip of Flanders and most of Belgium – including Brussels – was practically untouched, though the population did suffer during the occupation from lack of food and hundreds of men were forced to work in German factories.

The Belgian language divide

The Belgians are divided between two main groups, the **Walloons**, French-speakers concentrated in Brussels and the south of the country who account for around forty percent of the population, and to the north the **Flemings**, Dutch- or Flemish-speakers, who form about sixty percent out of a total population of some ten million. There are also, in the far east of the country, a few pockets of German-speakers around the towns of Eupen and Malmédy.

The Flemish-French **language divide** has troubled the country for decades, its significance rooted in deep class and economic divisions. When the Belgian state was founded in 1830, its ruling and middle classes were predominantly French-speaking and they created the new state in their linguistic image: French was the official language and Flemish was banned in schools. This Francophone domination was subsequently reinforced by the way the economy developed, with Wallonia becoming a major coal-mining and steel-producing area, while Flanders remained a predominantly agricultural, rural backwater. There were nationalist stirrings amongst the Flemings from the 1860s onwards, but it was only after World War II – when Flanders became the country's industrial powerhouse as Wallonia declined – that the demand for linguistic and cultural parity became irresistible. In the way of such things, the Walloons read Flemish "parity" as "domination", setting the scene for all sorts of inter-communal hassle.

As a response to this burgeoning animosity, a **Language Frontier** was formally drawn across the country in 1962, cutting the country in half, from west to east. The aim was to distinguish between the French- and Flemish-speaking communities and thereby defuse tensions, but it didn't work. In 1980, this failure prompted another attempt to rectify matters with the redrafting of the constitution and the creation of a federal system, with three separate **communities** – the Flemish North, the Walloon South and the German-speaking east – responsible for their own cultural and social affairs and education. At the same time, Belgium was divided into three **regions** — the Flemish North, the Walloon South and bilingual Brussels, with each regional authority dealing with matters like economic development, the environment and employment.

Although the niceties of this partition have undoubtedly calmed troubled waters, in **bilingual Brussels** and at national government level the division between

After the war, under the terms of the **Treaty of Versailles**, Belgium was granted extensive reparations from Germany. Domestically, the Belgian government extended the franchise to all men over the age of 21, a measure which subsequently ended several decades of political control by the Catholic party. The latter was now only able to keep power in coalition with the Liberals – usually with the Socialists, the third major party, forming the backbone of the opposition. The political lines were, however, increasingly fudged as the Catholic party moved left, becoming a Christian Democrat movement that was keen to cooperate with the Socialists on such matters as social legislation. The political parties may have been partly reconciled, but the economy staggered from crisis to crisis even before the effects of the Great Depression hit Belgium in 1929. The political class also failed to placate those Flemings who felt discriminated against. There had been a widespread feeling among the Flemish soldiers of World War I that they had borne the brunt of the fighting and now an increasing number of Flemings came to believe – not without justification – that the Belgian government was overly Walloon in its sympathies. Only reluctantly did the government make Flanders and Wallonia legally unilingual regions in 1930, and even then the linguistic boundary was left unspecified in the hope that French-speakers would come to dominate central Belgium. Inevitably, some

Flemish- and French-speakers still influences many aspects of working and social life. Schools, political parties, literature and culture are all segregated along linguistic lines, leading to a set of complex, face-saving regulations which can verge on the absurd. Government press conferences, for example, must have questions and answers repeated in both languages, one after the other. Across Belgium as a whole, bitterness about the economy, unemployment and the government smoulders within (or seeks an outlet through) the framework of this linguistic division, and individual neighbourhoods can be paralysed by language disputes. The communities of Fourons/Voeren, for instance, a largely French-speaking collection of villages in Flemish Limburg, almost brought down the government in the mid-1980s when the Francophone mayor, one Jose Happart, refused to take the Flemish language exam required of all Limburg officials. Dismissed, he stood again and was re-elected, prompting the prime minister at the time, Wilfred Martens, to offer his own resignation. The Fourons affair was symptomatic of the obstinacy that besets the country to this day with a sort of linguistic guerilla warfare continuing along the peripheries of the Language Frontier with, for example, Eddie de Block, the mayor of Merchtem, on the edge of Brussels, introducing a ban on the speaking of French in the town's schools in 2006. These various disputes give succour to the political right on both sides – namely the Vlaams Blok – now Vlaams Belang – on the Flemish side, and, for the French-speakers, the Front des Francophones (FDF).

All this said, it would be wrong to assume that Belgium's language differences have gone beyond the level of personal animosity and institutionalized mutual suspicion. Belgian **language extremists** have been imprisoned over the years, but very few, if any, have died in the fight for supremacy. Indeed, some might see a bilingual nation as a positive thing in a Europe where trading – and national – barriers are being increasingly broken down. Suggesting this to a Belgian, however, is normally useless, but there again the casual visitor will rarely get a sniff of these tensions. It's probably better to speak English rather than Flemish or French in the "wrong" part of Belgium, but if you make a mistake, the worst you'll get is a look of glazed indifference.

of this discontent was sucked into **Fascist** movements, which drew some ten percent of the vote in both the Walloon and Flemish communities, though for very different reasons: the former for its appeal to a nationalist bourgeoisie, the latter for its assertion of "racial" pride among an oppressed group.

World War II and the postwar period

The Germans invaded again in May 1940, launching a blitzkrieg that overwhelmed both Belgium and the Netherlands in short order. This time there was no heroic resistance by the Belgian king, now **Léopold III**, who ignored the advice of his government and surrendered unconditionally and in such great haste that the British and French armies were, as their Commander-in-Chief put it, "suddenly faced with an open gap of twenty miles between Ypres and the sea through which enemy forces might reach the beaches". It is true that the Belgian army had been badly mauled and that a German victory was inevitable, but the manner of the surrender infuriated many Belgians, as did the king's refusal to form a government in exile. At first the occupation was relatively benign and most of the population waited apprehensively to see just what would happen. The main exception – setting aside the king, who at best played an ambivalent role – was the right-wing edge of the Flemish Nationalist movement, which cooperated with the Germans and (unsuccessfully) sought to negotiate the creation of a separate Flemish state. Popular opinion hardened against the Germans in 1942 as the occupation became more oppressive. The Germans stepped up the requisitioning of Belgian equipment, expanded its forced labour schemes, obliging thousands of Belgians to work in Germany, and cracked down hard on any sign of opposition. By the end of the year, a Resistance movement was mounting acts of sabotage against the occupying forces and this, in turn, prompted more summary executions of both Resistance fighters and hostages.

The summer of 1942 witnessed the first round-ups of the country's **Jews**. In 1940, there were approximately 50,000 Jews in Belgium, mostly newly arrived refugees from Hitler's Germany. Much to their credit, many Belgians did their best to frustrate German efforts to transport the Jews out of the country – usually to Auschwitz; the Belgian police did not cooperate, Belgian railway workers left carriages unlocked and/or sidelined trains, and many other Belgians hid Jews in their homes for the duration. The result was that the Germans had, by 1944, killed about half the country's Jewish population, a much lower proportion than in other parts of occupied Europe. With the occupation hardening, the vast majority of Belgians were delighted to hear of the D-Day landings in June 1944. The **liberation** of Belgium began in September with the American troops in the south and the British and Canadian divisions sweeping across Flanders in the north.

After the war, the Belgians set about the task of **economic reconstruction**, helped by aid from the United States, but hindered by a divisive controversy over the wartime activities of King Léopold. Inevitably, the complex shadings of collaboration and forced cooperation were hard to disentangle, and the debate continued until 1950 when a referendum narrowly recommended his return as king from exile. Léopold's return was, however, marked by rioting across Wallonia, where the king's opponents were concentrated, and Léopold abdicated in favour of his son, **Baudouin**.

1950–2000

The development of the postwar Belgian economy followed the pattern of most of Western Europe – reconstruction in the 1950s; boom in the 1960s; recession in the 1970s; and retrenchment in the 1980s and 1990s. Significant events included the belated extension of the franchise to women in 1948; an ugly, disorganized and hasty evacuation of the Belgian Congo in 1960; and the transformation of Brussels from one of the lesser European capitals into a major player when it became the home of the **EU** and **NATO** – the latter organization was ejected from France on the orders of de Gaulle in 1967. There was also a right royal pantomime when Catholic King Baudouin abdicated for the day while the law legalizing abortion was ratified in 1990.

Yet, above all, the postwar period was dominated by increasing **tension between the Walloon and Flemish communities**, a state of affairs that was entangled with the economic decline of Wallonia, formerly the home of most of the country's heavy industry, as compared with burgeoning Flanders. One result of the tension was that every **national institution** became dogged by the prerequisites of bilingualism – speeches in parliament, for example, had, and still have, to be delivered in both languages – and in Brussels, the country's one and only **bilingual region**, every instance of the written word, from road signs to the yellow pages, has to be bilingual as well. Brussels has also been subtly affected by the **Language Divide** (or Language Frontier; see box, pp.260–261), which was formally delineated in 1962. Bilingual Brussels is now encircled by Flemish-speaking regions and, partly as a result, many Francophones living in the city have developed something of a siege mentality; the Flemish, on the other hand, can't help but notice the prevalence of the French language in what is supposed to be their capital city.

Bogged down by these linguistic preoccupations, the federal government often appears extraordinarily cumbersome, but there again much of the political class is at least partly reliant on the linguistic divide for their jobs and, institutionally speaking, has little incentive to see the antagonisms resolved. A rare moment of national unity came in 1996 when communities from both sides of the linguistic divide rose up in protest at the Belgian police, which proved itself at best hopelessly inefficient, at worst complicit in the gruesome activities of the child murderer and pornographer **Marc Dutroux**. Over 350,000 people took to the capital's streets, demanding the police and justice system be overhauled. This outburst of public protest peaked again two years later when, amazingly enough, Dutroux escaped his police guards, stole a car and headed out of the city. Although he was subsequently recaptured, most Belgians were simply appalled, though there was some relief when Dutroux was finally sentenced to life imprisonment in June 2004.

The present

There was some political spring-cleaning in the city in 2000 when the liberals were voted out of power in the elections to the **Brussels Regional Parliament**. They were replaced by a red-green coalition, but in the next election, in 2004, the coalition was itself replaced by a socialist-led alliance, who remain in power at time of writing. Nationally, **Guy Verhofstadt** cobbled together a centre-left coalition in 1999 and repeated this political feat after the federal elections of 2003. Matters might then have proceeded smoothly enough had it not been for a bitter conflict between French- and Flemish-speaking politicians over the electoral arrangements pertaining to **Brussels–Halle–Vilvoorde** (BHV for short). This extraordinarily complex dispute sapped the strength of the national government and, after the federal elections of 2007, no politician was able to construct a ruling coalition. Eventually, after several months, a government was formed, but at time of writing the Prime Minister – Yves Leterme – has just offered his resignation to the king and it looks like the horse trading will have to start all over again. The omens are not good: there's precious little goodwill between the French- and Flemish-speaking politicians and Belgium may indeed split into two (north and south), though neither side will want to surrender Brussels and the city may in itself, therefore, hold things together.

These political difficulties reflect deep inter-communal tensions. In essence, the **Walloons** fear that the wealthier and more numerous Flemings will come to dominate the state, and indeed they may make this a self-fulfilling prophecy with their reluctance to learn Flemish – bilingualism being a prerequisite for any national job. The **Flemings**, on the other hand, want political and cultural recognition, and many bristle at what they perceive as Wallonian cultural and linguistic arrogance. These tensions can, however, be exaggerated. In 2006, a Belgian TV station, RTBF, mounted an elaborate spoof, saying that the Dutch-speaking half of the country had declared independence. There were pictures of cheering crowds waving the Flemish flag and of trams stuck at the new international border, but few Belgians were jubilant and instead there was widespread alarm. Most polls indicate that a clear majority of Belgians want their country to survive, though few would give the same reason as the country's most popular writer, the recently deceased **Hugo Claus**, who wrote "I insist on being Belgian. I want to be a member of the pariah nationality, the laughing stock of the French and the object of contempt of the Dutch. It's the ideal situation for a writer."

An introduction to Belgian art

The following **outline** is the very briefest of introductions to a subject that has rightly filled volumes, and is designed to serve only as a quick reference. Inevitably, it covers artists that lived and worked in both the Netherlands and Belgium as these two countries have both been, for most of their history, bound together as the so-called Low Countries. For more in-depth and academic studies, see the recommendations in the "Books" section on p.273.

The Early Flemish Masters

Throughout the medieval period, Flanders was one of the most artistically productive parts of Europe with each of the cloth towns, especially Bruges and Ghent, trying to out-do its rivals with the quality of its religious art. Today, the works of these early Flemish painters, known as the **Flemish Primitives**, are highly prized and an excellent sample is displayed in both Ghent and Bruges as well as in Brussels. **Jan van Eyck** (1385–1441) is generally regarded as the first of the Flemish Primitives, and has even been credited with the invention of oil painting itself – though it seems more likely that he simply perfected a new technique by thinning his paint with (the newly discovered) turpentine, thus making it more flexible. His fame partially stems from the fact that he was one of the first artists to sign his work – an indication of how highly his talent was regarded by his contemporaries. Van Eyck's most celebrated work is the *Adoration of the Mystic Lamb*, a stunningly beautiful altarpiece displayed in St-Baafskathedraal in Ghent (see p.164). The painting was revolutionary in its realism, for the first time using elements of native landscape in depicting Biblical themes, and was underpinned by a complex symbolism which has generated analysis and discussion ever since. Van Eyck's style and technique were to influence several generations of Low Countries' artists.

Firmly in the Eyckian tradition was **Rogier van der Weyden** (1400–64), one-time official painter to the city of Brussels. Weyden's religious paintings do, however, show a greater degree of emotional intensity than those of van Eyck, while his serene portraits of the bigwigs of his day were much admired across a large swathe of western Europe. Among the many painters influnced by Van der Weyden, one of the most talented was **Dieric Bouts** (1415–75). Born in Haarlem in what is now the Netherlands but active in Leuven (see p.159), Bouts is recognizable by his stiff, rather elongated figures and horrific subject matter, all set against carefully drawn landscapes. **Hugo van der Goes** (d.1482) was the next Ghent master after van Eyck, most famous for the Portinari altarpiece in Florence's Uffizi. After a short painting career, he died insane, and his late works have implicit hints of his impending madness in their subversive use of space and implicit acceptance of the viewer's presence. Few doubt that **Hans Memling** (1440–94) was a pupil of Van der Weyden. Active in Bruges throughout his life, he is best remembered for the pastoral charm of his landscapes and the quality of his portraiture, much of which survives on the rescued side panels of triptychs. The Hospitaalmuseum in Bruges (see p.175) has a wonderful sample of his work.

Both **Gerard David** (1460–1523) and **Jan Provoost** (1465–1529) moved to Bruges at the end of the fifteenth century. Mostly they painted religious scenes, but their secular works are much more memorable, especially David's *Judgement of Cambyses*, exhibited in the Groeninge in Bruges (see p.174). David's best-known apprentice was **Adriaen Isenbrant** (d.1551), whose speciality was small, precisely executed panels. Isenbrant was the last of the great painters to work in that city before it was superseded by Antwerp – which itself became the focus of a more Italianate school of art in the sixteenth century.

Strikingly different, but broadly contemporaneous, was **Hieronymus Bosch** (1450–1516), who lived for most of his life in the Netherlands, though his style is linked to that of his Flemish contemporaries. His frequently reprinted religious allegories are filled with macabre visions of tortured souls and grotesque beasts, and appear at first faintly unhinged, though it's now thought that these are visual representations of contemporary sayings, idioms and parables. While their interpretation is far from resolved, Bosch's paintings draw strongly on subconscious fears and archetypes, giving them a lasting, haunting fascination.

The sixteenth century

At the end of the fifteenth century, Flanders was in economic and political decline and the leading artists of the day migrated to the booming port of Antwerp. The artists who worked here soon began to integrate the finely observed detail that characterized the Flemish tradition with the style of the Italian painters of the Renaissance. **Quentin Matsys** (1464–1530) introduced florid classical architectural details and intricate landscapes to his works, influenced perhaps by the work of Leonardo da Vinci. As well as religious works, he painted portraits and genre scenes, all of which have recognizably Italian facets, and paved the way for the Dutch genre painters of later years. **Jan Gossart** (1478–1532) made the pilgrimage to Italy too, and his dynamic works are packed with detail, especially finely drawn classical architectural backdrops. He was the first Low Countries artist to introduce the subjects of classical mythology into his works, part of a steady trend through the period towards secular subject matter, which can also be seen in the work of **Joachim Patenier** (d.1524), who painted small landscapes of fantastical scenery.

The middle of the sixteenth century was dominated by the work of **Pieter Bruegel the Elder** (c.1525–69), whose gruesome allegories and innovative interpretations of religious subjects are firmly placed in Low Countries settings. Pieter also painted finely observed peasant scenes, though he himself was well connected in court circles in Antwerp and, later, Brussels. **Pieter Aertsen** (1508–75) also worked in the peasant genre, adding aspects of still life; his paintings often show a detailed kitchen scene in the foreground, with a religious episode going on behind. Bruegel's two sons, **Pieter Bruegel the Younger** (1564–1638) and **Jan Bruegel** (1568–1625) were lesser painters: the former produced fairly insipid copies of his father's work, while Jan developed a style of his own – delicately rendered flower paintings and genre pieces that earned him the nickname "Velvet". Towards the latter half of the sixteenth century highly stylized Italianate portraits became the dominant fashion, **Frans Pourbus** the Younger (1569–1622) being the leading practitioner. Frans worked for the likes of the Habsburgs and the Médicis, his itinerant life in contrast to that of his grandfather, the Bruges-based **Pieter Pourbus** (1523–84), the founder of this artistic dynasty.

The seventeenth century

"Belgian" painting of the early seventeenth century was dominated by **Pieter Paul Rubens** (1577–1640), easily the most important exponent of the Baroque in northern Europe. Born in Siegen, Westphalia, Rubens was raised in Antwerp, where he entered the painters' guild in 1598. He became court painter to the Duke of Mantua in 1600, and until 1608 travelled extensively in Italy, absorbing the art of the High Renaissance and classical architecture. By the time of his return to Antwerp in 1608 he had acquired an enormous artistic vocabulary: the paintings of Caravaggio in particular were to influence his work strongly. His first major success was *The Raising of the Cross*, painted in 1610 and displayed today in Antwerp Cathedral (see p.152). A large, dynamic work, it caused a sensation at the time, establishing Rubens' reputation and leading to a string of commissions. *The Descent from the Cross*, his next major work (also in the cathedral), consolidated this success; equally Baroque, it is nevertheless quieter and more restrained.

The division of labour in **Rubens' studio**, and the talent of the artists working there (who included Antony van Dyck and Jacob Jordaens – see below) ensured a substantial output of outstanding work. The degree to which Rubens personally worked on a canvas would vary – and would determine its price. From the early 1620s onwards he turned his hand to a plethora of themes and subjects – religious works, portraits, tapestry designs, landscapes, mythological scenes, ceiling paintings – each of which was handled with supreme vitality and virtuosity. From his Flemish antecedents he inherited an acute sense of light, and used it not to dramatize his subjects (a technique favoured by Caravaggio and other Italian artists), but in association with colour and form. The drama in his works comes from the vigorous animation of his characters. His large-scale allegorical works, especially, are packed with heaving, writhing figures that appear to tumble out from the canvas.

The energy of Rubens' paintings was reflected in his **private life**. In addition to his career as an artist, he also undertook diplomatic missions to Spain and England, and used these opportunities to study the works of other painters and – as in the case of Velázquez – to meet them personally. In the 1630s, gout began to hamper his activities, and from this time his painting became more domestic and meditative. **Hélène Fourment**, his second wife, was the subject of many portraits and served as a model for characters in his allegorical paintings, her figure epitomizing the buxom, well-rounded women found throughout his work.

The followers of Rubens

Rubens' influence on the artists of the period was enormous. The huge output of his studio meant that his works were universally seen, and widely disseminated by the engravers he employed to copy his work. Chief among his followers was the portraitist **Antony van Dyck** (1599–1641), who worked in Rubens' studio from 1618, often taking on the depiction of religious figures in his master's works that required particular sensitivity and pathos. Like Rubens, van Dyck was born in Antwerp and travelled widely in Italy, though his initial work was influenced less by the Italian artists than by Rubens himself. Eventually van Dyck developed his own distinct style and technique, establishing himself as court painter to Charles I in England, and creating portraits of a nervous elegance that would influence portraiture there for the next hundred and fifty years. Most of his great portrait paintings remain in England, but his best religious works – such as the *Crucifixion* in Mechelen Cathedral (see p.146) – can be found in Belgium. **Jacob Jordaens** (1593–1678) was also an Antwerp native who studied under Rubens. Although he was commissioned to complete several works left unfinished by Rubens at the time of his death, his robustly naturalistic works have an earthy – and sensuous – realism that is quite distinct in style and technique.

Genre painting

As well as the Baroque creations of Rubens and his acolytes, another style emerged in the seventeenth century, that of **genre painting**. Often misunderstood, the term was initially applied to everything from animal paintings and still lifes through to historical works and landscapes, but later came to be applied only to scenes of everyday life. One of its early practitioners was **Frans Snijders** (1579–1657), who took up still-life painting where Aertsen left off, amplifying his subject – food and drink – to even larger, more sumptuous canvases, while doubling up as a member of the Rubens art machine, painting animals and still-life sections for the master's works. In the Spanish Netherlands (as Belgium was called from 1579–1713), the most skilful practitioner was **Adriaen Brouwer** (1605–38), whose peasant figures rivalled those of the painters Jan Steen and Adriaen van Ostade in the United Provinces (now the Netherlands) to the north. Brouwer's output was unsurprisingly small given his short life, but his riotous tavern scenes and tableaux of everyday life were deftly done, and were well received in their day, collected by, among others, Rubens and Rembrandt. Brouwer studied in Haarlem for a while under Frans Hals (and may have picked up much of his painterly technique from him), before returning to his native Flanders to influence **David Teniers the Younger** (1610–1690), who worked in Antwerp, and later in Brussels. Teniers' early paintings are Brouwer-like peasant scenes, although his later work is more delicate and diverse, including *kortegaardje* – guardroom scenes that show soldiers carousing.

The eighteenth century

By the end of the seventeenth century, French influences had overwhelmed Belgium's native artistic tradition with painters like **Jan Joseph Horemans I** and **Balthasar van den Bossche** modifying the Flemish genre painting of the previous century to suit Parisian tastes. Towards the end of the century, Neoclassicism came into vogue, a French-led movement whose leading light was **Jacques Louis David** (1748–1825), the creator of the *Death of Marat*, an iconic work displayed in Brussels' Musées Royaux des Beaux Arts (see p.78). **Laurent Delvaux** (1696–1778) was also an important figure during this period, a Flemish sculptor who produced a large number of works for Belgian churches, including the pulpit of Ghent's cathedral.

The nineteenth century

French artistic fashions ruled the Belgian roost well into the nineteenth century, and amongst them Neoclassicism remained the most popular. Of the followers of Jacques Louis David, **François Joseph Navez** (1787–1869) was the most important to work in Belgium, furthering the influence of the movement via his position as director of the Brussels academy. With Belgian independence (from the Netherlands) in 1830, came, as might be expected, a new interest in nationalism, and artists such as **Louis Galliat** (1810–87) and **Henri Dobbelaere** (1829–85) spearheaded a romantic interpretation of historical events, idealizing Belgium's recent and medieval history.

Antoine Wiertz (1806–65) – who has his own museum in Brussels (see p.84) – was much lauded for his grandiose amalgamation of romantic and Neoclassical themes in both his sculptures and paintings, while **Henri de Braekeleer** (1840–88) was highly regarded for his Dutch-inspired interiors and landscapes. Indeed, landscape painting underwent a resurgence of popularity in France in the mid-nineteenth century, and once again Belgian artists flocked to reflect that country's tastes. Perhaps more positively, **Emile Claus** (1849–1924) adapted French Impressionist ideas to create an individual style known as Luminism, and **Théo Rysselberghe** (1862–1926) followed suit. The talented **Fernand Khnopff** (1858–1921) developed his own style too, in his case inspired by the English Pre-Raphaelites.

One artist who stands out during this period is **Constantin Meunier** (1831–1905), a painter and sculptor whose naturalistic depiction of brawny workers and mining scenes was the perfect mirror of a fast-industrializing Belgium; Meunier is another artist to have his own museum in the capital – see p.100. The most original Belgian artist of the late nineteenth century was, however, **James Ensor** (1860–1949). Ensor, who lived in Ostend for most of his life, painted macabre, disturbing works, whose haunted style can be traced back to Bosch and Bruegel and which was itself a precursor of Expressionism. He was active in a group known as **Les XX** (*Les Vingt*; see box, p.105), which organized exhibitions of new styles of art from abroad, and greatly influenced contemporary Belgian painters.

The twentieth century

Each of the major modern art movements had its followers in Belgium, and each was diluted or altered according to local taste. **Expressionism** was manifest in a local group of artists established in a village near Ghent, with the most eye-catching paintings produced by **Constant Permeke** (1886–1952), whose bold, deeply coloured canvases can be found in many Belgian galleries. There was also **Jean Delville** (1867–1953), not as talented as Permeke perhaps, but an artist who certainly set about his religious preoccupations with gigantic gusto. **Surrealism** also caught on in a big way, perhaps because of the Belgian penchant for the bizarre and grotesque. **René Magritte** (1898–1967), one of the leading lights of the movement, was born and trained in Belgium and returned there after being involved in the movement's birth in 1927. His Surrealism is gentle compared to the work of Dalí or de Chirico: ordinary images are used in a dreamlike way, often playing on the distinction between a word and its meaning. His most famous motif was the man in the bowler hat, whose face was always hidden from view. Magritte lived in Brussels for many years and his old home and studio is now open to the public (see p.123). Also worthy of note is **Paul Delvaux** (1897–1994), who adopted his own rather salacious interpretation of the movement in a sort of "what-the-butler-saw" Surrealism.

Most of Belgium's interwar artists were influenced by van Doesburg and de Stijl in the Netherlands, though none figured highly in the movement. The abstract geometrical works of **Victor Severanckx** (1897–1965) owed much to de Stijl, and he in turn inspired the postwar group known as **La Jeune Peinture**, which gathered together some of the most notable artists working in Belgium, the antecedents of the Abstract Expressionists of the 1950s. A similar collective function was served by **CoBrA**, founded in 1948 and taking its name from the first letters of Copenhagen, Brussels and Amsterdam. While none of the Belgian participants in CoBrA achieved the fame of one of its Dutch members, Karel Appel, the name of **Pierre Alechinsky** (b. 1927) is certainly well known in his home town, Brussels. Probably the most famous recent Belgian artist is **Marcel Broodthaers** (1924–1976). He initially worked in the Surrealist manner, but soon branched out, quickly graduating from cut-paper geometric shapes into both the plastic arts and, most famously, sharp and brightly coloured paintings of everyday artefacts, especially casseroles brimming with mussels.

Books

M ost of the following **books** should be readily available in bookshops or online (Ⓦ www.amazon.com), though you may have a little more difficulty tracking down those few titles we mention which are currently out of print, signified o/p. Titles marked with the 🏃 symbol are especially recommended.

Travel and general

Eric Boschman and Nathalie Derny *Les Gouts des Belges*. Though only available in French, this is the definitive guide to Belgian food, cooking and tastes.

Charlotte and Emily Brontë (ed. Sue Lonoff) *The Belgian Essays*. The Brontë sisters left their native Yorkshire for the first time in 1842 to make a trip to Brussels; Charlotte returned the following year. This handsome volume – from Yale – reproduces the twenty-eight essays they penned (in French) during their journey and provides the English translation opposite. A delightful read; particular highlights are "The Butterfly", "The Caterpillar" and "The Death of Napoleon".

Guide Delta Bruxelles Over four hundred pages of detailed and perceptive hotel and restaurant reviews covering every corner of the capital. Only in French; available at leading bookshops in Brussels.

Michael Farr *Tintin: The Complete Companion* (o/p). A Tintinologist's treat, this immaculately illustrated book – written by one of the world's leading experts – explores every aspect of Hergé's remarkably popular creation. Particularly strong on the real-life stories that inspired Hergé, but you do have to be a serious fan to really enjoy this book.

Hergé *The Calculus Affair* and *The Making of Tintin: Cigars of the Pharaoh & the Blue Lotus*. Tintin comic strips come in and out of print at a rapid rate, usually in anthologies; there's a wide selection of audio cassettes too. The two anthologies listed here are as good a place as any to start.

Benoit Peeters *Tintin and the World of Hergé: an Illustrated History* (o/p). Examines the life and career of Hergé, particularly the development of Tintin, and the influences on his work. No fewer than three hundred illustrations, but sadly out of print.

🏃 **Luc Sante** *The Factory of Facts*. Born in Belgium but raised in the US, Sante returned to his native land for an extended visit in 1989, at the age of 35. Published in 1998, his book is primarily a personal reflection, but he also uses this as a base for a thoughtful exploration of Belgium and the Belgians – from their art to their food and beyond.

🏃 **Tim Webb** *Good Beer Guide to Belgium*. Detailed and enthusiastic guide to the best bars, beers and breweries. A good read, and extremely well informed to boot. Undoubtedly, the best book on its subject on the market. Published in 2005 by CAMRA (Campaign For Real Ale books).

History and politics

Neal Ascherson *The King Incorporated: Leopold the Second and the Congo.* Belgium's King Léopold II was responsible for one of the cruellest of colonial regimes, a savage system of repression and exploitation that devastated the Belgian Congo. Ascherson details it all.

Malcolm Balen *A Model Victory: Waterloo and the Battle for History.* Some twenty years after Waterloo, the British government asked Lieutenant William Siborne, a great fan of the Duke of Wellington, to prepare a scale model of the battle. They assumed that he would depict the start of the battle, but he chose the crisis instead – and this is where he came unstuck. After interviewing scores of Waterloo veterans, Siborne put the Prussians far in advance of what the Duke wanted, taking some of the glory from the British army. Siborne felt the full fury of Wellington's ire – and this much-praised book describes it all.

J.C.H. Blom (ed) *History of the Low Countries.* Belgian history books are thin on the ground, so this incisive, well-balanced volume is very welcome. A series of historians weigh in with their specialities to build a comprehensive picture of the region from the Celts and Romans through to the 1980s. Highly recommended, though hardly deckchair reading.

Paul van Buitenen *Blowing the Whistle: One Man's Fight Against Fraud in the European Commission.* All your worst fears about the EU confirmed. Buitenen was an assistant auditor in the EU's Financial Control Directorate in Brussels and this book, first published in 1998, exposed the fraud and corruption. Needless to say, the EU was far from grateful for his revelations and forced him to resign, but even so the stories of scandal became so widespread that the entire Commission was obliged to resign en masse. Since then, there have been earnest declarations that things are much better.

Christopher Hibbert *Waterloo.* Hibbert is one of Britain's leading historians, an astute commentator who writes in a fluent, accessible style. This book is divided into three parts. The first examines Napoleon's rise to power, the second looks at Wellington and his allies, and the third deals with the battle.

Adam Hochschild *King Leopold's Ghost.* Harrowing account of King Léopold's savage colonial regime in the Congo. A detailed assessment – perhaps a little too long – explains and explores its gruesome workings. Particularly good on Roger Casement, the one-time British consul to the Congo, who publicized the cruelty and helped bring it to an end. It was this same Casement, who ended up being hung by the British in 1916 for his active support of the Irish Republican movement. Hochschild's last chapter – "The Great Forgetting" – is a stern criticism of the Belgians for their failure to acknowledge their savage colonial history.

Geoffrey Parker *The Dutch Revolt.* Compelling account of the struggle between the Netherlands and Spain. Quite the best thing you can read on the period. The title may sound academic, but this book gives a fascinating insight into the Habsburg army that occupied the Low Countries for well over a hundred years – how it functioned, was fed and moved from Spain to the

Low Countries along the so-called Spanish Road. *The Army of Flanders and the Spanish Road 1567–1659* is by the same author.

Andrew Wheatcroft *The Habsburgs.* Excellent and well-researched trawl through the dynasty's history, from its eleventh-century beginnings to its eclipse at the end of World War I. Enjoyable background reading.

Geoffrey Wootten *Waterloo 1815.* About one-third of the length of Hibbert's *Waterloo* (see p.272), this 96-page book focuses on the battle, providing a clear, thorough and interesting account.

Art and architecture

Ulrike Becks-Malorny *James Ensor.* Eminently readable and extensively illustrated account of James Ensor's life and art. The often-neglected painter, from Ostend, was one of Belgium's finest.

Kristin Lohse Belkin *Rubens.* Too long for its own good, this book details Rubens' spectacularly success-ful career both as artist and diplomat. Belkin is particularly thorough in her discussions of technique and the workings of his workshop, and exten-sive reference is made to Rubens' letters. Excellent illustrations.

Robin Blake *Anthony van Dyck.* Whether or not van Dyck justifies 448 pages is a moot point, but he did have an interesting life and certainly thumped out a fair few paintings. This volume explores every artistic nook and cranny.

Aurora Cuito (ed) *Victor Horta* (o/p). Concise and readily digestible guide to the work of Belgium's lead-ing exponent of Art Nouveau (see pp.96–98).

R.H. Fuchs *Dutch Painting.* As complete an introduction to the subject – from Flemish origins to the present day – as you could wish for, in just a couple of hundred pages. First published in the 1970s.

R.H. Fuchs et al *Flemish and Dutch Painting (from Van Gogh, Ensor, Magritte and Mondrian to Contemporary).*

Excellent, lucid account giving an overview of the development of Flemish and Dutch painting from Van Gogh onwards.

Suzi Gablik *Magritte.* Suzi Gablik lived in Magritte's house for six months in the 1960s and this personal contact informs this text, which is lucid, perceptive and thoughtful. Most of the illustrations are, however, black and white. At 208 pages, much longer than the Hammacher version (see below).

Walter S. Gibson *Hieronymus Bosch* and *Bruegel.* Two wonder-fully illustrated Thames & Hudson titles on these exquisite allegorical painters. The former contains every-thing you wanted to know about Hieronymus Bosch, his paintings and his late fifteenth-century milieu, while the latter takes a detailed look at Pieter Bruegel the Elder's art, with nine well-argued chapters investigat-ing its various components.

A.M. Hammacher *René Magritte.* This well-written and beautifully illustrated book provides a detailed examination of Magritte's life, times and artistic output. It's concise too – at just 126 pages.

Craig Harbison *Jan van Eyck: The Play of Realism.* Not much is known about van Eyck, but Harbison has done his best to root out every detail. The text is accompanied by illustra-tions of all of Eyck's major paintings.

Literature

Mark Bles *A Child at War.* This powerful book describes the tribulations of Hortense Daman, a Belgian girl who joined the Resistance at the tender age of fifteen. Betrayed to the Gestapo, Daman was sent to the Ravensbruck concentration camp, where she was used in medical experiments, but remarkably survived. This is her story, though the book would have benefited from some editorial pruning.

Charlotte Brontë *Villette.* Bronte's Villette is a thinly disguised Brussels in this, her last novel, inspired by her lively experiences as a schoolteacher in the city.

Hugo Claus *The Sorrow of Belgium.* Claus is generally regarded as Belgium's foremost Flemish-language novelist, and this is generally regarded as his best novel. It charts the growing maturity of a young boy living in Flanders under the Nazi occupation. Claus' style is somewhat dense to say the least, but the book gets to grips with the guilt, bigotry and mistrust of the period, and caused a minor uproar when it was first published in the early 1980s. His *Swordfish* is a story of an isolated village rife with ethnic and religious tensions. The effects of this prove too much for a boy, precipitating his descent into madness. *Desire* is the strange and disconcerting tale of two drinking buddies, who, on an impulse, abandon small-town Belgium for Las Vegas, where both of them start to unravel. Claus, who was suffering from Alzheimers, chose to end his life in 2008.

Amelie Nothomb *Loving Sabotage.* English-language translations of modern Belgian writers (in both French and Dutch) are a rarity, but Nothomb, one of Belgium's most popular writers, has made the linguistic leap. This particular novel deals with the daughter of a diplomat stationed in Peking in the 1970s, a rite-of-passage story with a Maoist backdrop. *The Stranger Next Door,* perhaps Nothomb's most successful translated work, deals with weird and disconcerting happenings in the Belgian countryside, while *Fear and Trembling* is a sharply observed tale of the shoddy treatment meted out to a young Western businesswoman in a big corporation in Tokyo. Her latest novel, *Sulphuric Acid*, deals with a Big Brother-style show that turns into a bloodfest.

Georges Simenon *Maigret loses his Temper* and *Maigret and the Killer.* There can be no dispute that Simenon is Belgium's most famous crime writer, his main creation being the Parisian detective Maigret. There are dozens of books: these two ripping yarns can get you started.

Language

Language

Language

n Brussels, the majority of Belgians speak a dialect of French known as **Walloon**, as they do in the country's southern provinces, known logically enough as Wallonia. Walloon is almost identical to French, and if you've any knowledge of the language, you'll be readily understood. One peculiarity of the city is that French has **linguistic parity with Dutch**, which is spoken both here and across the northern part of Belgium in a variety of distinctive dialects commonly lumped together as **Flemish**. In Brussels, all manifestations of the written word have to be in both languages, though in this guidebook we have opted just for French – the language of the majority of city folk. Flemish may have parity with French, but the second most commonly spoken language in Brussels is actually **English**.

French isn't a particularly easy language, despite the number of words shared with English, but learning the bare essentials is not difficult and makes all the difference. Even just saying "Bonjour, Madame/Monsieur" when you go into a shop and then pointing will usually get you a smile and helpful service.

Differentiating words is the initial problem in understanding spoken French – it's very hard to get people to slow down. If, as a last resort, you get them to write it down, you'll probably find you know half the words anyway. Of the available **phrasebooks**, Rough Guide's own *French Dictionary Phrasebook* should sort you out better than most.

Pronunciation

Consonants

Consonants are pronounced much as in English, except:

c is softened to the s sound when followed by an "e" or "i", or when it has a cedilla (ç) below it

ch is always sh

g is softened to a French j sound when followed by "e" or "i", eg Gérard

h is silent

j is like the s sound in "measure" or "treasure"

ll is like the y in yes

qu is normally pronounced like a k (eg quatre)

r is growled (or rolled)

th is the same as t

w is v

Vowels

These are the hardest sounds to get right. Roughly:

a as in hat

e as in get

é between get and gate

è between get and gut

eu like the u in hurt

i as in machine

o as in hot

o, au as in over

ou as in food

u as in a pursed-lip version of use

More awkward are the combinations below when they occur at the ends of words, or are followed by consonants other than *n* or *m*:

in/im like the an in anxious

an/am, en/em as in don when said with a nasal accent

on/om like the don in Doncaster said by someone with a heavy cold

un/um like the u in understand.

Words and phrases

The basics

yes	oui
no	non
please	s'il vous plaît
(no) thank you	(non) merci
hello	bonjour
how are you?	comment allez-vous?/ ça va?
good morning/ afternoon	bonjour
good evening	bonsoir
good night	bonne nuit
goodbye	au revoir
see you later	à bientôt
now/later sorry	maintenant/plus tard pardon, Madame,

	Monsieur/je m'excuse
do you speak English?	parlez-vous l'anglais?
I (don't) understand	je (ne) comprends (pas)
women	femmes
men	hommes
men's/women's toilets	hommes/femmes
children	enfants
I want …	je veux…
I don't want	je ne veux pas
OK/agreed	d'accord

Cycling

tyre	pneu
puncture	pneu crevé
brake	frein
chain	chaîne
wheel	roué

pedal	pédale
pump	pompe
handlebars	guidon
broken	cassé

Travel and shopping

post office	la poste
stamp(s)	timbre(s)
money exchange	bureau de change
cashier	la caisse
ticket office	le guichet
how do I get to …?	comment est-ce que je peux arriver à …?
where is … ?	où est …?

how far is it to … ?	combien y a-t-il jusqu'à …?
when?	quand?
how much is …?	c'est combien …?
far/near	loin/près
left/ right	à gauche/ à droite
straight ahead	tout droit
platform	quai
here/there	ici/ là

good/bad	bon/mauvais	hot/cold	chaud/froid
big/small	grand/petit	with/without	avec/sans
open/closed	ouvert/fermé	a lot/a little	beaucoup/peu
push/pull	pousser/tirer	behind	derrière
new/old	nouveau/vieux	through traffic only	voie de traversée
cheap/expensive	bon marché/cher		

Numbers

0	zéro	19	dix-neuf
1	un	20	vingt
2	deux	21	vingt-et-un
3	trois	30	trente
4	quatre	40	quarante
5	cinq	50	cinquante
6	six	60	soixante
7	sept	70	soixante-dix (local usage is septante)
8	huit		
9	neuf	80	quatre-vingts
10	dix	90	quatre-vingt-dix (local usage is nonante)
11	onze		
12	douze		
13	treize	100	cent
14	quatorze	101	cent-et-un
15	quinze	200	deux cents
16	seize	500	cinq cents
17	dix-sept	1000	mille
18	dix-huit		

Days

Sunday	dimanche	night	la nuit
Monday	lundi	yesterday	hier
Tuesday	mardi	today	aujourd'hui
Wednesday	mercredi	tomorrow	demain
Thursday	jeudi	tomorrow morning	demain matin
Friday	vendredi	day	jour
Saturday	samedi	week	semaine
morning	le matin	month	mois
afternoon	l'après-midi	year	année
evening	le soir		

Months

January	janvier	April	avril
February	février	May	mai
March	mars	June	juin

July	juillet	**October**	octobre
August	août	**November**	novembre
September	septembre	**December**	décembre

Time

minute	minute	**What time is it?**	Quelle heure est-il?
hour	heure		

A French menu reader

Basic terms and ingredients

beurre	butter	pain	bread
chaud	hot	poisson	fish
dessert	dessert	poivre	pepper
escargots	snails	riz	rice
frappé	iced	salade	salad
fromage	cheese	sel	salt
froid	cold	sucre	sugar/sweet (taste)
gibiers	game	tourte	tart or pie
hors d'oeuvre	starters	tranche	slice
légumes	vegetables	viande	meat
oeufs	eggs		

Cooking terms and methods

à point	medium done	grillé	grilled
au four	baked	mijoté	stewed
bien cuit	well done	pané	breaded
bouilli	boiled	rôti	roast
frit/friture	fried/deep fried	saignant	rare
fumé	smoked	sauté	lightly cooked in butter

Starters and snacks

assiette anglaise	plate of cold meats	potage	thick soup, usually vegetable
bisque	shellfish soup		
bouillabaisse	fish soup from Marseilles	un sandwich/une baguette …	a sandwich …
bouillon	broth or stock	de jambon	with ham
consommé	clear soup	de fromage	with cheese
croque-monsieur	grilled cheese and ham sandwich	de saucisson	with sausage
		à l'ail	with garlic
crudités	raw vegetables with dressing	au poivre	with pepper
		oeufs …	eggs …

au plat	fried eggs	tomates	tomatoes
à la coque	boiled eggs	concombres	cucumbers
durs	hard-boiled eggs	crêpes …	pancakes …
brouillés	scrambled eggs	au sucre	with sugar
omelette …	omelette …	au citron	with lemon
nature	plain	au miel	with honey
au fromage	with cheese	à la confiture	with jam
salade de …	salad of …		

Meat and poultry

agneau	lamb	foie	liver
bifteck	steak	gigot	leg of venison
boeuf	beef	jambon	ham
canard	duck	lard	bacon
cheval	horsemeat	porc	pork
côtelettes	cutlets	poulet	chicken
cuisson	leg of lamb	saucisse	sausage
dindon	turkey	veau	veal

Fish and seafood

anchois	anchovies	maquereau	mackerel
anguilles	eels	morue	cod
carrelet	plaice	moules	mussels
crevettes roses	prawns	saumon	salmon
hareng	herring	sole	sole
lotte de mer	monkfish	truite	trout

Vegetables

ail	garlic	laitue	lettuce
asperges	asparagus	oignons	onions
carottes	carrots	petits pois	peas
champignons	mushrooms	poireau	leek
choufleur	cauliflower	pommes (de terre)	potatoes
concombre	cucumber	tomate	tomato
genièvre	juniper		

Sweets and desserts

crêpes	pancakes	parfait	frozen mousse, sometimes ice cream
crêpes suzettes	thin pancakes with orange juice and liqueur		
		petits fours	bite-sized cakes or pastries
glace	ice cream		
madeleine	small, shell-shaped sponge cake		

Fruits and nuts

amandes	almonds	noisettes	hazelnuts
ananas	pineapple	pamplemousse	grapefruit
cacahouètes	peanuts	poire	pear
cérise	cherry	pomme	apple
citron	lemon	prune	plum
fraise	strawberry	pruneau	prune
framboise	raspberry	raisins	grapes
marrons	chestnuts		

Drinks

bière	beer	thé	tea
café	coffee	vin ...	wine ...
eaux de vie	spirits distilled from various fruits	rouge	red
		blanc	white
jenever	Dutch/Flemish gin	brut	very dry
lait	milk	sec	dry
orange/citron pressé	fresh orange/lemon juice	demi-sec	sweet
		doux	very sweet

Glossaries

French terms

Abbaye Abbey or group of monastic buildings

Aéroport Airport

Auberge de la Jeunesse Youth hostel

Beaux Arts Fine arts

Beffroi Belfry

Béguinage Convent occupied by beguines, ie members of a sisterhood living as nuns but without vows and with the right of return to the secular world.

Bicyclette Bicycle

Bourse Stock exchange

Chapelle Chapel

Château Mansion, country house or castle

Cour Court(yard)

Couvent Convent, monastery

Dégustation Tasting (wine or food)

Donjon Castle keep

Eglise Church

Entrée Entrance

Est East

Etage Floor (of a museum, etc)

Fermé Closed

Fermeture Closing period

Fouilles Archeological excavations

Gare Train station

Gîte d'Etape Dormitory-style lodgings situated in relatively remote parts of the country which can house anywhere between ten and one hundred people

Grand-Place Central town square and the heart of most Belgian communities

Halle aux Draps Cloth hall – the building in medieval weaving towns where cloth would be weighed, graded, stored and sold

Halle aux Viandes Meat market

Halles Covered, central food market

Hôpital Hospital

Hôtel Either hotel, or – in its earlier sense – (private) town house

Hôtel de Ville Town hall

Jardin Garden

Jours Feriés Public holidays

Maison House

Marché Market

Moulin Windmill

Municipal Civic, municipal

Musée Museum

Nord North

Nôtre Dame Our Lady

Ouest West

Ouvert Open

Palais Palace

Place Square, market place

Pont Bridge

Porte Gateway

Quai Quay, or station platform

Quartier District or neighbourhood of a town

Reine Queen

Roi King

Rue Street

Sortie Exit

Sud South

Syndicat d'initiative Tourist office

Tour Tower

Trésor Treasury

Flemish terms

Abdij Abbey or group of monastic buildings

Begijnhof Convent occupied by beguines (*begijns*), ie members of a sisterhood living as nuns but without vows, retaining the right of return to the secular world

Beiaard Carillon (a set of tuned church bells, either operated by an automatic mechanism or played by a keyboard)

Belfort Belfry

Beurs Stock exchange

BG Begane grond – "ground floor"

Botermarkt Butter market

Brug Bridge

Burgher Member of the upper or mercantile classes of a town, usually with civic powers

Fiets Bicycle

Fietspad Bicycle path

Gasthof Inn

Gasthuis Hospital

Geen toegang No entry

Gemeente Municipal, as in Gemeentehuis (town hall)

Gerechtshof Law Courts

Gesloten Closed

Gilde Guild

Gracht Urban canal

Groentenmarkt Vegetable market

Grote Markt Central town square and the heart of most Belgian communities

Hal Hall

Hof Court(yard)

Huis House

Ingang Entrance

Jeugdherberg Youth hostel

K Kelder – "basement"

Kaai Quay

Kapel Chapel

Kasteel Castle

Kerk Church; Grote Kerk: the principal church of the town; Onze Lieve Vrouwekerk: church dedicated to the Virgin Mary

Koning King

Koningin Queen

Koninklijk Royal

Korenmarkt Corn market

Kunst Art

Kursaal Casino

Lakenhal Cloth hall – the building in medieval weaving towns where cloth would be weighed, graded and sold

Let Op! Attention!

Luchthaven Airport

Markt Marketplace

Molen Windmill

Noord North

OLV Church of Our Lady (Onze Lieve Vrouwekerk)

Ommegang Procession

Onze Lieve Vrouwekerk Church of Our Lady

Oost East

Paleis Palace

Plaats A square or open space

Plein A square or open space

Poort Gate

Raadhuis Town hall

Rijk State

Schatkamer Treasury

Schepenzaal Alderman's Hall

Schone Kunsten Fine arts

Schouwburg Theatre

Sierkunst Decorative arts

Spoor Track (as in railway) – trains arrive and depart on track (as distinct from platform) numbers

Stadhuis Town hall

Station (Train or bus) station

Stedelijk Civic, municipal

Straat Street

T/M Tot en met – "up to and including"

Toegang Entrance

Toren Tower

Tuin Garden

Uitgang Exit

Art and architectural terms

Ambulatory Interior covered passage around the outer edge of the choir of a church

Apse Semicircular protrusion at (usually) the east end of a church

Art Deco Geometrical style of art and architecture especially popular in the 1930s

Art Nouveau Style of art, architecture and design based on highly stylized vegetal forms. Particularly popular in the early part of the twentieth century

Balustrade An ornamental rail, running, almost invariably, along the top of a building

Baroque The art and architecture of the Counter-Reformation, dating from around 1600 onwards. Distinguished by extreme ornateness, exuberance and by the complex but harmonious spatial arrangement of interiors

Basilica Catholic church with honorific privileges

Carillon A set of tuned church bells, either operated by an automatic mechanism or played by a keyboard

Caryatid A sculptured female figure used as a column

Chancel The eastern part of a church, often separated from the nave by a screen (see "rood screen" p.286); contains the choir and ambulatory

Classical Architectural style incorporating Greek and Roman elements – pillars, domes, colonnades, etc – at its height in the seventeenth century and revived, as Neoclassical, in the nineteenth century

Clerestory Upper storey of a church with windows

Diptych Carved or painted work on two panels, often used as an altarpiece – both static and, more occasionally, portable

Expressionism Artistic style popular at the beginning of the twentieth century, characterized by the exaggeration of

shape or colour; often accompanied by the extensive use of symbolism

Flamboyant Florid form of Gothic

Fresco Wall painting – durable through application to wet plaster

Gable The triangular upper portion of a wall – decorative or supporting a roof

Genre painting In the seventeenth century the term "genre painting" applied to everything from animal paintings and still lifes through to historical works and landscapes, while in the eighteenth century, the term came only to be applied to scenes of everyday life

Gobelins A rich French tapestry, named after the most famous of all tapestry manufacturers, based in Paris, whose most renowned period was in the reign of Louis XIV; also loosely applied to tapestries of a similar style

Gothic Architectural style of the thirteenth to sixteenth century, characterized by pointed arches, rib vaulting, flying buttresses and a general emphasis on verticality

Misericord Shelf on the underside of a hinged choir stall seat, which, when the seat was upright, could help a worshipper keep on his feet; the shelves were often carved with secular subjects as bottoms were not thought worthy of religious carvings

Nave Main body of a church

Neoclassical Architectural style derived from Greek and Roman elements – pillars, domes, colonnades, etc – popular in the Low Countries during French rule in the early nineteenth century

Neo-Gothic Revived Gothic style of architecture popular between the late eighteenth and nineteenth centuries

Renaissance The period of European history – beginning in Italy in the fourteenth century – that marks the end of the medieval period and the rise of the modern world. Defined, amongst many criteria, by an increase in classical scholarship, geographical discovery, the rise of secular values and the growth of individualism. Also refers to the art and architecture of the period

Retable Altarpiece

Rococo Highly florid, light and intricate eighteenth-century style of architecture, painting and interior design, forming the last phase of Baroque

Romanesque Early medieval architecture distinguished by squat forms, rounded arches and naive sculpture

Rood loft Gallery (or space) on top of a rood screen

Rood screen Decorative screen separating the nave from the chancel; a rood loft is the gallery (or space) on top of it

Stucco Marble-based plaster used to embellish ceilings, etc

Transept Arms of a cross-shaped church, placed at ninety degrees to nave and chancel

Triptych Carved or painted work on three panels, often used as an altarpiece

Tympanum Sculpted, usually recessed, panel above a door

Vault An arched ceiling or roof

Travel store

D: Rough Guide
DIRECTIONS for
short breaks

Available from all good bookstores

For more information go to www.roughguides.com

ROUGH GUIDES

THE ROCCO FORTE COLLECTION

Brussels, Hotel Amigo

THE ART OF SIMPLE LUXURY IN KEY DESTINATIONS

Abu Dhabi (2010)   Berlin   Brussels   Edinburgh   Florence   Frankfurt   Geneva
Jeddah (2010)   London   Manchester   Marrakech (2009)   Munich   Prague (2008)
Rome   Sicily (2009)   St Petersburg

www.roccofortecollection.com

Small print and
Index

A Rough Guide to Rough Guides

Published in 1982, the first Rough Guide – to Greece – was a student scheme that became a publishing phenomenon. Mark Ellingham, a recent graduate in English from Bristol University, had been travelling in Greece the previous summer and couldn't find the right guidebook. With a small group of friends he wrote his own guide, combining a highly contemporary, journalistic style with a thoroughly practical approach to travellers' needs.

The immediate success of the book spawned a series that rapidly covered dozens of destinations. And, in addition to impecunious backpackers, Rough Guides soon acquired a much broader and older readership that relished the guides' wit and inquisitiveness as much as their enthusiastic, critical approach and value-for-money ethos.

These days, Rough Guides include recommendations from shoestring to luxury and cover more than 200 destinations around the globe, including almost every country in the Americas and Europe, more than half of Africa and most of Asia and Australasia. Our ever-growing team of authors and photographers is spread all over the world, particularly in Europe, the USA and Australia.

SMALL PRINT

In the early 1990s, Rough Guides branched out of travel, with the publication of Rough Guides to World Music, Classical Music and the Internet. All three have become benchmark titles in their fields, spearheading the publication of a wide range of books under the Rough Guide name.

Including the travel series, Rough Guides now number more than 350 titles, covering: phrasebooks, waterproof maps, music guides from Opera to Heavy Metal, reference works as diverse as Conspiracy Theories and Shakespeare, and popular culture books from iPods to Poker. Rough Guides also produce a series of more than 120 World Music CDs in partnership with World Music Network.

Visit www.roughguides.com to see our latest publications.

Rough Guide travel images are available for commercial licensing at www.roughguidespictures.com.

Rough Guide credits

Text editor: Natasha Foges
Layout: Ajay Verma
Cartography: Ashutosh Bharti
Picture editor: Emily Taylor
Production: Rebecca Short
Proofreader: Amanda Jones
Cover design: Chloë Roberts
Photographers: Roger Mapp, Jean-Christophe Godet and Anthony Cassidy
Editorial: London Ruth Blackmore, Andy Turner, Keith Drew, Edward Aves, Alice Park, Lucy White, Jo Kirby, James Smart, Róis'n Cameron, Emma Traynor, James Rice, Emma Gibbs, Kathryn Lane, Christina Valhouli, Monica Woods, Mani Ramaswamy, Joe Staines, Peter Buckley, Matthew Milton, Tracy Hopkins, Ruth Tidball; **New York** Andrew Rosenberg, Steven Horak, AnneLise Sorensen, Ella Steim, Anna Owens, Sean Mahoney, Paula Neudorf; **Delhi** Madhavi Singh, Karen D'Souza
Design & Pictures: London Scott Stickland, Dan May, Diana Jarvis, Mark Thomas, Nicole Newman, Sarah Cummins; **Delhi** Umesh Aggarwal, Jessica Subramanian, Ankur Guha, Pradeep Thapliyal, Sachin Tanwar, Anita Singh, Nikhil Agarwal

Production: Vicky Baldwin
Cartography: London Maxine Repath, Ed Wright, Katie Lloyd-Jones; **Delhi** Jai Prakash Mishra, Rajesh Chhibber, Rajesh Mishra, Animesh Pathak, Jasbir Sandhu, Karobi Gogoi, Alakananda Bhattacharya, Swati Handoo, Deshpal Dabas
Online: London George Atwell, Faye Hellon, Jeanette Angell, Fergus Day, Justine Bright, Clare Bryson, Áine Fearon, Adrian Low, Ezgi Celebi, Amber Bloomfield; **Delhi** Amit Verma, Rahul Kumar, Narender Kumar, Ravi Yadav, Debojit Borah, Rakesh Kumar, Ganesh Sharma
Marketing & Publicity: London Liz Statham, Niki Hanmer, Louise Maher, Jess Carter, Vanessa Godden, Vivienne Watton, Anna Paynton, Rachel Sprackett, Libby Jellie, Holly Dudley; **New York** Geoff Colquitt, Nancy Lambert, Katy Ball; **Delhi** Ragini Govind
Manager India: Punita Singh
Reference Director: Andrew Lockett
Operations Manager: Helen Phillips
PA to Publishing Director: Nicola Henderson
Publishing Director: Martin Dunford
Commercial Manager: Gino Magnotta
Managing Director: John Duhigg

Publishing information

This fourth edition published February 2009 by
Rough Guides Ltd,
80 Strand, London WC2R 0RL
345 Hudson St, 4th Floor,
New York, NY 10014, USA
14 Local Shopping Centre, Panchsheel Park,
New Delhi 110017, India
Distributed by the Penguin Group
Penguin Books Ltd,
80 Strand, London WC2R 0RL
Penguin Group (USA)
375 Hudson Street, NY 10014, USA
Penguin Group (Australia)
250 Camberwell Road, Camberwell,
Victoria 3124, Australia
Penguin Group (Canada)
195 Harry Walker Parkway N, Newmarket, ON,
L3Y 7B3 Canada
Penguin Group (NZ)
67 Apollo Drive, Mairangi Bay, Auckland 1310,
New Zealand

Cover concept by Peter Dyer.
Typeset in Bembo and Helvetica to an original design by Henry Iles.
Printed and bound in China
© Martin Dunford and Phil Lee, 2009
No part of this book may be reproduced in any form without permission from the publisher except for the quotation of brief passages in reviews.
304pp includes index
A catalogue record for this book is available from the British Library.
ISBN: 978-1-84836-033-4
The publishers and authors have done their best to ensure the accuracy and currency of all the information in **The Rough Guide to Brussels**, however, they can accept no responsibility for any loss, injury, or inconvenience sustained by any traveller as a result of information or advice contained in the guide.

1   3   5   7   9   8   6   4   2

Help us update

We've gone to a lot of effort to ensure that the fourth edition of **The Rough Guide to Brussels** is accurate and up to date. However, things change – places get "discovered", opening hours are notoriously fickle, restaurants and rooms raise prices or lower standards. If you feel we've got it wrong or left something out, we'd like to know, and if you can remember the address, the price, the hours, the phone number, so much the better.

Please send your comments with the subject line "**Rough Guide Brussels Update**" to ✉ mail@roughguides.com. We'll credit all contributions and send a copy of the next edition (or any other Rough Guide if you prefer) for the very best emails.
Have your questions answered and tell others about your trip at
Ⓦ community.roughguides.com

SMALL PRINT

ROUGH GUIDES

Acknowledgements

Martin Dunford Thanks to Caroline, Daisy and Lucy for as always being a willing team of volunteers, Heather for spending time with us in Brussels, and to Ging and Deb for dropping in to see us and braving the weather! Thanks also to Natasha Foges for smoothing the way so attentively.

Phil Lee Thanks to our editor, Natasha Foges, for her patient good humour and exemplary attention to detail during the preparation of this new edition of the Rough Guide to Brussels. Special thanks also to Anita Rampall of Tourism Flanders & Brussels; Pieter Vander Gheynst from the Conseil Bruxellois des Musées; Igor Daems from Toerisme Antwerpen; and Sophie Bouallegue of the Belgian Tourist Office - Brussels & Wallonia. I am especially grateful also for the assistance offered me by Romina Kennedy of Rocco Forte Hotels. Thanks also to my co-authors, Martin Dunford, Suzy Sumner and Loïk Dal Molin.

Readers' letters

SMALL PRINT

Thanks to all the readers who have taken the time to write in with comments and suggestions (and apologies if we've inadvertently omitted or misspelt anyone's name):

John Akhurst; Anthony Neil Ashworth; Richard Barker; Tom Baxter; Johan Bergstromallen-Allen; Otto Beuchner; Alexsandra Bilos; Lianne Bissell; Julia Bomken; Chris Burin; Richard Butler; Martin Connors; David Cox; Emmanuel David; John & Frances Davies; Nele Depoorter; Mike Dobson; Simon Evans; Franck Faraday; Anthea Finlayson; Sheina Foulkes; Catherine Froidebise; Patrick Gardinal; Eric Van Geertruyden; Johan De Geyndt; Pieter Van der Gheynst; Mike Gingell; J. Goodfellow; David Gruccio; Katrien Gysen; Tony Hallas; John Hammond; Helen Harjanto; Lucy Hartiss; Pat Hindley; Herman Hindricks; Jay Jones; Adam Kramer; John & Angela Lansley; Peter & Vivien Lee; Simon Loveitt; Heather McCann; Richard Madge; Loes Maveau; Heather McCann; Claudia Merges; Slávi Metz; Deirdre & David Mills; William Milne; Paul Mitchell; Bernadette & Michael Mossley; Ros Murphy; Mary Murray; B. E. Neale; Stuart Newman; Adolphe Nzeza; Isabel Payno; Susan Plowden; Johnny Pring; David Reeves; Kiron Reid; John A Rosenhof; Chris Serle; Silke; Simon Evans; Roel Smeyers; Tim Smith; William Smith; Phyllis Snyder; K. Tan; Warren Thomas; Christina Thyssen; Robin Tilston; Elisabeth Timenchik; David Trussler; Frederik Vlieghe; Mary Whitham; Brian & Suzanne Williams; Steve Willis; Stephen Wills; Melanie Winterbotham; Glenda Young.

Photo credits

All photos © Rough Guides except the following:

Cover
Above: Statue of Everard 't Serclaes, Grand-Place © Maisant Ludovic/Photolibrary
Front cover image: Antiques shop window, place du Grand Sablon © Peter Horree/Alamy
Back cover image: Statue, place des Martyrs © Chloë Roberts

Title page
Sculpture outside the Royal Library © World Pictures/Photoshot

Full page
Street scene, Brussels © Yvan Travert/Photolibrary

Introduction
The Atomium © Steve Vidler/eStock Photo
Hôtel Hannon © Bildarchiv Monheim/GmbH/Alamy
Flags of EU member countries © Julian Pottage/Robert Harding /DRR.net
The Grand-Place © Irek/SIME/4Corners Images
Bike riders at the Cinquantenaire Arch © Leslie Banks/iStock Photo

Things not to miss
04 Musées Royaux des Beaux-Arts © Belgian Tourist Office NYC/USA/www.visitbelgium.com
07 Mussels with wine © Belgian Tourist Office NYC/USA/www.visitbelgium.com
08 Centre Belge de la Bande Desinée © Daniel Fouss/Comics Center

Belgian food colour insert
Sweets in shop window, Brussels © Neil Emmerson/Jupiter Images
Patisserie, Brussels © Francesca Yorke/Axiom
Frites © FAN travelstock/Alamy
Wittamer chocolate shop, Belgium © Georgia Glynn Smith/Photolibrary
Rack of waffles © Tourism Flanders-Brussels/www.visitflanders.com

Belgian beer colour insert
Pouring a pint of Belgian beer © Etienne Ansotte/Rex Features
Belgian beer barrels © Tourism Flanders-Brussels/www.visitflanders.com
La Mort Subite © Tourism Flanders-Brussels/www.visitflanders.com
Belgian hop fields © Tourism Flanders-Brussels/www.visitflanders.com

Black and whites
p.42 Hôtel de Ville © Belgian Tourist Office NYC/USA/www.visitbelgium.com
p.44 Guild houses on the Grand-Place © Belgian Tourist Office NYC/USA/www.visitbelgium.com
p.97 Staircase, Musée Victor Horta © Belgian Tourist Office NYC/USA/www.visitbelgium.com
p.130 Alice & David Museum © Tourism Flanders-Brussels/www.visitflanders.com
p.136 The Wellington Museum © Rolf Richardson /Alamy
p.152 Antwerp town hall © Belgian Tourist Office NYC/USA/www.visitbelgium.com
p.160 Bench sculpture, Leuven © Belgian Tourist Office NYC/USA/www.visitbelgium.com
p.182 Hotel Amigo © Rocco Forte Hotels
p.184 Bemanos © Bemanos
p.185 Hotel Métropole © Franck Duez/Courtesy of the Métropole
p.188 L'Art de la Fugue © L'Art de la Fugue
p.216 The Jack Van Poll Trio at the Music Village © Michel Binstock/DRR.Net
p.220 Interior of the Théâtre Monnaie © Tourism Flanders-Brussels/www.visitflanders.com
p.226 Galeries St-Hubert © Belgian Tourist Office NYC/USA/www.visitbelgium.com
p.241 Dinosaurs inside the Muséum des Sciences Naturelles © Tourism Flanders-Brussels/www.visitflanders.com
p.248 Ommegang Festival © Belgian Tourist Office NYC/USA/www.visitbelgium.com

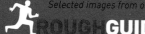

Index

Map entries are in colour.

N

O

P

Q

R

INDEX

302

Map symbols

maps are listed in the full index using coloured text

▬▬▬·	International boundary	⊥	Fountain
▬▬··	Provincial boundary	⊙	Statue
▬ ▬ ▬	Chapter boundary	◆	Point of interest
▬▬▬	Motorway	⊠	Post office
═══	Major road	@	Internet
═══	Minor road	ⓘ	Tourist office
▬▬▬	Pedestrianized road	🏛	Monument
⊪⊪⊪	Steps	▣	Restaurant
⋮⋮⋮	Tunnel	✈	Airport
	Tracks	★	Bus stop
▬▬▬	Railway line	Ⓜ	Metro station
────	River	Ⓟ	Prémétro station
⨾	Bridge	▮	Building
⊠	Gate	✚	Church
▲	Peak	░	Park

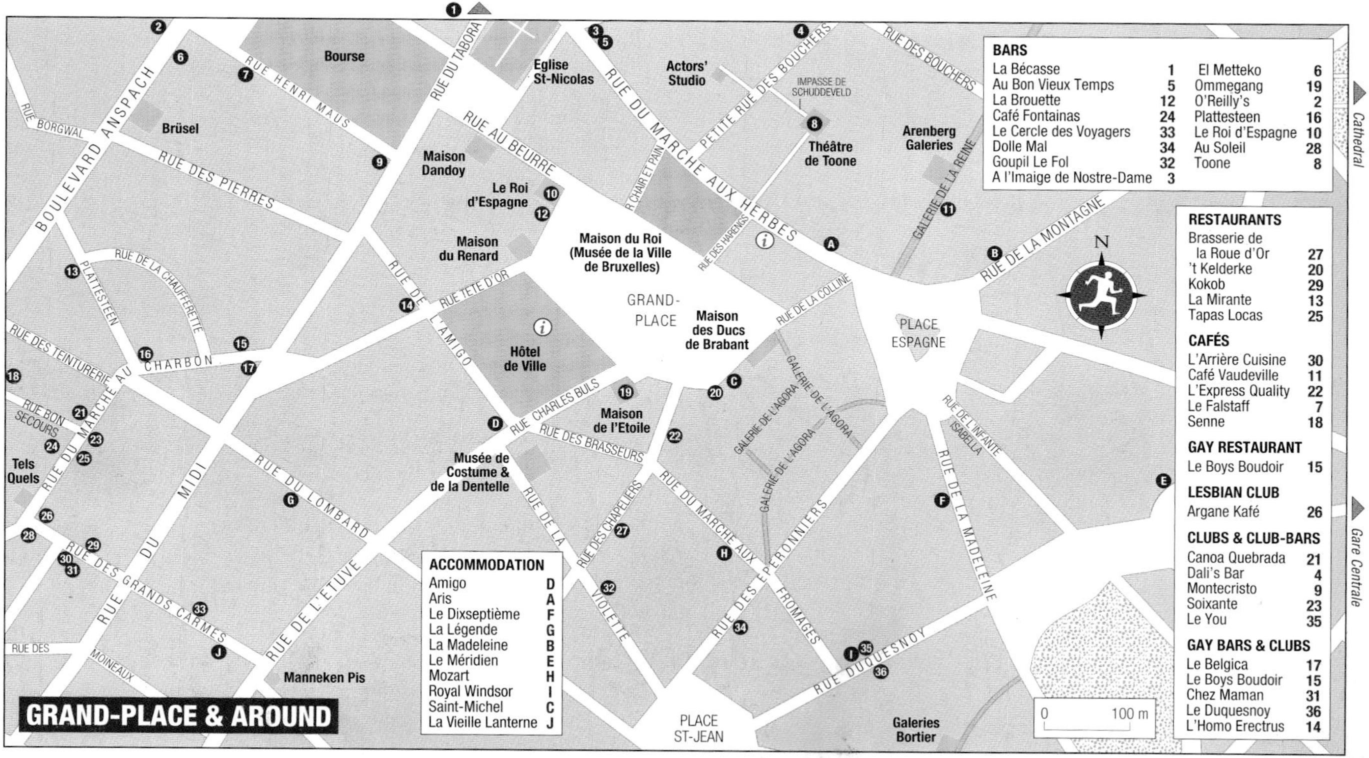

GRAND-PLACE & AROUND
BARS
La Bécasse 1
Au Bon Vieux Temps 5
La Brouette 12
Café Fontainas 24
Le Cercle des Voyagers 33
Dolle Mal 34
Goupil Le Fol 32
A l'Imaige de Nostre-Dame 3
El Metteko 6
Ommegang 19
O'Reilly's 2
Plattesteen 16
Le Roi d'Espagne 10
Au Soleil 28
Toone 8
RESTAURANTS
Brasserie de la Roue d'Or 27
't Kelderke 20
Kokob 29
La Mirante 13
Tapas Locas 25
CAFÉS
L'Arrière Cuisine 30
Café Vaudeville 11
L'Express Quality 22
Le Falstaff 7
Senne 18
GAY RESTAURANT
Le Boys Boudoir 15
LESBIAN CLUB
Argane Kafé 26
CLUBS & CLUB-BARS
Canoa Quebrada 21
Dali's Bar 4
Montecristo 9
Soixante 23
Le You 35
GAY BARS & CLUBS
Le Belgica 17
Le Boys Boudoir 15
Chez Maman 31
Le Duquesnoy 36
L'Homo Erectrus 14
ACCOMMODATION
Amigo D
Aris A
Le Dixseptième F
La Légende G
La Madeleine B
Le Méridien E
Mozart H
Royal Windsor I
Saint-Michel C
La Vieille Lanterne J
Cathedral
Gare Centrale
N
0
100 m
Bourse
Eglise St-Nicolas
Actors' Studio
Théâtre de Toone
Arenberg Galeries
Brüsel
Maison Dandoy
Le Roi d'Espagne
Maison du Renard
Maison du Roi (Musée de la Ville de Bruxelles)
GRAND-PLACE
Maison des Ducs de Brabant
Hôtel de Ville
Maison de l'Etoile
Musée de Costume & de la Dentelle
PLACE ESPAGNE
PLACE ST-JEAN
Galeries Bortier
Manneken Pis
Tels Quels
BOULEVARD ANSPACH
RUE DU TABORA
RUE HENRI MAUS
RUE BORGWAL
RUE DES PIERRES
RUE AU BEURRE
RUE DU MARCHE AUX HERBES
PETITE RUE DES BOUCHERS
RUE DES BOUCHERS
IMPASSE DE SCHUDDEVELD
GALERIE DE LA REINE
RUE DE LA MONTAGNE
R CHAIR ET PAIN
RUE DES HARENGS
RUE DE LA COLLINE
RUE TETE D'OR
RUE DE L'AMIGO
RUE DE LA CHAUFFERETTE
PLATTESTEEN
RUE DES TEINTURERIE
RUE AU CHARBON
RUE BON SECOURS
RUE DU MARCHE AU
RUE CHARLES BULS
RUE DES BRASSEURS
GALERIE DE L'AGORA
RUE DE L'INFANTE ISABELLA
RUE DE LA MADELEINE
RUE DU MIDI
RUE DU LOMBARD
RUE DES GRANDS CARMES
RUE DE L'ETUVE
RUE DE LA VIOLETTE
RUE DES CHAPELIERS
RUE DU MARCHE AUX FROMAGES
RUE DES EPERONNIERS
RUE DUQUESNOY
RUE DES MOINEAUX

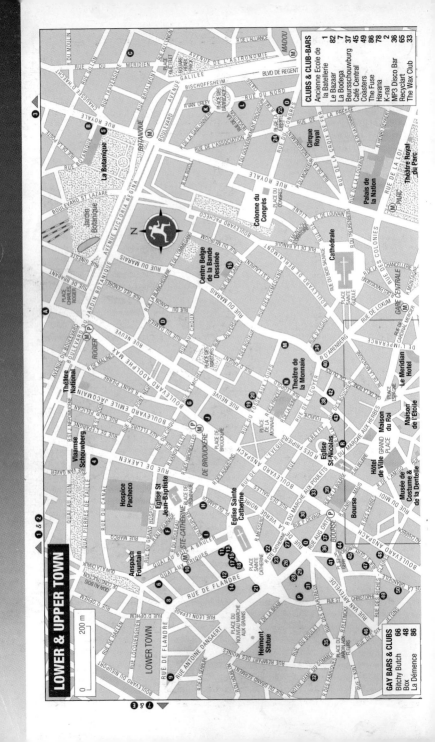

LOWER & UPPER TOWN

0 — 200 m

La Botanique

Jardin Botanique

Théâtre National

Vlaamse Schouwborg

Hospice Pacheco

Eglise St Jean-Baptiste

Eglise Sainte Catherine

Anspach Fountain

Helmont Statue

Centre Belge de la Bande Dessinée

Colonne du Congrès

Cirque Royal

Palais de la Nation

Théâtre Royal du Parc

Cathédrale

Théâtre de la Monnaie

Eglise St-Nicolas

Maison du Roi

Maison de l'Etoile

Hôtel de Ville

Musée du Costume & de la Dentelle

Bourse

Le Meridian Hotel

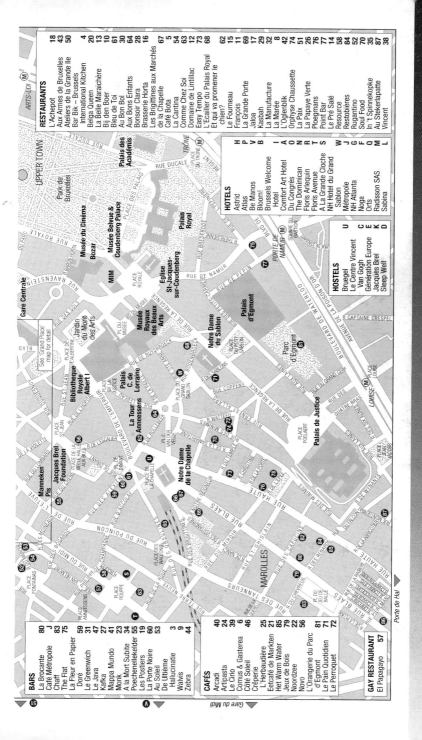

RESTAURANTS

L'Achepot	18
Aux Armes de Bruxelles	43
Ateliers de la Grande Ile	50
Bar Bik – Brussels	4
International Kitchen	20
Belga Queen	13
La Belle Maraîchère	10
Bij den Boer	61
Bleu de Toi	30
Au Bon Bol	64
Aux Bons Enfants	28
Bonsoir Clara	16
Brasserie Horta	67
Les Brigittines aux Marchés de la Chapelle	5
Café Bota	54
La Cantina	63
Comme Chez Soi	12
Domaine de Lintillac	73
Easy Tempo	68
L'Ecailler du Palais Royal	62
Et ou va promener le chien?	15
Le Fourneau	11
François	69
La Grande Porte	17
Jaloa	29
Kasbah	32
La Manufacture	8
La Marée	42
L'Ogenblik	74
Orphyse Chaussette	51
La Paix	26
La Papaye Verte	77
Ploegmans	76
Point Bar	14
Le Pré Salé	58
Resource	84
Restobières	52
Rugantino	70
Soul Food	35
In 't Spinnekopke	87
Au Stekerlapatte	38
Vincent	

HOTELS

Astrid	H
Atlas	P
Be Manos	V
Bloom!	B
Brussels Welcome Hotel	I
Comfort Art Hotel	A
Du Congrès	O
The Dominican	Q
Floris Arlequin	R
Floris Avenue	T
A La Grande Cloche	S
NH Hotel du Grand Sablon	U
Métropole	C
NH Atlanta	E
Noga	K
Orts	D
Radisson SAS	
Sabina	

HOSTELS

Bruegel	U
Le Centre Vincent	C
Van Gogh	E
Génération Europe	K
Jacques Brel	D
Sleep Well	

BARS

La Brocante	80
Café Métropole	J
Chaff	83
The Flat	75
La Fleur en Papier Doré	59
Le Greenwich	31
Le Java	47
Kafka	27
Mappa Mundo	41
Monk	23
A la Mort Subite	34
Poechenellekelder	55
Les Postiers	19
La Porte Noire	60
Au Soleil	53
De Ultième Hallucinatie	3
Walvis	9
Zebra	44

CAFÉS

Arcadi	40
Artipasta	24
Le Cirio	39
Comus & Gasterea	6
Côté Soleil	46
Crêperie L'Herbaudière	25
Eetcafé de Markten	21
Het Warm Water	85
Jeux de Bois	79
Noordzee	22
Novo	56
L'Orangerie du Parc d'Egmont	81
Le Pain Quotidien	71
Le Perroquet	72

GAY RESTAURANT

El Papagayo	57

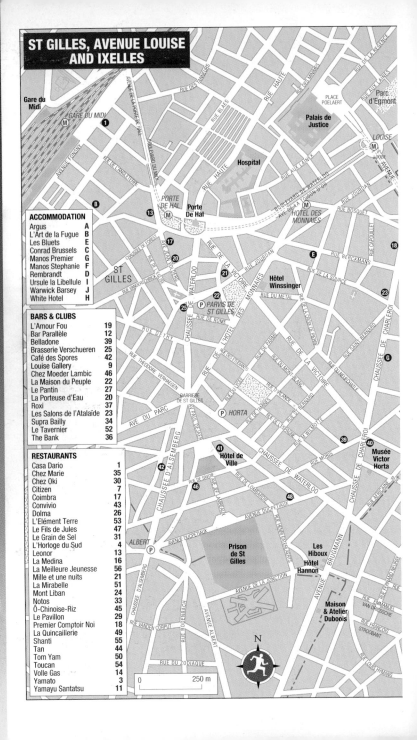

ST GILLES, AVENUE LOUISE AND IXELLES

Gare du Midi

GARE DU MIDI

Parc d'Egmont

PLACE POELAERT

Palais de Justice

LOUISE
PL. LOUISE

Hospital

PORTE DE HAL
Porte De Hal

HÔTEL DES MONNAIES

ST GILLES

Hôtel Winssinger

PARVIS DE ST GILLES

HORTA

Hôtel de Ville

Musée Victor Horta

ALBERT

Prison de St Gilles

Les Hiboux

Hôtel Hannon

Maison & Atelier Dubois

N

0   250 m

ACCOMMODATION

Argus	A
L'Art de la Fugue	B
Les Bluets	E
Conrad Brussels	C
Manos Premier	G
Manos Stephanie	F
Rembrandt	D
Ursule la Libellule	I
Warwick Barsey	J
White Hotel	H

BARS & CLUBS

L'Amour Fou	19
Bar Parallèle	12
Belladone	39
Brasserie Verschueren	25
Café des Spores	42
Louise Gallery	9
Chez Moeder Lambic	46
La Maison du Peuple	22
Le Pantin	27
La Porteuse d'Eau	20
Roxi	37
Les Salons de l'Atalaïde	23
Supra Bailly	34
Le Tavernier	52
The Bank	36

RESTAURANTS

Casa Dario	1
Chez Marie	35
Chez Oki	30
Citizen	7
Coimbra	17
Convivio	43
Dolma	26
L'Elément Terre	53
Le Fils de Jules	47
Le Grain de Sel	31
L'Horloge du Sud	4
Leonor	13
La Medina	16
La Meilleure Jeunesse	56
Mille et une nuits	21
La Mirabelle	51
Mont Liban	24
Notos	33
Ô-Chinoise-Riz	45
Le Pavillon	29
Premier Comptoir Noi	18
La Quincaillerie	49
Shanti	55
Tan	44
Tom Yam	50
Toucan	54
Volle Gas	14
Yamato	3
Yamayu Santatsu	11

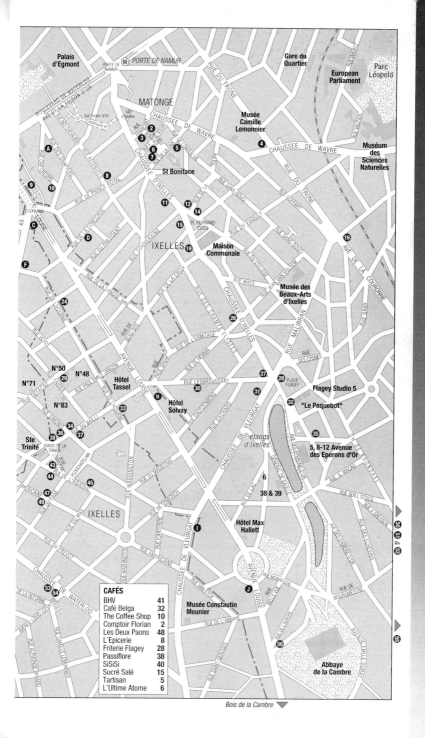

Palais
d'Egmont

Gare du
Quartier

European
Parliament

Parc
Léopold

PORTE DE NAMUR

PORTE DE
NAMUR

MATONGE

CHAUSSÉE DE WAVRE

Musée
Camille
Lemonnier

CHAUSSÉE DE WAVRE

Muséum
des
Sciences
Naturelles

St Boniface

IXELLES

PL. FERNAND
COCQ

Maison
Communale

Musée des
Beaux-Arts
d'Ixelles

N°50

N°48

N°71

N°83

Hôtel
Tassel

Hôtel
Solvay

PLACE
FLAGEY

Flagey Studio 5

"Le Paquebot"

Ste
Trinité

PARVIS DE LA
TRINITÉ

étangs
d'Ixelles

5, 8-12 Avenue
des Eperons d'Or

6

38 & 39

IXELLES

Hôtel Max
Hallett

CHAUSSÉE DE WATERLOO

Musée Constautin
Meunier

Abbaye
de la Cambre

CAFÉS	
BHV	41
Café Belga	32
The Coffee Shop	10
Comptoir Florian	2
Les Deux Paons	48
L'Epicerie	8
Friterie Flagey	28
Passiflore	38
SiSiSi	40
Sucré Salé	15
Tartisan	5
L'Ultime Atome	6

Bois de la Cambre

RUE DE LA CROIX DE FER
MADOU Ⓜ
RUE DE LA BIGORNE
RUE DE L'ARTICHAUT
RUE HYDRAULIQUE
RUE DE VERVERS
RUE DES GRIS
RUE DES GRAVELINES
RUE DES EBURONS

RUE DE LA LOUVAIN
RUE DE LA PRESSE
RUE HENRI BEY AERT
RUE MARIE THERESE
RUE DES DEUX EGLISES
RUE DU BERCEAU
RUE DU MARTEAU

Villa
Hôtel van Eetvelde Germaine

PACIFICATION
LE BON
AVENUE PALMERSTON

SQUARE MARIE LOUISE

RUE PHILIPPE LE BON
ORTELIUS
❸

RUE DE LA LOI
BOULEVARD DU REGENT
AVENUE DES ARTS
ARTS-LOI Ⓜ
RUE DE COMMERCE
AVENUE DES ARTS
JOSEPH II
RUE STEVIN
RUE LIVINGSTONE
RUE CHARLES MARTEL
RUE ST QUENTIN
❻
❾

Parc de Bruxelles

RUE DUCALE
RUE ZINNER
RUE DE LA LOI
RUE JOSEPH II
CHAUSSEE DE TACITURNE

Charlemagne
MAALBEEK Ⓜ
RUE DE LA

RUE DE L'INDUSTRIE
RUE GUIMARD
SQUARE FRÈRE ORBAN
RUE DE LA SCIENCE
RUE JACQUES
❿
DE LALAING
RUE DU TACITURNE
BOULEVARD CHARLEMAGNE

RUE LAMBERMONT
BOULEVARD DU REGENT
AVENUE DES ARTS
RUE DUCALE

BELLIARD
RUE D'ARLON
RUE DE TOULOUSE
Gare Schuman **Résidence Palace**

RUE MONTOYER
RUE DE COMMERCE
RUE MARIE DE BOURGOGNE
RUE DE TREVES
RUE DE PASCALE
CHAUSSEE D'ETTERBEEK

TRÔNE

RUE DU LUXEMBOURG
SQUARE DE MEEÛS
Ⓐ
Ⓒ
Gare du Quartier Léopold
⑫

RUE DU TRÔNE
RUE DE PARIS
RUE DE LUXEMBOURG
PLACE DU LUXEMBOURG

European Parliament

Bibliothèque Solvay

Parc Léopold

⑮
RUE DE FERLARS
RUE CAROLY
RUE DU PARNASSE
RUE DE TREVES
ⓘ
CHAUSSEE D'ETTERBEEK

RUE DU CHAMP DE MARS
⑰
PLACE DE LONDRES
RUE DE LONDRES

Ⓓ
⑱
RUE MAJOR RENE DUBREUCQ

Musée Camille Lemonnier

RUE D'IDALIE
RUE GODECHARLE

Muséum des Sciences Naturelles

PLACE JOURDAN
⑲ ⑳

CHAUSSEE DE WAVRE
RUE WIERTZ
RUE VAUTIER
Musée Wiertz

AVENUE DE MAELBEEK
RUE GRAY

RUE DE LA PAIX
DE LONGUE VIE
RUE DE GEORGES LORAND
CHAUSSEE DE WAVRE

RUE JULES BOUILLON
RUE DE LA TULIPE
RUE VAN AA
RUE DE LA CÔTE
SANS-SOUCI
RUE GOFFART
RUE DU VIADUC
RUE DU VIADUCT
RUE LAMBROECK
RUE UMALIE

RUE DU TRÔNE AVENUE
RUE WEYENBERG
RUE DU BROCHET

RUE SOUVERAINE
CHAUSSEE D'IXELLES
RUE MERCELIS
RUE DES CHAMPS
RUE COLLEGE
VENSE
VAN VOLSEM
RUE CLEMENTINE
RUE WERY
RUE GRAY
RUE DU VIVIER

RUE MAES

THE EU QUARTER & AROUND

0 ——————— 300 m

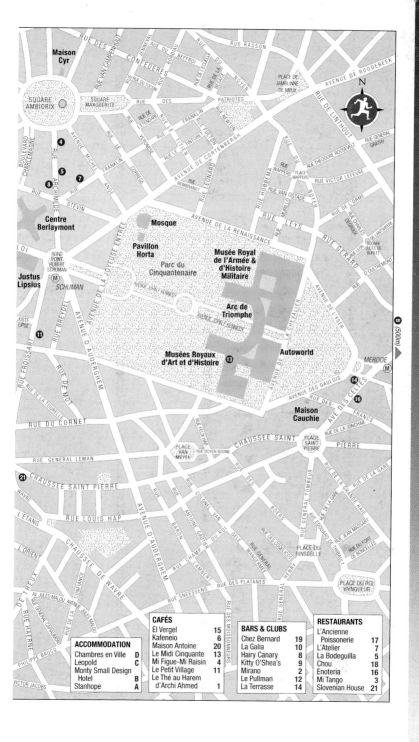

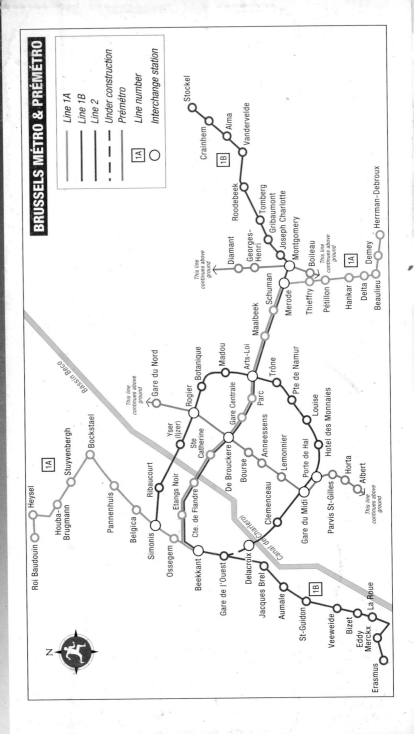

BRUSSELS MÉTRO & PRÉMÉTRO

Line 1A
Line 1B
Line 2
Under construction
Prémétro
1A Line number
○ Interchange station